The Western League

ALSO BY W.C. MADDEN

*Baseball's First-Year Player Draft,
Team by Team Through 1999*
(McFarland, 2001)

*The All-American Girls Professional
Baseball League Record Book:
Comprehensive Hitting, Fielding and Pitching Statistics*
(McFarland, 2000)

*The Women of the All-American Girls
Professional Baseball League:
A Biographical Dictionary*
(McFarland, 1997)

The Western League

A Baseball History, 1885 through 1999

W. C. MADDEN
and PATRICK J. STEWART

McFarland & Company, Inc., Publishers
Jefferson, North Carolina, and London

Library of Congress Cataloguing-in-Publication Data

Madden, W.C.
　　The Western League : a baseball history, 1885 through 1999 /
W.C. Madden and Patrick J. Stewart.
　　　　p.　　cm.
　　Includes bibliographical references and index.

　　ISBN-13: 978-0-7864-1003-3
　　ISBN-10: 0-7864-1003-5
　　(softcover : 50# alkaline paper) ∞

　　1. Western League (Baseball league)—History.　2. Minor
league baseball—West (U.S.)—History.　3. American League
of Professional Baseball Clubs—History.　I. Stewart, Patrick J.
II. Title.
GV875.W48 M33　　2002
796.357'64'0978—dc21　　　　　　　　　　　　　　　　2002001093

British Library cataloguing data are available

©2002 W.C. Madden and Patrick J. Stewart. All rights reserved

*No part of this book may be reproduced or transmitted in any form
or by any means, electronic or mechanical, including photocopying
or recording, or by any information storage and retrieval system,
without permission in writing from the publisher.*

Manufactured in the United States of America

*McFarland & Company, Inc., Publishers
　Box 611, Jefferson, North Carolina 28640
　　www.mcfarlandpub.com*

To Asa Stewart

*Human lives may end,
but not the forces they set in motion.*

Contents

Preface ix
Introduction 1
Abbreviations Used 3

1. The Inaugural Season 5
2. The Early Years (1886–1893) 13
3. The Johnson Years (1894–1899) 34
4. A New Century, A New League (1900–1937) 57
5. Class D Era (1939–1941) 200
6. After the War (1947–1958) 211
7. The Independent Phase (1995–Present) 270
8. League Records 293
9. League Officials 302
10. All-Time Players and Team 310

Bibliography 313
Index 315

Preface

The idea for this book came from Patrick Stewart, whose grandfather, Ace Stewart, played in the Western League in its infancy. Stewart had researched his grandfather extensively; however, he wasn't prepared to write a book on the Western League. He approached author Bill Madden, who had written about Ace in his first book, *The Hoosiers of Summer*. That union led to this book.

Bill and Pat are both members of the Society for American Baseball Research, and they turned to other members for help in preparing the book. Most of the photos for this book came from Jay Sanford, who has an extensive collection. Harold Dellinger was a great source of information, as his report of the league in 1885 was used extensively to write the first chapter of the book. Marc Okkonen, who wrote a book about minor league towns in Michigan, provided some valuable information about teams from there.

George Rugg, the curator of Joyce Sports Research Center at Notre Dame University, was very helpful in providing information about the league, using the center's collection of sports books. The Notre Dame Library also provided microfilm of *The Sporting News*. Tammy Carney from the Owen County Public Library helped with research on Ban Johnson. The Spencer Lion's Club showed the authors his grave and home. Howe Sportsdata was of great assistance by allowing the use of their statistics of the Independent Western League, 1995–1999, which were conveniently located on the Western League website. The current Western League was of great assistance, too, by providing a media guide, information and photos.

The information in this book was taken from many different sources, which are recorded at the end of the book in the bibliography. Many of the statistics came from Reach Guides and *The Encyclopedia of Minor League Baseball*. Many first names for the players were not available from the early days in the league, because the sports writers didn't always list first names.

Introduction

The Western League was one of the first minor leagues in baseball history. Its beginnings can be traced to the Northwestern League, which was formed in 1879. The league was the first league located west of the eastern seaboard, hence the name. Sometimes the Northwestern League was referred to as the Western League, but the year 1885 is considered the first year in which a league was called specifically the Western League.

The American League was a direct descendant of the Western League. Ban Johnson, a sports writer from Cincinnati, revitalized the Western League in 1894, then took the teams from the league to begin the American League in 1900. That fact was further explained in a book about the life of Charles Comiskey that was written in 1919. The book noted: "In order to confer the distinction of an honorable 'ancestry' on the American League, historians have endeavored to link the junior major organization with certain predecessors of more or less renown. Age might give it a greater respectability but the fact remains that it was the Western League, founded in 1894, which was expanded into the American League in 1900. The original Northwestern League, organized in 1879, and the Western Association, founded in 1888, cannot claim relationship."

Of course, not everyone agreed with that statement. The pamphlet titled "Through the Years with the Western League," which was published by the Western League in 1951, didn't consider Johnson's league the true Western League. Instead, it recognized the Western Association as the league and explained that the Western League was known as the Western Association during those years. The 1951 publication also failed to recognize the Western League that ran from 1939 to 1941, because it was a Class D league with teams that had originally come from the Nebraska State League. Those arguments are noted, but this book recognizes only those leagues with the name "Western League" and disregards geographical distinctions. Some baseball experts may disagree, but we are calling it like we see it. If it walks like a duck and talks like a duck, then it is a duck.

The Western League was renamed the American League at a meeting in October 1899, but Alfred H. Spink, the sports editor of the *St. Louis Post Dispatch*, laid claim to being the first to suggest the name of the league in 1898. After the American League was named, the new Western League in 1900 went back to its roots and started again with teams from earlier days. The league took on a Class A status in 1902, which was the highest classification at the time. Baseball was graded A, B, C and D. The minor leagues added a Class AA league later, but the Western league stayed at Class A.

The Western League became known as the longest running minor league until the Depression spelled its end. The teams were surrounded by the Dust Bowl in the 1930s and attendance dropped off. It folded in 1937. Then in 1939 the Nebraska State League borrowed the league's name. The Class D league operated until 1941. The day that will live in infamy— December 7, 1941—spelled the end of the league (and many other minor leagues), as the country and the players went off to fight a more important game. The war ended in 1945, and two years later the Western League was revived again as a Class A league. The league ran for a dozen years until the Major Leagues abandoned it. Without affiliations it could not operate financially.

The league was revived again in 1995 as an independent venture along the west coast. It still thrives today and consists of former major league players and players on their way up.

In the history of the Western League, 20 players who played in the league were eventually inducted into the National Baseball Hall of Fame. They were:

Jake Beckley
Mordecai "Three-Finger" Brown
Charles Comiskey
"Wahoo Sam" Crawford
Dizzy Dean
Hugh Duffy
Urban "Red" Faber
Jesse Haines
Carl Hubbell
Ban Johnson

Tony Lazzeri
Connie Mack
Heinie Manush
Joe "Iron Man" McGinnity
Charles "Kid" Nichols
"Big" Sam Thompson
Joe Tinker
Dazzy Vance
Arky Vaughn
Rube Waddell

Abbreviations Used

A—Assists
AB—At Bats
AL—Albuquerque
AM—Amarillo
Avg.—Average
BA—Bartlesville
BB—Base on Balls
BND—Bend
BUF—Buffalo
CH—Cheyenne
CHO—Chico
CLE—Cleveland
CO—Columbus
CG—Complete Games
CS—Colorado Springs
CSt—Caught Stealing
DA—Davenport
DE—Denver
DP—Double Plays
DT—Detroit
E—Errors
EM—Emporia
ER—Earned Runs
ERA—Earned Run Average
FW—Fort Wayne
G—Games
GB—Games Behind
GR—Grand Rapids
GRH—Grays Harbor

H—Hits
HA—Hastings
HR—Home Runs
IN—Indianapolis
IP—Innings Pitched
JO—Joplin
KC—Kansas City
L—Losses
LB—Long Beach
LE—Leavenworth
LI—Lincoln
LOB—Left on Base
ML—Milwaukee
MN—Minneapolis
MU—Muskogee
MV—Mission Viejo
NO—Norfolk
OM—Omaha
PAC—Pacific
PB—Passed Balls
Pct.—Percentage
PO—Putouts
POS—Position
PS—Palm Springs
R—Runs
RI—Rock Island
RNO—Reno
S—Sacrifices
SAL—Salinas

Abbreviations Used

SB—Stolen Bases
SC—Sioux City
SH—Sacrifice Hits
ShO—Shutouts
SJ—St. Joseph
SNC—Sonoma County
SO—Strikeouts
SP—St. Paul
SPG—Springfield
SUR—Surrey

SV—Saves
TB—Total Bases
TC—Total Chances
TH—Terre Haute
TO—Topeka
TOL—Toledo
TRI—Tri-City
W—Wins
WES—Western
ZI—Zion

1
The Inaugural Season

Professional baseball was not well organized in the 1880s. The first minor leagues were slow to develop. Many teams or leagues operated on a day-to-day basis. Just a handful of minor leagues operated before 1885. When the Union Association met on January 15, 1885, in Milwaukee for its annual meeting, only two teams attended, which led to its demise. Kansas City and Milwaukee were already financially committed to another baseball season, so closing up shop was out of the question. The teams decided that same day that a new league was needed. It would be called the Western League, although the area today is now considered the Midwest.

Tim Sullivan, the co-owner of the Kansas City club, wired Toledo and Indianapolis to inquire if the former American Association teams were interested in the new league. Toledo had no firm commitment from the Association, and Indianapolis had been dropped by the Association for poor attendance. Both showed interest.

Eight teams were desired, so more teams were contacted and an organizational meeting was set up in Indianapolis in early February. Delegates from Cleveland, Indianapolis, Kansas City, Milwaukee, Nashville, St. Paul and Toledo arrived. Attention also came from Columbus, Evansville, Minneapolis, Omaha and Springfield, Ohio. Cincinnati also showed some interest, although a National League team was already playing there. The first order of business was election of officers. A.V. Kim of Kansas City was named president, while C.M. Kipp was named vice president. Phillip Igae of Indianapolis became the secretary and treasurer. Directors included T.H. Whipple of Toledo, Joseph Swabacher of Indianapolis and T. Lawrence of Cleveland. The new league decided to become party to the National Agreement as a minor league. The agreement meant the league would not sign players banned or blacklisted by other agreement teams. Teams would be required to have enough money at start-up to finance the team for a month—about $1,800. In other business, visiting teams were guaranteed $75 or 30 percent of gate receipts, as they might elect. Admission in those days ranged anywhere from a dime to a quarter for the bleachers.

American Association playing rules were adopted, with a few exceptions, such as the restrictions on pitching delivery. Sunday play would be allowed; however, some teams were restricted by blue laws, such as Indianapolis. So some teams maintained a park outside the city to play on the Sabbath and skirt the law. The official ball would be made by A.J. Reach. Sullivan was appointed the head of the umpires committee. Umps would be paid $5 a game plus travel and expenses. Sullivan also became the traveling representative for the league.

At the end of February, Sullivan traveled to Philadelphia to complete the affiliation with the National Association. By then he had commitments from Cleveland, Indianapolis, Kansas City, Milwaukee, Nashville, St. Paul and Toledo. Nashville had to be dropped though because the city already possessed a Southern League club. The league would begin with six teams.

By late March, Grand Rapids, Keokuk, Omaha and Minneapolis were also being considered for the league. Of the four, only Omaha was admitted and became a replacement for St. Paul, which couldn't raise enough money. Omaha was behind the other teams, which already had signed enough players for spring training and exhibition games.

The season opened for the league on April 18 with a full slate of games, but the Cleveland-at-Toledo contest was rained out. Kansas City hosted Omaha at its new park on Southwest Boulevard at Broadway, which was on the outskirts of the city. Pastime Park held about 11,000 in the shape of an amphitheater, but a disappointing 3,000 fans attended the opener, which the Cowboys won 12–4 over the Omahas. Milwaukee opened in Indianapolis in foul weather, which held the crowd to 700 at the Washington Park Stadium. Milwaukee edged the Hoosiers 3–1 on five-hit pitching by Charles Baldwin.

Cleveland opened the season the following day at Toledo at the same stadium the team used the year before when it was with the American Association. Every Cleveland player got a hit in an 11–5 rout of the Avengers before 3,500 fans. Cleveland continued its mastery over Toledo and swept the four-game series. Kansas also swept its three-game set with Omaha. Indianapolis rebounded to whip Milwaukee the next three games that first week of the season.

In the second week of play, league-leading Cleveland traveled to Omaha, second-place Kansas City hosted Milwaukee and third-place Indianapolis laid out the red carpet for Toledo. Omaha held its games at a stadium located a considerable distance out of town, which hurt attendance for the series, and the teams split the series. Milwaukee and Kansas City also split their series, while Indianapolis swept their series with Toledo. The seven-game winning streak sent the Hoosiers atop the league after two weeks of play.

Indianapolis continued its winning ways in Week Three by whipping Omaha in three games and tying another contest to end its winning streak at 10 games. Omaha would have forfeited those games because Ed Kent was found to be blacklisted. He was immediately released, and Omaha would not be further penalized. Second-place Cleveland journeyed to Kansas City. The Cowboys were drawing the best crowds in the league and swept Cleveland to take over second place. Milwaukee also swept Toledo in a three-games series in the brewery town. One of the games was rained out.

The fourth week of play featured a series between the top two teams. Indianapolis traveled to Kansas City, who had yet to be on the road. The Cowboys won the opener in 10 innings but lost the next three. The second game drew some 10,000 fans. The wildest affair was the last game of the series. With Kansas City up a bunch, a small yellow dog jumped into the Indianapolis dugout and laid his head on J.W. McKeenan's knee. The dog changed the Hoosiers' luck as the team scored seven runs to tighten up the contest. The dog disappeared for a few innings before returning and bringing more luck to the team. Indianapolis scored another seven runs to win the game 17–12. Third-place Milwaukee continued its standing by taking three of four from Cleveland. The bottom dwellers fought each other, and Toledo finally won its first game of the season after 11 straight defeats. The teams split the series. The second game was a wild affair in which Toledo committed 18 errors! Still, it only lost by a run, 16–15.

The first half of the season ended with the following standings:

	W	L	T	Pct	GB
Indianapolis Hoosiers	13	2	1	.846	—
Kansas City Cowboys	10	5	0	.667	3
Milwaukee Cream Citys	9	6	0	.667	4
Cleveland Forest City	7	9	0	.438	6½
Omaha Omahogs	4	11	1	.267	9
Toledo Avengers	2	13	0	.133	11

The second half opened auspiciously, with the league taking on the court over Sunday baseball. Omaha traveled to Cleveland where police arrested three players for playing on Sunday to make a point, but curiously did not stop the game. The prosecutor decided only to take Cleveland catcher Andy Sommers to trial over the matter as a test case of the law. The defense insisted that the law was unconstitutional because it made no exception for those who held another day as the Sabbath. The jury found Sommers guilty. The club vowed to appeal the case to a higher court. The problem was not restricted to the Midwest; 45 other baseball players were arrested in New York City, too.

Cleveland completely overwhelmed Omaha the first week of the second half, scoring 52 runs to Omaha's 16 runs in four games. First-place Indianapolis continued in first by splitting a four-game series with Milwaukee. Toledo and Kansas City also split their games.

The following week was marred by the Sunday problem. The entire Cleveland team was arrested this time by Marshall Locke, who had unsuccessfully tried out for the team and played briefly with Omaha. Attendance was always bigger at Sunday games, so the league insisted on playing on the Sabbath. Cleveland lost three of four games to Toledo during the week.

Another problem developed in Kansas City. Owner Sullivan charged an umpire, who responded with a left to his jaw. The Cowboys managed only one win in four games with Milwaukee. Meanwhile, Indianapolis swept Omaha with ease. Attendance was down throughout the league, with the exception of Kansas City and Milwaukee. Some teams were losing money, and a turnaround was necessary soon if they were to continue.

Battles with umpires continued into June as Omaha pitcher Bob Black and umpire John Brennan fought in the lobby of the Lindell Hotel. Omaha had dropped four straight to Kansas City. Indianapolis also swept Cleveland, and Milwaukee took three of four games from Toledo.

Omaha's poor performance on the field was compounded by poor attendance and led the team to drop out of the league. The Milwaukee club was headed to Omaha to play when the team folded. However, the league was quick to admit Keokuk to the league, and Milwaukee took a detour to Iowa. Keokuk was well financed and had a second field, Crystal Glen Park, to play at on Sunday. On other days they played in Sportsmans Park. Keokuk won three of five games against Milwaukee.

Cleveland traveled to Kansas City and won the first game of the series before surprising the league by folding up the next day. The team cited huge losses—about $2,500—and not being able to play on Sunday as the reasons for its demise. In fact, later in the week Kansas City and Cleveland tried to play an exhibition game on Sunday, and law officers stopped the game after three innings.

More bad news came in Toledo, which folded after it was unable to make a $75 guarantee to Indianapolis. Toledo manager Dan O'Leary cited losses up to $8,000. In fact, players were paid in jewelry and apparel in lieu of salary. Some players were paid as little as $2.50 a day.

St. Joseph and St. Paul applied for membership to replace Toledo and Cleveland, but the league decided to go on with just four teams. Indianapolis played a series with Kansas City which lasted only two games because the Hoosiers sold its players to Detroit of the National League.

The remaining teams held a meeting on June 15 at the Indianapolis Grand Hotel and considered admission of teams from St. Joseph, St. Paul and Springfield, Illinois. The St. Joseph franchise was quickly eliminated from consideration when a Grand Jury indicted a number of players for playing on Sunday. Financial consideration ended any speculation with the other clubs. Players and managers jumped ship quickly for positions with other teams. The league disbanded. Keokuk went on to barnstorm another month before calling it "quits." Memphis took over the Kansas City club. Bad weather and restrictions on Sunday play had kept the league from becoming a success.

Final Standings

	W	L	T	Pct.	GB
Indianapolis Hoosiers	27	4	1	.852	—
Milwaukee Cream Citys	20	15	0	.750	9
Kansas City Cowboys	17	13	0	.765	9½
Omaha Omahogs/ Keokuk Hawkeyes	7	27	1	.206	21½
*Cleveland Forest City	13	16	0	.448	NA
*Toledo Avengers	8	21	0	.276	NA

*Teams disbanded before the end of the season.

Blacks Play in Western League

In the early days of baseball, no color line existed and a couple of black players were part of the Western League. Moses Walker was a "crack colored player" for Cleveland. He became the first African-American player in the majors when he caught for the Toledo Blue Stockings of the American Association in 1884.

Another black player in the league was John Fowler, a second baseman with Keokuk. Fowler is considered the first professional black ballplayer, beginning his career in 1878. He also played for Topeka the following season in the Western League.

By 1889, African-Americans were barred from most of organized baseball until Jackie Robinson broke the color barrier in 1947 with the

The 1885 Keokuk team joined the Western League shortly before it folded. The squad included John Fowler (center, standing), the first professional black player. (Photograph courtesy of the National Baseball Hall of Fame, Cooperstown, N.Y.)

Brooklyn Dodgers. Another African-American player would not play in the Western League again until 1950.

"Big" Sam Had Roots in League

"Big" Sam Thompson, an Indiana farm boy, began his professional career with Indianapolis and was one of the better hitters in the Western League in 1885. In 30 games he collected 14 extra base hits. After the league folded he went to Detroit and played there for four seasons.

At six-foot-two, the mustachioed ex-carpenter was considered a mammoth. He earned his nickname by clouting 20 home runs one season for Philadelphia, which was quite an accomplishment considering the ball and fields. In 15 major league seasons he hit 127 four baggers.

In 1974 the Veterans Committee named him to the Hall of Fame.

"Lady" Baldwin Was No Lady

Charles "Lady" Baldwin, who acquired the feminine name because he neither smoked, drank nor swore, pitched for Milwaukee before joining Detroit after the league ended.

The southpaw had a fantastic 42–13 record for the Detroit Wolverines in 1886 to lead the league in victories. In 1887 he was deadly in the World Series, winning four of five games against St. Louis.

Baldwin pitched for six seasons in the majors before retiring in 1890.

Veach Had Odd Nickname

Willie "Peek-a-Boo" Veach acquired his unusual nickname when he played for Kansas City of the Union Association in 1884. He was bothered by men on base, so his manager told him to look at the bench for a signal to indicate when he should throw to first. After he picked off two men, the opposition got wise to the signal. So the manager moved the signal to a person in the stands, but the other team figured out what was going on.

Veach led the Western League in wins that first season. He went on to play first base for Louisville in the American Association in 1887 and the National League in 1890. After baseball, Veach joined Teddy Roosevelt's Rough Riders in the Spanish-American War.

Batting Leaders
RUNS
Emmett Seery, KC—43
Thomas O'Brien, KC—41
Thomas Poorman, IN—41
Charles Collins, IN—38
Sam Thompson, IN—38

HITS
William O'Brien, KC—51

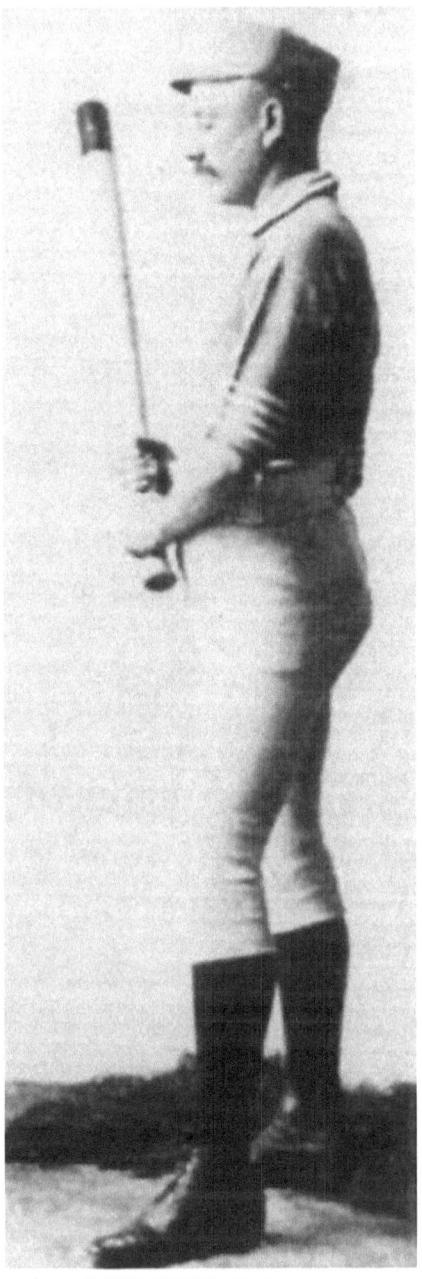

Charles "Lady" Baldwin pitched for Milwaukee in 1885. (Photograph courtesy of Jay Sanford.)

Eugene Moriarty, IN—46
Sam Thompson, IN—45
Emmett Seery, KC—41
Ernest Birch, KC—39
Thomas Poorman, IN -39

DOUBLES
William O'Brien, KC—15
Joe Morrison, TOL—11
Michael Kennedy, CLE—10
Eugene Moriarty, IN—10
William Query, IN—10

TRIPLES
Emmett Seery, KC—9
Eugene Moriarty, IN—6
Sam Thompson, IN—5
Harry Wheeler, CLE—5
Several with 4

HOME RUNS
J.W. Keenan, IN—3
Thomas Poorman, IN—2
Several with 1

Pitching Leaders

GAMES
William Veach, KC—18
William Stemmyer, TOL—17
Charles Baldwin, MI—16
Larry McKeon, IN—14
William O'Donnell, OM—13

GAMES STARTED
William Veach, KC—17
William Stemmyer, TOL—17
Charles Baldwin, MI—15
Larry McKeon, IN—14
Several with 11

COMPLETE GAMES
William Stemmyer, TOL—17
Larry McKeon, IN—14
William Veach, KC—14
Charles Baldwin, MI—14
Several with 11

WINS
Larry McKeon, IN—11
Charles Baldwin, MI—10
William Veach, KC—9
Daniel Casey, IN—9
Several with 7

LOSSES
Emmett Seery, KC—11
William O'Donnell, OM—9
William Veach, KC—8
Chuck Lauer, CLE—7

SHUTOUTS
Charles Baldwin, MI—2
Several with 1

2
The Early Years (1886–1893)

Ted Sullivan, who organized the Western League in 1885, decided to revive the dormant Northwestern League instead of continuing the Western League in 1886. So a group of men, including *The Sporting News* founder Al Spink, gathered in St. Joseph, Missouri, on January 18 to breathe life into the Western League again. League officials met again on March 28 in Leavenworth, Kansas, and decided on an 80-game schedule for the six-team league, which included teams in Denver and Leadville in Colorado; Leavenworth and Topeka in Kansas; Lincoln, Nebraska; and St. Joseph, Missouri. These teams were much further west than those in the previous league. Edward Murphy was named president.

1886

During an exhibition game in April, the league showed it was competitive with the National League as "Bond Hill" Billy Hart pitched a no-hitter against the St. Louis Maroons.

On July 4, Leadville and Denver were delayed 30 minutes by a snowstorm. That was a hazard in mountainous Colorado. The first full season of the league ended on Sept. 20 with Denver winning the pennant, four games ahead of an unlikely St. Joseph squad. Surprisingly, the Missouri team won second place while never fielding more than 10 players on the roster. Manager Nin Alexander performed double duty, serving as the team's catcher. The team had just two pitchers who alternated playing center field when they weren't on the mound. Denver, on the other hand, led the league in hitting by a wide margin thanks to Darby O'Brien, who led the hitting with a .348 average. Another one of the leading hitters was Lincoln's Perry Werden (.317). Perry also played for Topeka in 1887 and for Minneapolis in the 1890s.

The Western League

A trio of players pose in this 1886 photo of the Leadville Blues. (Photograph courtesy of Jay Sanford)

Beckley Develops Hidden-Ball Trick

One of the leading hitters in the league in 1886 was Leavenworth's Jake Beckley. He averaged .341 and showed some power. He bettered

The Early Years (1886–1893)

Denver's Darby O'Brien led the Western League in hitting with a .348 average in 1886. Later he played with Brooklyn in the National League. (Photograph courtesy of Jay Sanford)

himself the following season by hitting .401 with Leavenworth and Lincoln. He started his major league career with the Pittsburgh Pirates in 1888.

While Beckley wasn't the best fielding first baseman, he was clever and developed a hidden-ball trick. He would hide the ball under one corner of first base. When the runner took his lead, Beckley simply reached down, retrieved the ball and tagged him out.

The large first baseman would go on to distinguish himself in the majors and finished with a career .308 average. After 20 seasons in the majors, Beckley came back to play one more season in the Western League in 1910 with Topeka. In 1971 he was named to the Hall of Fame by the Veterans Committee.

Tebeau Brothers Start in League

The Tebeau brothers both started their professional careers in the Western League in 1886. Oliver played for St. Joseph and hit .294 as its second baseman, while his brother, George, played for Denver and was one of the leading hitters in the league with a .317 average.

The following season, Oliver, whose nickname was "Patsy," replaced his brother in Denver and hit .424 in 95 games. George took on the name "White Wings" and went to play for Cincinnati of the American Association, where he became the first player to hit a home run in his first major league at-bat.

Both players continued with careers in the majors. Patsy became a player-manager with the Cleveland Spiders in 1891. George went back to Denver to play and manage the team

Jake Beckley played first base for Leavenworth in 1886. He then played for the Pirates, Reds and Giants to earn a spot in the Hall of Fame.

Opposite Top: The Leadville Blues lasted only one year in the league. (Photograph courtesy of Jay Sanford)
Opposite Bottom: The Denver Mountain Lions won the pennant in 1886. Pictured are (standing) Fred O'Neil, Tom McAndries, Jack Ryan (middle), Billy Mountjoy, president George Higgins, manager W. Wallace, Tom Hogan, Frank Meinke; (sitting) Joe Straub, Ed Silch, Lanser, Dan Dugan; (lying down) Darby O'Brien and George Tebeau. (Photograph courtesy of Jay Sanford)

Oliver "Patsy" Tebeau played in the Western League in 1886 along with his brother, George. Later he played and managed Cleveland. (Photograph courtesy of Jay Sanford)

The Early Years (1886–1893)

George Tebeau played in the Western League before managing four different teams in the league from 1897 to 1901. (Photograph courtesy of Jay Sanford)

in the Western Association for a spell. In 1894 George joined his brother in Cleveland for a couple of seasons.

George returned to the Western League to manage several teams: Columbus, 1897–98; Grand Rapids, 1899; Denver, 1900; and Kansas City, 1901. He helped to turn the Western League into the American League, then he assisted in starting a new Western League in 1900.

After baseball, Patsy killed himself in 1918 in his own restaurant after his wife had left him. George became a millionaire and lived until 1923.

1886

Final Standings

	W	L	Pct.	GB
Denver Mountain Lions	54	26	.675	—
St. Joseph Reds	50	30	.625	4
Leadville Blues	39	41	.487	15
Topeka Capitals	35	45	.437	19
Leavenworth Soldiers	31	49	.387	23
Lincoln Tree Planters	31	49	.387	23

Team Batting

	AB	R	H	Avg.
Denver	2,763	629	774	.284
St. Joseph	2,655	560	692	.260
Leadville	2,732	575	754	.276
Topeka	2,753	530	674	.245
Leavenworth	2,702	464	656	.242
Lincoln	2,585	379	625	.242

Team Fielding

	PO	A	E	Pct.
St. Joseph	1730	1110	306	.962
Lincoln	1796	1404	322	.908
Topeka	1803	929	341	.889
Leavenworth	1782	1048	359	.889
Leadville	1814	1222	355	.887
Denver	1661	1103	376	.885

Individual Hitting Leaders
(240 At Bats Minimum)

	G	AB	H	Avg.
O'Brien, DE	77	294	102	.348
Harding, SJ	47	251	82	.338
Hall, SJ	70	272	87	.319
Tebeau, DE	89	306	97	.317
Werden, LI	67	262	83	.317

1887

Teams folded like bad poker hands in 1887. The Leadville franchise disbanded at the start of the 1887 season, but Omaha and Hastings in Nebraska, and Kansas City, Missouri, were added. Leavenworth was forced to quit after a game on July 8 due to lack of fan support. It was replaced by Wichita, which came over from the Kansas State League, on July 26. Two days later, St. Joseph ceased. It was replaced by Emporia, Kansas, on Aug. 13. Then Wichita folded on Sept. 5, followed quickly by Emporia on Sept. 9.

Topeka clinched the pennant on Sept. 24 by defeating Lincoln for its 17th straight victory and twenty-third out of twenty-four games won. The schedule went through Oct. 13, but the last game was played Oct. 2. Lincoln set an all-time offensive record during the season when it routed newcomer Wichita 46–7 on 50 hits. The record number of hits was inflated by the rule that counted a walk as a hit. That rule also propelled Percival Werden, who would play seven years in the majors, to a 35-game hitting streak during the season. The one-year rule ballooned batting averages of individuals and teams to record highs. And it hurt pitchers. At least one—James Conway of Topeka—was robbed of a no-hitter.

Long Played Twice in League

Herman "Germany" Long played left field for Emporia in 1887 and

The Early Years (1886–1893)   21

The Topeka Golden Giants won the Western League pennant in 1887. (Photograph courtesy of the National Baseball Hall of Fame, Cooperstown, N.Y.)

led the league in that position with a .915 fielding percentage—not very high by today's standards.

Long played for Kansas City in 1889 in the American Association before going to the National League the following year. In the majors he

Kid Nichols pitched for Kansas City in 1887. He returned to play in the Western League in 1902. He later was named to the Hall of Fame. (Photograph courtesy of Jay Sanford)

The Early Years (1886–1893) 23

Herman Long had two stints in the Western League. He was with Emporia in 1887 and later with Des Moines in 1905. (Photograph courtesy of Jay Sanford)

John Gaffney was an umpire in the Western League in 1887. (Photograph courtesy of Jay Sanford)

was switched to shortstop, where he committed a lot more errors, but fielders in those days didn't have the gloves or the ability of today's players. He became better as the years went by and he led the National League at that position for a couple of seasons.

In all, Herman played 16 seasons in the majors before returning to the Western League again in 1905 to manage Des Moines for a season. He contracted tuberculosis and died in 1909.

The Early Years (1886–1893)   25

RIVERFRONT PARK - DENVER, COLORADO 1887

An artist drew this action at Riverfront Park in Denver in 1887. (Drawing courtesy of Jay Sanford)

1887
Final Standings

	W	L	Pct.	GB
Topeka Golden Giants	83	24	.775	—
Lincoln Tree Planters	62	34	.645	15½
Denver Mountaineers	51	49	.510	23½
Kansas City Cowboys	49	53	.480	31½
Omaha Omahogs	36	65	.356	44
Hastings	33	62	.347	44
*Leavenworth Soldiers	27	27	.500	N/A
*St. Joseph Reds	21	48	.304	N/A
*Wichita Braves	7	32	.179	N/A
*Emporia	5	18	.217	N/A

*Disbanded during the season.
The final standings do not include games with Emporia or Wichita, as the league failed to recognize those games in the official final standings.

Team Batting

	AB	R	H	HR	SB	Avg.
Topeka	5060	1354	1975	56	449	.390
Lincoln	4561	1138	1684	85	224	.369
Denver	4884	1156	1772	50	237	.363
Kansas City	4763	1039	1663	46	346	.349
Hastings	4095	728	1314	57	178	.321
Omaha	4186	783	1291	27	362	.308

Team Fielding

	PO	A	E	DP	Pct.
Topeka	3025	1527	471	68	.906
Lincoln	2800	1370	458	47	.901
Denver	2944	1601	525	64	.896
Omaha	2766	1328	505	55	.890
Kansas City	3067	1473	585	72	.886
Hastings	2711	1403	579	63	.877

Individual Fielding Leaders
(Minimum 70 Games)

	POS	PO	A	E	DP	Pct.
Smith, DE	1b	1224	38	36	49	.972
McSorley, DE	2b	307	388	76	38	.904
Tebeau, DE	3b	162	195	47	9	.884
Phillips, DE	ss	118	373	63	34	.886
Hassamaer, KC	rf	206	52	33	7	.896
Gorman, DE	cf	159	23	24	2	.883
Welch, HA	lf	130	24	20	0	.878
Gunson, TO	c	352	79	19	3	.958

Individual Batting Leaders
(Minimum 357 at Bats)

	AB	H	Avg.
Macullar, James, TO	567	263	.464
Shaffer, George, LI	443	204	.460
Stearns, Daniel, TO	605	265	.438
Manning, James, KC	392	171	.436
Mansell, Thomas, KC	476	207	.435

Earned Run Average Leaders
(Minimum 20 Decisions)

	G	W	L	Pct.	ERA
Swartzel, LE/LI	51	31	15	.674	3.05
Nichols, KC	33	18	13	.581	3.22

The Early Years (1886–1893) 27

	G	W	L	Pct.	ERA
Conway, TO	43	32	9	.780	3.54
Sullivan, TO	47	36	9	.800	3.68
Fitzsimmons, LE/SJ/DE	29	19	10	.655	3.74

Batting Leaders

HOME RUNS
Beckley, LE/LI—16
Holliday, TO—16
Rowe, LI—14
Herr, LI—13
Mansell, KC—13

TRIPLES
Beckley, LE/LI—24
Joyce, LE/KC—25
Stearns, TO—20
Rowe, LI—18
Dolan, LI—17

DOUBLES
Hassamer, KC—38
Holliday, TO—37
Silch, DE—36
Beckley, LE/LI—33
Several with 32

HITS
Stearns, TO—265
Macullar, TO—263
Holliday, TO—231
McSorley, DE—229
Silch, DE—228

STOLEN BASES
Lillie, KC—69
Manning, KC—62
Stearns, TO—39
Hassamer, KC—38
Mansell, KC—32

RUNS
Stearns, TO—189
Holliday, TO—172
Macullar, TO—167
Silch, DE—165
Johnson, TO—152

Pitching Leaders

WINS
Sullivan, TO—36
Conway, TO—32
Swartzel, LE/LI—31
Hart, LI—28
Ehret, SJ/DE—20

LOSSES
Healey, OM—27
Ehret, SJ/DE—25
Wehrle, HA—25
Nichols, HA—23
Barston, SJ/OM—18

INNINGS PITCHED
Ehret, SJ/DE—405
Swartzel, LI/LI—401
Sullivan, TO—396
Wehrle, HA—377
Healey, OM—373.2

STRIKEOUTS
Swartzel, LE/LI—205
Sullivan, TO—142
Conway, TO—138
Ehret, SJ/DE—133
Healey, OM—129

WILD PITCHES
Healey, OM—27
Swartzel, LE/LI—27
Ehret, SJ/DE—23
Sullivan, TO—22
Bartson, SJ/OM—21

HIT BATTERS
Ehret, SJ/DE—24
Sullivan, TO—21
Conway, TO—19
Voss, DE—19
Barston, SJ/OM—17

Left: Bill Traffley played for Des Moines in 1888. He later managed the team when it moved to the Western Association. (Photograph courtesy of Jay Sanford)
 Right: Pitcher Burt "Cowboy" Jones pitched for Denver in 1888. (Photograph courtesy of Jay Sanford)

1888

The same month that the Western League was concluding play, owners in other cities were forming the Western Association. The Western League reorganized in February 1888 with just five teams comprising the league. New to the league were Hutchinson and Newton, both from Kansas. Kansas City departed for the Western Association, which included teams from Des Moines, St. Louis, St. Paul, Omaha, Milwaukee, Sioux City, Chicago and Davenport.

After a couple of weeks of play, the league began to unravel. Lincoln disbanded on June 6, followed by Newton on June 11. With only three teams remaining, the rest of the league dissolved on June 21. Some players were picked up by other teams, while others would have to wait another season. Denver was leading the league by a wide margin, and pitcher Avery was perfect with an 8–0 record.

Cal McVey, who played four years in the majors in its early days, played for the Denver Mountaineers in 1888. (Photograph courtesy of Jay Sanford)

Pitcher Bill Fagan helped the Denver team finish first in the shortened 1888 season. (Photograph courtesy of Jay Sanford)

1888

Final Standings

	W	L	Pct.	GB
Denver Mountaineers	18	6	.750	—
Leavenworth Soldiers	7	7	.500	6
Hutchinson	9	10	.474	6½
*Newton	3	5	.375	N/A
*Lincoln Tree Planters	2	11	.154	N/A

*Disbanded before the end of the season.

Individual Hitting
(Minimum 72 At Bats)

	AB	H	Avg.
Krehmeyer, DE	83	28	.337
Genins, DE	85	28	.329
Rafferty, HU	86	27	.313
J. Curran, LE	80	24	.300
Litz, DE	87	26	.298

Individual Fielding
(Minimum 10 Games)

	POS	PO	A	E	Pct.
White, HU	1b	206	3	11	.950
McAndries, DE	2b	55	47	10	.910
Larkin, LE	3b	23	5	7	.872
Rafferty, HU	ss	30	58	12	.880
Gorman, DE	of	25	1	1	.962
Corkhill, HU	of	40	17	7	.890
Whitely, HU	of	27	6	5	.868
Krehmeyer, DE	c	69	32	5	.952

Earned Run Average Leaders

	W	L	Pct.	ERA
Ware, LI	4	1	.800	1.50
Avery, DE	8	0	1.000	1.75
Murphy, LE	5	3	.625	2.25
Kane, HU	4	5	.444	2.30
Moore, LI	1	6	.143	2.42

1889–1891

The Western League was not to be heard from again until 1892. Meanwhile, the Western Association continued with limited success and absorbed some of the teams from the Western League. The players tried running their own professional league—the Players League—in 1890, but it lasted only one season.

These were hard times, as a depression had choked the country since 1883. In 1891 the Western Association dwindled to four teams, as four teams folded before the end of the season. The Sioux City Cornhuskers won the pennant that season and also won a post-season series from the Chicago White Stockings and St. Louis Browns of the National League.

1892

In 1892 the Western Association was gone and the Western League was revived, with clubs in Kansas City, Minneapolis, St. Paul, Omaha, Milwaukee, Toledo, Indianapolis and Columbus, Ohio. St. Paul dropped out in May and Fort Wayne took its place. Columbus won the first half of the season. Soon after that, Fort Wayne and Milwaukee folded and the league crumpled on July 11. Contributing factors to the league's demise included rainy weather and poor fan interest. Ironically, the Indianapolis team was inappropriately named Rainmakers. More than a third of Columbus' wins came at the hands of pitcher George Stephens, who led the league in wins with 18.

1892

Final Standings

	W	L	Pct.	GB
Columbus Reds	46	26	.697	—
Kansas City Cowboys	33	33	.500	13
Omaha Omahogs	31	31	.500	13
Toledo Black Pirates	28	29	.491	13½
Minneapolis Minnies	21	25	.457	15
Indianapolis Rainmakers	15	39	.278	25
*Milwaukee Brewers	32	21	.604	N/A
*St. Paul Saints/Fort Wayne	20	31	.392	N/A

*Disbanded before the end of the season

Individual Hitting Leaders
(Minimum 205 At Bats)

	G	AB	R	H	S	SB	Avg.
Sutcliffe, SP/FW	46	212	42	70	12	14	.330
McClellan, COL	59	215	34	65	16	18	.302

	G	AB	R	H	S	SB	Avg.
Manning, KC	49	222	62	67	7	30	.301
Sunday, KC	49	216	36	63	12	7	.291
O'Rourke, COL	58	217	36	62	13	28	.285

Individual Fielding Leaders

	POS	PO	A	E	Pct.
Motz, SP/FW	1b	556	14	2	.997
Manning, KC	2b	111	109	19	.943
O'Rourke, COL	3b	71	126	19	.912
McGarr, MIL	ss	85	150	22	.915
Lally, COL	rf	99	5	4	.963
Abbey, COL	cf	110	4	7	.944
Hogriever, SP/FW	lf	121	7	10	.927
McMahon, KC	c	221	61	5	.982

Batting Leaders

HITS
Sutcliff, SP/FW—70

STOLEN BASES
Ward, MIL—39

RUNS
Manning, KC—62

Pitching Leaders

WINS
George Stephens, COL—18

STRIKEOUTS
Jim Hughes, KC—111

WINNING PERCENTAGE
Fred Clausen, COL—.773, 17–5

1893

In 1893 the Western League was again dormant. The Western Association had plans to put teams in Omaha, Des Moines, St. Joseph, Lincoln, Rock Island, Quincy, Peoria and Jacksonville on the diamond, but the league never got off the ground. The depression continued to spell hard times for the economy and baseball.

3

The Johnson Years (1894–1899)

After a year with no Western League or Association, an organizational meeting was held on Nov. 20, 1893, at a secret session in the Grand Hotel in Detroit. Representatives came from Grand Rapids, Sioux City, Minneapolis, Milwaukee, Kansas City, Toledo, Indianapolis and Detroit. Cincinnati Reds manager Charles Comiskey persuaded the delegates to name Ban Johnson, a sports editor, as the president, secretary and treasurer of the new organization. "Mr. Ban Johnson, besides being an authority on baseball, is competent to fill the position to which we elected him," said D.A. Long, who represented Toledo. Johnson, the son of a college professor, would fit into the role because he was humorless and dictatorial. He received a salary of $2,500. Johnson set out to bring more honesty to the game, better umpiring and more of a family atmosphere.

The new Western League consisted of teams from Detroit, Grand Rapids, Indianapolis, Kansas City, Milwaukee, Minneapolis, Sioux City and Toledo. Some member cities had once fielded teams in the majors, including Detroit, which had been in the National League for eight seasons in the 1880s. George A. Vanderbeck was the president of the club, and it became known as the Tigers after the striped socks worn by the players.

Indianapolis had been in the National League, too. Its owner was John T. Brush, who also owned the Cincinnati Reds, so Indianapolis was going to be a strong contender with its direct links to the majors. Meanwhile, the teams from the old Western League formed the Western Association, along with four Illinois communities.

Johnson Brings New Life to Western League

Byron Bancroft "Ban" Johnson began to love the game of baseball as a child growing up in Cincinnati. He became a catcher in high school and played at Oberlin College. Johnson was on track to become a lawyer, but he quit college to join the *Cincinnati Commercial-Gazette*, much to his father's disliking.

Johnson quickly moved up from reporter to sports editor. He came

Ban Johnson lived in this home in Spencer, Indiana, before his death in 1930. (Photograph by W.C. Madden)

Joe Drescher cleans off the gravestone of Ban Johnson in Spencer, Indiana, where he is buried beside his wife. The Lions repaired the mausoleum and put a plaque on it to inform visitors that Johnson was the founder of the American League. (Photograph by W.C. Madden)

to know Charles Comiskey while covering the National League team. The two supposedly kicked around the idea of reviving the Western League at a local drinking establishment called the Ten-Minute Club, where patrons had to order drinks every ten minutes or be shown the door.

After the dream became a reality, Ban set out on a course to eventually turn the Western into the American League as a rival to the National League. He also went on a mission to clean up the game in his league and make it more respectable. Under his tutelage, the league became the best-run circuit in organized baseball.

After succeeding in turning the American League into a major league, he presided over it until his health forced him to retire in 1927. He died in 1930. Johnson became known as the "Czar of Baseball." Besides founding the American League, he helped establish baseball in Mexico in the 1920s.

1894

In the Western League's first season, Sioux City jumped out to a big lead before fizzling near the end, but it held on to take the pennant. The Cornhusters were sparked by George Hogriever, who led the league in stolen bases (93), and F. Genins (with a .385 average). Pitcher Pete Daniels won more than half of Kansas City's victories to lead the Blues to third. Indianapolis was never in the race. The Hoosiers got off to a slow start before Brush began sending some major league players to Indianapolis, a move which irked President Johnson.

The Sioux City Cornhuskers won the Western League pennant in 1894. (Photograph courtesy of the National Baseball Hall of Fame, Cooperstown, N.Y.)

The first season was a financial success, thanks to Johnson's approach to the game. The financial situation was helped by the National League, which compensated the league $500 for any player it drafted. That figure was raised to $1,000 the next season but dropped back to $500 after that.

"Iron Man" Pitches for the Blues

Joe "Iron Man" McGinnity's professional career started off slowly in the Western League, as the hurler was just 8–10 for the Kansas City Blues in 1894.

Joe went back to semipro ball for a couple of years and developed an underhanded pitch that was much harder to hit. He returned to pro ball in 1898 with the Western Association. The following season he was in the majors until the end of his career.

The righthander's best season came in 1904 when he was 35–8 for New York in the National League. He would go on to a 248–141 professional record, which landed him in the Hall of Fame in 1946.

"Moose" Clouts 43 Dingers

Minneapolis' Perry "Moose" Werden hit 43 homers in 1894, which was far more than other hitters in organized baseball. That was significant, because it occurred during the dead ball era.

He passed that milestone the next season by stroking 45 homers and topping the league with a .428 average. His home run record would stand until Babe Ruth topped it in 1920. He also had seven triples and 39 doubles. In one game in 1895 he hit four homers and a single in five trips to the plate. Changes to Athletic Park limited his production the next season, but he still managed 18 homers to lead the league.

After a year in the National League with Louisville in 1897, he returned to Minneapolis, but he broke a leg in an exhibition season and was out for a season. He came back to the Western League in 1901 to play for St. Paul–Des Moines.

Stewart Plays Nine Seasons in Western

Asa "Ace" Stewart began one of the longest careers of any player in the Western League with Sioux City in 1894. The second baseman set the league record for miscues when he recorded 102 errors that season. However, he made up for it by slugging 22 homers to push Sioux City to the title.

His power led him to being purchased by the Chicago Colts to play for Cap Anson in 1895. "Anson and Stewart didn't get along," said his grandson, Patrick Stewart. So Stewart returned to the Western League in 1896 with Indianapolis for four seasons. His fielding improved every season, and Ace helped the Hoosiers finish first or second in each of those seasons.

In 1900 the second baseman went to Kansas City for a while. The next season he was in Omaha for three seasons. During that time he convinced Mordecai "Three-Finger" Brown to play for

Ace Stewart played for Sioux City, Indianapolis, Kansas City and Omaha over nine seasons in the Western League. (Photograph courtesy of Patrick Stewart)

Omaha for a season before the pitcher went on to a long career in the majors.

1894
Final Standings

	W	L	Pct.	GB
Sioux City Cornhuskers	74	51	.592	—
Toledo White Stockings	67	55	.549	5½
Kansas City Blues	68	58	.540	6½
Minneapolis Millers	63	62	.504	10
Grand Rapids Rippers	62	64	.492	12½
Indianapolis Hoosiers	60	64	.484	13½
Detroit Wolverines	56	69	.448	18
Milwaukee Brewers	47	74	.388	24½

Individual Hitting Leaders
(Minimum 390 At Bats)

	G	AB	R	H	Avg.
Wright, GR	133	531	217	253	.476
Hines, MN	130	586	194	250	.427
George, GR	115	515	137	218	.423
Klusman, KC	127	562	168	235	.418
Werden, MN	114	518	140	216	.416

Individual Fielding Leaders
(Minimum 100 Games)

	POS	G	PO	A	E	Pct.
Motz, IN	1b	101	1023	36	16	.985
Conner, TO	2b	117	301	367	39	.945
Clingman, MIL	3b	110	155	246	29	.933
Wheelock, GR	ss	113	205	464	82	.891
Gilks, TOL	of	108	214	18	14	.943
Genins, SC	of	118	320	20	22	.939
Hogriever, SC	of	126	248	16	20	.930
Spies, GR	c	133	597	169	58	.930

Hitting Leaders

HOME RUNS
Perry Werden, MN—43

RUNS
William Wright, GR—217

STOLEN BASES
George Hogriever, SC—93

HITS
Wright, GR—253

Pitching Leaders

WINS
Pete Daniels, KC—36

STRIKEOUTS
Frank Foreman, TOL—190

WINNING PERCENTAGE
Pete Daniels, KC—.735, 36–13

1895

Although Sioux City was a winner on the field, the team was not a winner in the stands, so it was dropped for the 1895 season in favor of a franchise in St. Paul. "Despite the fact that it had a championship team to lure the fans, season attendance at Sioux City was only 42,000 paid admissions," explained President Johnson. That was the only change to the financially sound league, which was considered by baseball as the strongest minor league. Comiskey was granted the franchise, and he managed it as well.

The 1895 season opened on May 1 and some 5,000 fans showed up in Milwaukee for the team's first game against Minneapolis. Milwaukee won 4–3. And St. Paul won 4–3 in Kansas City. Veteran Tony Mullane played first base for St. Paul. The Toledo club received a fatal blow halfway through the season when the city put a ban on Sunday baseball there. The franchise was allowed to move to Terre Haute, Indiana, on July 4. On July 23 Perry Werden of Minneapolis slammed four homers and a single in one game.

One-hundred-twenty-four games were played in the 1895 season. Indianapolis made good on a promise to win the pennant to the *Sporting Life* before the season began when someone was quoted as saying, "Won't swear to it, but we are intending to put spikes on our shoes and climb for it." The Hoosiers did just that and pushed past the St. Paul Saints to win the 1895 pennant by four games. The Indianapolis team received lots of help from Cincinnati, as two key reinforcements—Bill Phillips and George Hogriever—were sent there. Phillips finished with a 12–4 record and Hogriever hit .402. The team caught the ire of the Kansas City press, which called the team "Cincinapolis" because of its connections. Cincinnati owner Brush continued the practice of sending players up and down from Indianapolis, thereby inventing the farm system long before it became a regular practice. The league tried to prevent Brush from "farming" players, but he continued the habit.

Co-founder Comiskey Leads St. Paul Franchise

Charles Comiskey was the co-founder of the Western League of 1894, but he couldn't participate the first year of the league because of his contract with Cincinnati. He had to wait until 1895 before getting a franchise with the league he helped organize.

"The Old Roman" was a first baseman when he first started playing the game in 1882. He is credited with getting pitchers to cover first base when the ball is hit to the right side. He helped start the Players' League in 1890, but it lasted only one season. Then he became a player-manager with the Cincinnati Reds, which is where he met Ban Johnson and the two conspired to start the Western League.

After the Western League transformed into the American League, the St. Paul franchise was moved to Chicago, where Comiskey would run the White Sox. In 1906 his "Hitless Wonders" would surprise the crosstown Cubs in the World Series. In 1910 he built a stadium named after him that was one of the wonders of the baseball world at the time.

However, the owner became a tightwad with his players, which led eight players to turn to gamblers in 1919 to make more money off the World Series. They were caught, which led to the infamous Black Sox Scandal. While all eight players were found not guilty in a trial, they were banned by baseball for life by Commissioner Kenesaw Mountain Landis. Comiskey blamed his old friend Johnson for the scandal, which added to their falling out. Comiskey died in 1931. He was named to the Hall of Fame in 1939.

1895

Final Standings

	W	L	Pct.	GB
Indianapolis Hoosiers	78	43	.645	—
St. Paul Apostles	74	50	.597	5½
Kansas City Blues	73	52	.584	7
Minneapolis Millers	64	59	.520	15
Detroit Tigers	59	66	.472	21
Milwaukee Brewers	57	67	.460	22½
Toledo Swamp Angels/ Terre Haute Hottentots	52	72	.419	27½
Grand Rapids	38	86	.306	41½

Team Batting

	G	AB	R	H	Avg.
Indianapolis	121	4039	1201	1641	.354
Minneapolis	123	4803	1282	1702	.350
Kansas City	125	4623	1071	1505	.338
Grand Rapids	124	4708	1060	1509	.333
St. Paul	124	4711	1185	1512	.321

The Western League

	G	AB	R	H	Avg.
Detroit	125	4700	993	1503	.319
Toledo	124	4480	831	1360	.305
Milwaukee	124	4722	901	1415	.300

Team Fielding

	G	PO	A	E	Pct.
Detroit	125	3254	1668	321	.939
Kansas City	125	3200	1539	342	.933
Toledo	124	3214	1519	339	.933
St. Paul	124	3190	1591	352	.931
Indianapolis	121	3195	1513	372	.927
Minneapolis	125	3218	1658	304	.925
Milwaukee	124	333	1540	408	.923
Grand Rapids	124	3221	1690	456	.915

Individual Fielding Leaders
(Minimum 100 Games)

	POS	G	PO	A	E	Pct.
Klusman, KC	1b	120	1059	3	20	.982
Manning, KC	2b	121	298	344	36	.947
Hatfield, KC	3b	117	138	249	41	.904
Taylor, ML	ss	124	241	429	89	.883
McCarthy, IN	of	120	296	14	20	.939
Gilks, TO	of	105	191	14	14	.930
Burns, MN/SP	of	118	213	17	18	.925
Roach, TO	c	102	448	98	22	.961

Individual Pitching Leaders

	G	ER	ERA
Mullane, SP	30	68	2.30
Fisher, IN	52	128	2.46
Hastings, KC	44	134	3.04
Jones, SP	30	93	3.10
Phillips, IN	18	56	3.11

Individual Hitting Leaders
(Minimum 94 Games)

	G	H	Avg.
Werden, MN	123	179	.428
Dungan, DT	125	149	.424

	G	H	Avg.
McCarthy, IN	121	146	.420
Motz, IN	117	162	.420
Carroll, GR/KC	122	154	.414

1896

The Terre Haute club was dropped in favor of putting a club in Columbus, Ohio, with Tom Loftus as the manager. The league was divided into Eastern and Western Divisions. Indianapolis, Detroit, Toledo and Columbus were put in the Eastern Division, and Milwaukee, St. Paul, Minneapolis and Kansas City comprised the Western Division.

The 1896 season opened in Detroit on April 28 with Charley Bennett being honored. The former star catcher for the 1887 Detroit National League champions had lost both lower legs in a tragic train accident. The park was being named in his honor. In July the St. Paul Apostles knocked out eight homers en route to a 41–8 thrashing of neighbor Minneapolis. Former major league player Jack Glasscock went 8-for-9 and scored seven

The 1896 Minneapolis Millers finished in first place behind the managing of Walter Wilmot, who is pictured in the center of this team photo. (Photograph courtesy of Jay Sanford)

runs. Glasscock, who had 17 years in pro baseball, came over from the National League to play for St. Paul and lead the Western in average with a .431 mark.

The Minneapolis Millers ran away with the pennant in 1896 by a nine-and-a-half-game margin over Indianapolis, despite the *Sporting Life* saying that the team would not be as strong as the previous season in a preseason article. The Millers showcased the best pitcher in the league in Bill Hutchinson, who won an all-time 38 contests. Werden also hit .377 that season in leading the Millers.

Connie Mack Jumps to Western

In 1896 President Johnson read that Connie Mack would not be offered another contract as manager of the Pittsburgh Pirates, so he offered him the managerial job with the Milwaukee Brewers in 1897. Mack accepted.

Connie became a player as well for his team, and appeared in 27 games for the last time in his career, which began professionally in 1886 with Washington in the National League. He played first base and caught during his playing career, but he was just an average hitter.

In 1901, when the American League became a major league, Mack took over as manager and part owner of the Philadelphia Athletics, a new franchise. "The Tall Tactician" became easy to identify on the field because he wore civilian attire instead of a uniform.

Mack became an institution in Philadelphia, as he managed there until 1950 and holds the all-time record for wins and losses in that time. He took the Athletics to nine pennants in 50 seasons and two world championships. On the other hand, his Athletics finished last 17 times during his reign. He was named to the Hall of Fame in 1937.

1896

Final Standings

	W	L	Pct.	GB
Minneapolis Millers	89	47	.654	—
Indianapolis Hoosiers	78	54	.591	9
Detroit Tigers	80	58	.580	10
St. Paul Apostles	73	63	.537	16
Kansas City Blues	69	66	.511	19½
Milwaukee Brewers	62	78	.443	29
Columbus Buckeyes	52	88	.371	39
Grand Rapids Gold Bugs	45	94	.324	45½

Playoffs

Minneapolis beat Indianapolis, 4 games to 2

Team Batting

	G	AB	H	Avg.
St. Paul	136	5282	1788	.339
Minneapolis	136	5005	1609	.321
Kansas City	135	4707	1455	.309
Indianapolis	132	4640	1393	.300
Detroit	138	4990	1486	.298
Milwaukee	140	5251	1566	.298
Columbus	140	5043	1493	.296
Grand Rapids	140	4989	1418	.284

Team Fielding

	G	TC	E	Pct.
Kansas City	135	5725	385	.933
Minneapolis	136	5729	397	.931
Grand Rapids	140	5812	406	.930
Indianapolis	132	5580	389	.930
St. Paul	136	5798	411	.929
Detroit	138	5804	430	.927
Columbus	140	6028	454	.925
Milwaukee	140	5933	444	.925

Individual Hitting Leaders
(Minimum 434 At Bats)

	G	AB	R	H	Avg.
Glasscock, SP	135	610	172	263	.431
George, SP	138	637	159	244	.383
Werden, MN	140	575	145	217	.377
Schriver, MN	137	563	120	206	.366
Weaver, ML	144	628	114	224	.357

Individual Fielding Leaders
(Minimum 100 Games)

	POS	G	PO	A	E	Pct.
Carney, GR	1b	134	1348	91	16	.989
Pickett, SP/MN	2b	120	383	342	45	.937
Hatfield, KC	3b	132	163	279	40	.917
Wheelock, CO/GR	ss	100	206	370	64	.900
McCarthy, IN	of	133	285	24	11	.966
Burns, SP	of	114	221	21	18	.943

	POS	G	PO	A	E	Pct.
Gilks, GR	of	106	221	15	16	.937
Schriver, MN	c	137	531	147	26	.963

Individual Pitching Leaders

	G	R	ER	ERA
Davis, IN	24	97	43	1.79
Dammann, IN	47	211	95	2.02
Bevis, KC	20	114	41	2.09
Phillips, IN	27	117	57	2.11
Mullane, SP	49	268	117	2.38

Batting Leaders

HITS
George, SP—244

RUNS
Glassock, SP—172

Pitching Leaders

WINS
Bill Hutchinson, MN—38

STRIKEOUTS
Roger Denzer, St. Paul—200

WINNING PERCENTAGE
Bill Hutchinson, MN—.731, 38–14

1897

The 1897 season opened on April 21 when Indianapolis shut out Grand Rapids 10–0. The Hoosiers opened the season with a four-game winning streak and continued to dominate through the season to win the pennant by a comfortable margin over Columbus. Indianapolis also won a postseason series against Columbus, three games to two. Each player was paid $75 for participating.

A trio of Indianapolis pitchers dominated the league. The Hoosiers Jot Goar, who was purchased from Pittsburgh in the National League, led the league in ERA (1.30) on his way to a 28–8 record. Frank Foreman was 27–9 and Bill Phillips was 30–10 to push the Hoosiers to the top. The league's leading hitter was McBride with St. Paul, with a .387 average.

Steinfeldt Played Third for Cubs

Harry Steinfeldt played for the Detroit Tigers in 1897 before going to the Cincinnati Reds the next season.

The third baseman went to the Cubs in 1906 and became the other player in the famous Tinker-to-Evers-to-Chance infield. In fact, that season was his best in the majors, as he hit .327 and led the league in hits and RBI. The sure-handed fielder was the best third baseman in the National

The Johnson Years (1894-1899) 47

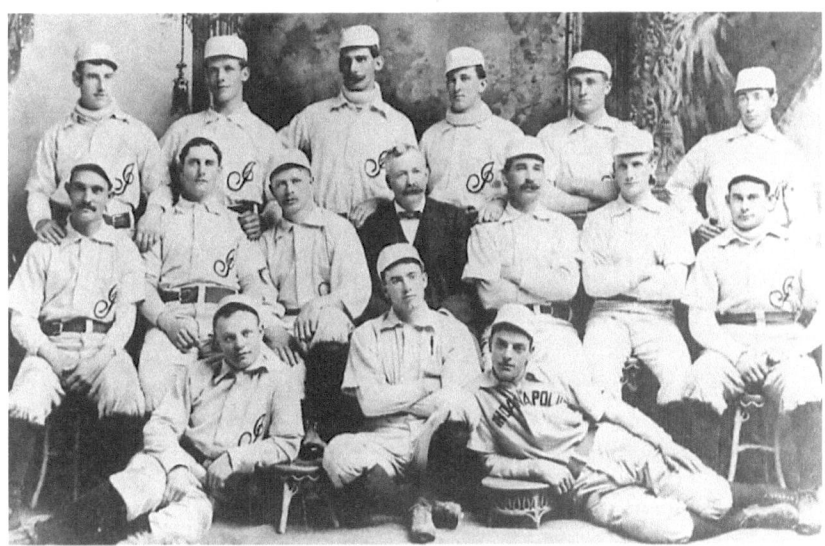

The Indianapolis Hoosiers won the Western League pennant in 1897. (Photograph courtesy of the National Baseball Hall of Fame, Cooperstown, N.Y.)

League as well, and would have won a gold glove if the award had been available at the time.

After 14 seasons, four pennants and two world championships, he retired after the 1911 season with Boston.

1897

Final Standings

	W	L	Pct.	GB
Indianapolis Hoosiers	98	37	.725	—
Columbus Senators	89	47	.654	9½
St. Paul Saints	86	51	.627	13
Milwaukee Creams	85	51	.625	13
Detroit Tigers	70	66	.514	28½
Minneapolis Millers	43	95	.311	56½
Kansas City Blues	40	99	.287	60
Grand Rapids Gold Bugs	35	100	.259	63½

Team Batting

	G	AB	H	Avg.
Indianapolis	136	4965	1559	.314

	G	AB	H	Avg.
Columbus	138	4936	1545	.313
Detroit	137	4966	1516	.305
St. Paul	139	5109	1545	.302
Milwaukee	138	4812	1416	.296
Minneapolis	138	4812	1292	.289
Grand Rapids	136	4840	1352	.279
Kansas City	142	4925	1360	.276

Team Fielding

	G	TC	E	Pct.
Columbus	138	5679	373	.934
Milwaukee	138	5962	417	.930
Indianapolis	136	5605	399	.929
Minneapolis	138	5715	482	.916
St. Paul	139	5867	507	.914
Kansas City	142	5857	508	.913
Detroit	137	5768	509	.912
Grand Rapids	136	5768	510	.912

Individual Hitting Leaders
(Minimum 440 At Bats)

	G	AB	R	H	SB	Avg.
McBride, SP	133	528	170	201	44	.387
Dungan, DET	137	548	143	207	20	.378
McFarland, IN	131	533	136	190	47	.357
Frank, CO	130	515	126	184	29	.357
Gray, IN	125	518	131	182	13	.351

Individual Fielding Leaders
(Minimum 100 Games)

	POS	G	PO	A	E	Pct.
Ganzel, GR	1b	125	1205	84	22	.983
Crooks, CO	2b	131	383	378	39	.951
Gray, IN	3b	125	145	218	37	.908
Lewee, ML	ss	126	276	462	57	.928
Weaver, ML	of	138	308	18	18	.948
Nicholl, DT	of	127	305	21	19	.945
McBride, SP	of	133	314	18	24	.933
Spires, SP	c	134	570	124	27	.962

Individual Pitching Leaders

	G	W	L	R	ER	ERA
Goar, IN	39	28	8	146	51	1.30
Jones, CO	31	17	6	127	45	1.45

The Johnson Years (1894–1899)

	G	W	L	R	ER	ERA
Foreman, IN	43	27	9	176	65	1.51
Fricken, SP	34	15	12	172	56	1.64
Mullane, SP	30	14	11	165	52	1.73

Batting Leaders

HOME RUNS
William Gray, IN—19

HITS
William George, SP—207

RUNS
Al McBride, SP—166

STOLEN BASES
Mertes, CO—97

TOTAL BASES
McFarland, IN-305

Pitching Leaders

WINS
Francis Foreman, IN—30

STRIKEOUTS
Tommy Thomas, DT—147

WINNING PERCENTAGE
Francis Foreman, IN—.769, 30-9

1898

After four disappointing years in the cellar and pitiful gate receipts, the Grand Rapids franchise moved to St. Joseph, Missouri, before the 1898

The magnates of the Western League that eventually became the American League were: (standing from left) R. Allen, Indianapolis; M.R. Killiea, Milwaukee; Connie Mack, Milwaukee; Charles A. Comiskey, St. Paul; G.H. Schmelz; (sitting from left) T.J. Loftus, Columbus; M.J. O'Brien; Ban Johnson, president; J.H. Manning, Kansas City; G.A. Vanderbeck, Detroit; and C.H. Saulpaugh, Minneapolis. (Photograph courtesy of the National Baseball Hall of Fame, Cooperstown, N.Y.)

season. President Johnson opened the season by announcing that he was withholding a portion of each player's pay until the last day of the season to try and cut down on drinking. A number of teams were rife with drunks. Johnson also kept the intoxicated fans out of the stands by ejecting them if they became rowdy, which improved the atmosphere at the parks. He hired a staff of competent umpires and backed them to avoid all the arguing that was prevalent in the National League.

Kansas City won the pennant in 1898 after defeating Indianapolis in the final game of the season. The Cowboys took the title by two-and-a-half games over the Hoosiers. The Cowboys pulled in some good crowds for the last series with the Hoosiers, including one numbering 10,781. KC was led by the best hitter in the league in Slagle, with a .378 batting average. Phillips of the Hoosiers had the best winning percentage (.748, 29–8), while Denzer of St. Paul chalked up the most victories (31).

Fans failed to support the St. Joseph franchise, so it was moved to Omaha, but it failed there as well and was not considered for the next season.

Williams Was Great Rookie

Jimmy Williams came to Kansas City in 1898 and was placed at third base as an experiment. The experiment worked and he won the job.

The next season he was purchased by Pittsburgh and had one of the best rookie seasons ever. He batted a .352 average, led the National League in triples (27), clobbered nine homers, knocked in 116 RBI and scored 126 runs. Unfortunately, his 11-year career in the majors was all downhill after that performance.

Jimmy Williams, here in a New York Highlanders uniform, played for KC in 1898. (Photograph courtesy of Jay Sanford)

The Johnson Years (1894–1899)   51

1898

Final Standings

	W	L	Pct.	GB
Kansas City Blues	88	51	.633	—
Indianapolis Hoosiers	84	50	.627	1½
Milwaukee Brewers	82	57	.590	6
St. Paul Apostles	81	58	.583	7
Columbus Senators	73	60	.549	12
Detroit Tigers	50	87	.365	37
Minneapolis Millers	48	92	.343	40½
St. Joseph Saints/ Omaha Omahogs	42	93	.311	44

Team Batting

	G	AB	R	H	Avg.
Kansas City	140	4,814	887	1,390	.287
Detroit	138	4,510	636	1,250	.275
Columbus	133	4,639	799	1,273	.274
Milwaukee	139	4,491	733	1,207	.260
St. Paul	139	4,911	858	1,203	.257
Indianapolis	134	4,505	742	1,150	.252
Minneapolis	141	4,916	696	1,212	.247
St. Joseph	136	4,643	511	1,073	.231

Individual Batting Leaders (Minimum 434 At Bats)

	G	AB	R	H	SB	Avg.
Slagel, KC	133	545	137	206	41	.378
Williams, ML	139	536	113	184	22	.343
Dungan, DT	131	532	88	173	15	.325
Glenalvin SP	131	515	102	167	24	.324
Frisbee, KC	138	549	104	173	28	.315

Individual Fielding Leaders

	POS	G	PO	A	E	Pct.
Motz, IN	1b	119	1329	54	20	.986
Viox, KC	2b	119	288	348	39	.942
Shoch, MIL	3b	118	131	250	39	.907
Allen, IN	ss	124	378	416	59	.931
Waldron, MIL	of	137	210	13	12	.953
Geier, SP	of	115	272	18	15	.951
Lally, CO	of	110	222	13	14	.944
Spires, SP	c	135	625	123	31	.960

Individual Pitching Leaders
(30 or more decisions)

	G	W	L	Pct.
Phillips, IN	37	29	8	.784
Denzer, SP	43	33	10	.767
Taylor, ML	41	28	13	.683
Gear, KC	39	25	14	.641
Jones, CO	41	26	15	.634

Attendance

Kansas City	180,000
Milwaukee	160,000
Indianapolis	120,000
St. Paul	90,000
Detroit	85,000
Columbus	60,000
St. Joseph/Omaha	50,000
Minneapolis	40,000

Batting Leaders

HOME RUNS
Frank Shugart, SP—12

HITS
Jimmy Slagle, KC—206

RUNS
Jimmy Slagle, KC—137

STOLEN BASES
Charles Campau, KC—60

Pitching Leaders

WINS
Roger Denzer, SP—33

WINNING PERCENTAGE
Bill Phillips, IN—.748, 29-8

COMPLETE GAMES
Bill Phillips, IN—39

1899

The 1899 season got under way on April 27. By July, Columbus had retired from the league and Grand Rapids took its place. Indianapolis won the pennant, although it didn't win as many games as Minneapolis. The Hoosiers finished with 75 victories, while the Millers had 76. However, Indianapolis had fewer losses, and its final winning percentage was .615 compared to .603 for Minneapolis. It was the Hoosiers' third pennant in five years.

Indianapolis had none of the hitting or pitching leaders in the league. Instead, it had the best infield in the league and relied more on teamwork than other teams. McFarland did hit .331 to lead the Hoosiers. Alfonso

The Kansas City Blues played in this stadium in 1899. (Photograph courtesy of the National Baseball Hall of Fame, Cooperstown, N.Y.)

Davis helped Minneapolis to second place, as he led the league in hits (176) and runs scored (126). The Millers also had Jock Menefee, who led the league in winning percentage (.781, 25-7).

Wacky Waddell Was with Western

Rube Waddell was quite a character, as well as being one of the best pitchers in the Western League in 1899. During a game against Indianapolis he turned a somersault in protest of a single by Ace Stewart. Such acts were usually reserved for the vaudeville stage.

The zany lefthander for Columbus–Grand Rapids tied with two other pitchers for the league lead in wins, with 27, and led Western hurlers with 200 strikeouts. Rube's performance earned him a call to Louisville at the end of the season where he was 7-2. In the off season he wrestled alligators in Florida.

The strikeout artist got used to leading the pack and led the American League in Ks six years in a row. He also had one of the lowest ERAs (2.16) in the history of the game during his 13 seasons in the majors. It earned him a spot in the Hall of Fame in 1946.

"Wahoo Sam" Plays Half Season in Western

"Wahoo Sam" Crawford came from the Canadian League in midseason in 1899 and hit .345, which was just two percentage points behind the league leader. The outfielder was signed by Cincinnati after the season and hit .307 in 31 games to earn himself a spot in the majors.

Crawford went from Cincinnati to Detroit where he played alongside Ty Cobb, and they became one of the most feared one-two hitting combinations. In fact, Cobb campaigned for his teammate to get into the Hall of Fame, which finally occurred in 1957. Of course, Crawford deserved it. He was most the prolific triples hitter in major league history, as he hit double-figure triples for 17 consecutive seasons and 312 lifetime.

He would have reached 3,000 hits had his Western League hits counted toward his major league totals. And he contended that they should, but they didn't.

1899

Final Standings

	W	L	Pct.	GB
Indianapolis Hoosiers	75	47	.615	—
Minneapolis Millers	76	50	.603	1
Detroit Tigers	64	60	.516	12
Columbus Senators/ Grand Rapids	63	62	.504	13½
St. Paul Saints	57	69	.452	20
Milwaukee Brewers	55	68	.447	20½
Kansas City Blues	53	70	.431	22½
Buffalo Bisons	53	70	.431	22½

Team Batting

	AB	R	Avg.
Detroit	4362	734	.289
Minneapolis	4511	828	.284
Milwaukee	4285	679	.267
Buffalo	4325	568	.265
St. Paul	4508	654	.263
Kansas City	4448	651	.263
Indianapolis	4172	654	.255
Grand Rapids	4372	676	.248

Team Fielding

	PO	A	Pct.
Milwaukee	3312	1699	.940
Indianapolis	3363	1697	.938
Minneapolis	3367	1671	.937
Grand Rapids	3268	1636	.936
Kansas City	3270	1630	.935

The Johnson Years (1894-1899)

	PO	A	Pct.
Buffalo	3234	1655	.935
Detroit	3283	1622	.927
St. Paul	3434	1625	.925

Individual Hitting Leaders
(Minimum 391 At Bats)

	G	AB	R	H	2b	Avg.
Dungan, DET	124	481	85	167	16	.347
Davis, MN	117	521	126	176	38	.338
Waldron, ML	115	484	98	161	40	.332
Barrett, DET	121	481	117	159	30	.331
McFarland, IN	119	460	79	152	25	.331

Individual Fielding Leaders
(Minimum 100 Games)

	POS	G	PO	A	E	Pct.
Motz, IN	1b	125	1340	54	17	.988
Hallman, BUF	2b	112	285	367	24	.965
Gray, MIL	3b	108	160	234	44	.900
Allen, IN	ss	101	222	357	53	.931
Waldron, ML	of	115	206	21	9	.962
Garry, BF	of	124	310	24	14	.959
Dungan, DT	of	124	219	23	12	.952
Spies, SP	c	127	510	114	23	.964

Individual Pitching Leaders

	G	W	L	Pct.
Waddell, CO/GR	34	26	8	.765
Croning, DT	38	26	12	.684
Menefee, MN	32	25	7	.781
Scott, MN	33	23	10	.697
Friend, MN	32	20	12	.625

Batting Leaders

HOME RUNS
Bob Stafford, MI—8

HITS
Alfonso Davis, MI—176

RUNS
Alfonso Davis, MI—126

Pitching Leaders

WINS
Jack Cronin, DET—26
Rube Waddell, CO/GR—26

STRIKEOUTS
Rube Waddell, CO/GR—200

WINNING PERCENTAGE
Jack Menefee, MN—.781, 25-7

Western Transitions Into American

The success of the Western League and turmoil in the National League paved the way for Ban Johnson to boldly move the league into a major league. At a meeting in the Northwestern Hotel in Chicago on October 11, 1899, Indianapolis Club President W.F.C. Golt made the motion to change the name to the American League, and James Franklin of Buffalo seconded it. The vote was unanimous. Surprisingly, Indianapolis shunned the new league and tried to secure a franchise with the National League. Those efforts failed and, as a result, Indianapolis stayed a minor league team the rest of the century. Comiskey's St. Paul club was moved to Chicago and became the White Sox.

The National League helped the American League in March 1900 by cutting back from 12 teams to eight teams and abandoning franchises in Washington, Cleveland, Baltimore and Louisville. The opening of those cities were quickly filled by the American League, except for Louisville. "Everything is booming all along the line, and I expect to see the most prosperous season in the history of the league," president Ban Johnson said in the *Sporting News*.

The National League refused to recognize the American League as its equal, so the American League was considered a minor league in 1900 (an effort is now being made to change this season to a major league season). The league then withdrew from the National Agreement, which meant it would not allow its players to be drafted by the National League. The American League wouldn't respect territorial rights or the reserve clause either. After raiding 111 players from National League teams by offering increased salaries of up to $5,000, the major league recognition finally came. In 1903 the American League put a franchise in New York, which led the National League to finally identify the league as its equal and sign a new National Agreement. The two leagues played their first postseason series in 1903, yet the first World Series was not established until 1905 between the leagues.

4
A New Century, A New League (1900–1937)

While the old Western League was changing colors like a chameleon and becoming a major league, a new Western League was being formed at a meeting in Omaha on March 27, 1900. Thomas Jefferson Hickey became its president, and George Tebeau his right-hand man. Three of the cities from the 1899 Western League would occupy the new league: Kansas City, Minneapolis and St. Paul. It then turned to the cities that had been in the Western League previously. Tebeau found ownership in Colorado Springs and Pueblo, Colorado.

1900

Omaha jumped off to an early lead in the first season of the new league, but the Omahogs faded halfway through the season and Denver Grizzlies and Des Moines Hawkeyes caught them. When the final standings were published in *The Des Moines Register and Leader*, Des Moines won the pennant by a half game. However, President Hickey had the final word. He had failed to keep the press informed of his rulings during the season on several disputed games. When he issued the final official standings, the Grizzlies won the pennant, with Des Moines a game and a half behind. Tebeau managed the Grizzlies to the comeback.

Denver was led by Elwood "Pop" Eyler and his 23 wins. Another strong pitching performance was turned in by Henry Maupin of St. Joseph, also with 23 victories. He had come from two unsuccessful seasons in the National League where he had been 0–5. Johnny "Noisy" Kling—noisy because of his constant chatter behind the plate—caught for St. Joseph before going to the Cubs at the end of the season. Kling earned a

Top: The 1900 Omaha team was nicknamed the Omahogs after the stockyards located in the city. (Photograph courtesy of Jay Sanford)

Bottom: Omaha's Pearl Barnes prepares for a pitch from a Denver pitcher during the opening day game at Denver's Broadway Park in 1900. (Photograph courtesy of Jay Sanford)

permanent position with Chicago and became part of the championship Cubs teams in the early 1900s. Jack Glasscock finished up his lengthy professional career with Sioux City in 1900. He was one of the best defensive shortstops in the majors during the 1880s. Hansen with Sioux City earned a suspension for the rest of the season when he pounded the Omaha catcher over the head with a bat.

Top: The 1900 Des Moines Hawkeyes finished in second place. (Photograph courtesy of Jay Sanford)
 Bottom: The 1900 Denver Bears consisted of players from many different teams, as evidenced by this spring training photo. The team won the pennant that season. The players were: (front row from left) Mons "Eddie" Webster, Walter "Wizard" Preston, Jack Sullivan, Pearl "Casey" Barnes, Clarence Leisenring (mascot), Joe Tinker, W.E. Harry McNeeley; (middle row from left) Pop Eyler, Dakin "Dusty" Miller, Tom "Tacks" Parrott, Charley Kight, Charles "Princeton Charlie" Reilly, Charlie Zeitz, W.E. "Bill" Hickey, Al Hickey; (top row from left) Len "Dad" Shirk, Walter Price, Walt Bissell, unknown, "Old Hoss" Hausen, Harry "Klondike" Kane, J.H. Vizard and Jack Holland. (Photograph courtesy of the National Baseball Hall of Fame, Cooperstown, N.Y.)

Every team turned a profit in 1900. The league had tried to limit salaries, but it had trouble establishing standards. Omaha paid its players $900 initially.

Tinker Played in Western Before Joining Evers and Chance

Joe Tinker came to Denver in 1900 where he wasn't so famous. The fame would come later when he went to the Chicago Cubs and became the shortstop in the Tinker-to-Evers-to-Chance double-play combination, which was made famous by a poem.

Tinker wasn't the best of fielders when he was with the Western League, so George Tebeau sent him to Butte, Montana, for more seasoning. He honed his skills and by 1905 he was the leading shortstop in the National League. He helped Chicago to four pennants and two world championships.

The famed shortstop moved across town in 1914 to play and manage the Chicago Whales of the Federal League. When the league folded he boomeranged back to manage the Cubs for a season. After baseball he retired to Orlando, Florida, where a field was named in his honor.

The 15-year major leaguer was named to the Hall of Fame in 1946 by the Veterans Committee. A year later he died.

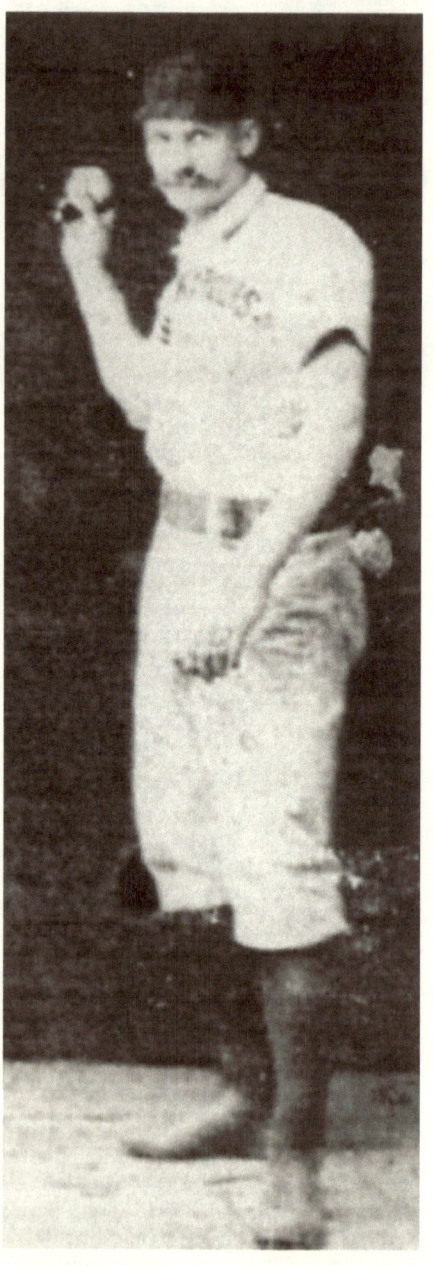

Jack Glasscock was an infielder for Sioux City in 1900. He also played for several teams in the majors. (Photograph courtesy of Jay Sanford)

A New Century, A New League (1900–1937)   61

1900

Final Standings

	W	L	Pct.	GB
Denver Bears	61	44	.581	—
Des Moines Hawkeyes	59	45	.567	1½
Sioux City Cornhuskers	49	48	.505	8
Omaha Omahogs	51	53	.490	9½
St. Joseph Saints	51	58	.468	12
Pueblo Indians	41	64	.390	20

Individual Batting Leaders
(Minimum 325 At Bats)

	G	AB	R	H	SB	Avg.
Hines, DM	99	392	90	132	31	.337
Schrall, SJ	108	445	68	149	14	.335
McHale, PU	98	422	86	135	51	.320
Preston, PU	104	432	101	137	35	.317

Individual Fielding Leaders
(Minimum 80 Games)

	POS	G	PO	A	E	Pct.
Davis, SJ	1b	82	845	18	18	.979
Bristow, SJ	2b	102	292	277	42	.947
Strang, SJ	3b	108	160	233	31	.926
Lewee, DE	ss	85	263	300	47	.922
Nagle, DM	of	90	178	20	8	.961
Schrall, SJ	of	108	228	9	14	.944
Miller, DE	of	100	236	17	17	.937
Cote, SC	c	88	407	113	8	.950

Batting Leaders

HOME RUNS
Dave Brain, SP—13

HITS
Dakin Miller, KC—153

RUNS
Bill Hartman, KC—101

Pitching Leaders

EARNED RUN AVERAGE
Parvin, SC—3.41
Schmidt, DN—4.14
Herman, SJ—4.70
McNeeley, DN—5.60
Maupin, SJ—5.65

WINS
Henry Maupin, SJ—31

STRIKEOUTS
Fred Glade, DM—196

WINNING PERCENTAGE
Bob Ewing, KC—.808, 21-5

1901

The league added two more franchises the next year, although it could have expanded to as many as 10 teams, as Indianapolis, Louisville and Milwaukee were interested in coming to the league. However, league officials decided that eight teams would be sufficient. Pueblo and Sioux City were replaced by Colorado Springs, Kansas City, Minneapolis and St. Paul. Teams would be limited to 14 players, and 120 games would be played.

Opening day was May 3, 1901. Kansas City jumped out to an early lead and never looked back. The Blues ran away with the pennant, while St. Paul and St. Joseph finished second and third, respectively. The Blues boasted the best pitcher in the league in Bob Ewing, who was 21–5. He signed with Cincinnati the next season and eventually pitched 11 seasons in the majors, posting a respectable 124–118 record.

St. Paul's Dave Brain led the league in homers with 13. That earned him a trip to the White Sox and seven years in the majors. The league's leading hitter was Frank Hemphill with last-place Colorado Springs. Hemphill had tests in the majors but failed both times to stick there. Des Moines pitcher Fred Glade was the best strikeout artist in 1901, as he painted 196 batters. Glade got a try in the majors with the Cubs the next season, then he pitched four full seasons with the Browns.

Top: Elwood Eyler led Denver to the pennant in 1900. (Photograph courtesy of Jay Sanford).
Bottom: Johnny Kling caught for St. Joseph in 1900. Then he went to the Chicago Cubs. (Photograph courtesy of Jay Sanford.)

A New Century, A New League (1900–1937)   63

The National Agreement went the way of the dinosaur when the National League announced it would no longer honor it because of competition from the American League, which had already decided not to  abide by it. With the national accords gone, Western League president Thomas J. Hickey called for a meeting of minor league presidents in Chicago on Sept 5, 1901, to form a new organization to protect its interests. The National Association of Professional Base Ball Leagues was born. It rated minor leagues in four classes: A, B, C and D. The Western League received a Class A rating, which it would hold through 1937. The National Association also established salary limits and a system for drafting players. A Board of Arbitration was given

Top: This was the first photo of Joe Tinker as a professional player with Denver. (Photograph courtesy of Jay Sanford)
Bottom: The 1901 Kansas City Blues won the pennant. (Photograph courtesy of Jay Sanford)

The 1901 St. Paul Saints finished in second place. (Photograph courtesy of Jay Sanford)

power to suspend players, clubs or officials for violations. Minor league teams had no direct connections with major league teams like they do today. Those affiliations would come in the 1930s.

Dooin Doodles with Shin Guards

Charles "Red" Dooin caught for St. Joseph in 1901, which was the year before he went to the majors with Philadelphia, where he played 13 of his 15 years in the majors.

The inventive catcher experimented with shin guards made of papier-mâché outside the uniform.

Later in Dooin's playing career he broke an ankle and leg, which slowed him considerably. He turned to managing after his playing days.

1901
Final Standings

	W	L	Pct.	GB
Kansas City Blues	79	44	.642	—
St. Paul Saints	69	54	.561	10
St. Joseph Saints	69	58	.543	12
Denver Grizzlies	60	69	.504	17
Omaha Omahogs	61	62	.496	18
Minneapolis Millers	56	62	.475	20½
Des Moines Millers	48	75	.390	31
Colorado Springs Millionaires	45	73	.381	31½

A New Century, A New League (1900–1937) 65

Individual Fielding Leaders

	POS	G	PO	A	E	Pct.
Davis, SJ	1b	82	845	18	18	.979
Bristow, SJ	2b	102	292	277	42	.947
Strang, SJ	3b	108	160	233	31	.926
Lewee, DE	ss	85	263	300	47	.922
Nagle, DM	of	90	178	20	8	.961
Schrall, SJ	of	108	228	9	14	.944
Miller, DE	of	100	236	17	17	.937
Cole, SC	c	88	407	113	8	.950

Batting Leaders

BATTING AVERAGE
Frank Hemphill, CS, .332

RUNS
Bill Hartman, KC, 101

HITS
Dakin Miller, KC, 153

HOME RUNS
Dave Brain, SP, 13

Pitching Leaders

WINS
Henry Maupin, SJ, 31

STRIKEOUTS
Fred Glade, DM, 196

WINNING PERCENTAGE
Bob Ewing, KC, .808, 21–5

1902

For the 1902 season, President Hickey and Tebeau wanted to form a new organization with the teams of the Western League and Western Association, but the owners opposed them and asked for their resignation, so they organized the independent American Association. The departed executives got revenge by placing teams in three of the same cities of the Western League, which led to the AA being branded as an outlaw league. It was not sanctioned by the National Association. The Western League countered by putting a team in Milwaukee, the American Association stronghold. James Whitfield of Kansas City took over as president of the Western League, but he died shortly after his election. Mike Sexton of Rock Island, Illinois, took over as president on April 17.

In a close race, Kansas City won the pennant on the last day of the season, with Omaha finishing second. The Cowboys had fewer wins but won the championship by .003 percentage points. Charles "Kid" Nicols managed and pitched the Cowboys to the pennant with his 27 wins. KC also had Jake Weimer, with the most strikeouts (209). Weimer went to the Cubs the next season and played seven seasons in the majors. The Cowboys also had Irv Waldron, one of the leading hitters in the league. Waldron had played in the American League the year before.

Roy Hartzell played infield and outfield with Indianapolis and Denver before going to the American League for 11 seasons with St. Louis and New York. (Photograph courtesy of Jay Sanford)

Gus Dundon of Denver was the best fielding third baseman in the league. He was signed by the White Sox in 1904 and played three seasons in Chicago.

Pitcher Only Needed Three Fingers

Mordecai "Three Finger" Brown acquired the nickname because he only had three full fingers on his right hand as a result of a farming accident when he was a boy growing up in Indiana. "All I know is that I had all the fingers I needed," he once said. The deformity gave him a natural sinker and curveball.

Brown was pitching for Terre Haute in the Three-I League when he signed a contract with Omaha for $125 a month. Omaha had to pay Terre Haute $300 to obtain Brown. Mordecai was worth every penny of that money, as he turned in 27 wins that season for Omaha.

The farm boy was purchased by the St. Louis Cardinals in 1903 and began his major league career. Although he had a losing record, Chicago Cubs manager Frank Selee saw his potential and traded 21-game winner Jack Taylor for Brown. Selee must have had a crystal ball. Brown led the Cubs to four pennants and two world championships. His achievements led him to the Hall of Fame.

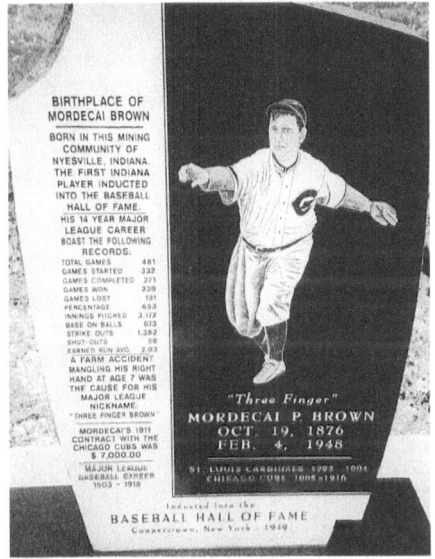

Top: Mordecai "Three-Finger" Brown won 27 games for Omaha in 1902. The pitcher with the mangled hand led the Chicago Cubs to a World Series and a spot in the Hall of Fame.

Bottom: This monument was dedicated in 1994 to honor Mordecai "Three Finger" Brown in his hometown of Nyesville, Indiana. (Photograph by Patrick Stewart)

Hugh Duffy played the outfield for two seasons for Milwaukee beginning in 1902. (Photograph courtesy of Jay Sanford)

After his playing days were over, he returned to Terre Haute, where he owned and operated a service station until his death.

Duffy Manages in Western

Player-manager Hugh Duffy led the Milwaukee Creams to a third-place finish in 1902. He began playing professional baseball in 1884, the year before the first Western League was formed.

The veteran played and managed for eight seasons and was a scout with Boston until his death in 1954. The outfielder set the all-time single season batting average of .440 in 1894 with Boston. He was named to the Hall of Fame in 1945 for his efforts and contributions to baseball.

1902

Final Standings

	W	L	Pct.	GB
Kansas City Blue Stockings	82	54	.603	—
Omaha Indians	84	56	.600	—
Milwaukee Creams	80	54	.597	1
Denver Grizzlies	81	57	.587	2
St. Joseph Saints	71	68	.511	12½
Colorado Springs Millionaires	63	75	.457	20
Des Moines Midgets	54	83	.394	28½
Peoria Distillers	35	103	.254	48

Team Batting

	AB	H	Avg.
Denver	4600	1322	.287
Kansas City	4625	1213	.262

A New Century, A New League (1900–1937)   69

	AB	H	Avg.
Milwaukee	4667	1218	.261
Colorado Springs	4632	1206	.260
Des Moines	4551	1144	.251
Omaha	4772	1174	.246
St. Joseph	4711	1153	.245
Peoria	4731	1101	.233

Team Fielding

	PO	A	E	TC	Pct.
Omaha	3797	1992	298	6087	.951
Kansas City	3657	1365	272	5294	.949
Milwaukee	3774	1692	318	5784	.945
Peoria	3666	1886	315	5866	.945
St. Joseph	3774	1733	328	5793	.943
Colorado Springs	3557	1885	342	5784	.941
Denver	3562	1674	335	5571	.940
Des Moines	3549	1741	335	5625	.940

Individual Hitting Leaders
(Minimum 421 At Bats)

	G	AB	R	H	TB	SB	Avg.
Frisk, DE	123	450	89	168	271	20	.373
Delehanty, DE	137	554	118	194	265	38	.350
Stone, PE/OM	138	573	94	193	316	34	.346
O'Brien, MI	142	560	125	191	244	36	.341
Waldron, KC	132	553	99	178	242	21	.322

Individual Fielding Leaders
(Minimum 100 Games)

	POS	G	PO	A	E	Pct.
Thornton, MI	1b	133	1305	86	29	.978
Quinn, DM	2b	135	256	375	26	.960
Rohe, SJ	3b	119	181	264	25	.947
Holingsworth, CS	ss	110	225	335	44	.927
Duffy, MI	of	140	302	12	11	.966
Stone, PO/OM	of	138	261	16	10	.965
Felsen, SJ	of	127	237	10	9	.965
Gonding, OM	c	129	676	165	18	.971

Batting Leaders

HOME RUNS
Emil Frisk, DE—14

HITS
George Stone, PE/OM—198

RUNS
John O'Brien, MI—125

STOLEN BASES
Dundon, DE—44

SACRIFICE HITS
Shannon, KC—36

TOTAL BASES
Stone, PE/OM—316

Pitching Leaders

WINS
Charles "Kid" Nichols, KC—27

Mordecai "Three-Finger" Brown, OM—27

WINNING PERCENTAGE
Charles "Kid" Nichols, KC—.794, 27-7

STRIKEOUTS
Jake Weimer, KC—209

1903

The fight between the American Association and Western League for dominance and fans continued into 1903, resulting in substantial losses on both sides. President Sexton struggled with the schedule until he cut the travel by 5,000 miles in a budget-cutting measure. The weather was no help either, as cold weather, rain and floods cancelled games for 10 consecutive days in the spring. Then poor weather and low attendance during the fall led Sexton to cancel the last two weeks of the season. By this time Milwaukee owned a seven-and-a-half game advantage, so the Creams—so named because Milwaukee was known as the Cream City—could not have been caught by Colorado Springs anyway. The Creams were led by pitcher Ed Kenna, who posted 28 victories that season.

Henry Schmidt pitched for Denver and spent 1903 with Brooklyn, where he was 22–13. (Photograph courtesy of Jay Sanford)

The league's leading hitter was Bill Congalton with the Colorado Springs Millionaires. Not only did he have the most hits (184), but he also had the highest batting average (.363). That was enough to move him back to the majors for a couple of years with Cleveland and Boston. Prior to coming to the Western League, Congalton spent a season with the Cubs.

A New Century, A New League (1900–1937) 71

Top: The 1903 Colorado Springs finished in second place. (Photograph courtesy of Jay Sanford)
Left: Bill Congalton, Colorado Springs, was the leading hitter in the league in 1903. (Photograph courtesy of Jay Sanford)
Right: Miller Huggins played infield for St. Paul from 1901 to 1903. Then he went to the Reds and Cardinals. (Photograph courtesy of Jay Sanford)

Omaha players come off the field as Denver players go out in a 1903 game in Omaha. (Photograph courtesy of Pat Stewart)

"Kid" Nichols Was Twice in Western

Charles "Kid" Nichols was the player-manager for KC for two seasons near the end of his playing career. He had the best winning percentage in 1902, with his 27–7 record, to lead the KC Cowboys to the pennant.

Nichols was actually on the roster of the Kansas City club in 1887, but he never played a game. "I don't think I weighed more than 135 pounds," he told a newspaper reporter. "Because of my size, they referred to me as the batboy. That's where my nickname of Kid came from, and it was to stick to me throughout my life."

He then went to the Southern League and Western Association before playing for a dozen years in the National League. He boomeranged back to the Western League in 1902 to play for two seasons. The hurler ended a 20-year professional career in 1906 with a 361–208 record. That led to him being enshrined in the Hall of Fame in 1949, four years before his death.

1903

Final Standings

	W	L	Pct.	GB
Milwaukee Creams	83	43	.659	—
Colorado Springs Millionaires	77	52	.597	7½
Kansas City Blue Stockings	65	61	.516	18
St. Joseph Saints	62	59	.512	20½
Denver Grizzlies	61	70	.466	24½
Peoria Distillers	57	69	.452	26
Des Moines Undertakers	55	76	.420	30½
Omaha Indians	49	79	.383	34½

Team Hitting

	AB	H	Avg.
Colorado Springs	4367	1229	.281
Des Moines	4516	1199	.266
Milwaukee	4094	1085	.265
St. Joesph	4080	1083	.265
Kansas City	4371	1144	.262
Denver	4372	1124	.257
Omaha	4126	1040	.252
Peoria	4260	1061	.249

Team Fielding

	PO	A	E	TC	Pct.
Peoria	3307	1600	247	5154	.952
Des Moines	3445	1617	257	5319	.952
St. Joesph	3169	1505	256	4930	.948
Colorado Springs	3320	1598	280	5198	.946
Omaha	3234	1537	279	5050	.945
Milwaukee	3167	1326	275	4768	.942
Denver	3383	1640	319	5341	.940
Kansas City	3262	1531	311	5104	.939

Individual Hitting Leaders
(Minimum 400 At Bats)

	G	AB	R	H	TB	SB	Avg.
Congalton, CS	123	507	84	184	245	30	.363
Fleming, CS	120	533	107	180	206	39	.338
O'Neill, MI	102	442	107	147	206	43	.338
O'Leary, DM	129	547	81	170	209	34	.311
Several with .310							

Individual Fielding Leaders
(Minimum 100 Games)

	POS	G	PO	A	E	Pct.
Everett, CS	1b	108	1099	87	14	.988
Quinn, DM	2b	127	284	359	16	.976
Cockman, MI	3b	118	154	198	32	.917
O'Leary, DM	ss	129	330	429	60	.927
Carter, DE/CS	of	108	186	17	7	.967
Belden, SJ	of	114	235	11	10	.961
Jones, DE	of	117	230	20	11	.958
Lucia, MI	c	114	562	132	22	.963

Batting Leaders

HOME RUNS
Mike Jacobs, KC—8

HITS
Bill Congalton, CS—184

RUNS
Tom Fleming, CS—107
Tom O'Neill, MI—107

SACRIFICES
McVicker, MI—37

TOTAL BASES
Congalton, CS—245

Pitching Leaders

WINS
Ed Kenna, MI—28

WINNING PERCENTAGE
Ed Kenna, MI—.757, 28-9

STRIKEOUTS
H.B. Cushman, DM—195

1904

A compromise was reached before the beginning of the 1904 season between the Western League and Western Association. The Western League withdrew franchises from Kansas City and Milwaukee in return for maintaining its rating as a Class A league, even though it fell below the population requirement for Class A ranking by the National Association. The rating assured that Western League players would get top pay and have a better chance of making it to the majors. A salary limit of $1,800 was put on all clubs, with the exception of the manager and captain. The league would remain at six teams for the next five seasons. Other Class A leagues at the time included the Eastern League, American Association and Pacific Coast League. Meanwhile, the Western Association got a Class C rating, so it would never compete with the Western League for players.

In 1904 the Omaha Rangers surged past Denver and Colorado Springs in the last month of the season to win the pennant. The Rangers were led by Del Howard, who ended up with the most hits (184) and homers (9) on the season.

Walter "Wizard" Preston played for Denver from 1900 to 1903. In 1904 he left for spring training from his home in Denver and was never heard from again. (Photograph courtesy of Jay Sanford)

Howard went to the Pittsburgh Pirates the next season and played five years in the majors. John "Jack the Giant Killer" Pfeister was the leading pitcher on the team. He would get back to the majors the next season, and appeared there for eight season with a career 71–44 record.

During the season, Buck Thiel of Des Moines assaulted a local reporter and was arrested. He pled guilty to the charge, then was traded to Omaha. Des Moines was nicknamed the Underwriters that season because the city was known as an insurance center.

Lobert Races Against Horses

After getting a try with Pittsburgh in 1903, Hans Lobert came to Des Moines in 1904. The speedy, bowlegged third baseman got a try with the Cubs the next season and finally cracked into the majors for good with Cincinnati the year after that.

The excellent base stealer became more famous for his off-the-field exhibits of speed against cars, horses and professional runners. He played 14 years before his speed finally sputtered, and along with it went his value. Then Lobert coached, managed and scouted the rest of his days.

1904

Final Standings

	W	L	Pct.	GB
Omaha Rangers	90	60	.600	—
Colorado Springs	85	58	.594	1½
Denver Grizzlies	87	61	.588	2
Des Moines Underwriters	79	69	.534	10
St. Joseph Saints	53	93	.365	35
Sioux City Soos	45	98	.315	41½

Individual Hitting Leaders
(Minimum 465 At Bats)

	G	AB	R	H	TB	SB	Avg.
Congalton, CS	129	538	113	176	240	22	.327
Howard, OM	144	582	113	184	299	30	.316
Kahl, CS	130	526	97	160	225	15	.304

Individual Fielding Leaders
(Minimum 100 Games)

	POS	G	PO	A	E	Pct.
Conery, DM	1b	143	1488	83	20	.987
Hallman, DE	2b	139	305	440	28	.964

	POS	G	PO	A	E	Pct.
Schelbeck, SJ	3b	124	161	265	29	.965
Smith, DE	ss	141	296	414	58	.924
Blake, CS	of	140	317	26	6	.983
Fanning, SC	of	102	232	11	10	.960
Hartman, SJ	of	141	343	17	16	.956
Lucia, DE	c	140	771	143	25	.973

Batting Leaders

HOME RUNS
Del Howard, OM—9

HITS
Del Howard, OM—184

RUNS
George Nill, CS—117

Pitching Leaders

STRIKEOUTS
Pfiester, OM—178
Hostetter, DE—175
Denna, DE—168
Lindeman, SJ—131
Cadwalder, SC—126

BASE ON BALLS
Pfiester, OM—124
Diehl, SJ—103
Clark, SJ—100
Kostal, SJ—98
Kenna, DE—98

WILD PITCHES
Clark, SJ -12
Cadwallader, SJ—8
Lindeman, SJ—7
Yollendorf, DE—7
Skopec, CS—6

HIT BATTERS
Cadwallader, SC—23
Diehl, SJ—19
Hodson, SJ—15
Skopec, CS—14
Kostal, SJ—14

1905

Sexton resigned as president and Norris "Tip" O'Neill took over as president of the league, where he would remain for a decade.

The Colorado Springs franchise faltered and was transferred in mid-season to Pueblo. Des Moines jumped into the league lead with two months to play with the help of a winning streak by pitcher Bill Chappelle. He won five games in five days—three of which were shutouts. The iron man threw a five-hitter on August 11 to win 16–0. Then two days later he pitched a doubleheader and won both with shutouts again. After a day's rest, he pitched both games in another doubleheader and won both. In all, he threw 43 innings in five days! Most pitchers today are lucky to throw that much in a month. The Des Moines Underwriters also had former major league player George Hogriever, who led the league in runs (122) that season. A couple of future major leaguers also sent the Underwriters to the top like foam on a beer. Claude Rossman led the league in hits and average, which earned him a promotion to the majors, where he played for five seasons and appeared in two World Series with the Detroit Tigers.

In a postseason series against Milwaukee of the American Association, Des Moines won the first two games before dropping three in a row and losing the series.

Leifield Lifts Underwriters to Pennant

Lefty Leifield of Des Moines led the Western League with his 26 victories in 1905 to help the Underwriters win the pennant.

His performance lifted him to the Pittsburgh Pirates in September that year. The left-handed hurler had some great years with the Pirates as he recorded winning seasons six years in a row. Lefty pitched a dozen years in the majors and finished his baseball career with a 124–97 record.

1905

Final Standings

	W	L	Pct.	GB
Des Moines Underwriters	95	52	.646	—
Denver Grizzlies	94	59	.614	4
Omaha Rourkes	86	62	.581	9½
Sioux City Packers	80	69	.537	16
Colorado Springs Millionaires/				
Pueblo Indians	52	93	.359	42
St. Joseph Saints	37	109	.253	57½

Individual Hitting Leaders
(Minimum 456 At Bats)

	G	AB	R	H	Avg.
Roseman, DM	150	640	105	229	.357
Hogriever, DM	146	506	122	165	.326
Gauley, DM	123	525	112	166	.317
Noblet, SC	144	549	86	174	.317
Long, DM	118	475	78	146	.307

Individual Fielding Leaders
(Minimum 100 Games)

	POS	PO	A	E	Pct.
Rossman, DM	1b	1701	66	33	.982
Martin, OM	2b	274	339	29	.955
Sheehan, SC	3b	214	253	24	.951
Long, DM	ss	237	341	43	.936
Hogriver, DM	of	162	13	2	.980
Noblit, SC	of	272	22	5	.983
Collins, SC/SJ	of	199	29	5	.978
Ziuran, SJ/DE	c	613	123	11	.985

Hitting Leaders

HOME RUNS
Bill Shipke, OM—10

HITS
Claude Rossman, DM—229

RUNS
George Hogriever, DM—122

Pitching Leaders

WINS
Lefty Leifield, DM—26

INNINGS PITCHED
Peter Manske, DM—357

1906

In 1906 Sunday baseball was again coming under attack as the Iowa Senate passed a bill prohibiting the game on Sunday. The Des Moines and Sioux City schedules had to be adjusted to comply with the law. However, the 1906 season was still a financial success, with no teams needing to move.

Des Moines, which changed its nickname to Champions, continued to dominate the league despite the sale of several of their best players to the majors midway through the season. The Champions assumed an early lead, and by midseason the result was never in doubt. Des Moines skated

The 1906 Denver Grizzlies were managed by Bill Everitt (standing in back row, center). (Photograph courtesy of Jay Sanford)

A New Century, A New League (1900–1937)

to a 23-game lead, the winningest margin in league history. The team also had ornate horse blankets made that read, "Des Moines, Champions of the Western League." The Champions' leading hitter was Mike Welday with a .359 batting average. He went on to play a couple of years for the White Sox, too. Roscoe Miller of Des Moines led the league with his 28 wins on the season. Miller pitched for four seasons in the majors before coming to the Western League. Des Moines also had veteran George Magoon, who had played five seasons in the majors.

The best hitters in the league actually played for the worst team, the Pueblo Indians. Bill McGilvray led the league with a .373 average. He later got a cup of coffee with the Reds. James Cook scored the most runs, while Henry Melchior had the most hits. It was all for naught, as the team was the worst in fielding and their pitching was miserable.

Cicotte Starts in Western, Ends in Shame

Eddie Cicotte pitched for Des Moines in 1906 and Lincoln in 1907. He became one of the players involved in the infamous Black Sox Scandal. (Photograph courtesy of Jay Sanford)

Eddie Cicotte helped Des Moines to a first-place finish in 1906, as he pitched in 27 contests. The next season he helped Lincoln to second place. The hurler's success in the Western League led him to the Boston Red Sox in 1908.

After a couple of marginal seasons, Boston traded him to the White Sox. He learned to throw the knuckleball, which earned him the nickname "Knuckles."

After a 29–7 season, he seemed destined for stardom. Then he got greedy. He became one of the eight players who threw the 1919 World Series in the infamous Black Sox Scandal. It led to his lifetime ban from baseball by Commissioner Kenesaw Mountain Landis. He was so ashamed of what he did he assumed another name to protect his family.

1906
Final Standings

	W	L	Pct.	GB
Des Moines Champions	97	50	.660	—
Lincoln Ducklings	75	74	.503	23

	W	L	Pct.	GB
Omaha Rourkes	73	74	.497	24
Sioux City Packers	69	81	.460	29½
Denver Grizzlies	68	81	.456	30
Pueblo Indians	63	85	.426	34½

Team Hitting

	AB	R	H	TB	SB	Avg.
Sioux City	5232	750	1421	1872	113	.271
Denver	5105	765	1373	1792	167	.263
Lincoln	4950	675	1287	1718	284	.260
Pueblo	5326	843	1593	2137	180	.209
Des Moines	4820	829	1417	1787	389	.204
Omaha	5152	658	1348	1805	194	.201

Team Fielding

	PO	A	E	TC	Pct.
Des Moines	3929	1804	297	6030	.951
Lincoln	3834	1820	324	5978	.946
Omaha	2984	2015	343	6342	.946
Denver	3925	1837	383	6145	.938
Sioux City	3941	2035	410	6386	.936
Pueblo	3848	1869	407	6124	.933

Individual Hitting Leaders
(Minimum 456 At Bats)

	G	AB	R	H	SB	Avg.
McGilvray, PU	139	531	109	198	32	.372
Welday, DM	120	549	93	197	31	.359
Melchoir, PU	149	622	108	220	30	.353
Quillin, LI	138	526	95	184	34	.350
Campbell, SC	150	602	132	211	12	.350

Individual Fielding Leaders
(Minimum 100 Games)

	POS	G	PO	A	E	TC	Pct.
Dolan, OM	1b	109	1054	57	22	1133	.981
Magoon, DM	2b	144	359	438	26	823	.968
Perring, OM	3b	150	211	342	47	600	.922
Newton, SC	ss	125	250	392	84	706	.900
Noblit, SC	of	149	270	38	7	315	.978
Ketchum, LI	of	146	250	19	9	287	.968
Cook, PU	of	143	267	17	10	294	.966
Zinran, LI	c	123	604	133	9	746	.987

Individual Pitching Leaders
(Minimum 25 Decisions)

	W	L	Pct.
Manske, DM	23	10	.697
Cicotte, DM	18	9	.667
McKay, DM/LI	20	10	.667
Miller, DM	28	15	.651
Eyler, LI	26	21	.553

Batting Leaders

HOME RUNS
George Noblitt, SC—11

HITS
Henry Melchior, PU—220

RUNS
James—Cook, PU—149

Pitching Leaders

GAMES
Jones, LI—46

WINNING PERCENTAGE
Mark Hall, SC—.900, 9-1

WINS
Roscoe Miller, DM—28

1907

Before the season began, the Western League offered the Western Association $3,000 for the right to the Topeka territory, but the measure was voted down. Sunday ball continued to be a problem plaguing the league, as the Nebraska Legislature killed a bill that would have allowed Sunday play, which meant Lincoln couldn't play on the Lord's day. However, the team tried to play on a Sunday later that season; the court fined every player a dollar and court costs.

Des Moines continued to be competitive, but the Omaha Rourkes—so named after their manager, William "Pa" Rourke—finally surged past the Champs with two weeks to go in the season to take the championship. The new Lincoln Tree Planters, named in honor of Arbor Day, which had originated in Nebraska, finished a surprising second. Excessive bad weather in 1907 reduced the season by a few games, but it didn't rain on the financial success.

Pueblo's McGilvray continued to pound out the hits to lead the league in that category as well as runs scored. But the Indians only improved to next-to-last.

First "Babe" Played in Western

Charles Adams of Denver had the most wins in the league, with 23 in 1907. The following season he went up to Louisville, where he picked up the nickname "Babe," supposedly the first player with that nickname.

The Hoosier then went to the Pirates. After a 12–3 record during the regular season, the manager picked Adams over the team's ace for the opener of the World Series. The Babe came through and ended up winning three World Series games, a record for a rookie.

Known for his control, Adams pitched a 21-inning game on July 17, 1914, without giving up a walk, which is a record that stands today. Adams returned to the Western League to manage briefly in 1917 before returning to the majors to pitch another five seasons. In all, Adams pitched 17 years in the majors and twice led the National League in shutouts.

1907

Final Standings

	W	L	Pct.	GB
Omaha Rourkes	84	63	.571	—
Lincoln Tree Planters	79	63	.556	2½
Des Moines Champs	76	63	.547	4
Denver Grizzlies	68	75	.476	14½
Pueblo Indians	66	74	.471	14½
Sioux City Packers	56	91	.381	27½

Team Hitting

	AB	R	H	SH	SB	Avg.
Denver	4793	595	1231	183	171	.257
Omaha	4935	644	1261	203	277	.256
Pueblo	4822	598	1231	156	200	.255
Sioux City	4990	588	1274	155	131	.255
Des Moines	5630	583	1176	163	232	.255
Lincoln	4973	616	1238	219	309	.249

Team Fielding

	PO	A	E	TC	Pct.
Omaha	4026	2085	265	6376	.958
Lincoln	4031	2046	271	6348	.957
Des Moines	3669	1967	283	5919	.952
Sioux City	3885	2051	299	6235	.952
Pueblo	3780	1774	324	5878	.945
Denver	3807	1733	356	5893	.940

Individual Hitting Leaders
(Minimum 456 At Bats)

	G	AB	R	H	SB	Avg.
Hogriever, DM	143	496	80	158	46	.319

	G	AB	R	H	SB	Avg.
Welch, OM	151	514	70	160	40	.311
McGilvary, PU	146	564	94	174	33	.308
Cassiday, DE	127	485	88	149	36	.307
Fenion, LI	138	516	72	154	42	.298

Individual Fielding Leaders
(Minimum 100 Game)

	POS	G	PO	A	E	Pct.
White, DE	1b	123	1205	38	15	.988
Fox, LI	2b	149	385	475	32	.964
Austin, OM	3b	151	216	479	36	.951
Granville, SC	ss	138	278	419	49	.934
Noblit, SC	of	147	277	26	9	.971
Autrey, OM	of	135	267	19	10	.966
Campbell, SC	of	138	190	9	7	.966
Gooding, OM	c	114	568	131	15	.979

Batting Leaders

HOME RUNS
John Thomas, LI—9

HITS
Bill McGilvray, PU -174

RUNS
Bill McGilvray, PU—94

Pitching Leaders

MOST GAMES
Jones, LI—46

Hutch, PU—43
Clark, DM—43
Cicotte, LI—39
Thompson, OM—39

MOST WINS
Charles "Babe" Adams, DE—23

WINNING PERCENTAGE
Charles "Babe" Adams, DE—.657, 23-12

1908

Omaha's hopes of winning a second consecutive pennant in 1908 were dashed by the Sioux City Soos in a close race. Omaha's Dusty Rhodes hurled a no-hitter in late August; however, the Soos put on a 12-game winning streak to boost their efforts. The pennant came down to the final season series. On the next to the last day of the schedule the Soos swept a doubleheader from Omaha before the largest crowd (10,000) in league history. Sioux City clinched the pennant the last day with another victory over Omaha. The Soos where guided by James "Ducky" Holmes, a major leaguer for 10 seasons.

More than a third of the Soos' victories came from Al Furchner, with his 30 wins. He had one more victory than the Rourkes' Pat Reagan. Lin-

The police came out for the game in Des Moines in 1908. The team finished last that season. (Photograph courtesy of Jay Sanford)

coln finished third on the season and was still prevented from playing Sunday ball. Roy Witherup won 20 games with last place Des Moines, and earned a trip to the majors for three seasons.

Speedy "Pepper" Steals Show

Omaha's Jimmy "Pepper" Austin led the league in stolen bases two years in a row: 63 for 1907 and 97 in 1908. He led third basemen in fielding in 1907, too.

That speed led him to the New York Highlanders the next season. For the next 10 seasons the Wales-born player stole double digit bases each season for New York, then for the St. Louis Browns. Then he coached and filled in as manager for the Browns for number of years.

1908

Final Standings

	W	L	Pct.	GB
Sioux City Soos	88	57	.607	—
Omaha Rourkes	86	59	.593	2
Lincoln Greenbackers	74	73	.503	15
Denver Grizzlies	72	74	.493	17½
Pueblo Indians	62	79	.440	23
Des Moines Boosters	54	94	.365	35½

Team Hitting

	AB	R	H	SH	SB	Avg.
Omaha	4661	623	1231	198	285	.264

	AB	R	H	SH	SB	Avg.
Denver	4860	696	1254	219	197	.259
Pueblo	4722	669	1205	192	339	.255
Sioux City	4692	698	1185	183	268	.253
Des Moines	4775	631	1190	132	204	.249
Lincoln	4830	574	1112	214	221	.230

Team Fielding

	PO	A	E	TC	Pct.
Lincoln	3885	1915	260	6060	.957
Sioux City	3840	1831	261	5914	.956
Omaha	3822	1817	269	5908	.954
Des Moines	3817	1913	332	6062	.945
Pueblo	3785	1815	334	5934	.944
Denver	3883	1724	356	5963	.940

Individual Hitting Leaders
(Minimum 450 At Bats)

	G	AB	R	H	SB	Avg.
Welch, OM	147	497	69	180	26	.362
Autrey, OM	147	534	91	171	31	.320
Matticks, PU	143	563	93	179	45	.318
Dwyer, DM	139	532	77	169	28	.318
Belden, OM	145	537	94	164	22	.305

Individual Fielding Leaders
(Minimum 90 Games)

	POS	G	PO	A	E	Pct.
Dwyer, DM	1b	135	1454	69	21	.986
Fox, LI	2b	147	349	370	27	.964
Autrey, OM	3b	146	256	325	36	.942
Gagnier, LI	ss	149	388	495	45	.952
Welch, OM	of	147	279	14	6	.981
Campbell, SC	of	146	178	8	7	.964
Cassady, DE	of	149	233	24	10	.963
Zinran, LI	c	92	652	105	13	.983

Individual Pitching Leaders
(Minimum 35 Decisions)

	W	L	Pct.
Regan, OM	29	7	.800
Furchner, SC	30	11	.732
Bonno, LI	23	17	.575

	W	L	Pct.
Johnson, LI	19	16	.543
Witherup, DM	20	20	.500

Batting Leaders

HOME RUNS
Ira Belden, DE—7
Hamilton Patterson, PU—7
John Thomas, LI—7

STOLEN BASES
Jim Austin, OM—97

HITS
Harry Welch, OM—180

RUNS
Tom Campbell, SC—113

1909

The Western League finally obtained Topeka for a franchise and added Wichita as well to increase the league to eight teams. The switch led President Shively of the Western Association to withdraw the pennant Topeka won in 1908. The addition of Wichita and Topeka increased attendance all over the circuit, and profits went up as well.

The Sioux City Soos again had a strong franchise and fought with the Des Moines Boosters for the pennant. The race came down to the last day of the season. The Soos faced Omaha, a team out for revenge and who wanted to stop Sioux City from winning the title. Des Moines was playing Lincoln. The Soos lost the first game of a double dip; but in the second game they were ahead 3–0, and Lincoln was leading Des Moines, so Sioux City fans were making plans for a victory parade back home. Their hopes were quickly deflated when Omaha struck back to take the lead and won 7–5, while Des Moines rallied to beat Lincoln 5–3. Ironically, Sioux City ended up with more victories than Des Moines but lost the pennant by two percentage points.

The Boosters were led by Fred Lange with his 29 victories and 328 league-leading strikeouts. He never pitched in the majors, though. Omaha's Harry Welch led the circuit in hitting with his .373 average. Omaha also had the leading run leader in Tony Smith, who played three years in the majors. However, Smith failed to hit above the Mendoza Line (.200) in the majors.

1909

Final Standings

	W	L	Pct.	GB
Des Moines Boosters	93	59	.612	—
Sioux City Soos	94	60	.610	—

A New Century, A New League (1900-1937)   87

	W	L	Pct.	GB
Omaha Rourkes	84	68	.553	9
Topeka Jayhawks	76	73	.510	15½
Wichita Jobbers	71	82	.464	22½
Denver Grizzlies	69	82	.460	23½
Lincoln Greenbackers	61	89	.407	31
Pueblo Indians	58	93	.384	34½

Team Hitting

	AB	R	H	HR	SB	Avg.
Des Moines	5165	745	1343	26	242	.260
Denver	5182	787	1378	28	224	.266
Lincoln	5036	646	1272	19	241	.253
Omaha	4928	799	1392	24	344	.283
Pueblo	4852	688	1302	41	199	.268
Sioux City	5076	921	1445	60	294	.285
Topeka	4999	692	1308	29	218	.262
Wichita	5208	710	1352	48	174	.260

Team Fielding

	G	PO	A	E	Pct.
Omaha	152	3963	1957	270	.956
Sioux City	154	4069	1976	302	.952
Topeka	149	3930	1926	313	.949
Des Moines	152	4090	1855	329	.948
Denver	151	3969	1728	318	.947
Wichita	153	4063	1855	359	.943
Lincoln	150	3989	1988	386	.939
Pueblo	151	3803	1802	363	.939

Individual Hitting Leaders
(Minimum 450 At Bats)

	G	AB	R	H	HR	SB	Avg.
Welch, Harry, OM	151	527	81	196	7	51	.372
Smith, SC	156	557	135	183	6	52	.329
Jones, DE	152	586	110	191	8	43	.326
Edmonson, SC	125	454	90	147	11	25	.324
Kane, OM	153	558	101	176	1	33	.315

Individual Fielding Leaders
(Minimum 100 Games)

	POS	G	PO	A	E	Pct.
Hunter, SC	1b	156	1558	85	24	.986
Fox, LI/OM	2b	148	318	400	27	.963

	POS	G	PO	A	E	Pct.
Maag, DE	3b	120	169	211	24	.941
Gagnier, LI	ss	133	371	370	49	.934
Waldron, LI	of	150	202	15	2	.991
Cassidy, DE	of	154	262	24	7	.976
Belden, DE	of	153	267	19	8	.973
Towne, SC	c	109	594	88	10	.986

Individual Pitching Leaders
(Minimum 20 Decisions)

	G	W	L	Pct.
Olmstead, DE	37	24	8	.750
Lange, Fred, DM	52	29	12	.707
Alderman, SC	47	22	10	.688
Wright, TO	37	21	10	.677
Atchison, WI	58	18	11	.621

Batting Leaders

HOME RUNS
Hunter, SC—13
Pettigrew, TO—12
Pennell, WI—12
Edmondson, SC—11
Thomas, LI—11

STOLEN BASES
Fisher, OM—88
Niehoff, DM—63
Hunter, SC—59
Smith, SC—52
Welch, OM—51

HITS
Welch, OM—196
Jones, DE—191
Smith, SC—183
Waldron, LI—183
Cassidy, DE—182

DOUBLES
Welch, OM—41
Hunter, SC—39
Jones, DN—38
Jehl, PU—36
Thomas, LI—11

TRIPLES
Kane, OM—16

Welch, OM—15
Davidson, LI—15
Jones, DE—14
Matticks, DM—13

RUNS
Smith, SC—135
Hunter, SC—132
Fisher, OM—127
Maag, DE—123
Andreas, SC—120

Pitching Leaders

GAMES
Kaufmann, TP—58
Lange, DM—52
Shaner, WI—50
Miller, DM—47
Alderman, SC—47

WINS
Lange, DM—29
Miller, DM—24
Olmstead, DE—24
Kaufmann, TO—22
Alderman, SC—22

LOSSES
Kaufmann, TO—26
Swift, PU—23
Galgano, PU—21

Shaner, WI—21
Johnson, LI/SC—19
STRIKEOUTS
Lange, DM—328
Miller, DM—265
Adams, DE—192
Alderman, SC—184
Swift, PU—174
BASES ON BALLS
Shaner, WI—165
Adams, DE—148
Hollenbeck, OM—165
Alderman, SC—126
Swift, PU—122

WILD PITCHES
Shaner, WI—14
Miller, DM—12
Alderman, SC—11
Olmstead, DE—10
Clarke, DM/SC—8

HIT BATTERS
Alderman, SC—32
Adams, DE—27
Shaner, WI—23
Lange, DM—21
Freeman, SC—21

1910

The minor Western League took on a major schedule in 1910 by scheduling 168 games. The experimental season began April 22 and ran through October 3 with no problems. The season was quite successful financially, considering the unfavorable business conditions of the era.

The change produced the first Western League team to win more than 100 games in a season. In fact, two teams—Sioux City and Denver—exceeded the century mark. The Sioux City Packers won the crown handily by five-and-a-half games over Denver. At the bottom of the pile was Topeka, which set a club record for futility by losing 125 games and finish-

The 1910 Des Moines team was nicknamed the Boosters, and it finished next to last in the league. (Photograph courtesy of Jay Sanford)

John "Red" Corriden (right) played for Omaha in 1910 before going to the Detroit Tigers and Chicago Cubs. (Photograph courtesy of W.C. Madden)

ing 64 games behind the Packers. And Des Moines was kept on the road for six weeks because of lean fan support at home.

The Packers were led by Art Fenlon, who also led the league with a .365 hitting mark, and Marty O'Toole, the league leader in winning percentage with a 19–5 mark. O'Toole once struck out 18 in a game, only to

A New Century, A New League (1900–1937)   91

lose. He traveled to the Pittsburgh Pirates the next season, but he never achieved much success during five seasons in the majors. John Thomas helped Lincoln to a third-place finish with his 22 long balls, while Denver's Cozy Dolan swiped 80 bases to lead the circuit.

1910

Final Standings

	W	L	Pct.	GB
Sioux City Packers	108	60	.643	—
Denver Grizzlies	102	65	.611	6½
Lincoln Railsplitters	95	71	.572	12
Wichita Jobbers	89	78	.533	18½
Omaha Rourkes	84	82	.506	23
St. Joseph Drummers	76	91	.455	31½
Des Moines Boosters	72	96	.429	36
Topeka Jayhawks	42	125	.251	65½

Team Hitting

	AB	R	H	SB	HR	Avg.
Des Moines	5431	625	1329	259	30	.245
Denver	5536	943	1567	385	69	.283
Lincoln	5447	789	1437	254	52	.264
Omaha	5525	835	1458	321	40	.264
St. Joseph	5477	774	1403	348	34	.256
Sioux City	5770	1068	1732	305	73	.300
Topeka	5522	563	1293	132	33	.248
Wichita	5568	801	1491	233	49	.268

Team Fielding

	G	PO	A	E	Pct.
Wichita	167	4426	2195	284	.959
Lincoln	166	4459	2180	318	.954
Omaha	166	4471	2160	331	.952
Sioux City	168	4505	2179	348	.951
Denver	167	4480	2067	341	.950
St. Joseph	167	4407	2128	394	.943
Des Moines	168	4337	2089	421	.939
Topeka	167	4248	2105	446	.934

Individual Fielding Leaders
(Minimum 100 Games)

	POS	G	PO	A	E	Pct.
Stem, SC	1b	169	1659	111	27	.985

	POS	G	PO	A	E	Pct.
Hughes, WI	2b	161	407	457	34	.962
Westerzil, WI	3b	147	188	324	45	.929
Gagnier, LI	ss	156	465	466	52	.947
Cassidy, DE	of	160	299	25	6	.982
Mattick, DM	of	161	380	24	13	.969
Beall, DM	of	170	417	20	15	.967
Miller, SC	c	132	883	186	30	.973

Individual Pitching Leaders
(Minimum 20 Decisions)

	G	W	L	Pct.	BB	SO
O'Toole, SC	30	19	5	.792	73	207
Rhodes, OM	31	17	5	.773	90	134
McGrath, LI	26	16	7	.696	86	86
Hammond, SC	38	19	9	.679	80	95
Schreiber, DE	39	21	11	.656	77	157

Batting Leaders

BATTING AVERAGE
Art Fenlon, SC—.365

HOME RUNS
Thomas, LI—22
Cassiday, DE—18
Beall, DE—14
Quillen, SC—14
Welch, OM—12

STOLEN BASES
Dolan, DE—80
Corridon, OM—63
Lindsay, DE—62
Neihoff, DM—62
R. Jones, SJ—60

HITS
Neighbors, SC—206
Beall, DE—202
Quillen, SC—197
Stem, SC—195
Jones, SJ—192

DOUBLES
Fenlon, SC—48
Quillen, SC—43
Jones, SJ—38
Westerzil, WI—38
Neighbors, SC—35

TRIPLES
Curtis, DM—20
Powell, SJ—20
Beall, DE—19
Neihoff, DM—15
Jones, SJ—14

RUNS
Andreas, SC—137
Quillen, SC—133
Beall, DE—128
Dolan, DE—128
Linsey, DE—126

Pitching Leaders

GAMES
Herche, DM—50
Jackson, TO/WT—49
Olmstead, DE—48
Wright, TO/WI—47
Keeley, OM—47

WINS
Durham, WI—24
Olmstead, DE—22
Schreiber, DE—21
Aitchison, WI—20
O'Toole, SC—19

LOSSES
Jackson, TO/WI—26

Fugate, TO—24
Wright, TO/WI—22
Kaufman, TO/SJ—21
Johnson, SJ—19

BASES ON BALLS
Herche, DM—176
Jackson, TO/WI—157
Freeman, SC—141
Biersorfer, DM—140
Wright, TO/WI—124

STRIKEOUTS
Freeman, SC—248
O'Toole, SC—207
Jackson, TO/WI—207

Wilson, SC—202
Herche, DM—191

WILD PITCHES
Herche, DM—12
Alderman, SC—12
Chabek, SC—11
K.M. Hagerman, DE—10
Durham, WI—9

HIT BATTERS
Alderman, SC—44
Freeman, SC—33
Fugate, TO—25
Kaufman, TO/SJ—23
Biersorfer, DM—21

1911

The league continued the 168-game schedule in 1911, but Sunday prohibition continued to be a problem. This time the issue came up in Wichita and forced the league to move the franchise to Pueblo, which had dropped out of the league the year before.

The 1911 Denver Grizzlies were tops in the league. Members of the team were (front row) Kenworth, Weldensaul, mascot, Lloyd, McMurray; (middle row) Quillen, Gilmore, Hendricks, Hagerman, O'Brien, Cassidy, Spahr; (back row) president J.C. McGill, Harris, Kinsella, Coffey, Lindsay, Ehman, Beall and Lee Hayes, secretary. (Photograph courtesy of Jay Sanford)

Red Faber hurled for three seasons in the Western League, beginning in 1911 with Pueblo. Then he went to Des Moines for two years. He later was named to the Hall of Fame. (Photograph courtesy of Jay Sanford)

Denver improved on its second-place finish the year before by earning an all-time league record 111 victories. The Grizzlies secured the pennant with about a month to go and finished with an 18-game lead over the St. Joseph Drummers. To boost attendance, the Drummers did Ladies Day one better by making Mondays free for all children during the entire season.

The Denver Grizzlies were led to the pennant by Bucky O'Brien's 26 wins on the season. He also led the league in strikeouts. O'Brien moved to the Boston Red Sox and won 20 games the next season. He also pitched in the World Series but lost both games. Unable to maintain his stuff, O'Brien was dealt to the Cubs in 1913, which was his last year in the majors.

The league leader in RBI was St. Joseph's Dutch Zwilling, who went to the Federal League for two seasons and the Cubs for another. He also has the distinction of being the last player on the player register.

1911

Final Standings

	W	L	Pct.	GB
Denver Grizzlies	111	54	.673	—
St. Joseph Drummers	93	72	.564	18
Wichita Jobbers/				
Pueblo Indians	92	75	.551	20
Sioux City Packers	85	80	.515	26
Omaha Rourkes	85	80	.515	26
Lincoln Railsplitters	84	81	.509	27
Topeka Kaws	60	104	.365	50½
Des Moines Boosters	49	113	.302	60½

Team Hitting

	AB	R	H	SB	HR	Avg.
Pueblo	5686	876	1612	174	38	.284
Denver	5535	890	1558	353	64	.281
Sioux City	5488	863	1503	279	39	.274
Omaha	5644	781	1510	326	36	.268
St. Joseph	5281	712	1371	351	21	.259
Lincoln	5476	698	1416	303	40	.259
Topeka	5537	640	1391	163	18	.251
Des Moines	5445	577	1287	234	12	.236

Team Fielding

	G	PO	A	E	Pct.
Denver	165	4465	2126	249	.964
Lincoln	165	4459	2173	266	.961
St. Joseph	165	4358	2155	280	.959
Sioux City	165	4336	2013	277	.958
Pueblo	167	4551	2301	299	.958
Omaha	165	4558	2248	382	.947
Des Moines	162	4264	2107	376	.944
Topeka	164	4291	2069	413	.940

Individual Fielding Leaders
(Minimum 100 Games)

	POS	G	PO	A	E	Pct.
Lindsay, SJ	1b	163	1564	124	17	.990
Lloyd, DE	2b	164	414	512	38	.961
Quillen, DE	3b	166	177	250	26	.943
Gagnier, LI	ss	156	382	501	40	.957
Belden, PU	of	158	267	17	5	.983

The Western League

	POS	G	PO	A	E	Pct.
Zwilling, SJ	of	147	291	23	7	.978
Curtis, DM	of	162	323	17	9	.974
Clemons, PU	c	154	613	188	15	.982

Individual Pitching Leaders
(Minimum 35 Games)

	G	W	L	Avg.	BB	SO
Chellette, SJ	51	27	12	.692	87	202
O'Brien, DE	37	26	7	.788	77	261
Ellis, PU	47	22	11	.667	42	139
Jackson, PU	54	22	20	.528	168	208
Barber, SC	46	19	14	.573	69	132

Individual Batting Leaders
(Minimum 450 At Bats)

	G	AB	R	H	HR	SB	RBI	Avg.
Thomason, OM/TO	163	638	102	218	1	43	76	.342
Zwilling, SJ	150	531	89	181	5	36	92	.341
Kane, OM	171	642	108	218	8	73	80	.340
Cassidy, DE	169	639	112	213	7	40	91	.333
King, OM/TO	152	573	69	182	1	28	46	.318

Batting Leaders

HOME RUNS
Thomas, LI—12
Reilly, SC—11
Williams, OM—10
Several with 9

STOLEN BASES
Kane, OM—73
Coffey, DE—68
Kelly, SJ—63
Reilly, SJ—61
Niehoff, OM—60

HITS
Thomason, OM/TO—218
Kane, OM—218
Cassidy, DE—213
Lloyd, DE—201
Berger, PU—198

DOUBLES
Belden, PU—43
Berger, PU—41
Reilly, SC—37
Cobb, LI—36
Hartman, SC—36

TRIPLES
Berger, PU—17
Zwilling, SJ—16
Kane, OM—16
Beall, DE—16
Several with 15

RUNS
Berger, PU—128
Lloyd, DE—123
Andreas, SC—123
Kelly, SJ—115
Cassidy, DE—112

Pitching Leaders

GAMES
Jackson, PU—54
Chellette, SJ—51
Hueston, DM—48

Ellis, PU—47
Durbin, OM/TO—47
WINS
Chellette, SJ—27
O'Brien, DE—26
Ellis, PU—22
Jackson, PU—22
Barber, SC—19
LOSSES
Hueston, DM—28
Jackson, PU—20
Perry, PU—20
Owens, DM—20
Hall, OM—17
BASES ON BALLS
Jackson, PU—168
Hageman, LI—132
Clark, SC—127

Hall, OM—116
Hueston, DM—110
STRIKEOUTS
O'Brien, DE—261
Jackson, PU—208
Chellette, SJ—202
Hageman, LI—193
Hall, OM—190
WILD PITCHES
Robinson, OM—14
Durbin, OM/TO—12
Several with 8
HIT BATTERS
Freeman, SJ—19
Chellette, SJ—18
Applegate, LI—16
Hall, OM—16
Durbin, OM/TO—16

1912

Wichita regained control of the franchise from Pueblo in 1912. While 168 games were again scheduled, Mother Nature cut it back by five or six

The 1912 Des Moines team finished fourth in the league. (Photograph courtesy of Jay Sanford)

games for most teams. Class AA was added and several leagues moved up, but the Western League remained as a Class A team.

Denver continued its dominance and again won the pennant over St. Joseph. The race wasn't decided until the last week of the season. Although this was still the dead ball era, John Beall hit a league-record 18 homers in the light air of the mile-high Colorado city. Beall also led the league in total bases when he pounded out 33 triples and 26 doubles as well. He played parts of four seasons in the majors after that summer, but he never achieved the same success. Babe Borton, who led the league in average with a .364 mark, left St. Joseph after the season for four seasons in the majors, too. Sioux City's Elmer Brown tied with Omaha's Mark Hall for the most victories on the season, with 25. In the postseason Western Championship, the Grizzlies faced Minneapolis of the American Association and whipped the Millers soundly.

1912

Final Standings

	W	L	Pct.	GB
Denver Grizzlies	99	63	.610	—
St Joseph Drummers	94	72	.566	7
Omaha Rourkes	92	71	.564	7½
Des Moines Boosters	82	80	.506	17
Lincoln Railsplitters	83	81	.506	17
Sioux City Packers	74	85	.466	23½
Wichita Jobbers	75	89	.458	25
Topeka Jayhawks	51	109	.318	47

Western Championship

Denver defeated Minneapolis, four games to one.

Team Fielding

	G	PO	A	E	Pct.
Lincoln	169	4490	2105	278	.960
Des Moines	169	4550	2150	293	.958
Omaha	165	4430	2164	296	.957
Sioux City	164	4327	2131	314	.954
Denver	166	4372	1993	308	.954
Wichita	167	4438	2301	324	.954
St. Joseph	171	4566	2148	331	.953
Topeka	163	4250	1903	347	.937

Individual Batting Leaders
(Minimum 500 At Bats)

	G	AB	R	H	SB	Avg.
Thomason, OM	164	620	102	213	41	.344
Watson, SJ	162	631	138	216	49	.342
Zwilling, SJ	162	607	109	207	35	.341
Beall, DE	162	602	135	203	25	.337
Myers, SC	162	667	98	224	41	.336

Individual Fielding Leaders
(Minimum 100 Games)

	POS	G	PO	A	E	Pct.
Lindsay, DE	1b	145	1307	68	17	.988
Andreas, SC	2b	137	385	355	29	.962
Niehoff, OM	3b	165	224	418	50	.928
Meinke, SJ	ss	171	423	529	43	.957
Thomason, OM	of	164	319	22	10	.972
McCormick, LI	of	145	269	12	8	.972
Cassidy, DE	of	155	226	20	8	.969
Gossett, SJ	c	135	794	210	24	.977

Individual Pitching Leaders
(Minimum 20 Decisions)

	G	W	L	Pct.	BB	SO
Hicks, OM	42	18	5	.783	60	132
Hall, OM	49	25	9	.735	121	206
Leonard, DE	35	22	9	.710	62	226
Johnson, SJ	49	23	10	.697	72	191
Schreiber, DE	44	20	9	.690	77	188

Batting Leaders

HOME RUNS
Beall, DE—18
Johnson, OM—16

TOTAL BASES
Beall, DE—349

RUNS
Powell, SJ—139
Kelly, SJ—137

STOLEN BASES
Nieoff, LI—70
Mullen, LI—63
Powell, SJ—49
Watson, SJ—49
Kelly, SJ—46

SACRIFICES
Cassidy, DE—50
Lindsay, DE—44
Coyle, OM—42
Powell, SJ—40
Several with 39

Pitching Leaders

GAMES
Hagerman, LI—51
Brown, SC—51
Hueston, DM—50

Jackson, WI—50
Hall, OM—49

WINS
Hall, OM—25
Brown, SC—25
Johnson, SJ—23
Hagerman, LI—23
Leonard, DE—22

LOSSES
Jackson, WI—23
Hagerman, LI—18
Brown, SC—17
Durham, WI—17
Hornsby, TO—17

BASES ON BALLS
Hagerman, LI—145

Hall, OM—121
Perry, WI—115
Brown, SC—110
Crutcher, SJ—103

STRIKEOUTS
Hagerman, LI—315
Crutcher, SJ—254
Leonard, DE—226
Douglas, DM—211
Hall, OM—206

WILD PITCHES
Hall, OM—20
Brown, SC—14
Beebe, OM—13
Northrup, DM—13
Hagerman, LI—12

1913

Denver changed its name to the Bears and made it a hat trick in 1913 by winning its third pennant in a row thanks to manager Jack Hendricks, who was to manage in the majors for seven years. This time the Bears gained 104 victories and finished 10 games better than Des Moines. In the Minor League Championship Series, the Bears lost the seven-game series, four games to two, to the Milwaukee Brewers.

The best hitter for the Bears that season was Les Channell, who briefly played with the New York Yankees, with 26 homers to top the league. He also scored the most runs (137). St. Joseph's George Boehler led the league in wins (27). He departed for the majors for nine seasons, where he took on the role of reliever. Art Nehf pitched for Sioux City, and two years later he was pitching for the Boston Braves. He went on to a 15-year career and 184–120 record. Edd Roush played for Lincoln in 1913 before going to the Federal League the next season. The outfielder had a great career that landed him in the Hall of Fame in 1962. George Watson of St. Joseph was the early hitting leader with a .393 average, but he broke his leg after playing 33 games and was out the rest of the season.

In 1913 the Topeka management placed a value of $25,000 on its franchise. The year also marked the beginning of the Federal League, which first began as an independent minor league, reminiscent of the American League's beginnings. The Federalists raided the Western League, capturing some of its stars and managers in a move to become a major league in 1914. Even umpires, like Ollie Anderson, jumped to the Federals for higher pay.

Faber Leads White Sox to Crown

Urban "Red" Faber pitched the most innings in the league and won 20 games for the second-place Des Moines Boosters in 1913. It was his second year with the league, as he played for Pueblo in 1911.

The White Sox purchased him the following season for $3,500 and he began his major league career. The following season the spitballer was 24–14 for the Southsiders and led the league in games started.

In 1917 he won three World Series games to lead the Sox to the world championship. He had nothing to do with the Black Sox Scandal in 1919. In fact, he didn't pitch because of an injury.

Faber rebounded the following season and won more than 20 contests three years in a row, plus he led the league in ERA two of those years. He pitched 20 seasons and gained 254 victories, which finally led to his election to the Hall of Fame in 1964.

1913

Final Standings

	W	L	Pct.	GB
Denver Bears	104	62	.627	—
Des Moines Boosters	94	72	.568	10½
St. Joseph Drummers	89	79	.531	15½
Lincoln Greenbackers	87	90	.522	17½
Omaha Rourkes	79	86	.478	24½
Sioux City Packers	73	92	.442	30½
Topeka Jayhawks	73	92	.442	30½
Wichita Jobbers	65	101	.389	39

Team Batting

	AB	R	H	HR	SB	Avg.
Denver	5655	943	1667	77	221	.295
Sioux City	5653	849	1617	46	196	.286
Omaha	5660	809	1536	40	163	.272
Des Moines	5572	821	1493	58	176	.268
Lincoln	5539	795	1479	40	187	.267
St. Joseph	5653	808	1505	33	241	.266
Wichita	5587	722	1480	20	190	.265
Topeka	5567	769	1459	28	178	.260

Team Fielding

	G	PO	A	E	Pct.
Des Moines	168	4446	2042	260	.961
St. Joseph	169	4473	2136	314	.955
Lincoln	169	4411	1988	302	.955
Denver	168	4447	2044	316	.953
Topeka	166	4359	2165	334	.951
Omaha	166	4380	2127	341	.950
Sioux City	168	4401	2157	354	.948
Wichita	166	4358	2232	359	.948

Individual Fielding Leaders
(Minimum 100 Games)

	POS	G	PO	A	E	Pct.
Muellen, LI	1b	100	919	59	9	.992
Andreas, DM	2b	115	283	311	21	.966
Quillen, DE	3b	158	189	251	59	.938
Meinke, SJ	ss	165	386	495	59	.938
Middleton, WI	of	150	336	27	5	.986
Channell, DE	of	160	356	24	9	.977
McCormick, LI	of	164	325	18	16	.959
Johnson, OM	c	137	724	156	20	.980

Earned Run Average Leaders
(Minimum 150 Innings Pitched)

	G	W	L	IP	ERA
Hicks, OM	30	7	10	156-⅔	2.27
Boehler, SJ	54	27	13	345	2.32
Musser, DM	23	15	6	179-⅔	2.36
Faber, DM	50	21	20	373-⅓	2.48
Rogge, DM	45	25	17	360-⅔	2.70

Individual Batting Leaders
(Minimum 500 At Bats)

	G	AB	R	H	HR	SB	Avg.
Middleton, WI	150	573	100	212	1	46	.370
Congalton, OM	164	649	117	227	19	15	.349
Channell, DE	162	624	137	210	26	38	.337
Forsythe, TO	159	646	117	217	4	28	.334
Thomason, OM	160	608	128	202	5	13	.332

Batting Leaders

HOME RUNS
Channell, DE—26
Congalton, OM—19
McCormick, LI—15
Jones, DM—15
Several with 12

TOTAL BASES
Channel, DE—368
Congalton, OM—342
McCormick, LI—304
Jones, DM—294
Zwilling, SJ—291

STOLEN BASES
Kelly, SJ—68
Middleton, WI—46
Coffey, DE—39
Channel, DE—38
Cooney, SC—37

HITS
Congalton, OM—227
Forsythe, TO—217
Middleton, WI—212
Channell, DE—210
Kelly, SJ—209

DOUBLES
Clark, SC—50
Congalton, OM—50
McLarry, TO—48
Smith T., SC—46
Channell, DE—44

TRIPLES
Westerzil, SJ—20
McCormick, LI—19
Channell, DE—18
Thomason, OM—15
Zwilling, SJ—15

RUNS
Channell, DE—137
Kelly, SJ—136
Thomason, OM—128
Smith T., SC—124
Cooney, SC—119

Pitching Leaders

GAMES
Boehler, SJ—55

Closman, OM—51
Faber, DM—50
Crutcher, SJ—46
Robinson, OM—46

WINS
Boehler, SJ—27
Hagerman, DE—26
Rogge, DM—25
Ehman. LI—23
Wolfgang, DE—23

BASES ON BALLS
Perry, WI—123
Reynolds, TO—122
Boehler, SJ—118
Closman, OM—116
Crutcher, SJ—115

STRIKEOUTS
Johnston, SJ—265
Boehler, SJ—244
Crutcher, SJ—211
Hagerman, DE—203
Rogge, DM—189

WILD PITCHES
Boehler, SJ—13
Crutcher, SJ—13
McConnanghey, SJ—10
Cochreham, TO—10
Lafferty, DM—10

HIT BATTERS
Closman, SJ—30
Rogge, DM—24
Faber, DM—21
Robinson, OM—20
Several with 19

INNINGS PITCHED
Faber, DM—373.1
Rogge, DM—360.2
Boehler, SJ—345
Closman, OM—317.2
Ehman, LI—314.2

1914

Denver's bid for a record fourth pennant was put in doubt right away when manager Jack Hendricks left for Indianapolis and the American

Dazzy Vance pitched for St. Joseph in 1914 before he went on to a successful career in the majors that led him to the Baseball Hall of Fame. (Photograph courtesy of Jay Sanford)

Association. He was replaced by Jack Coffey, a former major league player. The doubt turned to a certainty as Sioux City recorded 105 victories. Sioux City, which took "Indians" as a nickname, were guided to the title by Josh Clarke, brother of Fred Clarke, who played for the Pittsburgh Nationals. St. Joseph finished third after a close battle with Des Moines and Lincoln.

The Indians were led by Larry LeJeune's league-leading .361 batting average and 124 runs scored. Major league veteran Jim Kane had the most hits (221) in the league to aid the Indians' efforts. However, Denver had the best hurler, as Buck Sterzer recorded 28 wins. And, as usual, the Bears had the best home run hitter in the league, with Bill Fisher slamming 21.

Denver represented the Western League in the Minor League Championship Series. The Bears were downed by the Indianapolis Indians, four games to two. A drop in attendance in the league mirrored a general decline in baseball enthusiasm.

1914

Final Standings

	W	L	Pct.	GB
Sioux City Indians	105	60	.636	—
Denver Bears	96	72	.571	10½
St. Joseph Drummers	89	75	.543	15½
Des Moines Boosters	82	81	.503	22
Lincoln Tigers	81	87	.480	25½
Omaha Rourkes	77	87	.470	27½
Topeka Jayhawks	68	97	.412	37
Wichita Wolves	63	102	.382	42

Team Batting

	AB	R	H	HR	SB	BB	SO	LOB	Avg.
Denver	5907	966	1751	86	184	466	622	1285	.296
Sioux City	5545	962	1609	48	319	742	750	1186	.290
St. Joseph	5489	819	1519	19	234	552	673	1161	.277
Omaha	5593	805	1529	33	210	457	738	1036	.273
Des Moines	5627	790	1506	57	149	618	623	1172	.268
Topeka	5553	742	1471	31	181	524	623	1095	.265
Wichita	5544	723	1446	38	210	511	790	1110	.261
Lincoln	5623	679	1415	24	236	515	777	1192	.252

Team Fielding

	G	PO	A	E	DP	PB	Pct.
Sioux City	167	4485	2249	250	137	18	.964
Des Moines	167	4428	2104	280	89	25	.959
Lincoln	170	4523	2223	332	115	14	.953
Omaha	165	4378	2004	315	108	31	.953
Topeka	165	4421	2034	323	112	26	.952
St. Joseph	165	4331	2046	324	88	23	.952
Wichita	166	4351	2296	362	132	22	.948
Denver	171	4521	2037	290	124	7	.858

Individual Fielding Leaders (Minimum 100 Games)

	POS	G	PO	A	E	Pct.
Jones, W., DM	1b	163	1660	77	14	.992
Cooney, SC	2b	167	487	510	24	.976

	POS	G	PO	A	E	Pct.
Baird, SC	3b	108	146	227	32	.921
Coffey, DE	ss	164	338	461	55	.939
Clarke, J., SC	of	121	183	15	4	.980
Cassidy, DE	of	157	249	22	6	.970
Nicholson, WI	of	153	272	26	8	.974
Haley, DM	c	146	677	167	14	.984

Earned Run Average Leaders
(Minimum 150 Innings Pitched)

	G	W	L	IP	ER	BB	SO	ERA
Scoggins, LI	44	19	14	283	81	73	179	2.58
Reisigi, TO	35	17	13	259	76	92	152	2.64
Grover, TO	39	11	16	243	72	106	161	2.67
Harrington, DE	39	21	13	268	86	96	180	2.89
Willis, OM	46	18	13	307	100	112	99	2.96

Individual Batting Leaders

	G	AB	R	H	HR	SB	Avg.
Lejeune, SC	151	521	124	188	11	50	.361
Kane, SC	167	658	118	221	11	24	.336
Butcher, DE	156	581	110	195	5	28	.336
Congalton, OM	136	516	97	173	11	18	.335
Coffey, DE	165	628	116	207	7	34	.330

Batting Leaders

HOME RUNS
Fisher, DE—21
W. Jones, DM—20
Bills, WI—17
Hunter, DM—13
Several with 11

TOTAL BASES
Kane, SC—313
W. Jones, DM—292
Lejeune, SC—289
Butcher, DE—289
Coffey, DE—287

HITS
Kane, SC—221
Coffey, DE—207
Hahn, DM—202
Thomason, OM—201
Forsythe, TO—201

DOUBLES
Koerner, TO—46
Patterson, SJ—46
Bills, WI—43
Lejeune, SC—40
P. O'Rourke, WI—40

TRIPLES
Butcher, DE—23
Tallion, TO—18
Fox, SJ—18
Coffey, DE—15
Lejeunne, SC—14

RUNS
Hahn, DM—198
Lejeune, SC—124
Koerner, TO—123
Fox, SJ—122
Kane, SC—118

STOLEN BASES
McGaffigan, LI—64

Nicholson, WI—60
G. Watson, SJ—53
Lejeune, SC—50
Krug, OM—47

Pitching Leaders

GAMES
Sterzer, SJ—51
Willis, OM—46
Scoggins, LI—44
C.R. Clarke, TP/SC—44
D. Thomas, SJ—43

WINS
Sterzer, SJ—51
Gaskell, DE—27
Gasper, SC—25
Harrington, DE—21
Mogridge, DM—21

LOSSES
Grover, TO—16
Ehman, LI—16
Lakaff, DM—16
Mogridge, DM—15
Scoggins, LI—14

INNINGS PITCHED
Sterzer, SJ—332
Gaskell, DE—322

Mogridge, DM—314
Willis, OM—307
Ehman, LI—291-2/3

BASES ON BALLS
Tipple, OM—142
Sterzer, SJ—134
Willis, OM—112
Grover, TO—106
Lakaff, DM—105

STRIKEOUTS
Sterzer, SJ—206
Tipple, OM—202
Harrington, DE—180
Scoggins, LI—179
Grover, TO—161

WILD PITCHES
Brown, TO/SJ—18
Mogridge, DM—16
Purcell, SJ—13
Tipple, OM—10
Wetzel, DE—10

HIT BATTERS
Lakaff, DM—24
Durham, WI—16
Several with 15

1915

The 168-game schedule was cut down to the major league limit of 154 games, and opening day came on April 21. However, the salary limit was raised to $3,200.

Des Moines took the league lead in June, but the pennant wasn't decided until the next to the last day of the season when Des Moines won the second game of a doubleheader over Sioux City. Denver finished second.

Pitcher George Mogridge, who helped the Des Moines Boosters to the pennant with his league-tying 24 victories, went on to pitch 15 years in the majors. The Boosters also had the best run scorer in Tex Jones. The second place Denver team was led by slugger Harry "Moose" McCormick and his sixteen dingers. For the second year in a row, LeJeune with Sioux City led the league with his .355 batting average.

Dazzy Dizzies Western Batters

Dazzy Vance burned 199 batters for last-place St. Joseph in 1915 to lead the league. It earned him a try with Pittsburgh, but he flopped.

The following season he was back with St. Joseph and won 17 games, which earned him another trial with the New York Yankees. Unfortunately, elbow problems the next season kept him in the minors.

Finally, in 1922 he became a regular starter for the Brooklyn Dodgers at age 30. Two years later he devastated the competition and went 28–6 while leading the league in strikeouts. He was named the league's Most Valuable Player.

The next season he again led the National League in wins and strikeouts. His career ended in 1935 with a 197–140 record. Vance's achievements were finally rewarded with his election to the Hall of Fame in 1955.

1915

Final Standings

	W	L	Pct.	GB
Des Moines Boosters	87	53	.621	—
Denver Bears	82	55	.599	3½
Topeka Jayhawks	75	63	.543	11
Omaha Rourkes	71	69	.507	16
Lincoln Tigers	70	69	.504	16½
Sioux City Packers	66	68	.493	18
Wichita Wolves	57	80	.416	28½
St. Joseph Drummers	43	94	.314	42½

Team Batting

	AB	R	H	HR	SB	BB	SO	LOB	Avg.
Denver	4592	723	1295	75	175	421	573	897	.282
Sioux City	4451	638	1205	31	164	495	582	881	.270
Lincoln	4788	646	1274	16	138	523	570	1105	.266
Des Moines	4649	642	1239	40	142	466	509	1010	.266
Omaha	4765	641	1241	27	142	379	494	865	.260
Topeka	4573	627	1187	25	196	415	559	893	.260
Wichita	4580	580	1177	16	136	469	558	913	.257
St. Joseph	4522	489	1081	11	157	382	578	891	.239

Team Fielding

	G	PO	A	E	DP	PB	Pct.
Des Moines	141	3723	1790	228	105	25	.960
Sioux City	135	3559	1737	246	93	16	.956

A New Century, A New League (1900–1937)   109

	G	PO	A	E	DP	PB	Pct.
Topeka	140	3682	1611	251	100	16	.955
Lincoln	142	3790	1863	262	103	18	.955
Denver	138	3668	1766	264	119	6	.954
Omaha	142	3707	1838	269	112	20	.954
St. Joseph	137	3579	1812	281	99	26	.950
Wichita	139	3646	1885	288	103	23	.950

Individual Fielding Leaders
(Minimum 100 Games)

	POS	G	PO	A	E	Pct.
Jones, DM	1b	141	1468	53	19	.987
Lattimore, TO	2b	136	443	353	21	.974
Tannehill, DM/OM	3b	124	132	243	22	.945
McGaffigan, LI	ss	142	349	423	53	.936
Smith, OM	of	138	290	20	7	.978
Hunter, DM	of	138	263	15	7	.975
McIntyre, LI	of	119	165	19	5	.974
Monroe, TO	c	103	523	113	20	.970

Earned Run Average Leaders
(Minimum 200 Innings)

	G	W	L	IP	R	BB	SO	ERA
Mogridge, DM	42	24	11	307	93	88	175	1.93
Dawson, LI	30	13	14	220	87	62	108	2.01
Thomas, DM	48	22	13	292	120	97	110	2.09
Blodgett, OM	46	24	15	321	119	47	126	2.27
Dashner, TO	46	16	14	258	104	86	174	2.58

Individual Batting Leaders
(Minimum 500 At Bats)

	G	AB	R	H	HR	SB	Avg.
Galloway, DE	134	507	95	176	14	12	.347
Forsythe, OM	138	527	83	178	4	22	.338
Spencer, DE	135	550	93	185	4	20	.336
Jones, DM	141	532	103	170	14	11	.320
Kane, SC	131	462	81	147	3	21	.318

Batting Leaders

HOME RUNS
McCormick, DE—16
Galloway, DE—14
LeJeune, SC—14
Jones, DM—14
Shields, DE—10

TOTAL BASES
Galloway, DE—281
Jones, DM—267

Forsythe, OM—239
Spencer, DE—236
LeJeune, SC—223

HITS
Spencer, DE—185
Forsythe, OM—178
Galloway, DE—176
Jones, DM—170
Hahn, DM—164

DOUBLES
Jones, DM—43
Tydeman, WI/TO—39
LeJeune, SC—36
Kane, SC—36
Bills, DM—35

TRIPLES
Galloway, DE—17
Kelleher, DE—17
Krug, OM—14
Forsythe, OM—10
Tydeman, WI/TO—8

RUNS
Jones, DM—103
Wolfe, LI—101
Lattimore, TO—97
Galloway, DE—95
Spencer, DE—93

STOLEN BASES
McGaffigan, LI—44
Wolfe, LI—31
G. Watson, SJ/SC—30
Hensling, SC—28
Sawyer, DM—28

Pitching Leaders

GAMES
Thomas, DM—48
Grover, TO—47
Blodgett, OM—46
Dashner, TO—46
Mogridge, DM—42

WINS
Mogridge, DM—24
Blodgett, OM—24
Thomas, DM—22
Mitchell, DE—22
Grover, TO—20

LOSSES
Hoffman, OM/LI—17
Grover, TO—16
Geist, WI—16
Vance, SJ—15
Blodgett, OM—15

INNINGS PITCHED
Blodgett, OM—321
Mogridge, DM—307
Thomas, DM—292.1
Grover, TO—284.2
Vance, SJ—264

BASES ON BALLS
Harrington, DE—126
Grover, TO—117
Vance, SJ—110
Southern, WI—106
Musser, DM—100

STRIKEOUTS
Vance, SJ—199
Musser, DM—179
Mogridge, DM—175
Dashner, TO—174
Southern, WI—156

WILD PITCHES
Vance, SJ—12
Southern, WI—11
Wideman, SJ—11
Brown, SJ/WI—10
Several with 8

HIT BATTERS
Vance, SJ—25
Cockran, WI—23
Mogridge, DM—23
Thomas, DM—22
Several with 19

1916

Before the season began, O'Neill was replaced as president by Frank Zehrung, the former mayor of Lincoln, Nebraska. The league owners were tired of O'Neill refusing to move his office from Comiskey Park in Chicago to a Western League location. With the end of the Federal League, the Western League received some of its players and managers. Rebel Oakes, who had managed the Pittsburgh Federals, took over the reins of the Denver Bears.

Last-place Wichita had trouble attracting fans, so the franchise moved to Colorado Springs on September 10. Omaha had no problem attracting fans, as the team won 92 games on the road to the pennant. The Rourkes would have won the title by more games, but it lost six out of its last seven.

Denver did a turn-about, winning six out of its last eight games to finish fourth with a winning record. The Bears had the best hitter in Hank Butcher, who had played with the Cleveland Indians for two seasons before coming to the Western league. Denver also had another veteran from the National League and Federal League in Rebel Oakes, who was one of the leaders in hits (205) during the season. And Ben Dyer, who led the league in homers (16), went on to three seasons in the majors with Detroit. While Denver had the best hitters, the Rourkes won the league with its good pitching. The Rourkes' Otto Merz led the league in ERA (2.45).

Omaha could manage only one win in the Minor League Championship Series against Louisville.

1916

Final Standings

	W	L	Pct.	GB
Omaha Rourkes	92	57	.617	—
Lincoln Tigers	87	63	.580	5½
Sioux City Indians	79	71	.527	13½
Denver Bears	78	75	.510	16
Des Moines Boosters	75	75	.500	17½
Topeka Savages	70	84	.455	24½
St. Joseph Drummers	67	86	.438	27
Wichita Wolves/ Colorado Springs Millionaires	57	94	.377	36

Team Batting

	AB	R	H	HR	SB	BB	SO	LOB	Avg.
Denver	5176	832	1575	66	257	418	655	953	.304

The Western League

	AB	R	H	HR	SB	BB	SO	LOB	Avg.
Sioux City	5162	775	1492	33	200	488	632	1079	.289
Omaha	5046	806	1441	50	174	455	545	991	.286
Wichita	4950	719	1406	43	109	522	547	1026	.284
Lincoln	5027	777	1419	38	203	473	495	929	.282
Des Moines	5038	708	1386	36	133	480	557	1034	.275
Topeka	5207	704	1392	27	156	440	684	944	.267
St. Joseph	4992	535	1328	18	177	373	606	961	.266

Team Fielding

	G	PO	A	E	DP	PB	Pct.
Sioux City	152	4007	1814	204	105	8	.966
Denver	154	3973	2011	229	128	32	.963
Topeka	156	4054	2004	247	92	24	.961
St. Joseph	154	4030	1896	242	87	17	.961
Lincoln	150	4039	2016	257	116	25	.959
Des Moines	151	3976	1934	256	91	50	.958
Omaha	152	4068	1940	274	114	23	.956
Wichita	151	3837	1979	281	105	18	.954

Individual Fielding Leaders
(Minimum 90 Games)

	POS	G	PO	A	E	Pct.
Jones, DM	1b	151	1605	60	16	.990
Lattimore, TO/LI	2b	128	308	388	31	.957
Dyer, DE	3b	115	134	281	26	.941
Hartford, DM	ss	146	317	477	55	.935
Gilmore, SC	of	130	322	8	5	.985
Lejeune, SC	of	123	291	32	5	.985
Butcher, DE	of	116	225	16	4	.984
Krueger, OM	c	103	434	93	15	.972

Earned Run Average Leaders
(Minimum 20 Decisions)

	G	W	L	Pct.	IP	ER	BB	SO	ERA
Mers, OM	35	18	11	.621	250	68	22	39	2.45
C.R. Clark, SC	39	16	13	.552	272	80	56	131	2.65
C. Thompson, OM	33	17	10	.630	239	72	39	68	2.71
Musser, DM	47	22	14	.636	330	101	111	249	2.75
J. Williams, SJ	47	19	16	.543	327	92	71	186	2.80

Individual Batting Leaders
(Minimum 475 At Bats)

	G	AB	R	H	HR	SB	Avg.
Butcher, DE	145	541	116	204	15	32	.377

	G	AB	R	H	HR	SB	Avg.
Kirkman, SJ	151	585	67	205	6	18	.350
R. Miller, OM	151	570	119	196	10	23	.344
Oakes, DE	152	599	104	205	1	22	.342
Gilmore, SC	130	538	104	183	2	21	.340

Batting Leaders

HOME RUNS
Dyer, DE—16
Butcher, DE—15
Litschi, WI—14
Johnson, LI—13
Several with 12

TOTAL BASES
Butcher, DE—320
R. Miller, OM—287
Kirkham, SJ—283
Dyer, DE—275
Connolly, SC—267

HITS
Kirkman, SJ—205
Oakes, DE—205
Butcher, DE—204
Watson, SC—198
R. Miller, OM—196

DOUBLES
Jones, DM—47
R. Miller, OM—45
Carlisle, LI—44
Connolly, SC—42
Litschi, WI—40

TRIPLES
Butcher, DE—20
Gilmore, SC—17
Kirkham, SJ—16
Watson, SC—15
McCabe, SJ—15

RUNS
Carlisle, LI—121
R. Miller, OM—119
Watson, SC—118
Butcher, DE—116
Oakes, DE—104

STOLEN BASES
Shields, DE—62

Watson, SC—49
McCabe, SJ—37
A.C. Miller, DE—35
Several with 32

Pitching Leaders

GAMES
Sommers, SJ—53
Koestner, WI/SJ—48
Musser, DM—47
J. Williams, SJ—47
Manser, DE—46

WINS
East, LI—24
Halla, LI—23
Musser, DM—22
Grover, TO/SC—20
Several with 19

LOSSES
Sommers, SJ—20
Koestner, WI/SJ—19
Hovlik, SJ—18
Baker, DM—17
J. Williams, SJ—16

BASES ON BALLS
Hovlik, SJ—155
Koestner, WI/SJ—126
East, LI—123
Musser, DM—111
Hall, TO—109

STRIKEOUTS
Musser, DM—249
Hovlik, SJ—176
Koestner, WI/SJ—169
East, LI—157
Grover, TO/SC—154

WILD PITCHES
Musser, DM—19
Hovlik, SJ—16
Koestner, WI/SJ—15

Grover, TO/SC—13
Several with 9

HIT BATTERS
Sommers, SJ—22
Sterser, DE—18
Gregory, LI—17
East, LI—16
Grover, TO/SC—14

INNINGS PITCHED
Sommers, SJ—350
Halla, LI—335
Musser, DM—330
Baker, DM—313
Koestner, WI—311

1917

Baseball was receiving more competition from new golf courses and fans going to movies, but, more importantly, the nation's attention turned toward the war in Europe when the country joined the effort in April 1917. Some players went off to war voluntarily.

Joplin replaced the Topeka franchise. Then the lack of public interest forced the league to go to a split season after the season had already begun. The hope was to tighten races, create a four-team playoff and raise more interest.

More interest was certainly raised in the first half, as the race went down to the last day with Des Moines nipping Lincoln. The St. Joseph franchise moved to Hutchison at the beginning of the second half. Sioux City moved to St. Joseph two weeks later. Zehrung resigned as president halfway through the financially rocky season and was replaced by E.W. Dickerson, who had been the president of the Central League. For the second half, Hutchinson ended up with the exact same record as Joplin, 33-24. The regular season ended on September 16, two weeks later than the original schedule. Hutchinson won three straight over Joplin in a best-of-five playoff to face Des Moines for the championship. Apparently, the extra contests drained the Wheatshockers and the team ran out of gas against Des Moines. The Boosters,

BROADWAY THEATRE PROGRAM

BASEBALL
WESTERN LEAGUE

DENVER
—— *vs.* ——

WICHITA -   May 29-30-30-31
LINCOLN - - June 8- 9-10-11
DES MOINES - June 12-13-14-15
OMAHA -   - June 16-17-18

——— *Games Called* ———
Sundays 3 P. M.   Week Days 3:30 P. M.

Schedule for Denver from 1917. (Photograph courtesy of Jay Sanford)

A New Century, A New League (1900–1937)   115

managed by Jack Coffey, won the postseason finals over Hutchinson, four games to two.

Hank Butcher of Denver was the triple-crown winner as he led the league in average (.321), hits (183) and home runs (13). He could have led the league in RBI as well, but no statistics were kept. His efforts didn't help the Bears much, as they finished next to last in the league. Butcher played with the Cleveland Indians before coming to the Western League. Des Moines was led by pitcher Rudy Kallio's 25 wins and Paul Musser's 23 victories. Kallio was promoted to the Detroit Tigers the next season, but he couldn't find the same success there and spent only three seasons in the majors. Musser, who led the league in strikeouts in 1917, had a brief stint in the majors before and after playing in the Western League. Lincoln's Howard Gregory finished with a 23–8 record and the best winning percentage (.742). He had a cup of coffee with the Browns.

O'Doul Better Hitter Than Pitcher

Frank "Lefty" O'Doul was a pitcher for Des Moines in 1917 and went 8–6. Two years later he damaged his arm and was moved to the outfield. It was probably for the best.

He developed into a solid hitter in the Pacific Coast League, which led him back to the majors after several unsuccessful tries. After a season with the Yankees he was traded to Philadelphia. The Baker Bowl had a small right field which was ideal for the left-handed hitter. He made the most of it as he led all hitters with a .398 average on his way to breaking Rogers Hornsby's record of 250 hits in a season.

O'Doul's major league career ended after the 1934 season with a .349 career average, fourth best in the history of the game. He has not been elected to the Hall of Fame, probably because he played only eight full seasons in the majors.

1917

Final Standings
First Half

	W	L	Pct.	GB
Des Moines Boosters	55	35	.611	—
Lincoln Links	54	37	.593	1½
Sioux City Indians	50	40	.556	5
Joplin Miners	47	44	.516	8½
Omaha Rourkes	47	45	.511	9
Denver Bears	44	48	.478	12

	W	L	Pct.	GB
St. Joseph Drummers	33	56	.371	21½
Wichita Witches	33	58	.368	22½

Second Half

	W	L	Pct.	GB
Hutchinson Wheatshockers	32	24	.571	—
Joplin Miners	32	24	.571	—
Sioux City Indians/ St. Joseph Drummers	30	26	.536	2
Lincoln Links	29	27	.518	3
Des Moines Boosters	29	27	.518	3
Wichita Witches	28	28	.500	4
Omaha Rourkes	26	30	.464	6
Denver Bears	18	38	.321	14

Playoffs

Hutchinson defeated Joplin, three games to one, to decide the second-half winner.

Finals

Des Moines defeated Hutchinson, four games to two.

Team Batting

	AB	R	H	HR	SB	BB	SO	Avg.
Sioux City/St. Joseph	4839	654	1314	21	175	415	545	.272
Omaha	4789	664	1257	27	177	380	602	.262
Denver	5041	667	1313	30	164	382	629	.260
Des Moines	4770	631	1216	24	195	426	486	.255
St. Joseph/Hutchinson	4832	519	1222	25	166	421	657	.253
Joplin	4864	683	1217	20	171	446	555	.252
Wichita	4918	597	1230	25	91	446	739	.250
Lincoln	4727	624	1139	20	195	531	567	.241

Team Fielding

	G	PO	A	E	DP	PB	Pct.
Des Moines	146	3881	1753	233	178	18	.960
Sioux City/St. Joseph	146	3852	1783	265	193	8	.955
Lincoln	147	3913	1900	285	103	21	.953
Denver	149	3878	1840	290	79	17	.952
St. Joseph/Hutchinson	147	3908	1757	301	73	19	.950
Joplin	147	3840	1797	298	94	9	.950
Wichita	148	3896	2078	336	88	14	.947
Omaha	148	3909	1944	331	77	20	.946

Individual Fielding Leaders
(Minimum 100 Games)

	POS	G	PO	A	E	Pct.
Mills, DE	1b	149	1558	75	22	.987
Coffey, DM	2b	139	329	346	27	.962
Ewoldt, DM	3b	129	166	253	22	.950
Hartford, DM	ss	143	262	391	48	.932
Butcher, DE	of	118	202	29	2	.991
Gilmore, SC/SJ	of	136	272	13	5	.983
McCabe, SJ/HU	of	111	249	31	5	.982
Shestak, DE	c	113	539	156	12	.983

Individual Pitching Leaders
(Minimum 30 Decisions)

	G	W	L	Pct	IP	AB	H	BB	SO
Gregory, LI	39	23	8	.742	319	1188	304	60	86
Kallio, DM	38	25	9	.735	306	1118	219	107	179
Adams, HU	35	20	13	.606	308	1114	244	34	197
Sanders, JO	45	18	12	.600	327	1004	239	120	125
Musser, DM	48	23	18	.561	346	1186	215	134	337

Individual Batting Leaders
(Minimum 455 At Bats)

	G	AB	R	H	HR	SB	Avg.
Butcher, DE	148	570	92	183	13	33	.321
Jones, WI	127	471	73	150	4	14	.319
Connolly, SJ	136	491	69	151	6	23	.308
Gilmore, SJ	136	551	116	169	6	42	.307
Cochran, JO	147	551	109	166	6	55	.301

Batting Leaders

HOME RUNS
Butcher, DE—13
E. Smith, OM—9
McCabe, HU—8
Several with 6

TOTAL BASES
Butcher, DE—285
Mills, DE—231
Gilmore, SJ—230
Cochrane, Jo—225

HITS
Butcher, DE—183
Gilmore, SJ—169
Cochran, JO—166
Cass, DM—166
Several with 158

DOUBLES
Mills, DE—37
Jones, WI—36
Butcher, DE—35
Crosby, SJ—35
L. Lamb, JO -33

TRIPLES
Kelleher, DE—16
Butcher, DE—14
McCabe, HU—12

Mills, DE—12
E. Smith, OM—11

RUNS
Gilmore, SJ—116
Cochran, JO—109
Cass, DM—94
Carlisle, JO—94
Butcher, DE—92

STOLEN BASES
Healey, SJ—56
Cochran, JO—55
Gilmore, SJ—42
Cass, DM—32
Watson, SJ—31

Pitching Leaders

GAMES
Hall, JO—52
Musser, DM—48
Koestner, WI—46
Sanders, JP—45
Several with 43

WINS
Merz, OM—26
Kallio, DM—25
Several with 23

LOSSES
Lyons, WI—21
R. Wright, HU—21
Clemons, WI—19
Several with 18

INNINGS PITCHED
Musser, DM—346
Hall, JP—343
Merz, OM—335
Koestner, WI—329
Sanders, JP—327

BASES ON BALLS
Koestner, WI—151
Musser, DM—134
Nabors, DE—124
Sanders, JO—120
Smithson, HU—119

STRIKEOUTS
Musser, DM—337
Adams, HU—197
Kallio, DM—179
Grover, SJ—170
Baker, WI—167

HIT BATTERS
Sanders, JO—16
Grover, SJ—12
Bremmerhoff, SJ—11
Rose, SC/SJ—11
Several with 11

WILD PITCHES
Hovlik, HU—17
Sander, JP—14
Koestner, WI—13
Grover, SJ—10
Several with 9

1918

The problem of low attendance continued into 1918 as the war in Europe continued. Denver and Lincoln dropped out of the league before the beginning of the season. By the end of May the Topeka franchise was in such bad shape that it was moved to Hutchinson.

A work-or-fight order helped put the league out of business by July 7, with the Wichita Jobbers in first place. Baseball was not considered as work by many. All other minor leagues suspended operations as well, and the major leagues cut back the season. The World Series was held earlier. Several league players joined the military, including President Dickerson, who went overseas.

Wichita's rise to the top was helped by one of the best pitchers in the league in Ed Hovlik. He tied for the most wins (13) and struck out the most hitters (128). With the Western League stopped, he signed with the Washington Senators and pitched in eight games later that season. The next year he flopped in three appearances and never pitched in the majors again.

Haines' Knuckler Baffles Batters

Jesse Haines got off to a great start in 1918 with 13 wins for Topeka/Hutchinson before the league suspended operations due to the war. He also led the league in ERA (1.59).

The following season he moved up to Kansas City in the American Association where he was one of the leading pitchers, with a 21-5 record. That propelled him to the majors, where he starred as one of the best pitchers during the Roaring 20s, winning 20 or more games three times during the decade.

A knuckleball provided Haines longevity in the majors until age 44. He finished with 210-158 record. The Veterans Committee elected him to the Hall of Fame in 1970.

1918

Final Standings

	W	L	Pct.	GB
Wichita Jobbers	41	24	.631	—
Topeka Kaw-nees/ Hutchinson Salt Packers	37	31	.544	5½
Des Moines Boosters	36	31	.537	6
Joplin Miners	34	31	.523	7
Omaha Rourkes	33	32	.508	8
Hutchinson Salt Packers/ Oklahoma City Indians	33	37	.471	10½
St. Joseph Saints	30	38	.441	12½
Sioux City Indians	22	42	.344	18½

Team Batting

	AB	R	H	TB	SB	Avg.
Oklahoma City	2194	285	587	806	81	.268
Wichita	2176	304	578	782	73	.265
Hutchinson	1919	255	498	625	103	.259
Omaha	1742	256	420	519	75	.241
Joplin	2194	268	521	703	66	.237

	AB	R	H	TB	SB	Avg.
St. Joseph	1784	193	422	536	64	.237
Des Moines	2085	296	491	608	114	.235
Sioux City	1685	171	362	456	45	.215

Individual Batting Leaders
(Minimum 200 At Bats)

	G	AB	R	H	TB	SB	Avg.
Berger, WI	61	203	31	59	88	6	.290
Daniels, SJ	54	200	23	57	74	7	.285
Kiltz, OK	45	201	29	57	85	6	.284
McBride, WI	57	211	24	59	67	0	.280
Falk, OK	56	212	32	59	93	13	.278

Team Fielding

	G	PO	A	E	DP	PB	Pct.
Hutchinson	59	1605	764	76	30	10	.968
Wichita	65	1733	722	98	47	2	.961
Joplin	64	1696	820	112	44	5	.957
Omaha	55	1446	704	108	35	5	.952
Sioux City	51	1376	703	117	48	7	.947
St. Joseph	55	1501	750	129	36	7	.946
Des Moines	67	1625	779	157	39	13	.939
Oklahoma City	68	1770	890	227	57	7	.921

Individual Fielding Averages
(Minimum 45 Games)

	POS	G	PO	A	E	Pct.
Bradley, HU	1b	59	671	30	4	.994
Benson, OK	2b	60	150	187	9	.979
Conroy, OK	3b	58	85	140	12	.949
Berger, WI	ss	56	114	181	14	.955
Wolfe, WI	of	47	84	1	1	.988
Williams, OM	of	55	56	7	1	.984
Nolte, HU	of	48	94	7	2	.981
Manion, HU	c	50	222	62	4	.986

Batting Leaders

HOME RUNS
Bob Murphy, DM—8

HITS
McClelland, OK—66
Pitts, HU/OK—62

McBride, WI—59
Berger, WI—59
Falk, OK—59

RUNS
Murphy, DM—40
Bashang, OM—40
Donica, OM—38

Washburn, WI—34
Bradley, HU—34

STOLEN BASES
Bashang, OM—23
Coffey, DM—21
Cleveland, HU—18
McCelland, OK—17
Murphy, DM—17

Pitching Leaders

WINS
Haines, TO/HU—13
Hovik, WI—13

ERA
Haines, TO/HU—1.59

INNINGS PITCHED
Hovlik, WI—146
Salisbury, TO/HU—142
Graham, HU/OK—138
Haines, TO/HU—132
Allison, SC—131

BASES ON BALLS
Fletcher, SC—58
Tedeschi, HU/OK—57
Luschen, SJ—57
Musser, DM—55
Delburn, DM—53

STRIKEOUTS
Hovlik, WI—107
Haines, TO/HU—71
Musser, DM—63
Tedeschi, HU/OK—61
Kopp, OM—56

WILD PITCHES
Koestner, WI—6
Graham, HT/OK—4
Sparks, WI/OK—3
Several with 2

HIT BATTERS
Waldbauer, WI—7
Hubbell, JO—6
Kotzelnick, TO/HU—6
Musser, DM—6
Several with 5

1919

When President Dickerson's return was delayed, club owners decided to pick Al Tearney, the Three-I president, to resurrect the league. The Western League returned to normal with eight teams competing. Tulsa took the place of Hutchinson.

The campaign featured a close race between St. Joseph, Tulsa and Wichita. St. Joseph compiled only one more win than Tulsa, but manager Alvin Dolan's Saints had six fewer losses. The two teams met in a seven game playoff series, and Tulsa jumped out to a three-game-to-one advantage before inclement weather struck. A lack of fan support resulted in the rest of the series being called off.

The Saints featured some of the best pitching in the league, with Louis North chalking up 23 wins. The St. Louis Cardinals signed him after the season and he pitched five years in the majors. He once led the National League in game appearances because of his relief efforts.

Wichita had the best hitters in the league, as Joe Wilhoit, who was in the majors for three years before coming to the league, recorded one of the highest batting averages (.422) in league history. His average was helped by a 69-game hitting streak, the longest in league history. During the hitting steak he hit a phenomenal .505, while collecting five homers, eight triples and 23 doubles. He also led the league in runs (126) and hits (222). The Red Sox signed him after the season, and he appeared in six games, which were his last in the majors. The Jobbers also had the home run leader, Clarence "Yam" Yaryan, with 12 dingers. He played a couple of seasons with the White Sox later.

Second-place Tulsa was led by pitcher Bill "Beverly" Bayne, who went 18–8. That record lifted him to the Browns at the end of the season. He went on to pitch nine seasons in the majors, ending with a 31–32 record.

1919

Final Standings

	W	L	Pct.	GB
St. Joseph Saints	78	57	.578	—
Tulsa Oilers	77	63	.550	3½
Wichita Jobbers	75	65	.536	5½
Des Moines Boosters	71	67	.514	8½
Oklahoma City Indians	69	69	.500	10½
Sioux City Indians	68	70	.493	12½
Joplin Miners	57	78	.422	21
Omaha Rourkes	56	80	.412	22½

Team Batting

	AB	R	H	HR	SB	BB	SO	Avg.
Wichita	4741	773	1383	42	66	428	222	.292
Sioux City	4789	745	1366	24	138	512	546	.285
Des Moines	4709	612	1303	18	161	364	546	.277
Tulsa	4758	653	1294	22	117	259	400	.272
St. Joseph	4466	644	1214	23	107	452	529	.272
Joplin	4656	628	1222	38	100	351	535	.262
Oklahoma City	4587	601	1184	21	103	443	694	.258
Omaha	4510	563	1131	15	86	464	491	.250

Team Fielding

	G	PO	A	E	DP	Pct.
Wichita	140	3699	1774	150	109	.973
Tulsa	141	3722	1825	222	106	.962
Des Moines	140	3712	1746	229	110	.960
St. Joseph	135	3605	1600	228	83	.958
Oklahoma City	138	3629	1772	209	118	.948

	G	PO	A	E	DP	Pct.
Omaha	136	3613	1805	307	95	.946
Sioux City	140	3725	1962	332	124	.945
Joplin	138	3626	1790	337	112	.940

Individual Fielding Leaders
(Minimum 100 Games)

	POS	G	PO	A	E	Pct.
Beall, SJ	1b	113	1041	51	14	.987
Coffey, DM	2b	123	339	334	29	.959
Brubaker, SJ	3b	115	119	223	15	.958
Berger, WI	ss	101	202	343	30	.948
McBride, WI	of	136	256	12	6	.978
Wilhoit, WI	of	128	301	27	13	.962
Griffin, OK	of	126	353	28	17	.957
Griffith, OK	c	109	486	136	16	.975

Individual Batting Leaders
(Minimum 435 At Bats)

	G	AB	R	H	HR	SB	Avg.
Wilhoit, WI	128	526	126	222	7	13	.422
Kelleher, SJ	118	460	91	149	5	14	.323
Lindimore, OK	135	497	78	157	2	16	.315
Moeller, SJ/WI	136	532	93	167	2	13	.314
Defate, SC	125	453	102	141	8	16	.311

Pitching Leaders
(Minimum 20 Decisions)

	G	W	L	Pct
North, SJ	33	23	9	.719
Bayne, TU	38	18	8	.692
Williams, SJ	42	20	11	.645
Bowman, WI	35	17	11	.607
Payne, DM	32	15	10	.600

Batting Leaders

HOME RUNS
Yaryan, WI—12
Collins, JO—10
Davis, TU—9
Defate, SC—8
Several with 7

TOTAL BASES
Wilhoit, WI—304
Moeller, SJ/WI—246
Hasbrook, DM—231
Kelleher, SJ—222
Lindimore, OK—221

HITS
Wilhoit, WI—222
Moran, SC—173
Hasbrook, DM—172
Moeller, SJ/WI—167
Goodwin, TU/SC—164

DOUBLES
Moeller, SJ/WI—51
Wilhoit, WI—41
Walker, SC/SJ—35
Hasbrook, DM—35
Defate, SC—34

TRIPLES
Lindimore, OK—15
Washburn, WI—14
Kelleher, SJ—14
Moeller, SJ/WI—11
Berger, WI—11

RUNS
Wilhoit, WI—126
Moran, SC—124
Defate, SC—102
Moeller, SJ/WI—93
Kelleher, SJ—91

STOLEN BASES
Hasbrook, DM—37
Coffey, DM—32
Moran, SC—31
Several with 23

Pitching Leaders

GAMES
Rasmussen, SC—44
Lyons, WI/SC—43
Several with 42

WINS
North, SJ—23
Williams, SJ—20
Rasmussen, SC—20
Several with 18

LOSSES
Marks, JO—17
Kopp, OM—16
Townsend, OM—16
Fuhr, OM—16
Several with 15

BASES ON BALLS
Musser, DM—118
Lyons, WI/SC—112
Stoner, OK—107
Bowman, WI—102
East, SC/WI—100

STRIKEOUTS
Musser, DM/WI—212
North, SJ—184
Williams, SJ—154
Dennis, OK—134
Mopel, JO—133

INNINGS PITCHED
Gregory, SC/WI—295
Salisbury, TU/OK—284
Rasmussen, SC—281
Kopp, OM—277
Williams, SJ—272

1920

The season began April 20, and the race between Tulsa and Wichita was as close as a clean shave. In the end, those Oilers from Oklahoma were a game better in the loss column than the Jobbers from Kansas.

Wichita had the best hitter in the league, as Yaryan led the league in just about everything. He proved the dead ball era was over with his 41 roundtrippers, and he led the league in batting average (.357), hits (206) and runs (124). (He likely led the league in RBI, but that statistic was not recorded.) The catcher went to the Chicago White Sox the next season to spend a couple of years in the majors. Omaha's Emilio Palmero, who had been sent back to the minors after a couple of unsuccessful seasons with the New York Giants, recorded the most wins on the season with 28. The

Cuban hurler was called back to the majors for three seasons, but he never achieved the success he had in the Western League. Oklahoma's C.A. Ramsey had the best winning percentage (.821), with a 23–5 record.

When the dust cleared on the season, nearly all the teams had made money. This success continued and it brought stability to the league for the next several years. The league roared into the 1920s like the rest of the nation. Baseball was prosperous everywhere. Prohibition did cut into profits at ballparks, but the hot dog and a Coke became a popular staple among fans.

Jim Bottomley was a first baseman for Sioux City in 1920. He was later named to the Hall of Fame. (Photograph courtesy of Jay Sanford)

1921

Final Standings

	W	L	Pct.	GB
Tulsa Oilers	92	61	.601	—
Wichita Jobbers	92	62	.597	½
Oklahoma City Indians	82	68	.547	8½
Omaha Rourkes	76	77	.497	16
St. Joseph Saints	74	80	.481	18½
Joplin Miners	73	81	.474	19½
Sioux City Packers	63	88	.417	28
Des Moines Boosters	58	93	.384	33

Team Batting

	AB	R	H	HR	BB	SO	Avg.
Wichita	5302	900	1537	114	193	581	.290
Tulsa	5135	805	1411	73	371	507	.275
St. Joseph	5273	702	1444	35	361	425	.274
Joplin	5167	702	1407	18	399	408	.272
Oklahoma City	5054	783	1366	17	435	506	.270
Sioux City	5177	665	1377	40	459	690	.266

	AB	R	H	HR	BB	SO	Avg.
Omaha	5074	718	1305	27	412	388	.257
Des Moines	5070	593	1262	31	367	493	.249

Team Fielding

	DP	PB	PO	A	E	Pct.
Tulsa	125	21	4020	1820	253	.958
St. Joseph	92	18	4141	1882	261	.958
Wichita	114	8	4028	2148	296	.954
Des Moines	95	22	3951	1993	294	.953
Omaha	78	15	4058	1887	313	.950
Oklahoma City	110	10	3943	1914	315	.949
Joplin	98	18	4050	1821	316	.949
Sioux City	108	24	3938	2027	375	.941

Fielding Leaders
(Minimum 100 Games)

	POS	G	PO	A	E	Pct.
Lelivelt, OM	1b	149	1500	81	26	.984
Coffey, DM	2b	133	338	412	37	.953
McDermott, DM	3b	137	167	245	24	.945
Tierney, TU	ss	130	318	339	46	.935
O'Connor, DM	of	119	290	22	4	.980
Connelly, TU	of	150	403	17	8	.981
Lamb, JO	of	127	248	26	8	.972
Crosby, SJ	c	114	483	99	11	.981

Pitching Leaders
(Minimum 20 Decisions)

	G	W	L	Pct.
Ramsey, OK	36	23	5	.821
Morris, TU	50	27	9	.750
Palmero, OM	40	28	10	.737
Gregory, WI	45	25	13	.658
Musser, WI	36	20	11	.645

Individual Batting Leaders
(Minimum 520 At Bats)

	G	AB	R	H	HR	Avg.
Yaryan, WI	151	577	124	206	41	.357
Tierney, TU	153	576	108	193	11	.335
Bogart, JO	153	545	101	181	4	.332
Beck, WI	150	572	106	190	30	.332
Pitt, OK	145	592	113	196	4	.331

Batting Leaders

HOME RUNS
Yaryan, WI—41
Beck, WI—30
Davis, TU—20
Platte, OM—15
East, WI—14

STOLEN BASES
Pitt, OK—41
Lee, OM—39
Kelleher, SJ—36
Hughes, OK—35
Emerick, SJ—28

HITS
Yaryan, WI—206
Pitt, OK—196
Tierney, TU—193
Beck, WI—190
Lindimore, OK—189

DOUBLES
Metz, SC—53
Tierney, TU—48
Beck, WI—47
Butler, WI—44
Several with 42

TRIPLES
Bogart, JO—16
Walker, SJ—16
Wagner, JO—15
Pitt, OK—13
Tierney, TU—13

TOTAL BASES
Yaryan, WI—376
Beck, WI—335
Tierney, TU—300
Platte, OM—279
Davis, TU—257

SACRIFICES
Weldell, OM—53
Kelleher, SJ—36
Marr, SC—33
Washburn, WI—33
Several with 30

RUNS
Yaryan, WI—124
Berger, WI—119
Pitt, OK—113
Gislason, OM—112
Tierney, TU—108

Pitching Leaders

GAMES
Morris, TU—50
Fletcher, DM—48
Gregory, WI—45
Fuhr, OM—44
Several with 43

WINS
Palmero, OM—28
Morris, TU—27
Gregory, WI—25
Bowman, WI—23
Ramsey, OK—23

LOSSES
Fletcher, DM—23
Kopp, OM—23
Lyons, SC—20
Merz, DM—18
Several with 17

INNINGS PITCHED
Fuhr, OM—338
Boehler, JO—334
Palmero, OM—334
Gregory, WI—320
Morris, TU—316

BASES ON BALLS
Lyons, SC—123
Musser, WI—117
Bowman, WI—101
Richmond, TU—100
Morris, TU—98

STRIKEOUTS
Boehler, JO—258
Palmero, OM—193
Musser, WI—179
Fuhr, OM—171
Williams, SJ—161

HIT BATTERS
McLoughlin, SJ—23
Sanders, JO—16

Richmond, TU—16
Morris, TU—14
Several with 13

WILD PITCHES
Davenport, SC—12

Lyons, SC—10
Bowman, WI—9
Lynch, DM—9
Schenberg, JO—8

1921

The financial success in 1920 led the league to go back to the 168-game slate it had used a decade earlier. Fans were coming back to baseball like perennials, but the season began on April 13 before flowers came to bloom.

Wichita changed its nickname to "Witches" and put a spell on the rest of the league. The witchcraft worked on the Oilers, who dropped all the way to last place. The Witches also ran away with the pennant by winning a league record 19 straight contests at the end of the season to easily claim the flag. Omaha edged out Oklahoma City for second.

Wichita again had some of the best hitters in the league, as it led the league in club batting with a .319 average. In one game the Witches brewed up 23 runs behind a league record five doubles by Jim Blakesley and three homers by Carlton East. Fred Beck slammed 35 homers for the Witches, while teammate Royce Washburn burned the bases for 170 runs. Omaha's Jack Lelivelt led all hitters with a .416 average, 274 hits and 70 doubles. The veteran had played six seasons in the majors long before he came to the Western League. He took over as manager for the team, too. His brother Bill also was a pitcher, so baseball ran in the family. Oklahoma City's Roy Allen notched the most wins (25) on the season. Tulsa's Phil Todt hit for the cycle, plus another single, in a game against St. Joseph.

In one game during the season, Des Moines was credited with 33 assists for an all-time league record. The shortstop Rhyne had 13 himself. The league was not as successful financially in 1921, as huge unemployment around the country kept some fans away.

1921

Final Standings

	W	L	Pct.	GB
Wichita Witches	106	61	.635	—
Omaha Buffaloes	95	73	.565	11½
Oklahoma City Indians	93	75	.554	13½
Sioux City Packers	81	83	.494	23½

	W	L	Pct.	GB
St. Joseph Saints	79	88	.473	27
Joplin Miners	76	91	.455	30
Des Moines Boosters	71	92	.436	33
Tulsa Oilers	65	103	.387	41½

Team Batting

	AB	R	H	HR	BB	SO	Avg.
Wichita	5940	1180	1892	149	583	559	.319
Omaha	5836	1034	1831	64	515	393	.314
Joplin	5754	910	1721	33	485	464	.299
St. Joseph	5891	885	1724	33	520	515	.293
Tulsa	5827	856	1691	106	449	643	.290
Des Moines	5687	836	1637	67	453	608	.288
Sioux City	5682	897	1615	59	655	645	.284
Oklahoma City	5745	823	1608	44	500	553	.280

Team Fielding

	DP	PB	PO	A	E	Pct.
Wichita	161	5	4631	2268	249	.965
St. Joseph	117	13	4368	2098	286	.958
Oklahoma City	126	11	4484	2093	292	.957
Sioux City	135	31	4346	2065	295	.956
Omaha	115	14	4491	2283	335	.953
Tulsa	141	11	4327	2146	331	.951
Des Moines	121	14	4530	2265	354	.950
Joplin	139	15	4375	2027	358	.947

Fielding Leaders
(Minimum 100 Games)

	POS	G	PO	A	E	Pct.
Beck, WI	1b	166	1759	90	26	.986
Krueger, JO	2b	144	370	470	37	.958
Butler, WI	3b	156	193	310	24	.954
Berger, WI	ss	165	323	603	51	.948
Corridon, SJ	of	136	246	14	4	.985
Harper, OK	of	168	486	29	9	.983
O'Connor, DM	of	140	226	22	5	.980
Haley, WI	c	145	527	139	14	.979

Pitching Leaders
(20 Decisions or More)

	G	W	L	Pct.
Beebe, WI	40	19	9	.679
Allen, OK	52	25	13	.658

	G	W	L	Pct.
Sellars, WI	52	21	12	.636
Gregory, WI	48	22	13	.629
Salisbury, OK	51	17	12	.586

Individual Batting Leaders
(Minimum 520 At Bats)

	G	AB	R	H	HR	Avg.
Lelivelt, OM	166	659	149	274	14	.416
Harper, OK	168	606	130	238	19	.393
East, WI	168	663	156	255	26	.385
Metz, SC	167	621	114	229	20	.369
Davis, TU	144	549	93	200	21	.364

Batting Leaders

HOME RUNS
Beck, WI—35
Washburn, WI—30
Todt, TU—28
East, WI—26
Blakesley, WI—25

STOLEN BASES
Haney, OM—48
Pitt, OK—34
Smith, WI—33
Lee, OM—32
Several with 28

HITS
Lelivelt, OM—274
East, WI—255
Harper, OK—238
Robertson, JO—238
Metz, SC—229

DOUBLES
East, WI—69
Metz, SC—62
Berger, WI—61
Griffith, OM—60
Harper, OK—50

TRIPLES
Robertson, JO—16
Fisher, SJ—15
Haney, OM—15
Smith, WI—14
Gislason, OM—13

TOTAL BASES
East, WI—418
Lelivelt, OM—404
Washburn, WI—377
Beck, WI—372
Harper, OK—367

SACRIFICES
Haney, OM—49
Washburn, WI—45
Beatty, SJ—37
Grant, DM—31
O'Brien, OM—31

RUNS
Washburn, WI—170
Smith, WI—160
East, WI—156
Berger, WI—155
Lelivelt, OM—149

Pitching Leaders

GAMES
Glassier, OM—62
Black, DM—57
Davenport, OM—53
Berger, JO—53

WINS
Allen, OK—25
Glasier, OM—22
Gregory, WI—22
Sellars, WI—21
Tesar, SC—21

A New Century, A New League (1900–1937) 131

LOSSES	BASES ON BALLS
Black, DM—23	Tesar, SC—138
Lukanovic, TU—21	Berger, JO—136
Merz, DM—21	Young, JO—136
Tesar, SC—21	Hovlik, SJ—128
Boehler, TU—20	Sellars, WI—128

INNINGS PITCHED	STRIKEOUTS
Allen, OK—346	Tesar, SC—163
Glasier, OM—331	Black, DM—146
Tesar, SC—324	Berger, JO—140
Black, DM—320	Hovlik, SJ—139
Merz, DM—305	Lukanovic, TU—128

1922

Before the season began, Denver took Joplin's place in the schedule. The only Colorado entry had to give visiting clubs an additional share of the gate receipts to make up for the extra travel.

Club owners met in Kansas City on July 10, planning to split the season, but President Tearney won over enough votes to kill the measure. In defeating the bush league tactics, he accused some owners of putting financial gain ahead of sportsmanship by advocating a divided campaign.

Sioux City transferred its September games to Lincoln, but the Iowa club retained the franchise. The pennant race came down to the last week of the season, with Wichita, St. Joseph and Tulsa battling for the crown. Tulsa charged past the other teams to win the pennant, which surprised many, as the team had finished last the previous season. Since the Oilers placed in second in 1920, their ride was reminiscent of a roller coaster, too. Tulsa was much too good for Mobile in a postseason seven-game series. The Oilers won the series four games to one. The Southern and Texas League presidents then decreed no more outside series for the Dixie Series winner, so the postseason series was axed.

The Oilers had a team loaded with ex-major leaguers that season and led the league in hitting and pitching. Tulsa's best hitter was Yank Davis, who powered 35 homers on the season. Many times he knocked in Herschel Bennett, who led the league in runs scored with 177. Bennett was signed by the St. Louis Browns the next season and played outfield there for five seasons. Oilers' Lyman Lamb, who was with the Browns for the previous two seasons, also led the league in doubles (68). On the mound, Tulsa's George Boehler led the league in wins and tied an all-time Western League record of 38 victories, while setting the all-time record amount of innings (441). Boehler was an ex–Browns player who had pitched seven years in the majors before coming to the Western League. He played two more years in the majors after the 1922 season.

East improved on his .385 batting average from the year before to lead the league with a .391 average, keeping Wichita in the hunt. During two games against Denver he put together a string of 11 consecutive hits, which included three homers and two doubles. East had a cup of coffee in the majors with two teams. Another coffee drinker in the majors was Omaha's Dan Tipple with the Yankees. He led the league in winning percentage (.793) with his 23-6 record.

A railroad strike cut into the profits of the league in 1922.

Manush Mashes Ball to Get to Hall

Heinie Manush slugged 20 triples and homers for Omaha in 1922, which resulted in his promotion to the Detroit Tigers the next year.

Manager Ty Cobb turned him into a line-drive hitter, and he became one of the leading hitters in Major League baseball. He ended up averaging .330 for his career.

The outfielder was named to the Hall of Fame in 1964 by the Veterans Committee.

Heine Manush played the outfield for Omaha in 1922 before a great career in the majors and a spot in the Hall of Fame in 1964. (Photograph courtesy of Jay Sanford)

1922

Final Standings

	W	L	Pct.	GB
Tulsa Oilers	103	64	.617	—
St. Joseph Saints	98	70	.584	5½
Wichita Witches	94	73	.568	9
Omaha Buffaloes	91	77	.549	12½
Sioux City Packers	86	79	.518	16

A New Century, A New League (1900–1937) 133

	W	L	Pct.	GB
Oklahoma City Indians	73	94	.435	30
Denver Bears	63	105	.374	40½
Des Moines Boosters	61	107	.363	42½

Team Batting

	AB	R	H	HR	BB	SO	Avg.
Tulsa	6029	1184	1945	160	578	503	.323
Wichita	6033	1190	1907	110	679	616	.316
Sioux City	5926	1071	1821	81	570	613	.307
Omaha	5794	1003	1765	101	466	609	.305
St. Joseph	5867	975	1750	62	580	582	.298
Oklahoma City	5832	914	1720	36	587	616	.295
Denver	5695	856	1617	60	499	684	.284
Des Moines	5825	811	1647	72	446	719	.283

Team Fielding

	G	DP	PB	PO	A	E	Pct.
Tulsa	168	106	14	4460	1972	238	.964
Sioux City	167	171	36	4395	2165	256	.962
St. Joseph	169	113	19	4410	2085	296	.956
Wichita	168	159	12	4445	2112	310	.955
Denver	168	150	22	4288	2241	317	.954
Omaha	168	128	14	4367	2010	325	.952
Oklahoma City	168	125	8	4404	2120	330	.952
Des Moines	168	119	23	4565	2116	395	.944

Individual Fielding Leaders
(Minimum 100 Games)

	POS	G	PO	A	E	Pct.
Metz, SC	1b	166	1609	77	15	.991
Bauman, TU	2b	143	363	480	33	.962
Patterson, DE	3b	157	161	321	22	.956
Berger, WI	ss	159	309	526	57	.933
Lamb, TU	of	156	359	35	10	.975
Manush, OM	of	166	391	16	11	.974
Bennett, TU	of	161	327	15	9	.974
Crosby, TU	c	156	839	119	12	.988

Individual Pitching Leaders
(20 Decisions or More)

	G	W	L	Pct.
Tipple, OM	39	23	6	.793
Boehler, TU	62	38	13	.745

	G	W	L	Pct.
Grover, SJ	34	16	6	.727
Maun, WI	37	18	7	.720
Williams, SC	29	16	7	.696

Individual Batting Leaders
(Minimum 520 At Bats)

	G	AB	R	H	HR	Avg.
East, WI	168	690	157	270	30	.391
Manush, OM	167	652	148	245	20	.376
Bennett, TU	161	717	177	265	24	.370
Levlivelt, TU	154	594	114	219	16	.369
Berger, WI	159	634	150	229	6	.361

Batting Leaders

HOME RUNS
Davis, TU—35
Lamb, TU—32
East, WI—30
Bennett, TU—24
Washburn, WI—23

STOLEN BASES
Eish, SC—52
Smith, L. WI—48
Pitt, OK—37
Grantham, OM—33
Gislason, OM—31

HITS
East, WI—270
Bennett, TU—265
Manush, OM—245
Fisher, SJ—242
Berger, WI—229

DOUBLES
Lamb, TU—68
Metz, SC—65
Blakesley, WI—60
Baumann, TU—56
Bennett, TU—56

TRIPLES
East, WI—20
Long, DE—18
Fisher, SJ—17
Several with 13

TOTAL BASES
East, WI—433
Bennett, TU—419
Lamb, TU—406
Davis, TU—403
East, WI—389

SACRIFICES
Lamb, TU—33
Corriden, SJ—30
Bauman, TU—27
Berger, WI—27
Bonowitz, SJ—27

RUNS
Bennett, TU—177
Davis, TU—162
Fisher, SJ—160
Grantham, OM—157
East, WI—157

Pitching Leaders

GAMES
Boehler, TU—62
Tesar, SC—56
Allen, OK—50
Roetiger, SC—50
Okrie, OM—48

WINS
Boehler, TU—38
Tipple, OM—23
Gregory, WI—22
Allen, OK—21
Tesar, SC—21

LOSSES
Tesar, SC—24
Allen, OK—20
Hall, DE—20
Salisbury, DE—19
Gross, DE—18

INNINGS PITCHED
Boehler, TU—441
Tesar, SC—356
Allen, OK—322
Gregory, WI—302
Roetiger, SC—294

BASES ON BALLS
Roetiger, SC—237
Sellers, WI—156
Tesar, SC—143
Tipple, OM—139
Wilson, SC—137

STRIKEOUTS
Roetiger, SC—207
Tesar, SC—200
Tipple, OM—194
Sellers, WI—145

WILD PITCHES
Black, DM/TU—14
Boehler, TU—14
Roetiger, SC—12
Tipple, OM—12
Several with 11

HIT BATTERS
McLaughlin, DM/TU—21
Roetiger, SC—19
Wetzel, DE—17
Boehler, TU—12
Lynch, DM—12

1923

While there were no changes in franchises in 1923, the league had its share of troubles. Oklahoma City twice had its park severely damaged by floods. Sioux City had problems attracting enough fans to make it profitable, but there was no place it could move. The league bailed out the team's backers by taking over the franchise for the balance of the season. The Packers didn't help their efforts when the team finished next to last. The league planned to move Sioux City to Kansas City, Kansas. The location was across the border from Kansas City, Missouri, which had a team in the American Association. However, the move never materialized. A modified draft plan kept surplus major leaguers in the league and helped to attract fans and improve the competition.

The race for the flag was a photo finish between Oklahoma City, Tulsa and Wichita. Each of the teams ended up with more than 100 victories. However, Oklahoma City ended with fewer losses and edged the Oilers by two games.

Pitching carried the Indians to the title, as the Oilers still led the league in hitting. Oklahoma City's best pitcher was Emil Yde, who compiled a 28–12 record on the season. Yde hit an unbelievable .389 on the season to help his own efforts. He went to the Pittsburgh Pirates the next season and led the league in winning percentage with a 16–3 mark. He pitched a handful of seasons in the majors.

Opening day ceremonies in Denver in 1923 were captured in these photos. The Denver Bears' owner Milk Ansfinger holds onto the mascot, a live bear. The team finished last that season. (Photographs courtesy of Jay Sanford)

The leading hitter in the league was Joe Horan of Des Moines with a .411 average. Wichita's Jim McDowell slammed the most homers (37). Neither slugger ever played in the majors. Teammate Ernest Maun garnered the best winning percentage (.703) in the league with his 26–11 record. Later he spent two seasons in the majors. Karl Black of Tulsa recorded the most wins (29) on the season. Three players hit for the cycle that year: Mabion Higbee of Denver, Glenn McNally of Oklahoma City and Eddie Palmer of Sioux City.

This Babe Hit for Average

Babe Herman hit .416 in 92 games for Omaha in 1923, which showed he was ready for the majors, but that didn't occur until 1926 when he moved up to the Brooklyn Dodgers.

After a sophomore slump, he surged ahead like a bull market and reached a .393 batting average in 1930. Herman set the major league record for hitting for the cycle, as he did it twice in 1931 and once in 1933. However, he also tied a dubious record of hitting into three double plays in one game. He played 13 years in the majors and averaged .324.

1923

Final Standings

	W	L	Pct.	GB
Oklahoma City Indians	102	64	.614	—
Tulsa Oilers	101	67	.601	2
Wichita Izzies	100	68	.595	3
Omaha Buffaloes	92	74	.554	10
Des Moines Boosters	87	79	.527	15
St. Joseph Saints	65	101	.392	37
Sioux City Packers	59	105	.358	42
Denver Bears	59	107	.355	43

Team Batting

	AB	R	H	HR	BB	SO	Avg.
Tulsa	5986	1175	1956	134	416	446	.326
Des Moines	5861	969	1831	90	492	502	.312
Sioux City	5733	888	1769	74	494	540	.309
Wichita	5850	1021	177	9	544	571	.304
Omaha	5563	916	1668	92	443	352	.300
Oklahoma City	5711	970	1708	74	556	581	.299
Denver	5749	789	1642	65	497	632	.286
St. Joseph	5636	770	1595	52	494	588	.283

Team Fielding

	G	DP	PB	PO	A	E	Pct.
Denver	169	175	4	4496	2197	219	.968
Omaha	166	112	8	4395	2028	243	.964
Oklahoma City	168	146	12	4381	2036	248	.963
Wichita	170	150	16	4445	2015	269	.960
Denver	169	127	15	4314	2139	286	.958
Sioux City	165	140	22	4151	2072	272	.958
Des Moines	169	144	13	443	2045	288	.957
St. Joseph	168	156	13	4304	2211	302	.956

Individual Fielding Leaders
(Minimum 100 Games)

	POS	G	PO	A	E	Pct.
Olsen, SJ/SC	1b	129	1307	78	12	.991

	POS	G	PO	A	E	Pct.
McNally, OK	2b	147	411	484	21	.977
Butler, WI	3b	168	186	340	37	.934
Lee, TU	ss	160	443	567	43	.959
O'Connor, OM	of	108	185	18	3	.985
Blakesley, WI	of	168	310	14	6	.982
Bonowitz, OM	of	166	430	28	9	.981
Crosby, TU	c	160	616	136	8	.989

Individual Pitching Leaders
(20 Decisions or More)

	G	W	L	Pct.
Maun, WI	43	26	11	.703
Yde, OK	47	28	12	.700
Black, TU	58	29	13	.690
Songer, OK	40	18	9	.667
Speece, OM	49	26	14	.650

Individual Batting Leaders
(Minimum 520 At Bats)

	G	AB	R	H	HR	Avg.
Horan, DM	153	632	122	256	23	.411
Bauman, TU	158	611	129	229	4	.375
Palmer, SC	158	665	119	243	12	.365
McLarry, DM	160	656	149	238	16	.363
Luderus, OK	140	525	95	190	13	.362

Batting Leaders

HOME RUNS
C. McDowell, WI—37
Blakesley, WI—36
Davis, TU—32
Horan, DM—23
Several with 22

STOLEN BASES
L. Smith, WI—56
Conlan, WI—44
Kerr, OM—34
Butler, WI—30
Felber, OK—29

HITS
Horan, DM—256
Blakesley, WI—246
Palmer, SC—243
Lamb, TU—241
Davis, TU—240

DOUBLES
Lamb, TU—71
Palmer, SC—62
Horan, DM—57
Davis, TU—54

TRIPLES
Blakesley, WI—16
Lewan, SJ—15
Murphy, DM -13
McNally, OK—12
Several with 11

TOTAL BASES
Blakesley, WI—439
Davis, TU—402
Horan, DM—400

Lamb, TU—370
Palmer, SC—355
SACRIFICES
Corriden, DM—35
Lamb, TU—35
McNally, OK—35
McPhell, DE—35
Several with 32
RUNS
Blakesley, WI—151
D. Lee, TU—142
Davis, TU—141
Conlan, WI—135
Bauman, TU—129

Pitching Leaders
GAMES
Black, TU—58
Allen, OK—54
Payne, OK—54
May, OM—51
Voight, DE—51
WINS
Black, TU—29
Yde, OK—28
Maun, WI—26
Speece, OM—26
Payne, OK—24
LOSSES
Voight, DE—22
Hall, DE—21
Rasmussen, SC—21
Several with 18

SHUTOUTS
Payne, OK—6
McLaughlin, TU—4
Maun, WI—3
Yde, OK—3
Several with 2

INNINGS PITCHED
Voight, DE—332
McLaughlin, TU—322
Payne, OK—321
Speece, OM—314
Hovlik, WI—310

BASES ON BALLS
Yde, OK—169
Jones, DM—125
Hovlik, WI—120
Williams, SC—119
Sellers, WI—116

STRIKEOUTS
Hovlik, WI—161
Sellers, WI—153
Maun, WI—145
Lynch, DM—134
Speece, OM—129

HIT BATTERS
Williams, SC—25
McLaughlin, TU—20
Sellers, WI—18
Lindberg, SJ—17
Yde, OK—17

1924

Before the season began, the troubled Sioux City franchise was moved to Lincoln. The Links ended up finishing last in the standings that year.

During the season, Tulsa manager Jack Lelivelt was the first manager to be punished for allowing a non-pitcher on the mound when he had a first baseman pitch in a game. The league fined the field boss $100. In June rumors surfaced that Oklahoma City and Tulsa were plotting to quit the Western League and move to the Texas League. Financially troubled St. Joseph wasn't helped by a fire on September 18 that destroyed part of the grandstand. Damage was estimated at $15,000. After the season ended, Davenport, Springfield, Pueblo, Colorado Springs, Muskogee and Okmulgee all bid for the St. Joseph franchise. The close competition continued from the previous season, with a trio of teams again going down to the finish. Art Griggs guided his Omaha squad over Denver and Tulsa for the pennant. Omaha won the title with a strong pitching staff that included Bill Bailey, who led the league in 191 Ks. He also won 23 games. Bailey was a veteran of 11 years in the majors before coming to the Western League.

Tulsa's George Blaeholder recorded the best winning percentage (.750) in the league with his 18–6 record. The Oilers also had Royce Washburn, who set the league record for homers up to that point with his 48 four-base hits. Washburn also led the league in runs scored and total bases. Tulsa's Lyman Lamb set the all-time record for doubles with a phenomenal 100! He also led the circuit in hits (261). During a four-game series with Wichita, he was 18-for-22. Lamb was with the Browns for two seasons before coming to Tulsa. Herb Hall, who had a try in the majors, kept the Denver Bears close with his 26 victories. Bott of Wichita hit for the cycle, plus an extra double to boot, in a game against Tulsa. D.C. "Mutt" Williams of Denver set the all-time league record for successive shutout innings when he went 32 without giving up a run.

The Western League had its own version of the Tinkers-to-Evers-to-Chance double-play combination. Omaha's combination was third baseman Jimmy Wilcox to second baseman Fresco Thompson to first baseman Nick Cullop. The trio pulled off four double plays in one game on August 12, 1924.

The highest scoring game in league history occurred in 1924. Wichita beat Des Moines by a score that sounded more like a football game, 30–16. In fact, Wichita scored 11 runs in one inning! Another strange game occurred in 1924. Tulsa shut out Omaha 22–0, which became the all-time league record for a shutout margin.

Lazzeri Had Unusual Nickname

Tony Lazzeri played for the first part of the 1924 season in the Western League before earning a promotion back to Class AA after hitting .329.

Ping Bodie roamed the outfield for Des Moines in 1924 in the twilight of his career, which included the Yankees and White Sox.

Lazzeri had quite an unusual nickname. Fans would yell "Poosh 'Em Up," which meant hit, every time he came to bat, and it became his nickname. After a 60 home run season with the Salt Lake City Bees in 1925, he was promoted to the Yankees.

The versatile infielder played in the shadow of Babe Ruth and Lou Gehrig. He became the first hitter in history to hit two grand-slam homers in the same game. The Veterans Committee finally named him to the Hall of Fame in 1991.

1924

Final Standings

	W	L	Pct.	GB
Omaha Buffaloes	103	61	.628	—
Denver Bears	100	67	.599	4½
Tulsa Oilers	98	69	.587	6½
St. Joseph Saints	86	79	.521	17½
Oklahoma City Indians	82	86	.488	23
Wichita Izzies	79	88	.473	25½
Des Moines Boosters	59	106	.358	44½
Lincoln Links	57	108	.345	46½

Team Batting

	AB	R	H	R	BB	SO	Avg.
Tulsa	6113	1260	1992	198	610	574	.326
Denver	5902	1138	1815	100	645	586	.306
Wichita	6005	1057	1846	113	554	499	.307
Omaha	5826	986	1725	119	570	597	.296
Oklahoma City	5824	870	1628	71	501	639	.280
St. Joseph	5662	862	1572	57	560	568	.278
Lincoln	5880	880	1628	110	522	695	.277
Des Moines	5766	780	1587	91	475	536	.275

Team Fielding

	G	DP	PB	PO	A	E	Pct.
Denver	168	160	19	4485	2092	261	.962
St. Joseph	170	150	30	4484	2148	271	.961
Tulsa	169	168	10	4418	2170	271	.960
Oklahoma City	169	159	15	4439	2096	272	.959
Omaha	166	169	24	4430	1960	273	.959
Wichita	169	112	10	4466	2145	307	.956
Des Moines	169	182	26	4374	2217	304	.956
Lincoln	168	130	18	4379	2039	361	.947

Individual Batting Leaders
(Minimum 527 At Bats)

	G	AB	R	H	HR	Avg.
Miller, SJ	155	558	108	215	19	.385
Lelivelt, TU	155	594	124	228	11	.384
Washburn, TU	169	658	184	247	48	.375
Lamb, TU	168	699	149	261	19	.373
Ginglardi, DE	163	645	151	238	15	.369

Batting Leaders

HOME RUNS
Washburn, TU—48
Davis, TU—42
Cullop, OM—40
Beck, WI—38
Bodie, DM—32

STOLEN BASES
Smith, WI—56
L. Thompson, WI—39
Corrigan, SJ—34
Gorman, DE—31
Felber, OK—30

HITS
Lamb, TU—261
Washburn, TU—247
Ginglardi, DE—238
Dunning, WI—233
Several with 231

DOUBLES
Lamb, TU—100
Butler, WI—70
Dunning, WI—64
Knight, DE—56
Lelivelt, TU—56

TRIPLES
Roche, DE—18
O'Brien, DE—16
Ginglardi, DE—14
L. Thompson, OM—13
Several with 12

TOTAL BASES
Washburn, TU—458
Lamb, TU—426
Davis, TU—408
Cullop, OM—374
Butler, WI—369

SACRIFICES
Berger, DE—47
Butler, WI—37
Bonowitz, OM—34
Flippin, TU—28
Corrigan, SJ—28

RUNS
Washburn, TU—184
Ginglardi, DE—151
L. Thompson, OM—150
Lamb, TU—149
Davis, TU—148

Pitching Leaders

GAMES
Black, TU—59
Allen, OK—58
Hall, DE—57
Vorhies, DE—55
Bailey, OM—55

WINS
Hall, DE—26
Lee, OM—25
Bailey, OM—23
Koupal, OM—22
Songer, OK—22

LOSSES
Stokes, LI/DM—27
Grover, LI—18
R. Johnson, OK/TU—18
Several with 17

SHUTOUTS
Allen, OK—5

Davenport, SJ—4
Lee, OM—4
Songer, OK—4
Several with 3
INNINGS PITCHED
Bailey, OM—340
Lee, OM—325
Hovlik, WI—317
Hall, DE—315
Black, TU—300
BASES ON BALLS
Black, TU—139
Bailey, OM—134
Stokes, LI/DM—124
Tesar, TU—123
Songer, OK—118

STRIKEOUTS
Bailey, OM—191
Lee, OM—181
Hall, DE—154
Black, TU—144
Songer, OK—144
WILD PITCHES
Stokes, LI/DM—12
Black, TU—10
Ross, SJ—9
Several with 8
HIT BATTERS
Hall, DE—17
Allen, OK—15
Koupal, OM—15
Love, SJ—15

1925

St. Joseph remained in the Western League despite its continued financial problems. The Des Moines Demons and Denver Bears fought it out all season long, with the Demons winning the crown by a single game over the Bears. Tulsa slipped to a disappointing fifth place. The Demons had the largest representation on the All-Star Team, with five players: Charles Stuvengen, Elton Langford, F.A. Griffin, Homer Haworth and Herm Holzhouser. Despite coming in second, the Bears were not represented on the All-Star squad. However, the team had one of the league's best pitchers in Byrd Hodges, who led the league in wins (26).

Third-place Oklahoma City had four All-Stars. One was Joe Brown, who had the best winning percentage (.824, 14–3). Brown had a cup of coffee with the White Sox later. Walter Shaner led the league in triples for the lowly Lincoln Links, who finished last again in the league. Shaner's efforts led to his move up to the majors again for four seasons in all. Wolgamot of Oklahoma City hit for the cycle in a game against Tulsa. St. Joseph's Harold Haid was also named to the All-Star Team. He later pitched for a handful of seasons as a reliever in the majors.

During the season, Des Moines had one strange game against St. Joseph in which every hitter got exactly one hit and one hit only, which occurs about as often as a lunar eclipse.

Hubbell Was All-Star in Western

Carl Hubbell pitched for Oklahoma City and was named to the All-Star Team in 1925. Pitcher Lefty Thomas taught him the sinker, then he learned to throw a new pitch called a screwball.

Hall of Famer Carl Hubbell got his start in the Western League in 1924 with Oklahoma City. (Photograph courtesy of Jay Sanford)

He was signed by the Detroit Tigers the next season, but they kept him in the minors. After he threatened to quit baseball, the Tigers sold him to the New York Giants. The Tigers didn't realize what they had and probably regretted the sale for a long time, as the lefty led the American League three times in wins and ERA, and twice he was named Most Valuable Player. Hubbell had a winning season every year except his last, when he was 4–4. He finished his 16-year career with a 253–154 record and appeared in three World Series. "King Carl" was named to the Hall of Fame four years after he retired from baseball.

1925

Final Standings

	W	L	Pct.	GB
Des Moines Demons	98	70	.583	—
Denver Bears	97	71	.577	1
Oklahoma City Indians	88	76	.537	8
Wichita Izzies	80	84	.488	16
St. Joseph Saints	77	87	.470	19
Tulsa Oilers	75	91	.452	21½
Omaha Buffaloes	74	89	.454	22
Lincoln Links	70	91	.435	24½

Team Batting

	AB	R	H	HR	SB	BB	SO	Avg.
Wichita	5960	1159	1889	123	149	582	499	.317
Denver	5908	1165	1845	101	162	671	580	.312
Omaha	5812	1080	1799	122	71	556	574	.310
Tulsa	5935	1094	1826	140	114	515	551	.308
Des Moines	5824	1057	1790	112	133	622	379	.307
Oklahoma City	5707	969	1662	94	141	549	546	.291
Lincoln	5672	892	1621	40	165	500	522	.286
St. Joseph	5653	894	1609	30	174	534	415	.285

Team Fielding

	G	DP	PO	A	E	Pct.
Des Moines	170	135	4437	1980	250	.963
Tulsa	167	155	4332	1977	250	.962
Denver	171	132	4458	2034	274	.960
St. Joseph	166	133	4347	2086	265	.960
Lincoln	163	107	4183	1974	278	.957
Oklahoma City	166	138	4373	2083	297	.956
Wichita	166	151	4358	2167	304	.955
Omaha	163	120	4200	2042	320	.951

Individual Fielding Leaders
(Minimum 100 Games)

	POS	G	PO	A	E	Pct.
Griggs, OM	1b	132	1212	52	8	.994

The Western League

	POS	G	PO	A	E	Pct.
McNally, OK	2b	162	463	535	28	.973
Graff, WI	3b	137	124	283	24	.944
Flippin, TU	ss	167	355	414	43	.947
Demaggio, SJ	of	165	374	19	7	.983
Riggert, TU	of	160	295	18	7	.978
E. Moore, LI	of	127	312	18	10	.971
Smith, DE	c	129	515	98	10	.984

Individual Pitching Leaders
(Minimum 20 Decisions)

	G	W	L	Pct.
Thomas, DM	44	19	6	.760
Hodges, DE	56	26	9	.743
Holthauser, DM	37	19	8	.704
Moon, DM	53	22	13	.629
Hall, DE	52	23	14	.622

Individual Batting
(Minimum 500 At Bats)

	G	AB	R	H	HR	SB	Avg.
Osborn, OM	163	659	158	245	21	5	.372
Payne, WI	150	615	144	226	33	10	.367
O'Brien, DE	164	648	124	233	17	22	.360
Shaner, LI	163	642	145	230	14	34	.358
Bliss, SJ	139	530	81	188	8	10	.355

All-Star Team

1b—Charles Stuvengen, DM
2b—John Monroe, OK
3b—Joe Tate, OK
ss—George Corrigan, WI
of—Leo Payne, WI
of—Elton Langford, DM
of—F.A. Griffin, DM
c—F.J. WIlder, OK
c—Homer Haworth, DM
Utility—Luke Stuart, TU
p—Carl Hubbell, OK
p—Herm Holzhouser, DM
p—Ken Penner, WI
p—Claude Thomas, DM
p—Carl Christian, LI
p—Harold Haid, SJ

Batting Leaders

RUNS
Langford, DM—160
Osborn, OM—158
Ginglardi, DE—154
Several with 151

HITS
Osborn, OM—245
O'Brien, DE—233
Riggert, TU—234
Shaner, LI—230
Stuvengen, DM—229

DOUBLES
Riggert, TU—57
Knight, DE—56
Osborn, OM—55
McNally, OK—55
Felber, OK—47

TRIPLES
Shaner, LI—30
O' Brien, DE—23
Hock, OK—22
Dunning, SJ—19
Stuvengen, DM—18

HOME RUNS
Payne, WI—33
Wetzel, DM—32
McNally, OK—32
Griggs, OM—28
Wano, WI—25

STOLEN BASES
Gorman, DE—62
Hock, OK—53
Morehart, WI—44
Shaner, LI—34
DeMaggio, SJ—34

Pitching Leaders

WINS
Hodges, DE—26
Hall, DE—23
Moon, DM—22
Jolley, WI—22
Davenport, SJ—21

LOSSES
Jolley, WI—21
Davenport, SJ—21
Black, TU—20
Bailey, OM—19
Love, SJ—19

GAMES
Jolley, WI—57
Hodges, DE—56
Black, TU—56
Freeman, DE—54
Moon, DM—53

INNINGS PITCHED
Hodges, DE—330
Davenport, SJ—326
Jolley, WI—322
Haid, SJ—317
Bailey, OM—307

BASE ON BALLS
Bailey, OM—144
Bolen, TU—143
Pillette, LI—137
Haid, SJ—129
Moon, DM—125

STRIKE OUTS
Bolen, TU—184
Bailey, OM—149
Hall, DE—135
Davenport, SJ—133
Moon, DM—127

HIT BATTERS
Pillette, LI—22
Hall, DE—15
Hodges, DE—14
May, OK—14
Several with 13

WILD PITCHES
Hall, DE—9
Love, SJ—8
Moon, DM—7
Songer, OK—7
Carson, LI—7

1926

Several changes in leadership occurred in 1926 as Dale Gear, a former pitcher-manager, took over as league president. Also, former major leaguer Shano Collins became the manager for Des Moines. A rookie rule was adopted that required each club to have six players, including two pitchers, with no previous experience above Class B. The limit of 16 players was retained, but the salary limit was shaved from $5,500 to $4,500 per month.

John "Shano" Collins played first base for Des Moines in 1926 and 1927. He also played for the White Sox and Red Sox. (Photograph courtesy of Jay Sanford)

The Iowa team made it two pennants in a row when it edged Oklahoma City. Strangely enough, the Indians had one more win than the Des Moines Demons, but had two more losses. The Demons now had won the pennant six times during the century, more than any other franchise. St. Joseph, Tulsa and Denver battled for third place in the league. Oklahoma City brought charges against several teams of conspiring to help Des Moines win the pennant. Minor league president Mike Sexton, a former Western League leader, cleared Des Moines, Lincoln, Omaha and Tulsa of any wrongdoing.

Des Moines faced Springfield of the Three-I league for a Mid-Western Championship after the season ended. The Indians were down three games to one when the series was called due to cold weather. Des Moines had just two players on the All-Star Team and no leaders in any categories, but they had a solid pitching staff led by Pat Malone and Leo Moon, with 28 and 24 victories, respectively. Malone, who led the league that year in strikeouts, was signed by the Cubs two seasons later and led the National League twice in wins. He pitched 10 years in the majors and participated in three World Series.

Denver's Herb Hall was named the league's Most Valuable Player and received $500. Hall was the winningest pitcher in the league with his 29 victories. Three players from Oklahoma City made the All-Star Team, including Joe Brown, who was 14–10 on the season. Indians pitcher Frank Tubbs led the league in winning percentage with his 9–2 mark. The other All-Star was Eddie Hock, who had three tries at the majors without ever staying for long. Tulsa's Guy Sturdy was the triples leader, and his 49 homers set a new league record, which helped him lead the league in total bases (452) and runs scored (163). Sturdy played the next two seasons with the Browns and led the American League in pinch hits in 1928.

1926

Final Standings

	W	L	Pct.	GB
Des Moines Demons	99	64	.607	—
Oklahoma City Indians	100	66	.602	½
St. Joseph Saints	89	75	.543	10½
Tulsa Oilers	88	80	.524	13½
Denver Bears	86	78	.524	13½
Omaha Buffaloes	77	89	.464	23½
Lincoln Links	64	101	.388	36
Wichita Izzies	58	108	.349	42½

Team Batting

	AB	R	H	HR	SB	BB	SO	Avg.
Omaha	5890	1113	1817	140	179	529	658	.308
Tulsa	5873	1064	1807	133	92	545	521	.308
Oklahoma City	5844	999	1775	52	178	561	584	.304
Denver	5878	1004	1728	68	172	596	568	.294
Wichita	5860	983	1711	103	129	588	620	.292
Lincoln	5667	922	1653	50	102	543	550	.292
Des Moines	5584	967	1623	77	289	530	471	.291
St. Joseph	5618	887	1624	41	170	506	454	.289

Team Fielding

	G	DP	PO	A	E	Pct.
Oklahoma City	166	128	4426	2057	251	.963
Des Moines	163	128	4302	1968	244	.963
St. Joseph	165	136	4390	1959	258	.961
Tulsa	165	149	4254	2042	271	.959
Lincoln	165	116	4230	2105	279	.958
Wichita	168	149	4310	2100	284	.958
Omaha	168	145	4325	2026	290	.956
Denver	168	125	4457	2127	341	.951

Individual Fielding Leaders
(Minimum 100 Games)

	POS	G	PO	A	E	Pct.
McDaniel, OK	1b	161	1551	72	21	.987

	POS	G	PO	A	E	Pct.
Gislason, DM	2b	149	416	501	31	.967
F. Moore, OK	3b	166	189	345	18	.967
F. Haley, LI	ss	143	304	413	50	.935
Riggert, TU	of	143	251	22	5	.982
Patterson, TU	of	165	384	16	8	.980
O'Brien, DE	of	165	346	20	9	.976
Groft, OK	c	148	614	160	15	.981

Individual Pitching Leaders
(Minimum 30 Games)

	G	W	L	Pct.
Moon, DM	37	24	8	.750
F. Newton, SJ	51	19	8	.703
May, OK	58	26	12	.684
Malone, DM	52	28	13	.682
Blaeholder, TU	50	27	13	.675

Individual Batting Leaders
(Minimum 500 At Bats)

	G	AB	R	H	HR	SB	Avg.
Blakesley, OM	140	541	129	208	39	15	.384
Henry, OM	166	670	150	247	27	35	.369
O'Brien, DE	165	636	132	229	17	15	.360
Ginglardi, DE	168	644	154	230	11	18	.357
Patterson, TU	165	678	147	239	4	14	.353

All-Star Team

1b—Guy Study, TU
2b—Walter Nufer, SJ
3b—Pee Wee Lewis, TU
ss—Eddie Hock, OK
of—Jim Blakesley, OM
of—Ray O'Brien, DE
of—F.A. Griffin, DM
c—Peter Groft, OK
c—F. Meyers, OM
Utility—Ray Falk, DE
p—George Blaeholder, TU
p—Herbert Hall, DE
p—Pat Malone, DE
p—George Perry, SJ
p—Leo Moon, DM
p—Joe Brown, OK

Batting Leaders

HOME RUNS
Sturdy, TU—49
Blakesley, OM—39
Henry, OM—27
McNally, WI—25
Casey, TU—20

TOTAL BASES
Sturdy, TU—452
Henry, OM—417
Blakesley, OM—394
Wetzel, OM—394
H. Brown, OM—345

RUNS
Sturdy, TU—163
Ginglardi, DE—154

Henery, OM—150
H. Brown, OM—150
Patterson, TU—147

HITS
Henry, OM—247
Patterson, TU—239
Sturdy, TU—233
Gingiardi, DE—230
Hock, OK—230

DOUBLES
F. Lewis, TU—59
Wetzel, DM—58
Henry, OM—57
H. Brown, OM—57
Sturdy, TU—54

TRIPLES
Purdy, LI—21
Funk, OK—21
A. Smith, SJ—20
Several with 16

STOLEN BASES
Funk, OK—55
Hughes, DM—36
Henry, OM—35
Hock, OK—31
H. Brown, OM—30

Pitching Leaders

GAMES
Pallas, LI—59
May, OK—58
Greer, DE—58
Hall, DE—56
Schwartz, SJ—55

INNINGS PITCHED
Pallas, LI—350
Malone, DM—349
Greer, DE—344
Hall, DE—341
Blaeholder, TU—330

HITS
Pallas, LI—428
Hall, DE—385
Carney, WI—379

Greer, DE—369
Jolley, WI—367

RUNS
Pallas, LI—226
Jolley, WI—210
A. Campbell, WI—207
Pillette, OK—200
Montgomery, WI—192

BASE ON BALLS
Beck, TU—170
Pillette, OK—156
Walker, OM/DE—139
Blaeholder, TU—121
Crockett, LI—119

STRIKE OUTS
Malone, DM—190
Greer, DE—184
Walker, OM/DE—174
Blaeholder, TU—158
Schwartz, SJ—142

WILD PITCHES
Malone, DM—10
M. Thomas, OM—10
J. Davenport, OM—9
Blaeholder, TU—8
Beck, TU—8

WINS
Hall, DE—29
Malone, DM—28
Blaeholder, TU—27
May, OK—26
Moon, DM—24

HIT BATTERS
Beck, TU—21
M. Thomas, OM—16
Malone, DM—15
Pillette, OK—13
Jolley, WI—12

LOSSES
Pallas, LI—21
A. Campbell, WI—21
Jolley, WI—20
Carney, WI—19
Several with 18

1927

In 1927 the rookie rule from the year before was abolished. The schedule was reduced from 168 to 154 games, the same number as the major leagues. St. Joseph decided to move to the Western Association, so Amarillo, Texas, was given a franchise despite its smaller size; however, the new owners felt a new ball park would attract enough fans. This was the first time the Western League had acquired a Texas city, because most of those teams were part of the Texas League, also a Class A league.

After being rained out on opening day, Tulsa went on a winning path that led the Oilers to win the championship by a wide margin. The Oklahoma team had a strong lineup and led the league with a record .333 batting average, which was 32 points better than Des Moines. Wichita finished second, also by a wide margin over third-place Des Moines. Tulsa played Waco, the runner-up in the Texas League, in a postseason series and lost three games to two.

Four members of the Oilers were picked for the All-Star Team, and several led the league in their strengths. The Oilers' Joe Munson led the circuit in homers with 32. Munson, who had Napoleon as one of his middle names, had come from two seasons with the Chicago Cubs. Teammate Karl Black had the best winning percentage (.857, 12–2).

Joe Rabbit of Omaha ran like one on the bases and led the league with 49 stolen bases. He also hit a league record seven homers in three days to propel him to the top in runs scored and hits for the season. The speedster had a trial with Cleveland before coming to the Western League. Elton "Sam" Langford of Des Moines led all hitters with his .409 average. And Bill Allington with Wichita hit for the cycle, plus an extra homer, in a game against Omaha. Allington played several seasons in the league. He would later become the winningest manager in the All-American Girls Professional Baseball League. Also hitting for the cycle that season was Amarillo's Stormy Davis and Ray Gonzales.

Oklahoma City and Tulsa had threatened in years prior to desert the Western League and join the rival Texas League. After the season ended, the two teams announced that they were making the move. However, the National Board of Arbitration voted on December 5 that the two Oklahoma teams had to remain in the Western League.

Blaeholder Perfected Slider

George Blaeholder had two great seasons, winning 53 games for Tulsa before finally earning a permanent position with the St. Louis Browns.

Credited as being one of the first pitchers to perfect the slider, the righthanded pitcher led the American League with four shutouts in 1929, but he still had a losing record at 14–15. In fact, he never chalked up a winning mark with the lowly Browns. It was not until he went to Cleveland in his last season that he compiled a winning mark of 8–4. In all, Blaeholder pitched 11 seasons in the majors and ended with a 104–125 record.

1927

Final Standings

	W	L	T	Pct.	GB
Tulsa Oilers	101	53	0	656	—
Wichita Larks	91	63	0	.591	10
Des Moines Demons	82	72	0	.532	19
Denver Bears	77	75	1	.507	23
Oklahoma City Indians	68	86	2	.442	33
Amarillo Texans	66	87	0	.431	34½
Omaha Buffaloes	66	88	1	.429	35
Lincoln Links	63	90	2	.412	37½

Team Batting

	AB	R	H	HR	SB	BB	SO	Avg.
Tulsa	5545	1142	1844	149	79	503	517	.333
Des Moines	5445	965	1640	64	158	488	426	.301
Omaha	5469	913	1613	72	136	457	547	.298
Amarillo	5339	891	1559	37	133	523	488	.292
Wichita	5277	855	1534	84	85	520	571	.291
Denver	5316	803	1539	41	86	488	459	.290
Oklahoma City	5439	759	1526	22	91	471	507	.281
Lincoln	5526	755	1513	24	111	423	427	.274

Team Fielding

	G	DP	PO	A	E	Pct.
Lincoln	155	130	4107	1951	230	.963
Wichita	154	118	4101	2066	254	.960
Denver	153	130	4062	1834	253	.959
Amarillo	153	105	4013	1855	253	.959
Tulsa	154	127	4089	1853	263	.957
Des Moines	154	125	4110	1935	280	.956
Oklahoma City	156	80	4146	1838	288	.954
Omaha	155	161	4076	1970	308	.952

Individual Fielding Leaders
(Minimum 100 Games)

	POS	G	PO	A	E	DP	Pct.
Kuhel, LI	1b	141	1476	73	16	95	.990

	POS	G	PO	A	E	DP	Pct.
McNally, WI	2b	154	373	519	40	72	.957
Gottleber, LI	3b	155	161	290	17	29	.964
Browner, OK	ss	143	281	438	57	46	.927
Comorosky, WI	of	133	350	19	10	3	.974
O'Brien, DE	of	153	331	19	10	8	.972
Bliss, LI/WI	of	135	253	9	8	1	.970
Haley, WI	c	111	429	76	11	4	.979

Individual Pitching Leaders
(Minimum 20 Decisions)

	G	W	L	Pct.
Campbell, WI	38	19	6	.760
Blaeholder, TU	42	26	9	.743
Smithson, TU	31	14	6	.700
Walker, DE	39	19	9	.679
Davenport, DM	51	21	10	.677

Individual Batting Leaders
(Minimum 435 At Bats)

	G	AB	R	H	HR	SB	Avg.
Langford, DM	149	611	132	250	8	31	.409
Comorosky, WI	133	518	113	206	11	14	.398
Bennett, TU	153	608	151	234	21	11	.383
Munson, TU	154	583	146	223	32	17	.382
Sturdy, TU	148	605	144	226	23	17	.374

All-Star Team

1b—Guy Sturdy, TU
2b—Otis Branson, TU
3b—George Gottleher, LI
ss—Lou Brower, OK
of—Fred Bennett, TU
of—Adam Comonosky, WI
of—Elton Langford, DM
c—Joe Sprinz, DM
c—Pete Groft, OK
Utility—Al Vancamp, DM
p—George Blaeholder, TU
p—Dixie Walker, DE
p—Ed "Bear Tracks" Greer, DE
p—Lester Berry, WI
p—Clarence Griffin, LI
p—Fred Ortman, DM
p—John Smithson, TU

Batting Leaders

HOME RUNS
Munson, TU—32
Sturdy, TU—23
Bennett, TU—21
Rabbitt, OM—20
McNally, WI—19

TOTAL BASES
Rabbit, OM—399
Munson, TU—385
Bennett, TU—380
Langford, DM—377
Sturdy, OM—367

HITS
Rabbitt, OM—251
Langford, DM—250
Bennett, TU—234

Sturdy, TU—226
Reagan, DE—218

DOUBLES
Bennett, TU—55
Davis, OM/AM—49
Munson, TU—48
Langford, DM—47
Bliss, LI/WI—47

TRIPLES
Langford, DM—28
Rabbitt, OM—26
Swansboro, AM—20
Gottleber, LI—19
Allington, WI—19

RUNS
Rabbitt, OM—172
Bennett, TU—151
Munson, TU—146
Sturdy, TU—144
Swansboro, AM—136

STOLEN BASES
Langford, DM—31
Swansboro, AM—31
Knothe, DM—27
F. Griffin, DM—26
Reagan, DE—26

Pitching Leaders

GAMES
Graig, OK—60
Tubbs, OK—52
C. Davenport, DM—51
Darrow, OK—49
Jolley, WI—46

WINS
Blaeholder, TU—26
C. Davenport, DM—21

Ortman, DM—21
Campbell, WI—19
Walker, DE—19

LOSSES
Greer, DE—22
Lahaie, OK—18
F. Newton, AM—17
V. Roberts, OM—17
Tubbs, OK—17

BASES ON BALLS
Thomas, OM—121
Darrow, OK—101
Ellis, OK—101
Walker, DE—100
Tubbs, OK—97

STRIKEOUTS
Walker, DE—193
Greer, DE—152
S. Bolen, TU—133
Blaeholder, TU—123
Lahale, OK—110

WILD PITCHES
Ellis, OK—11
Thomas, OM—9
Strelecki, LI—8
A. Crandall, OM—8
V. Roberts, OM—8

HIT BATTERS
Ellis, OK—11
Thomas, OM—9
Several with 8

INNINGS PITCHED
Blaeholder, TU—313
C. Davenport, DM—289
Greer, DE—277
Jolley, WI—266
Lahaie, OK—264

1928

The Western League decided to split the season in 1928, with 82 games scheduled for each half. The winners of each half would then play a seven-game championship, unless the same team won both halves.

Before the 1928 season began, the infield at Merchants Park got a facelift. From the street, a sign showed passing motorists the field. The park featured a 457-foot centerfield, which only three players—Babe Ruth, Josh Gibson and Judy Cline—ever cleared. Denver purchased the park in 1923 and played there until 1946. (Photographs courtesy of Jay Sanford)

The Oklahoma City Indians won the first half by a handful of games over Pueblo. The Tulsa Oilers poured it on in the second half to win by a game over Wichita. Manager Marty Berghammer's Oilers faced the Indians in the playoffs and kept up the momentum they had in the second half by winning the series four games to one. One game was ruled no contest.

Tulsa was led by Munson, who continued to pound the ball as he led hitters with a .385 average and scored 171 runs. Another All-Star player with Tulsa was Chad Kimsey, a pitcher. Kimsey led the league in winning percentage (.767, 23–7). The notoriety led him to the Browns the next season, and he pitched six seasons in the sun. Oklahoma City was helped by Barney Bornholdt's 24 league leading wins. He also led the league in strikeouts (154). Bornholt was one of five players from the Indians to be named to the All-Star Team.

Oklahoma City got back one of the pitchers it had signed in 1926. The Indians had purchased a pitcher by the name of Collins from Ottumwa to be delivered in the spring of 1927. However, Collins never reported. Collins turned out to be Fay Thomas, who was already pitching in the National League for the New York Giants. Baseball Commissioner Kennesaw Mountain Landis forced Thomas to repay his $2,500 bonus to New York and report to Oklahoma City, with a year's suspension to boot. Thomas didn't return to the majors until 1931, remaining for three more seasons there.

The home run king that season was Wichita's Jim Stoner, who also led the league in hits and runs scored. Ironically, he wasn't even named to the All-Star Team. A year later he had a test with the Pittsburgh Pirates.

1928

Final Standings
First Half

	W	L	Pct.	GB
Oklahoma City Indians	51	29	.638	—
Pueblo Steel Workers	45	36	.556	6½
Wichita Larks	42	38	.525	9
Tulsa Oilers	43	39	.524	9
Denver Bears	41	41	.500	11
Amarillo Texans	36	39	.480	12½
Omaha Crickets	32	46	.410	18
Des Moines Demons	28	50	.359	22

Second Half

	W	L	Pct.	GB
Tulsa Oilers	53	30	.639	—
Wichita Larks	52	32	.619	1½
Oklahoma City Indians	44	38	.537	8½
Omaha Crickets	39	40	.494	12
Pueblo Steel Workers	40	42	.488	12
Denver Bears	40	43	.482	12½
Des Moines Demons	34	48	.422	18½
Amarillo Texans	24	54	.308	21½

Playoffs

Tulsa defeated Oklahoma City, four games to one.

Team Batting

	AB	R	H	HR	SB	BB	SO	LOB	Avg.
Tulsa	5878	1222	1896	193	56	576	604	1026	.323
Wichita	5989	1205	1884	183	97	618	637	1287	.315
Oklahoma City	5782	1056	1814	53	103	512	452	1212	.314
Omaha	5436	892	1654	89	178	481	459	1100	.304
Pueblo	5722	981	1720	80	75	545	500	1282	.301
Amarillio	5190	312	1522	51	95	387	550	1048	.293
Des Moines	5536	845	1582	66	82	565	532	1227	.286
Denver	5658	903	1605	49	72	545	532	1220	.284

Team Fielding

	G	DP	PO	A	E	Pct.
Pueblo	164	222	4285	2049	208	.968
Denver	165	136	4203	1934	245	.962
Oklahoma City	163	168	4279	1829	259	.959
Tulsa	165	152	4295	2050	275	.958
Amarillo	153	109	3902	1640	243	.958
Des Moines	164	126	4207	1894	271	.957
Wichita	166	141	4320	2045	285	.957
Omaha	158	147	4098	1872	311	.950

Individual Fielding Leaders
(Minimum 100 Games)

	POS	G	PO	A	E	DP	Pct.
Huffman, OK	1b	159	1333	96	23	132	.984
P. Kelly, DE	2b	151	355	474	24	78	.972
Tierney, PU	3b	160	165	303	20	28	.959
Knothe, PU	ss	164	380	587	43	165	.957

	POS	G	PO	A	E	DP	Pct.
Parker, DE	of	161	418	23	8	3	.982
R. Seeds, AM	of	140	404	19	10	8	.977
Neitzke, PU	of	135	441	5	13	2	.972
Burns, OM	c	134	621	134	18	14	.977

Individual Pitching Leaders
(Minimum 20 Decisions)

	G	W	L	Pct.
Kimsey, TU	47	23	7	.767
Hargrove, PU	39	21	8	.724
Bornholdt, OK	64	24	11	.686
Sanders, AM/WI	43	23	11	.676
Fette, PU	37	20	10	.667

Individual Batting Leaders
(Minimum 500 At Bats)

	G	AB	R	H	HR	SB	Avg.
Munson, TU	165	611	171	235	39	9	.385
Bennett, TU	136	507	136	188	35	5	.371
Stroner, WI	166	695	171	255	42	11	.367
Bliss, WI	165	635	150	224	21	5	.353
Crabtree, OK	133	544	114	192	7	16	.353

All-Star Team

1b—Fred "Snake" Henry, OM
2b—Jack Salzgaver, OK
3b—Oscar Grimes, TU
ss—George Knothe, PU
of—Joe Munson, TU
of—Leon Riley, PU
of—Estel Crabtree, OK
c—Arndt Jorgens, OK
c—Irving "Jack" Burns, OM
Utility—Joe Mayes, TU
p—Chad Kimsey, TU
p—William Hargrove, PU
p—Barney Bornholdt, OK
p—Lou Fette, PU
p—George Darrow, OK
p—Max Thomas, OM

Batting Leaders

HOME RUNS
Stroner, WI—42
Munson, TU—39
Bennet, TU—35
Allington, WI—34
Grimes, TU—24

TOTAL BASES
Stroner, WI—443
Munson, TU—418
Allington, WI—399
Grimes, TU—374
Bliss, WI—353

RUNS
Munson, TU—171
Stroner, WI—171
Grimes, TU—170
Saltzgaver, OK—169
Allington, WI—167

HITS
Stroner, WI—255
Munson, TU—235
Grimes, TU—233
Saltzgaver, OK—232
Wano, PU—225

DOUBLES
Wetzel, OM—61
R. O'Brien, DE—55
Bliss, WI—54
Grimes, TU—49
Allington, WI—47

TRIPLES
Eckhardt, AM/WI—27
Wano, PU—23
Saltzgaver, OK—22
Huffman, OK—21
Van Camp, DM—19

STOLEN BASES
Hetherly, OM—38
James, OM—30
Harvel, OM—28
Swansboro, AM/WI—25
Eckhardt, AM/WI—20

Pitching Leaders

GAMES
Tubbs, OK—73
Black, TU/OK—70
Bornholdt, OK—64
Day, OM—52
Naylor, TU—51

INNINGS PITCHED
Day, OM—313
Tubbs, OK—302
Kimsey, TU—297
Greer, DE—287
Evans, DE—285

HITS
Evans, DE—357
Jolley, DE—346
Sanders, AM/WI—337
Day, OM—335
Peery, WI—334

RUNS
Pillette, OM—201
Sanders, AM/WI—197
Peery, WI—197
Naylor, TU—188
Alter, WI—186

BASE ON BALLS
Bornholdt, OK—160
Tubbs, OK—152
Shanklin, WI—128
Alter, WI—121
Pillette, OM—121

STRIKE OUTS
Bornholdt, OK—154
Tubbs, OK—136
Day, OM—126
Greer, DE—126
Darrow, OK—125

WILD PITCHES
Tubbs, OK—12
Bornholdt, OK—11
M. Thomas, OM—11
Evans, DE—10
Day, OM—8

WINS
Bornholdt, OK—24
Kimsey, TU—23
Sanders, AM/WI—23
Several with 21

HIT BATTERS
Ferguson, DM—14
Carraway, AM—14
Several with 12

LOSSES
Greer, DE—20
Day, OM—18
Morgan, AM—18
Jolley, DE—17
Rush, DM—17

1929

The experiment with a Texas team ended as the Amarillo franchise was switched to Topeka. This saved teams a lot of travel money. The split season was discarded, too. Instead, a unique schedule was formulated that would allow for a seven-game series between natural rivals the last week of the season. The pairings were: Des Moines vs. Omaha; Tulsa vs. Oklahoma City; Wichita vs. Topeka; and Pueblo vs. Denver.

Tulsa and Oklahoma City battled for the title again as each held the league lead early in the season. In July the Tulsa Oilers took the lead for good and eased to their third consecutive pennant and fifth in 10 years. Tulsa won the title despite losing its manager, Marty Berghammer, who went to Milwaukee. The new Topeka club finished sixth.

The Oilers continued to have the best hitting in the league. Munson again led the league in runs scored. Teammate Lin Storti led the league in hits (167). And Jack Burns powered 36 homers to lead the league. His performance landed him with the Browns the next season, and he played seven seasons in the majors. On the mound the Oilers had Joe O'Dowd, who led the league in winning percentage with his 15–5 record. Wichita's Glen Spencer and Omaha's John McGrew each had 24 wins to tie for the league lead. Spencer went to the Pirates the next season and pitched five seasons in the majors. Two players hit for the cycle that season: Elwood Wirtz of Omaha and Leon Riley of Pueblo.

After the season ended the stock market crash of October 29 marked the end of postwar prosperity and the beginning of a long depression that would negatively affect baseball.

1929

Final Standings

	W	L	Pct.	GB
Tulsa Oilers	95	66	.590	—
Oklahoma City Indians	88	68	.564	4½
Omaha Crickets	81	75	.519	11½
Wichita Aviators	77	79	.494	15½
Denver Bears	73	81	.474	18½
Topeka Jayhawks	75	85	.469	9½
Des Moines Demons	72	86	.456	21½
Pueblo Steelworkers	69	90	.434	25

Team Batting

	AB	R	H	HR	SB	BB	SO	Avg.
Tulsa	5643	1116	1732	202	91	655	498	.307
Wichita	5374	956	1623	85	99	613	435	.302
Denver	5359	871	1539	47	105	640	481	.287

	AB	R	H	HR	SB	BB	SO	Avg.
Omaha	5157	910	1481	58	205	676	520	.287
Oklahoma City	5421	847	1543	46	87	490	409	.285
Pueblo	5391	819	1461	78	101	612	550	.271
Des Moines	5286	736	1398	76	101	511	486	.264
Topeka	5367	702	1406	55	136	469	451	.262

Team Fielding

	G	DP	PO	A	E	Pct.
Denver	154	151	4034	1897	221	.964
Oklahoma City	156	114	4133	1703	218	.964
Topeka	161	103	4355	1853	239	.963
Tulsa	161	162	4225	2074	276	.958
Des Moines	158	114	4165	1856	269	.957
Wichita	156	133	4078	1909	278	.956
Pueblo	160	134	4129	1919	282	.955
Omaha	156	116	4028	1764	271	.955

Individual Fielding Leaders
(Minimum 100 Games)

	POS	G	PO	A	E	DP	Pct.
Oglesby, DM	1b	153	1489	77	12	96	.992
Palmer, DE	2b	144	436	483	25	103	.974
Carroll, TO	3b	149	198	274	20	19	.959
M. Smith, DE	ss	121	210	388	33	70	.948
Honea, TO	of	161	478	13	8	4	.984
Zaepfel, DM	of	127	348	9	6	3	.983
Riley, PU	of	159	366	9	8	3	.979
D. Smith, TU	c	107	340	69	7	7	.983

Individual Pitching Leaders
(Minimum 20 Decisions)

	G	W	L	Pct.
O'Dowd, TU	35	15	5	.750
Spencer, WI	41	24	9	.727
McGrew, OM	42	24	10	.706
Stiles, TU	45	22	11	.667
Ketchum, TU	32	16	8	.667

Individual Batting Leaders
(Minimum 500 At Bats)

	G	AB	R	H	HR	SB	Avg.
Munson, TU	161	569	167	210	32	8	.369
Bratcher, DE	154	624	142	226	12	10	.362

	G	AB	R	H	HR	SB	Avg.
Mosolf, WI	142	566	106	205	7	14	.362
O'Brien, DE	154	583	102	203	9	7	.348
Guppy, OK	152	585	121	203	9	10	.347

Batting Leaders

HOME RUNS
I. Burns, TU—36
Munson, TU—32
Gullic, TU—32
L. Storti, TU—28
Circle, DM—26

TOTAL BASES
L. Storti, TU—389
I. Burns, TU—377
Munson, TU—356
Riley, PU—352
Bratcher, DE—337

RUNS
Munson, TU—167
I. Burns, TU—148
L. Stori, TU—146
Faber, OM—143
Bratcher, DE—142

HITS
L. Storti, TU—230
Bratcher, DE—226
I. Burns, TU—210
Munson, TU—210
Saltzgaver, OC—206

DOUBLES
L. Storti, TU—61
O'Brien, DE—50
Guppy, OC—46
Swansboro, WI—43
Gullic, TU—43

TRIPLES
Riley, PU—27
Parker, DE—22
Bratcher, DE—18
Brower, OK—15
Saltzgaver, OK—14

STOLEN BASES
Honea, TO—46
Griffin, OM—45
Swansboro, WI—41
Walker, DE—40
Windle, OM—33

Pitching Leaders

WINS
Spencer, WI—24
McGrew, OM—24
Stiles, TU—22
Herring, OK—19
Caraway, TO—19

LOSSES
Pillette, OM/DM—20
Cottey, PU—19
Greer, DE—19
Freeman, TO/WI—18
Caraway, TO—17

GAMES
Tubbs, OK—49
Herring, OK—48
Greer, DE—47
Darrow, OK—45
Several with 44

INNINGS PITCHED
Caraway, TO—305
McGrew, OM—294
Stiles, TU—290
H. Sanders, WI—277
Holmes, TO—264

BASE ON BALLS
W. Brown, OM—133
Bartholomew, OM—128
Stiles, TU—127
Tubbs, OK—125
Pillette, OM/DM—115

STRIKE OUTS
Caraway, TO—159
W. Brown, OM—131
Herring, OK—127
Morgan, TO—118
Cottey, PU—112

WILD PITCHES
Spencer, WI—12
W. Brown, OM—9
Several with 8

HIT BATTERS
Holmes, TO—18
Piercy, WI/DE—14
Pillette, OM/DM—11
Stiles, TU—10
Caraway, TO—10

1930

Tulsa's old park was declared unsuitable by the city and the club became involved in a squabble with the city commission, which prevented the team from building stands on a site the club had purchased. The league moved the Tulsa franchise to Topeka, where that franchise had shifted to St. Joseph. The player limit was also increased from 16 to 17.

The country and baseball faced some lean times due to the Stock Market crash in 1929. However, night baseball saved the day for the league. Lee Keyser at Des Moines installed lighting for $19,000 and was attempting to be the first team in professional ball to have night baseball. Unfortunately, the Independence Producers (Kansas) in the Western Association rigged up temporary lights to beat out Keyser by four days on May 2. The first twi-night doubleheader came on August 1 in Oklahoma City. By the end of the season all teams had lights except for St. Joseph, Wichita and Pueblo. The first night game in the majors wouldn't come until May 24, 1934, in Cincinnati.

Wichita and Omaha competed for first place most of the season until Omaha wilted in the dog days of summer. Oklahoma City put on a late season surge to finish third. The St. Joseph Saints were pathetic and finished last. The pennant-winning Aviators had three men named to the All-Star Team. One was outfielder Forrest Jensen, who led the league in hits (207) and average (.354). Another was pitcher Charles Wood, who led the league in wins (22) and strikeouts (197). Wood went to the Pirates at the end of the season and spent two seasons in the majors. The third All-Star was Gus Dugas, who also received a promotion to Pittsburgh. The outfielder spent four seasons in the majors, but a .053 average in 1934 meant his doom there. Although Oklahoma City finished third, the Indians had more All-Stars, with four. One of them was the ERA leader Walter Brown. The leading home run hitter that season was Des Moines' Stan Keyes with 35. He also led the league in RBI. Keyes never made it to the majors, though. Perhaps the strangest feat of the year was achieved by Omaha's Carl Dunagan, who hit home runs from both sides of the plate in successive at bats. This rare occurrence was even more bizarre because Dunagan was a pitcher!

Dizzy Dean Was All-Star in Western

Despite being a member of a last-place St. Joseph team, Dizzy Dean compiled a 17–8 record, which earned him a spot on the All-Star Team and a promotion to the Texas League, where he was 8–2. Dean moved up to the majors with the Cardinals, who let him pitch the last day of the season. He beat the Pittsburgh Pirates.

The country boy pitched another year in the Texas League before becoming a regular with the Cardinals. In his first season with St. Louis he dazzled everyone by winning 18 games. He topped that the next year with 20 wins, including a game in which he struck out 17 Cubs to set a major league record.

Dean's brother, Paul, joined him the next season, and they accounted for 48 wins for the Cardinals. Dizzy won 30! The deadly duo took the Gashouse Gang to the World Series and won two games apiece for the title. During the series Dizzy pinch ran and was hit in the head by a relay throw. He was carried off the field. Later he told the press, "The doctors x-rayed my head and found nothing."

Dizzy Dean pitched for a season in the Western League before he went on to a stellar career in the majors with the Cardinals, Cubs and Browns. (Photograph courtesy of Jay Sanford)

His career was all downhill after that season. He ended with a 150–83 career mark, which landed him in the Hall of Fame in 1955. After his playing career ended, he became a major league broadcaster.

1930

Final Standings

	W	L	Pct.	GB
Wichita Aviators	89	56	.614	—
Omaha Packers	76	66	.535	11½
Oklahoma City Indians	79	71	.527	12½
Des Moines Demons	77	71	.520	13½
Pueblo Braves	75	75	.500	16½
Denver Bears	74	74	.500	16½
Topeka Senators	66	84	.440	25½
St. Joseph Saints	53	92	.366	36

Team Batting

	AB	R	H	HR	BB	SO	Avg.
Wichita	5080	878	1527	120	498	458	.301
Denver	5063	870	1522	47	554	457	.301
Pueblo	4951	860	1424	83	567	515	.288
Des Moines	5077	882	1453	94	554	594	.286
Omaha	4691	853	1314	53	603	537	.280
Oklahoma City	5134	740	1424	50	442	513	.277
St. Joseph	5039	702	1396	65	428	491	.277
Topeka	5028	764	1331	73	637	617	.265

Team Fielding

	G	DP	PB	PO	A	E	Pct.
Wichita	146	120	11	3787	1639	231	.959
Denver	148	128	25	3811	1740	240	.959
Pueblo	150	123	15	3802	1703	241	.958
Oklahoma City	151	149	11	3954	1734	252	.958
Omaha	143	124	39	3651	1643	234	.956
Topeka	151	109	27	3923	1802	265	.956
Des Moines	148	102	12	3863	1635	268	.954
St. Joseph	147	103	39	3796	1653	281	.951

Individual Fielding Leaders
(Minimum 100 Games)

	POS	G	PO	A	E	DP	Pct.
Lowell, OK	1b	151	1426	86	12	122	.992

	POS	G	PO	A	E	DP	Pct.
Faber, OM	2b	130	322	432	24	74	.969
Vigare, WI	3b	117	120	247	24	15	.939
Bondurant, SJ/OM	ss	101	219	274	28	45	.946
Allington, OM	of	116	190	8	2	6	.990
H. Kelly, TO	of	143	394	19	6	4	.986
Jensen, WI	of	138	336	11	8	2	.977
Fitzpatrick, OK	c	137	653	108	14	17	.982

Earned Run Average Leaders
(Minimum 20 Decisions)

	G	W	L	Pct.	ERA
W. Brown, OK	29	16	6	.727	2.57
Wood, WI	25	22	3	.880	2.65
Jennings, PU	40	15	16	.484	3.33
Tubbs, OK	49	14	13	.519	3.39
Dunagan, OM	34	18	11	.621	3.54

Individual Batting Leaders
(Minimum 453 At Bats)

	G	AB	R	H	HR	Avg.
Jensen, WI	139	585	115	207	14	.354
Dugas, WI	143	582	111	203	26	.349
O'Brien, DE	129	468	91	163	7	.348
Van Camp, DM	129	469	96	161	18	.344
Lindimore, WI	144	572	126	195	11	.341

All-Star Team

1b—Jim Oglesby, Des Moines
2b—J. Faber, Omaha
3b—Hetherly, Omaha
ss—Lou Brower, Oklahoma City
of—Stan Keyes, Des Moines
of—Forrest Jensen, Wichita
of—Gus Dugas, Wichita
c—John Fitzpatrick, Oklahoma City
c—Jack Mealey, Wichita
Utility—Dewey Bondurant, Omaha
p—Walter Brown, Oklahoma City
p—Charles Wood, Wichita
p—Dizzy Dean, St. Joseph
p—Andy Bednar, Wichita
p—John Jones, Oklahoma City
p—Bud Tinning, Des Moines

Batting Leaders

HOME RUNS
Keyes, DM—35
Dugas, WI—26
Swansboro, WI—26
L. Riley, PU—20
Van Camp, DM—18

STOLEN BASES
Hinson, PU—76
Frey, PU—64
McIssac, PU—35
Hetherly, OM—33
Adair, DE—30

HITS
Jensen, WI—207
Dugas, WI—203
Lindimore, WI—195

Frey, PU—189
Lowell, OK—185
DOUBLES
Jensen, WI—41
Naj, OM—41
Clift, OK—38
Zaepfel, OM—38
Hughes, DM—35
TRIPLES
Hall, OK—19
Jensen, WI—19
Keyes, DM—18
L. Riley, PU—18
Adair, DE—17
TOTAL BASES
Keyes, DM—358
Dugas, WI—339
Jensen, WI—328
L. Riley, PU—298
Swansboro, WI—298
RUNS
Frey, PU—133
Hinson, PU—132
E. Parker, DE—127
Lindimore, WI—126
Keyes, DM—123

Pitching Leaders

GAMES
Tubbs, OK—49
Jolley, DE—44
Jennings, PU—40
Greer, DE—39
Jones, OK—39
WINS
Wood, WI—22
Greer, DE—19

Bednar, WI—18
Dunagan, OM—18
Several with 17
LOSSES
Halzlip, TO—18
Jennings, PU—16
Jolley, DE—16
Several with 13
INNINGS PITCHED
Jennings, PU—257
Jolley, DE—256
Greer, DE—238
Cooney, TO—237
Dunagan, OM—234
BASES ON BALLS
Birkofer, DM—124
Cooney, TO—121
Larsen, SJ/OM—112
Greer, DE—108
Tubbs, OK—105
STRIKEOUTS
Wood, WI—197
Greer, DE—154
Birkofer, DM—142
W. Brown, OK—142
Dean, SJ—134
WILD PITCHES
W. Brown, OK—11
Ostermueller, SJ—11
Cooney, TO—9
Several with 8
HIT BATTERS
Piercy, DE—15
Dean, SJ—12
Jolley, DE—11
Zahn, DM—11
Tinning, DM—10

1931

The Kansas squad continued its winning ways when it won the first half of a split-season format. Second place Des Moines pulled past the Aviators in the second half to finish first, just ahead of Wichita. The two

A New Century, A New League (1900–1937)   169

Emil "Dutch" Leonard pitched for St. Joseph in 1931 before laboring with the Washington Senators and Chicago Cubs. (Photograph courtesy of Jay Sanford)

teams met in a seven-game playoff, and the Demons proved they were the best, winning the series four games to two.

Des Moines was led to the title by triple crown winner Stan Keyes. The all-star outfielder led the league in average, home runs, RBI, total bases and hits. His hits included 36 doubles, 24 triples and 38 homers! The Demons also had a great pitcher, Bud Tinning, who was again named to the All-Star Team. The righthander led the league in wins (24), ERA (3.14) and winning percentage (.923), which was second best in league history. His performance earned him a promotion to the Chicago Cubs the next season, where he threw for four seasons and compiled a 22–15 record. Another All-Star for the second consecutive season was first baseman Jim Oglesby with Des Moines. He got a cup of coffee with the Philadelphia Athletics in 1936. Demons pitcher John Niggeling, who would go on to pitch nine seasons in the majors, missed pitching a no-hitter that season as he failed to cover first base on a grounder to the right side. He still won 6–0.

Des Moines showed off its hitting prowess in a doubleheader against Omaha late in the season. A 31-hit attack led the Demons to a 29–6 victory in the first game. Then they won the second contest by a 22–9 margin. The doubledip drubbing was the highest scoring in league history.

Wichita, the only club which didn't have lights, had a couple of good players. All-Star second baseman Tony Piet got called up to the Pirates in August for the rest of the season. He stayed in the majors for another nine seasons. John Kroner, with Oklahoma City, was named to the All-Star Team. In 1935 he finally got a shot at the majors and played four seasons there with Boston and Cleveland. Hal McCain split his time between the White Sox and Pueblo in 1931. He had pitched three previous seasons with Chicago without much success.

Arky Vaughn was an infielder for Wichita in 1931. He later became a Hall of Famer with the Pittsburgh Pirates. (Photograph courtesy of Jay Sanford)

Arky Strings Together Nine Hits

Arky Vaughn, with Wichita, led the league in runs scored in 1931. He had quite a hitting streak over two games in September when he strung together nine consecutive hits, two of which were homers. In the playoffs he hit a fantastic .444.

The next season the Pittsburgh Pirates made Vaughn their regular shortstop. He became a run scorer there as well, and led the National League in that category three times during his 14-year career in the majors. His best season came in 1935 when he hit .385 with 19 homers and 99 RBI. He also was a career .318 hitter. The overlooked player was finally named to the Hall of Fame in 1985.

1931

Final Standings
First Half

	W	L	Pct.	GB
Wichita Aviators	44	27	.620	—
Des Moines Demons	39	26	.600	3
Denver Bears	34	29	.540	6
St. Joseph Saints	31	32	.492	9
Pueblo Braves	31	34	.477	10
Oklahoma City Indians	33	38	.465	11
Omaha Packers	29	38	.438	13
Topeka Senators	25	42	.378	17

Second Half

	W	L	Pct.	GB
Des Moines Demons	55	25	.688	—
Wichita Aviators	48	31	.606	6½
St. Joseph Saints	48	32	.600	7
Pueblo Braves	45	35	.562	10
Oklahoma City Indians	37	42	.468	17½
Topeka Senators	33	44	.429	20½
Denver Bears	30	48	.385	24
Omaha Packers	20	59	.254	34½

Playoffs

Des Moines defeated Wichita, four games to two.

Team Batting

	AB	R	H	HR	BB	SO	Avg.
Wichita	5376	1060	1645	164	571	504	.306
Des Moines	5224	996	1590	91	541	530	.304

The Western League

	AB	R	H	HR	BB	SO	Avg.
Denver	5070	860	1488	42	575	540	.293
Pueblo	4999	850	1434	52	526	582	.287
St. Joseph	5022	792	1433	57	615	572	.286
Oklahoma City	5354	769	1487	37	408	745	.278
Topeka	4920	724	1341	31	565	625	.273
Omaha	4921	755	1321	33	631	581	.268

Individual Batting Leaders
(Minimum 453 At Bats)

	G	AB	R	H	HR	Avg.
Keyes, DM	132	550	144	203	38	.369
Hostetler, TO	119	528	117	189	4	.358
H. Kelly, DE	129	508	117	181	8	.356
Neitzke, PU	135	501	100	172	8	.348
Oglesby, DM	144	487	119	200	6	.341

Earned Run Average Leaders
(Minimum 20 Decisions)

	G	W	L	Pct.	ERA
Tinning, DM	29	24	2	.923	3.11
Knight, DM	26	17	7	.708	3.30
Jacobs, WI	41	25	7	.781	3.41
Thomas, OK	39	13	15	.464	3.41
Grant, DM	30	12	11	.522	3.48

Individual Fielding Leaders
(Minimum 100 Games)

	POS	G	PO	A	E	DP	Pct.
Goldberg, TO	1b	137	1242	67	12	81	.993
Swanson, DM	2b	146	351	483	30	106	.965
Kroner, OK	3b	110	127	238	21	28	.946
Cronin, DM	ss	118	231	354	30	86	.951
Stoneham, WI	of	151	255	13	2	3	.993
E. Johnson, WI/DM	of	105	215	11	4	1	.983
Munson, DM/TO	of	119	205	10	4	0	.982
Clark, PU	c	106	492	51	9	8	.984

All-Star Team

1b—Jim Oglesby, Des Moines
2b—Tony Piet, Wichita
3b—John Kroner, Oklahoma City
ss—Angus McIsaac, Pueblo
of—Stan Keyes, Des Moines
of—Ernie Parker, Denver
of—Mike Kreevich, Des Moines
c—Andy Vargas, Denver
c—Benny Warren, Wichita
Utility—Lem Young, Wichita

A New Century, A New League (1900-1937) 173

p—Bud Tinning, Des Moines
p—Harold McKain, Pueblo
p—Rufus Meadows, Topeka
p—Elmer Knight, Des Moines
p—Ed "Bear Tracks" Greer, Denver
p—Arthur Jacobs, Wichita

Batting Leaders

HOME RUNS
Keyes, DM—38
Swansboro, WI—26
Schino, OM/WI—24
F. Vaughan, WI—21
Prather, SJ—19

TRIPLES
McIsaac, PU—27
Keyes, DM—24
Schalk, OK—17
F. Vaughan, WI—16
Riley, PU—16

DOUBLES
Eggert, DM/TO—49
Young, WI—41
Zaepfel, OM—40
Schalk, OK—39
Vigare, OM/WI—39

TOTAL BASES
Keyes, DM—401
Stoneman, WI—290
F. Vaughan, WI—283
Oglesby, DM—278
Schalk, OK—279

HITS
Keyes, DM—203
Oglesby, DM—200
Young, WI—195
Schalk, OK—194
Stoneman, OM—193

STOLEN BASES
F. Vaughan, WI—43
Piet, WI—42
Frey, PU—30
H. Kelly, DE—25
Several with 21

BASES ON BALLS
O'Brien, DE—104
Stoneham, WI—91
Zaepfel, OM—91
Prather, SJ—89
Eggert, DM—81

RBI
Keyer, DM—160
H. Kelly, DE—138
Schino, OM/WI—123
Stoneham, WI—123
Several with 112

Pitching Leaders

WINS
Jacobs, WI—25
Tinning, DM—24
Darrow, PU—18
McKain, PU—18
Tullis, OK—18

LOSSES
Tullis, OK—18
Meadows, TO—17
Wyckoff, PU—16
Thomas, OK—15
Carlsen, OM—15

GAMES
McKain, PU—43
Dunagan, OM/DM—42
Tubbs, OK—42
Jacobs, WI—41
Several with 40

INNINGS PITCHED
McCain, PU—254
Jacobs, WI—253
Tubbs, OK -252
Niggeling, DM—244
Singleton, TO—235

BASES ON BALLS
Richardson, SJ—160
Meadows, TO—125
Tubbs, OK—124
Jacobs, WI—112
Niggeling, DM—107

STRIKEOUTS
Meadows, TO—177
Richardson, SJ—170

Greer, DE—152
Tubbs, OK—134
McKain, PU—132

1932

The Western League received some assistance from the Major Leagues as three teams became farm clubs. Tulsa was the only farm club of the Pittsburgh Pirates, while Denver was one of 11 for the St. Louis Cardinals. Wichita was affiliated with the Chicago Cubs. By this time, every club was equipped with lights for night games, which helped dwindling attendance due to the depressed economy. It was so rough that for some people a hot dog at the ballpark was their only meal of the day. Some teams lowered prices to a nickel to get people to come to games.

Tulsa returned to competition in the league after a two-year hiatus, during which it fielded no team. The Oilers won the first half of the season handily over second-place Denver. The second half wasn't so easy. Oklahoma City rose from the ashes—it had finished in seventh in the first half—to challenge Tulsa for first. The two ended up in a tie for first, so a three-game playoff was scheduled. If Tulsa won the playoff, it would have won the pennant outright, inasmuch as it won the first half as well. However, the Indians won the playoff two games to one to necessitate another playoff for the league title. The seven-game championship was decided quickly when Tulsa won four straight. In all, the two teams played each other 13 successive times at the end of the season.

Tulsa was led by a good pitching staff and dominated the All-Star Team, contributing five members. Pitcher Andy Bednar led the league in wins and winning percentage (.846, 22–4). Another All-Star pitcher was Ralph Birkofer, who led the league in strikeouts. The Pittsburgh Pirates took a brief look at Bednar, while they made Birkofer a member of their pitching staff for five seasons.

Oklahoma City had only one All-Star player: Roy Schalk. The second baseman was rewarded with a call from the Yankees at the end of the season. He later played two seasons in the majors with the White Sox during World War II. Oklahoma City won one game by forfeit when manager Frank Haley of St. Joseph knocked a watch from the umpire's hand.

In December, Tulsa and Oklahoma City finally got their wish and were admitted to the Texas League. Tulsa had won the Western League title six times.

1932
Final Standings
First Half

	W	L	Pct.	GB	Affiliations
Tulsa Oilers	46	22	.676	—	St. Louis Cardinals
Denver Bears	42	32	.568	7	Pittsburgh Pirates
Des Moines Demons	36	30	.545	9	None
Omaha Packers	36	37	.493	12½	None
St. Joseph Saints	35	36	.493	12½	None
Wichita Aviators	33	37	.471	14	Chicago Cubs
Oklahoma City Indians	31	41	.431	17	None
Pueblo Braves	25	49	.338	24	None

Second Half

	W	L	Pct.	GB
Tulsa Oilers	52	26	.667	—
Oklahoma City Indians	52	26	.667	—
Denver Bears	41	32	.562	8½
St. Joseph Saints	37	39	.487	14
Pueblo Braves	37	41	.474	15
Des Moines Demons	35	42	.455	16½
Wichita Aviators	30	49	.380	22½
Omaha Packers	22	51	.301	27½

Playoffs
Oklahoma City defeated Tulsa, two games to one, for the second-half title.

Finals
Tulsa defeated Oklahoma City, four games to none.

Team Batting

	AB	R	H	HR	BB	SO	Avg.
Denver	5247	995	1641	46	577	499	.313
Pueblo	5329	977	1592	49	669	597	.299
Tulsa	5162	1066	1526	70	687	536	.296
Des Moines	5019	893	1445	59	546	604	.288
Omaha	5145	827	1468	51	556	639	.286
Oklahoma City	5182	903	1478	51	585	659	.285
Wichita	5137	865	1457	107	523	549	.284
St. Joseph	4954	851	1374	30	665	549	.278

Team Fielding

	G	DP	PB	PO	A	E	Pct.
Oklahoma City	151	171	16	3926	1834	243	.960

	G	DP	PB	PO	A	E	Pct.
Des Moines	144	169	10	3724	1596	224	.960
Denver	147	153	12	3815	1652	245	.957
Tulsa	146	136	15	3799	1634	247	.957
St. Joseph	147	132	27	3748	1610	258	.954
Wichita	149	124	10	3752	1506	267	.952
Pueblo	153	143	14	3941	1683	284	.952
Omaha	147	136	35	3759	1588	297	.948

Individual Fielding Leaders
(Minimum 90 Games)

	POS	G	PO	A	E	DP	Pct.
Stoeven, DE	1b	141	1238	87	17	123	.988
Swanson, DM	2b	144	338	431	29	110	.964
Eggert, TU	3b	99	123	195	27	18	.922
Dean, OM/PU	ss	109	217	295	34	69	.938
Zoellers, SJ	of	142	292	10	3	2	.990
Allington, PU	of	153	371	9	6	1	.984
Brown, OM	of	130	213	12	4	3	.983
Vargas, DE	c	118	530	66	7	3	.988

Individual Pitching Leaders
(Minimum 20 Games)

	G	IP	R	SO	W	L	Pct.
Bednar, TU	33	234	106	93	22	4	.846
C. Taylor, TU/OK	29	135	71	35	12	3	.800
Lang, TU	30	180	110	75	12	5	.706
Bivin, TU	35	206	85	92	15	7	.682
Dailey, OM	28	117	88	81	6	3	.667

Individual Batting Leaders
(Minimum 453 At Bats)

	G	AB	R	H	HR	Avg.
Allington, PU	153	569	167	213	9	.374
Nydahl, DE	147	632	146	231	4	.366
E. Parker, DE	138	508	135	182	6	.358
Schino, TU	138	525	129	186	18	.354
E. Brown, OM	147	579	110	204	1	.352

All-Star Team

1b—Jim Oglesby, Des Moines
2b—Roy Schalk, Oklahoma City
3b—Russell Rollings, Denver
ss—George Binder, Denver
of—Stan Schino, Tulsa
of—Ernie Parker, Denver
of—John Soneham, Tulsa
c—Horton, Wichita

c—Tony Rego, Tulsa
p—Andy Bednar, Tulsa
p—Ralph Birkofer, Tulsa
p—Ed "Bear Tracks" Greer, Denver

Nydahl, DE—145
Swanson, DM—144
Stoneham, TU—138

Batting Leaders

HOME RUNS
Goldberg, WI—30
Harvel, WI—22
Lillard, WI -19
Schino, TU—18
Stoneham, TU—18

STOLEN BASES
Allington, PU—36
Harrell, SJ—30
Nydahl, DE—25
Schalk, OK—21
Several with 20

HITS
Nydahl, DE—231
Schalk, OK—223
Allington, PU—213
Rollings, DE—208
E. Brown, OM—204

DOUBLES
Schalk, OK—56
Rollings, DE—55
E. Brown, OM—52
Harvel, WI—52
Allington, PU—49

TRIPLES
Allington, PU—23
Wagner, DM—22
E. Parker, DE—20
Stoneham, TU—20
Oglesby, DM—19

TOTAL BASES
Allington, PU—335
Schalk, OK—326
Stoneham, TU—318
Harvel, WI—317
Rollings, DE—312

RUNS
Allington, PU—167
Hipps, TU—147

Pitching Leaders

GAMES
G. Brown, OM/PU—45
Benton, OK—43
Carlsen, PU—41
Matuzak, OK—41
Richardson, SJ—41

WINS
Bednar, TU—22
Greer, DE—21
E. Nelson, WI—18
Matuzak, OK—17
R. Jones, PU/OK—17

LOSSES
G. Brown, OM/PU—16
Richardson, SJ—16
Carlsen, PU—15
Matuzak, OK—14
E. Nelson, WI—14

INNINGS PITCHED
Greer, DE—261
E. Nelson, WI—255
May, SJ—249
Matuzak, OK—247
Jones, PU/OK—236

BASES ON BALLS
Richardson, SJ—168
Benton, OK—135
Estrada, PU—134
Matuzak, OK—125
Birkofer, TU—122

STRIKEOUTS
Birkofer, TU—186
E. Nelson, WI—169
Matuzak, OK—155
Richardson, SJ—139
Benton, OK—130

WILD PITCHES
M. Brown, DM—12
Birkofer, TU—11

Richardson, SJ—11
Benton, OK—10
Kennedy, SJ—10

HIT BATTERS
Birkofer, TU—22

Richardson, SJ—16
E. Nelson, WI—16
Matuzak, OK—12
Several with 11

1933

Denver and Pueblo were dropped to cut down on travel requirements for the financially troubled league. Denver owner Mike Anfenger sued the league for $150,000 for the loss of the franchise, but he lost. New franchises were awarded to Muskogee, Oklahoma; Hutchinson, Kansas; and Joplin and Springfield, Missouri.

The season was tough for a couple of teams. The Wichita Oilers were 6–13 when they moved to Muskogee, Oklahoma, on June 6. But the team was evicted from their park and became a road team on July 31. The Oilers became one of the worst teams in league history, with a 26–95 mark for a .215 winning percentage.

Rube Marquard pitched for Wichita in 1933. He later was named to the Hall of Fame. (Photograph courtesy of Jay Sanford)

The Hutchinson Wheatshockers were tied with Omaha for first by mid-June, but neither team could hold on to the lead as the St. Joseph Saints passed both teams and finished first in the first half. Hutchinson became the Bartlesville Bronchos on July 7. The second half was a totally different story. Topeka, which had finished in seventh place the first half, took the league lead in late July and held that position until late August when Springfield grabbed first for a brief time. Up until the last day of the season, Springfield, Topeka and Des Moines all had a shot at the second-half championship, but Topeka beat Joplin to secure the pennant. The Saints breezed by the Senators in the playoffs, winning the seven-game series in five games.

The Saints were led by none other than their own manager, Mike Ryba, who appeared in 114 games. The versatile leader caught 87 games, hit .380 and won three games he pitched. St. Joseph had the best pitching staff that season, with Herbert May garnering the most wins on the season and the best winning percentage with his 24–6 mark. The Saints also had the strikeout king, Cy Blanton, with 284 Ks. Blanton left for the majors the next season and led the National League in ERA in 1935. He pitched nine seasons in the big leagues for Pittsburgh and Philadelphia.

The season was marred by the death of a player. Jake Batterson, the second baseman for the Springfield Cardinals, died on July 3 after suffering injuries when he was hit in the head by a pitch thrown by Floyd Carlson of Omaha the previous day.

1933

Final Standings
First Half

	W	L	Pct.	GB	Affiliations
St. Joseph Saints	36	21	.632	—	None
Des Moines Demons	35	23	.603	1½	None
Joplin Miners	33	26	.559	4	St. Louis Browns
Springfield Cardinals	30	28	.517	6½	St. Louis Cardinals
Omaha Packers	29	28	.509	7	None
Hutchinson Wheatshockers/ Bartlesville Bronchos	25	32	.439	11	None
Topeka Senators	23	33	.411	12½	Cincinnati
Wichita Oilers/ Muskogee Oilers	18	38	.321	17½	None

Second Half

	W	L	Pct.	GB
Topeka Senators	45	22	.672	—
Springfield Cardinals	43	22	.662	1
Des Moines Demons	46	24	.657	1½
St. Joseph Saints	41	26	.612	4
Omaha Packers	34	33	.507	11
Hutchinson Wheatshockers/ Bartlesville Bronchos	26	38	.406	17½
Joplin Miners	22	43	.338	22
Wichita Oilers/ Muskogee Oilers	8	57	.123	36

Playoffs

St. Joseph beat Topeka, four games to one.

Team Batting

	AB	R	H	HR	BB	SO	Avg.
Springfield	4341	831	1300	71	519	620	.300
Topeka	4234	722	1235	68	383	604	.292
Omaha	4210	765	1215	44	518	531	.289
Joplin	4267	708	1207	46	415	504	.283
St. Joseph	4259	746	1199	47	474	637	.282
Des Moines	4236	798	1178	60	482	551	.278
Bartlesville	4166	682	1138	35	499	690	.273
Muskogee	4024	590	1058	54	389	590	.263

Team Fielding

	G	DP	PB	PO	A	E	Pct.
Topeka	123	92	9	3140	1376	197	.958
St. Joseph	124	102	20	3193	1263	217	.954
Joplin	124	86	15	3198	1355	223	.954
Omaha	124	124	13	3144	1442	229	.953
Springfield	123	102	17	3189	1265	230	.951
Des Moines	128	91	12	3250	1353	267	.945
Muskogee	121	80	13	2894	1319	266	.941
Bartlesville	121	90	22	3093	1515	297	.940

Individual Fielding Leaders
(Minimum 100 Games)

	POS	G	PO	A	E	DP	Pct.
Kentling, BA	1b	111	1056	66	12	66	.989
Williamson, JO	2b	116	336	349	38	51	.947
Tutaj, OM	3b	120	107	223	29	30	.919
Wise, TO	ss	119	226	342	43	57	.930
McFarland, JO/SJ	of	122	296	14	3	2	.990
Breese, TO	of	106	191	15	3	1	.986
Scaling, TO	of	119	282	11	7	2	.977
Knox, OM	of	114	606	88	11	11	.984

Individual Pitching Leaders
(Minimum 20 Decisions)

	G	IP	R	SO	W	L	Pct.
May, SJ	35	244	102	153	24	6	.800
Blanton, SJ	35	256	86	284	21	7	.750
Dailey, OM	32	226	108	155	20	9	.690
Gizelbach, DM	40	230	115	203	18	10	.643
Clay, DM	31	227	144	119	15	10	.600

Individual Batting Leaders
(Minimum 403 At Bats)

	G	AB	R	H	HR	Avg.
Ryba, Dominic, SP	114	418	82	159	5	.380
Tutaj, Stanley, OM	122	475	85	175	4	.368
Carson, Walter, SJ	122	411	117	186	13	.364
Patton, Dallas, SPG	123	507	115	175	11	.345
Howard, Frank, SPG	123	468	89	159	9	.340

All-Star Team

1b—Vic Shiell, Topeka
2b—Richard Harrell, St. Joseph
3b—Stanley Tutaj, Omaha
ss—John Keane, Springfield
of—Dallas Patton, Springfield
of—Walter Carson, St. Joseph
of—Leo Ogorek, Des Moines
c—Mike Ryba, Springfield
p—Herbert May, St. Joseph
p—Cy Blanton, St. Joseph

Batting Leaders

HOME RUNS
Shiell, Victor, TO—22
Brightwell, Glenn, TO—21
Frierson, William, JO—17
Hudson, Roy, MU/DM—16
Orwoll, Ossie, DM—15

STOLEN BASES
Ogorek, Leo, DM—60
Seitz, Grover, BA—51
Carson, Walter, SJ—37
Lick, Eddie, DM/SPG—34
Barton, Lawrence, SPG—33

HITS
Carson, Walter, SJ—186
Patton, Dallas, SPG—175
Tutaj, Stanley, OM—175
Several with 159

DOUBLES
Carson, Walter, SJ—43
Breese, Eldon, TO—42
Ryba, Dominic, SPG—42
Keane, John, SPG—41
Howard, Frank, SPG—40

TRIPLES
Frierson, William, JO—19
Catchings, Ben, BA—17
Bates, Charles, SJ—16
Holliday, Hugh, BA—14
Patton, Dallas, SPG—14

TOTAL BASES
Carson, Walter, SJ—294
Patton, Dallas, SPG—265
Howard, Frank, SPG—244
Bates, Charles, SJ—241
Shiell, Victor, TO—239

RUNS
Keane, John, SPG—118
Carson, Walter, SJ—117
Patton, Dallas, SPG—115
Ogorek, Leo, DM—108
McFarland, Howard, JO/SJ—105

Pitching Leaders

GAMES
Berry, JO—49
Copeland, SP—41
Gizelbach, DM—40
Wilson, JO/TO—40
Several with 38

WINS
May, SJ—24
Blanton, SJ—21
Berry, JO—20
Dailey, OM—20
Gizelbach, DM—18

LOSSES
Evans, BA—18
Richardson, SJ/MU—16
Berry, JO—15

Young, JO—15
Several with 14

INNINGS PITCHED
Berry, JO—280
Copeland, SPG—259
Blanton, SJ—256
Wilson, JO/TO—256
Evans, BA—247

BASES ON BALLS
Clay, DM—116
Godels, SPG—107
House, BA—100
Blanton, SJ—97
Several with 93

STRIKEOUTS
Blanton, SJ—284
Copeland, SPG—242
Gizelbach, DM—203
Dailey, OM—155
May, SJ—153

WILD PITCHES
Barnhart, SJ/TO—11
McCutcheon, BA -11
Evans, BA—10
Godels, SPG—9
Copeland, SPG—8

1934

The Western League continued to shrink its territory in 1934 as the four newcomers from 1933 were replaced by teams in Rock Island, Illinois, and three teams in Iowa: Cedar Rapids, Davenport and Sioux City.

The closest race in Western League history occurred in the first half of the 1934 season. Des Moines, St. Joseph and Sioux City finished in a dead heat. None of those teams could manage to win the second half, as fifth-place Davenport surged past all of them for the second-half crown. An unusual playoff had to be devised because of the triple tie in the first half. Davenport was paired with Des Moines, while Sioux City and St. Joseph met in the other five-game series. Davenport and St. Joseph won the first round of the playoffs and met in the seven-game finals. The finals went down to a seventh and final contest at Davenport. Herman Drefs, a 22-year-old southpaw, tossed a no-hitter to give St. Joseph the title. Drefs had won only one game since the middle of July and had been chased from the mound earlier in the playoffs, so he saved his best for last. Ironically, manager Earle Brucker had almost left the lefthander at home before going to Davenport for the last two games of the series.

The St. Joseph team was led by two good hitters: Howard McFarland and Charles Bates, who tied for the most hits in the season. Both got shots at the majors, but neither stuck. The best pitcher that season was Davenport's Frank Lamanski. He led the league in wins (24) and strikeouts (216).

1934

Final Standings
First Half

	W	L	Pct.	GB	Affiliations
Des Moines Demons	36	23	.610	—	None
St. Joseph Saints	36	23	.610	—	None
Sioux City Cowboys	36	23	.610	—	None
Rock Island Islanders	29	29	.500	6½	None
Davenport Blue Sox	29	30	.492	7	None
Cedar Rapids Raiders	24	34	.414	11½	None
Omaha Packers	24	35	.407	12	None
Topeka Senators	21	38	.356	15½	Cincinnati Reds

Second Half

	W	L	Pct.	GB
Davenport Blue Sox	41	23	.641	—
Topeka Senators	38	26	.594	3
Sioux City Cowboys	38	27	.585	3½
Des Moines Demons	32	33	.492	9½
St. Joseph Saints	29	33	.468	11
Rock Island Islanders	29	36	.446	12½
Omaha Packers	25	38	.397	15½
Cedar Rapids Raiders	23	39	.371	17

Playoffs

St. Joseph defeated Sioux City, three games to one.
Davenport defeated Des Moines, three games to one.

Finals

St. Joseph defeated Davenport, four games to three.

Team Batting

	AB	R	H	HR	BB	SO	LOB	Avg.
Des Moines	4452	751	1296	59	450	552	1016	.291
St. Joseph	4146	713	1149	42	551	650	956	.277
Rock Island	4207	630	1151	22	421	506	928	.274
Omaha	4273	616	1153	56	414	641	944	.270
Cedar Rapids	4154	585	1116	42	456	611	987	.269
Davenport	4201	658	1123	42	525	545	973	.267
Sioux City	4158	644	1104	85	409	602	874	.266
Topeka	4172	598	1051	65	426	705	861	.252

Team Fielding

	G	DP	PB	PO	A	E	Pct.
Topeka	123	105	14	3219	1408	200	.959
Des Moines	124	91	14	3259	1348	205	.957
Omaha	122	105	25	3172	1463	218	.955
Sioux City	124	93	7	3218	1465	226	.954
Rock Island	123	99	11	3186	1349	218	.954
Davenport	123	88	21	3212	1305	235	.951
St. Joseph	121	94	16	3152	1525	257	.948
Cedar Rapids	120	83	26	3133	1357	250	.947

Individual Fielding Leaders
(Minimum 100 Games)

	POS	G	PO	A	E	DP	Pct.
Shiell, Victor, TO	1b	120	1053	90	11	94	.990
Williford, Edward, TO	2b	124	330	363	26	72	.964
Crossley, Clarence, DA	3b	112	126	191	18	16	.946
Anderson, Harold, CR	ss	121	253	348	34	52	.946
Whitehouse, Harry, DA/SC	of	121	230	25	4	4	.985
Mizeur, William, CR	of	118	215	9	4	2	.982
Breese, Elden, TO	of	107	233	6	5	1	.980
Snyder, Morgan, TO	c	119	627	72	10	8	.986

Winning Percentage Leaders

	G	W	L	Pct.
Wehde, Wilbur, SC	16	10	2	.833
Lamanski, Frank, DA	37	24	7	.774
Hemenway, Emil, SC	10	5	2	.714
Tubbs, Frank, DA	34	17	7	.708
Thomas, Marlon, SC	31	17	8	.680

Individual Batting Leaders
(Minimum 384 At Bats)

	G	AB	R	H	HR	RBI	Avg.
Patterson, Floyd, RI	122	445	90	163	2	74	.366
McFarland, Howard, SJ	119	472	108	164	6	85	.347
Dickshot, John, RI/CR	117	423	112	145	16	79	.343
Bates, Charles, SJ	122	485	98	164	8	81	.338
McNeely, Albert, OM	108	438	75	143	9	92	.326

All-Star Team

1b—Malcom Pickett, Omaha
2b—Hugh Luby, Sioux City
3b—Clarence Crossley, Davenport
ss—Angus McIsaac, St. Joseph
of—Floyd Patterson, Rock Island
of—Albert McNeely, Omaha

of—John Dickshot, Rock Island/Cedar Rapids
c—Morgan Snyder, Topeka
p—Frank Lamanski, Davenport
p—Max Thomas, Sioux City

Attendance
Sioux City—87,196
Davenport—48,920
Cedar Rapids—47,360
St. Joseph- 43,772
Rock Island—36,619
Omaha—34,675
Des Moines—30,797
Topeka—28,889
Total—358,228

Batting Leaders
HOME RUNS
Johnson, Vern, SC—24
Willingham, Hugh, SC—19
Dickshot, John, RI/CR—16
Several with 15

RUNS BATTED IN
Hudson, Roy, DM—94
Gaffke, Fabian, DM—93
McNeely, Albert, OM—92
Mizeur, William, CR—91
Several with 88

STOLEN BASES
Ogorek, Leo, DM—38
Luby, Hugh, SC—35
McFarland, Howard, SJ—31
Corssley, Clarence, DA—27
Olsen, Russell, DA—24

HITS
Bates, Charles, SJ—164
McFarland, Howard, SJ—164
Ogorek, Leo, DM—164
Gaffke, Fabian, DM—163
Patterson, Floyd, RI—163

DOUBLES
Bates, Charles, SJ—37
McNeely, Albert, OM—37
McFarland, Howard, SJ—33
Several with 32

TRIPLES
Bates, Charles, SJ—20
Gaffke, Fabian, DM—17
Hall, Ermal, DA—15
McFarland, Howard, SJ—14
Several with 13

TOTAL BASES
Gaffke, Fabian, DM—269
Bates, Charles, SJ—265
McFarland, Howard, SJ—243
Dickshot, John, RI/CR—230
Mizeur, William, CR—224

RUNS
Dickshot, John, RI/CR—112
McFarland, Howard, SJ—108
Ogorek, Leo, DM—108
Breese, Elden, TO—106
Gaffke, Fabian, DM—105

Pitching Leaders
GAMES
Wilson, William, CR—40
Van Fleet, Dwight, CR—38
Lamanski, Frank, DA—37
Graf, Kinner, SC—36
Tubbs, Frank, DA—34

WINS
Lamanski, Frank, DA—24
Thomas, Marion, SC—17
Tubbs, Frank, DA—17
Sams, Ralph, DM—16
Several with 15

LOSSES
Evans, Ernest, CR/OM—15
Toubey, Gorden, RI—15
Van Fleet, Dwight, CR—15
Wilson, William, CR—15
Several with 13

INNINGS PITCHED
Lamanski, Frank, DA—262
Wilson, William, CR—229
Sams, Ralph, DM—228
Graf, Kinner, SC—222
Several with 218

BASES ON BALLS
King, Donald, SC/SJ—119
Toubey, Gorden, RI—114
Mills, Dale, TO—104
Hari, John, CR—95
Yelovic, John, TO—94

STRIKEOUTS
Lamanski, Frank, DA—216
Piechota, Al, DA—162

Van Fleet, Dwight, CR—157
Thomas, Marlon, SC—155
Toubey, Gorden, RI—145

WILD PITCHES
Piechota, Al, DA—19
Hari, John, CR—12
Yelovic, John, TO—12
Drefs, Herman, SJ—11
Hallett, John, SJ/CR—11

1935

Financial problems caused by the Depression took a toll on the league in 1935. Openers in the league drew from two to three thousand fans, which was not a good sign. Omaha decided to transfer to Council Bluffs on June 25. Then Rock Island withdrew on July 18. On the field, Keokuk jumped out to a 10–4 record before being caught by the Davenport Blue Sox in July. The Blue Sox led the league the rest of the way.

With the split season gone, the league went to a Shaughnessy playoff (first vs. fourth; second vs. third) for the first time. Davenport and St. Joseph swept their opponents in the first round to meet each other in the finals. St. Joseph made it three in a row in the playoffs as they beat Sioux City four games to three in the playoffs. The Blue Sox couldn't manage a win in the playoffs against fourth-place Sioux City, which was managed that season by the future Hall of Famer Hack Wilson, who set the Major League record for RBI in a season.

The greatest star in the league was St. Joseph's Earle Brucker, who was named Most Valuable Player. He was the best fielding catcher in the league. He went on to five seasons with the Philadelphia Athletics.

Harold Epps, with Cedar Rapids, batted .346 on the season, which helped propel him to the majors in 1938, where he played four seasons during the war. Another player with major league experience was Sioux City's Wilbur Wehde, who had a try with the White Sox before joining the Western League.

Pat Malone, who would later go on to pitch for the Cubs, had a long day during the season when he tried to pitch a doubleheader for Des Moines. He won the first game 4–0. In the second game against St. Joseph, he pitched 14 innings before finally running out of gas. The game went 18 innings and Des Moines won.

During the season an umpire took exception to Davenport's Hugh Morse's delivery. He called three balks in a row to send a batter home all the way from first base.

A New Century, A New League (1900–1937)

Des Moines had a devilish name in 1935 and finished in third place that season. (Photograph courtesy of Jay Sanford)

Passeau Wore Number 13

Claude Passeau of Des Moines led the league in wins and strikeouts. His performance led to his promotion to the Philadelphia Phillies the next season.

Pitching for a last-place team led him to a losing record over the next three seasons. Then he was traded in May 1939 to Chicago, who were much better than the lowly Phillies. The trade transformed him immediately into a winning pitcher. The righthander reached a career-high 20 wins in 1940.

He pitched throughout the war and in 1945 pitched in the World Series. Passeau was marvelous, as he threw a one-hit shutout. Wearing number 13, he pitched for 13 seasons and ended up with a 162–150 record.

1935
Final Standings

	W	L	Pct.	GB
Davenport Blue Sox	70	46	.603	—
St. Joseph Saints	58	48	.547	7
Des Moines Demons	58	55	.513	10½
Sioux City Cowboys	54	52	.509	11
Cedar Rapids Raiders	53	57	.482	14
Keokuk Indians	49	66	.426	20½
*Omaha Packers/ Council Bluffs	55	46	.545	NA
*Rock Island Islanders	19	46	.292	NA

*Disbanded before the end of the season.

Playoffs

St. Joseph defeated Des Moines, three games to none.
Sioux City defeated Davenport, three games to none.

Finals

St. Joseph defeated Sioux City, four games to three.
MVP—Earle Brucker, St. Joseph

Team Batting

	AB	R	H	HR	BB	SO	SB	LOB	Avg.
Council Bluffs	3453	605	977	52	380	446	59	755	.283
Cedar Rapids	3862	588	1074	60	331	510	90	807	.278

	AB	R	H	HR	BB	SO	SB	LOB	Avg.
Davenport	3988	598	1102	44	391	465	74	854	.276
Des Moines	3914	621	1061	49	391	530	91	834	.271
Keokuk	3929	545	1043	42	348	591	59	790	.265
St. Joseph	3597	534	955	33	400	498	83	816	.265
Sioux City	3631	490	957	72	343	552	115	774	.264
Rock Island	2046	249	515	12	157	289	60	399	.252

Team Fielding

	G	PO	A	E	DP	Pct.
Sioux City	107	2816	1379	184	113	.958
Des Moines	113	2947	1133	180	74	.958
Keokuk	115	2954	1312	195	105	.956
Cedar Rapids	111	2880	1305	192	92	.956
St. Joseph	106	2733	1195	184	88	.955
Davenport	116	3018	1164	213	77	.952
Rock Island	65	1560	740	120	40	.950
Council Bluffs	101	2554	1115	204	98	.947

Individual Fielding Leaders
(Minimum 74 Games)

	POS	G	PO	A	E	DP	Pct.
Shiell, Victor, KE/SJ	1b	109	990	69	12	80	.989
Williford, Edward, KE	2b	114	293	320	25	67	.961
Willingham, Hugh, SC	3b	94	107	176	16	21	.946
Falk, Peter, DM	ss	97	178	239	26	38	.941
Rye, Eugene, DA	of	76	148	3	1	0	.993
Goodman, David, SJ/KE	of	107	180	17	3	2	.985
Ogorek, Leo, DM	of	93	181	9	3	1	.984
Brucker, Earle, SJ	c	79	461	41	7	8	.984

Individual Pitching Leaders

	G	W	L	Pct.	IP	R	SO
Underwood, Floyd, CB	14	6	2	.750	82	46	31
Plechota, Al, DA	25	17	6	.729	209	70	157
Ehlers, Raymond, CB	14	5	2	.714	81	61	29
Anderson, William, SJ	19	11	5	.688	138	65	74
Taylor, Howard, DM/CR	35	18	9	.667	220	140	97
Graf, Kinner G., SC	30	18	9	.667	201	91	108

Individual Batting Leaders
(Minimum 360 At Bats)

	G	AB	R	H	HR	RBI	Avg.
Clements, Charles, CS	96	391	86	129	4	46	.330

	G	AB	R	H	HR	RBI	Avg.
Bocek, Milton, CR	111	447	93	147	16	74	.329
Packett, Harold, SJ	94	377	80	121	5	43	.321
Webb, James, CR	111	472	88	151	8	44	.320
Riley, Leon, DA	112	413	83	132	12	67	.320

Batting Leaders

HOME RUNS
Willingham, Hugh, SC—20
Bocek, Milton, CR—16
Luther, August, DM—15
Barton, Lawrence, CB—13
Williford, Edward, KE—13

RUNS BATTED IN
Vezelich, Louis, SJ/CB—78
Hall, Ermal, DA—76
Bocek, Milton, CR—74
Willingham, Hugh, SC—74
Williford, Edward, KO—73

STOLEN BASES
Bocek, Milton, CR—27
Ogorek, Leo, DM—25
Luby, High, SC—24
Packett, Harold, SJ—23
Several with 21

HITS
Webb, James, CR—151
Bocek, Milton, CR—147
Ogorek, Leo, DM—144
Hall, Ermal, DA—135
Williford, Edward, KE—133

DOUBLES
Hassler, Ben, CB—31
Clements, Charles, CB—27
Howard, James F., CB—27
Larson, Albert, CR—27
Polly, Nicolas, DA—27

TRIPLES
Clements, Charles, CB—15
Luther, August, DM—14
Holder, Brooks, DM—13
Epps, Harold, CR—11
Brucker, Earle, SJ—11

TOTAL BASES
Bocek, Milton, CR—239
Webb, James, CR—213

Williford, Edward, KE—206
Riley, Leon, DA—205
Several with 201

RUNS
Bocek, Milton, CR—93
Ogorek, Leo, DM—92
Vezelich, Louis, SJ/DB—90
Webb, James, CR—88
Clements, Charles, CB—86

Pitching Leaders

GAMES
Wehde, Wilbur, SC—40
Passeau, Claude, DM—37
Taylor, Howard, DM/CR—35
Tubbs, Frank, DA- 32
Phebus, Raymond, DA—31

WINS
Passeau, Claude, DM—20
Taylor, Howard, DM/CR—18
Graf, Kinner, SC—18
Plechota, Al, DA—17
Several with 15

LOSSES
Lott, Robert, KE—15
May, Herbert, SJ—14
Crampton, Elwyn, KE—12
Lyons, James, CR—12
Several with 11

INNINGS PITCHED
Passeau, Claude, DM—244
Taylor, Howard, DM/CR—220
Plechota, Al, DA—209
Chelini, Italo, KE—208
Graf, Kinner, SC—201

STRIKEOUTS
Passeau, Claude, DM—239
Plechota, Al, DA—157
Phebus, Raymond, DA—151

Drefs, Herman, SJ—143
Lamanski, Frank, DA—134

WILD PITCHES
Several with 9

BALKS
Morse, Hugh, DA—5
Petraborg, SC—4
Mead, Ralph, CR—2
Crampton, Elwyn, KE—2
Johnson, Lyle, KE—2

1936

Money was getting so tight in 1936 that just one club was profitable. Before the season began, the league dropped to six teams, its lowest total since 1908. Former major league player Dave Bancroft took over as manager at Sioux City. The split-season was again adopted.

On the field, Cedar Rapids jumped out to a lead after the first week of play, but it was soon caught and passed by Davenport. Omaha was in contention, but was struck by a couple of tragedies caused by Mother Nature. Omaha's park was first wrecked by a windstorm, so the Robin Hoods had to play some games in Lincoln. Then the park was destroyed by a fire, so the franchise moved to Rock Island and became a traveling team the rest of the year. The major leagues also dipped into the league's pockets quite a bit for players. Brooklyn took seven Western Leaguers, one from Omaha and the rest from Davenport, which was one of its farm clubs. The White Sox, Cardinals and other major league teams also purchased players. Most were pitchers. Davenport easily won the first half. The second half was more of a struggle, as Cedar Rapids kept the race close and finished a half game behind the Blue Sox.

While Davenport dominated the league, only one of its players, Nick Polly, was named to the All-Star team. Polly got a couple of shots at the majors, but neither lasted. Manager Celtus Dixon was also named to the special team. Cedar Rapids was helped defensively by James "Skeeter" Webb at short. Webb went on to 11 seasons in the majors. The Raiders also had strikeout leader James Hayes, who was given a try with the Senators the year before. Agrus "Dutch" Prather, who played for Omaha and Rock Island, was named MVP after leading the league in homers (22) and runs scored (102). Omaha also had 45-year-old Hank Severeid, who had caught for 15 years in the majors. Hal Turpin of Des Moines was the best hurler in the league. He won 20 contests and had the best winning percentage (.667, 20-10). Hugh Luby with Sioux City was called up to Philadelphia after the season, but he didn't stay there. He finally got a full season with the New York Giants in 1944.

1936
Final Standings
First Half

	W	L	Pct.	GB	Affiliations
Davenport Blue Sox	39	26	.600	—	Brooklyn Dodgers
Sioux City Cowboys	35	30	.538	4	None
Omaha Robin Hoods/ Rock Island Rocks	33	29	.532	4½	None
Cedar Rapids Raiders	35	31	.530	4½	St. Louis Cardinals
Des Moines Demons	33	33	.500	6½	None
Waterloo Hawks	25	41	.379	14½	None

Second Half

	W	L	Pct.	GB
Davenport Blue Sox	35	26	.574	—
Cedar Rapids Raiders	35	27	.565	½
Des Moines Demons	31	31	.500	4½
Omaha Robin Hoods/ Rock Island Rocks	29	35	.453	7½
Sioux City Cowboys	26	34	.433	8½
Waterloo Hawks	25	38	.397	11½

Team Batting

	AB	R	H	HR	SB	BB	SO	Avg.
Rock Island	4251	701	1188	63	76	530	591	.279
Cedar Rapids	4376	662	1176	62	123	455	616	.269
Sioux City	4305	644	1156	66	107	493	576	.269
Davenport	4306	668	1153	43	61	450	504	.268
Des Moines	4367	676	1151	67	66	419	553	.264
Waterloo	4266	560	1023	52	70	490	705	.240

Team Fielding

	G	DP	PB	PO	A	E	Pct.
Davenport	126	116	13	3297	1395	193	.961
Sioux City	125	132	9	3251	1532	211	.958
Waterloo	129	96	15	3325	1507	220	.956
Cedar Rapids	128	103	5	3293	1408	216	.956
Rock Island	126	91	18	3214	1380	229	.953
Des Moines	128	122	12	3311	1516	247	.951

Individual Fielding Leaders
(More Than 100 Games)

	POS	G	PO	A	E	DP	Pct.
Monahan, Peter, SC	1b	122	1072	71	9	107	.995

	POS	G	PO	A	E	DP	Pct.
Luby, Hugh, SC	2b	120	360	406	36	101	.955
Seghl, Philip, SC	3b	125	155	280	28	28	.940
White, Ray, DA	ss	125	228	396	32	79	.951
Scaritt, Russell, RI	of	113	236	5	5	1	.980
Goodman, David, SI	of	126	212	10	5	1	.978
Plummer, Irving, WA	of	129	290	16	8	3	.975
Wilson, William, DM	c	128	635	75	11	10	.985

Earned Run Average
(15 or More Innings)

	G	W-L	Pct.	IP	R	ER	ERA
Bonnetti, Julio, DM	35	14–13	.519	232	129	69	2.56
VanFleet, Dwight, CR	33	17–10	.630	224	98	66	2.65
Turpin, Harold, DM	34	20–10	.667	259	124	79	2.74
Taylor, Howard, CR	41	19–10	.655	267	112	82	2.76
Lotz, John N., SC	33	9–6	.600	150	88	51	3.06

Individual Batting Leaders
(Minimum 340 At Bats)

	G	AB	R	H	HR	SB	RBI	Avg.
Prerost, Joseph, DA	96	390	65	133	4	14	87	.341
Prather, Argus, RI	126	435	102	140	22	8	101	.322
Luby, Hugh, SC	120	486	91	155	11	40	62	.319
Goodman, David, RI	126	478	101	152	11	30	92	.318
Howard, James, CR	127	489	90	154	18	14	96	.315

All-Star Team
1b—Argus "Dutch" Prather, Rock Island
2b—Hugh Luby, Sioux City
3b—Nick Polly, Davenport
ss—James "Skeeter" Webb, Cedar Rapids
lf—Goldie Howard, Cedar Rapids
cf—James Asbell, Des Moines
rf—Dave Goodman, Rock Island
c—William Wilson, Des Moines
rhp—Hal Turpin, Des Moines
lhp—Richard Elston, Cedar Rapids
utility—Joe Spadafore, Rock Island
manager—Cletus Dixon, Davenport

Batting Leaders
HOME RUNS
Prather, Argus, RI—22
Keyes, Stanley, DM—20
Seghl, Philip, SC—14
Asbell, James, DM—13
Howard, James, CR—13

RUNS BATTED IN
Seghl, Philip, SC—104
Prather, Argus, RI—101
Howard, James, CR—96
Goodman, David, RI—92
Prerost, Joseph, DA—87

STOLEN BASES
Luby, Hugh, SC—40
Goodman, David, RI—30
Webb, James, CR—25
DeForrest, Russell, CR—23
Catchings, Ben, DM—21

HITS
Luby, Hugh, SC—155

Seghl, Philip, SC—153
Goodman, David, RI—152
Webb, James, CR—149
Van Camp, Albert, DM—148

DOUBLES
Prerost, Joseph, DA—35
Williford, Edward, RI—34
Denning, Otto, DA—34
Goodman, David, RI—33
Piet, Frank, DM—32

TRIPLES
Goodman, David, RI—14
Van Camp, Albert, DM—14
Catchings, Ben, DM—13
Rye, Eugene, DM—13
Leach, Frank, SC—12

TOTAL BASES
Goodman, David, RI—246
Howard, James, CR—238
Prather, Argus, RI—238
Keyes, Stanley, DM—233
Seghl, Philip, SC—224

RUNS
Prather, Argus, RI—102
Goodman, David, RI—101
Webb, James, CR—97
Leach, Frank, SC—95
Schinski, John, SC—93

BASES ON BALLS
Prather, Argus, RI—79
Goodman, David, RI—68
Riley, Leon, DA—64
Schinski, John, SC—58

Pitching Leaders

GAMES
Taylor, Howard, CR—41
Ludsick, John, DM—38
Zahn, George, SC—38
Bonnetti, Julio, DM—35
Several with 34

COMPLETE GAMES
Turpin, Harold, DM—28
Taylor, Howard, CR—25
Bonnetti, Julio, DM—20

Ludsick, John, DM—20
Graf, Kinner, SC—19

BALKS
Chody, Byron, DA—2
Papish, Frank, RI—2
Several with 1

WINS
Turpin, Harold, DM—20
Taylor, Howard, CR—19
Willoughby, C.W., DA—17
VanFleet, Dwight, CR—17
Several with 16

LOSSES
Papish, Frank, RI—16
King, Donald, WA—15
Stanceu, Charles, WA—14
Bonnetti, Julio, DM—13
Several with 12

INNINGS PITCHED
Taylor, Howard, CR—267
Turpin, Harold, DM—259
Bonnetti, Julio, DM—232
Ludsick, John, DM—231
Graf, Kinner, SC—227

BASE ON BALLS
Hayes, James, CR—118
King, Donald, WA—116
Nichols, Edward, RI—111
Papish, Frank, RI—103
Wolfe, Charles, RI—90

STRIKEOUTS
Hayes, James, CR—172
Taylor, Howard, CR—134
Wolfe, Charles, RI—133
Papish, Frank, RI—125
Turpin, Harold, DM—124

WILD PITCHES
Wolfe, Charles, RI—13
Taylor, Howard, CR—10
Doljack, Joe, WA—9
Mills, Dale, RI—8
Several with 7

1937

The league was in near collapse after the 1936 season, but the owner of the Cedar Rapids club, Harry Johnson, helped to iron out problems in the league and keep it afloat for another season. The attorney, who took no salary from his own club, obtained major league contracts for four of the league clubs, including his own. Tom Fairweather, who was president of the Three-I League and Western Association, was named president following the death of McLaughlin.

Johnson's Cedar Rapids Raiders surged past Sioux City into the league lead in late May and won the first half of the season by a wide margin over Des Moines. Rock Island dropped out on July 6, and its players were sold to other teams in the league or other leagues. The Raiders faced a team of All-Stars from the rest of the league on July 7 and lost 7–4 before 3,200 fans at Cedar Rapids. President Fairweather lifted the suspension of Howard Taylor from Cedar Rapids. Taylor had charged umpire Lynn Kelly and knocked him down. With Rock Island gone, the second-half schedule had a lot of holes. The league filled in some of those gaps by playing exhibition games against teams from the Negro American League or other barnstorming teams—without much success in the win column. In one game, Davenport was thrashed 14–2 by Ray Doan's Colored All-Stars.

The second half of the season turned into a two-horse race between Cedar Rapids and Waterloo. Talk of expansion was in the air for the next season, but Davenport already had an eye on going to the Three-I League. The Raiders finished the second half with a two-game lead over Waterloo. Since Cedar Rapids had won both halves, no playoff was necessary. Instead, the Raiders faced Moline from the Three-I league for a best of five series. Moline won the first game, 10–9, while the Raiders won the second, 3–2. The third contest ended in a tie as rain was the winner after seven innings. Cedar Rapids won the next two games to close the series.

Four players from Cedar Rapids were named to the All-Star Team, as well as manager Clarence "Cap" Crossley. The Raiders' Dwight Van Fleet was named for winning the most games during the season. Michael "Shotgun" Chartak was named for his hitting abilities. He later played in the majors during the war. The Raiders also had Dykes Porter, who led the league in ERA (2.28) and strikeouts (138). And Cal Lahman led the league in homers and RBI. Davenport had several good players, too. Pitcher Oadis Swigart chalked up 14 wins. He later pitched two seasons with the Pirates. Second baseman Frank Hall was named to the All-Star team as well. Sioux City's Arnold Thesenga won 14 games during the season. He got a cup of coffee with Washington during the war.

The league came to an end after the 1937 season due to financial woes. The Great Depression had claimed another victim. Waterloo and Cedar Rapids dropped down a class to join the Three-I League, which helped that struggling league boost its membership to eight teams. Sioux City went to the Nebraska State League. Davenport, Des Moines and Rock Island fielded no teams the next season. The Class A circuit, which had once had four leagues in the 1920s, was now down to one league, as more than half of the minor leagues went out of business during the depression.

1937
Final Standings
First Half

	W	L	Pct.	GB	Affiliations
Cedar Rapids Raiders	47	18	.723	—	St. Louis Cardinals
Des Moines Demons	32	31	.508	14	St. Louis Brown
Sioux City Cowboys	31	30	.508	15	Detroit Tigers
Waterloo Reds	32	33	.492	15	None
Davenport Blue Sox	29	33	.468	17½	Brooklyn Dodgers
Rock Island Islanders	20	46	.303	27½	None

Second Half

	W	L	Pct.	GB
Cedar Rapids Raiders	31	20	.608	—
Waterloo Reds	29	22	.569	2
Davenport Blue Sox	28	26	.519	4½
Des Moines Demons	25	31	.446	8½
Sioux City Cowboys	19	33	.365	12½

Rock Island withdrew July 7

Team Batting

	AB	R	H	HR	SB	BB	SO	Avg.
Cedar Rapids	4045	751	1137	75	115	524	535	.281
Sioux City	3830	586	1051	54	124	482	538	.274
Waterloo	4028	615	1100	36	103	462	473	.273
Des Moines	4094	619	1082	56	121	534	560	.264
Rock Island	2254	286	554	21	32	266	378	.246
Davenport	3878	489	942	54	75	458	444	.245

Team Fielding

	G	DP	PB	PO	A	E	Pct.
Davenport	116	90	8	3078	1406	179	.962

A New Century, A New League (1900-1937)

	G	DP	PB	PO	A	E	Pct.
Cedar Rapids	116	81	4	3061	1232	189	.958
Des Moines	119	77	17	3124	1364	204	.957
Rock Island	66	58	8	1708	741	119	.954
Waterloo	116	89	17	3038	1387	223	.952
Sioux City	113	106	6	2867	1352	260	.942

Individual Fielding Leaders
(More Than 100 Games)

	POS	G	PO	A	E	DP	Pct.
Clarke, Gordon, DA	1b	104	1007	38	13	68	.988
Hall, Frank, DA	2b	116	277	364	30	70	.955
Backer, Leonard, WA	3b	115	134	226	19	23	.950
Kennoy, Justin, CR	ss	116	200	309	42	48	.924
Lahman, Calvin, CR	of	111	204	8	3	2	.986
Chartak, Michael, CR	of	110	261	18	9	6	.969
VanCamp, Al, DA	of	102	169	18	6	2	.969
Clark, Keith, RI	c	95	458	81	13	8	.976

Individual Batting Leaders
(Minimum 340 At Bats)

	G	AB	R	H	HR	SB	RBI	Avg.
Mack, Joe, WA	108	415	83	140	7	16	85	.337
Hall, Ed, SC	112	423	79	141	12	27	77	.333
Schinski, John, SC/RI/WA	96	376	55	123	0	14	55	.327
Lahman, Calvin, CR	112	396	87	128	22	9	101	.323
Flood, Ray, DA	113	425	95	135	18	10	78	.318

Earned Run Average
(150 Or More Innings)

	G	W–L	Pct.	IP	R	ER	ERA
Potter, William, CR	29	18–6	.750	197	65	50	2.28
Swigart, Oadis, DA	28	14–12	.538	226	86	67	2.67
VanFleet, Dwight, CR	32	22–7	.759	226	90	71	2.83
Prince, William, DA	26	14–9	.609	199	64	56	2.89
Schmidt, Guenther, WA	24	12–8	.600	171	89	56	2.95

All-Star Team

1b—Russell DeForrest, Cedar Rapids
2b—Frank Hall, Davenport
3b—Leonard Backer, Waterloo
ss—Justin Keenoy, Cedar Rapids
lf—Ray Flood, Davenport
cf—Michael Chartak, Cedar Rapids
rf—Ed Hall, Sioux City
c—Armand Payton, Des Moines
rhp—Dwight VanFleet, Cedar Rapids
lhp—Arthur McDougal, Des Moines
utility—Walter Menke, Des Moines
manager—C.F. Crossley, Cedar Rapids

Batting Leaders

HOME RUNS
Lahman, Calvin, CR—22
Flood, Ray, DA—18
Chartak, Michael, CR—15
Hall, Ed, SC—12
Martinez, Henry, DM—12

RUNS BATTED IN
Lahman, Calvin, CR—101
DeForrest, Russell, CR—86
Mack, Joe, WA—85
Flood, Ray, DA—78
Howard, James, CR—78

STOLEN BASES
Allaire, Robert, DM—34
Huff, Kenneth, SC—29
Martinez, Henry, DM—28
Hall, Ed, SC—27
DeForrest, Russell, CR—22

HITS
Howard, James, CR—142
Hall, Ed, SC—141
Mack, Joe, WA—140
Flood, Ray, DA—135
Chartak, Michael, CR—133

DOUBLES
Backer, Leonard, WA—32
Chartak, Michael, CR—31
Lahman, Calvin, CR—31
Flood, Ray, DA—28
Several with 26

TRIPLES
Flood, Ray, DA—16
Mack, Joe, WA—14
Chartak, Michael, CR—14
Several with 12

TOTAL BASES
Flood, Ray, DA—249
Chartak, Michael, CR—237
Lahman, Calvin, CR—237
Hall, Ed, SC—221
Mack, Joe, WA—212

RUNS
Chartak, Michael, CR—113
Howard, James, CR—102
Flood, Ray, DA—95
Allaire, Robert, DM—94
Lahman, Calvin, CR—87

BASES ON BALLS
Hughes, Harry, DM—109
Allaire, Robert, DM—95
Chartak, Michael, CR—95
Lahman, Calvin, CR—93
Monahan, Peter, SC—79

STRIKEOUTS
Martinez, Henry, DM—107
Huff, Kenneth, SC—100
Keenoy, Justin, CR—87
Getting, Fritz, RI—68
Chartak, Michael, CR—67

Pitching Leaders

GAMES
Gebo, Gilbert, DM—36
Hemenway, Emil, WA—34
VanFleet, Dwight, CR—32
Thesenga, Arnold, SC—31
McDougall, Arthur, DM—30

COMPLETE GAMES
McDougall, Arthur, DM—24
Swigart, Oadis, DA—22
VanFleet, Dwight, CR—19
Prince, William, DA—18
Pyle, Ewald, DM—18

BALKS
Schmidt, Guenther, WA—4
Bastien, Edward, WA—3
Several with 2

WINS
VanFleet, Dwight, CR—22
Potter, William, CR—18
McDougall, Arthur, DM—16
Several with 14

LOSSES
Gebo, Gilbert, DM—15
Cauble, Vance, RI—13
LeGault, Steve, WA—13
Several with 12

INNINGS PITCHED
McDougall, Arthur, DM—233
Swigart, Oadis, DA—226
VanFleet, Dwight, CR—226
Gebo, Gilbert, DM—216
Prince, William, DA—199

BASE ON BALLS
Hayes, James, CR—126
Helser, Roy, WA—115
Bastien, Edward, WA—107
Cauble, Vance, RI—104
Finck, Lloyd, DM—101

STRIKEOUTS
Potter, William, CR—138
Krupski, Al, CR—130
Swigart, Oadis, DA—129
VanFleet, Dwight, CR—125
Several with 111

WILD PITCHES
Elston, Richard, CR—16
McDougall, Arthur, DM—14
Gebo, Gilbert, DM—12
Pyle, Ewald, DM—12
Cauble, Vance, RI—11

5
Class D Era (1939–1941)

In 1939 the Nebraska State League, which had been operating continuously since 1928, changed its name to the Western League and continued operation as a Class D league. J. Roy Carter was the president. The league had six teams. Sioux City and Lincoln were the only cities in the league that came from the old Western League. The other teams were the Mitchell Kernels, Norfolk Elks, Sioux Falls Canaries and Worthington Cardinals. All of the teams were farm clubs of the majors except Mitchell.

Few players from these teams ever made it to the major leagues. (However, even taking all Class D teams together, only about one in ten players made it to the majors.) The Class D leagues of yesteryear are comparable to the rookie leagues of today.

1939

The season got under way on May 11 with Sioux City at Lincoln before 1,000 shivering fans. Sioux City beat the Links, 4–2. On the same day, the 1938 champion Norfolk Elks whipped Worthington, 25–16. Norfolk continued its winning ways throughout the season and won the pennant by a wide margin. The Cowboys, who finished third in the regular season, edged Norfolk in the first round of the playoffs and won the finals over Lincoln.

Norfolk fielded the leading home run hitter, William Morgan, and leading hitter, Wendell Finders. Both were named to the All-Star Team. Lincoln's John Miller led the league in wins (21) and strikeouts (208).

1939 All-Star Team

of - Ed Wernet

of - William Morgan   of - Hans Krueger

2b - Wendell Finders

ss - Floyd McDaniel

3b - Ted Kakaloris   p - John Miller   1b - Pete Monahan
                     Leonard Bobeck

utility - Gottlieb Leipelt   manager - Elmer "Doc" Bennett

c - Karl Hower

1939
Final Standings

	W	L	Pct.	GB	Affiliations
Norfolk Elks	75	44	.630	—	New York Yankees
Sioux Falls Canaries	66	52	.559	8½	Chicago Cubs
Sioux City Cowboys	63	52	.548	10	Detroit Tigers
Lincoln Links	64	55	.538	11	St. Louis Browns
Mitchell Kernels	49	69	.415	25½	None
Worthington Cardinals	36	81	.308	38	St. Louis Cardinals

Playoffs

Sioux City defeated Norfolk, three games to two.
Lincoln defeated Sioux Falls, three games to two.

Finals

Sioux City defeated Lincoln, four games to two.

Team Batting

	R	H	RBI	Avg.
Lincoln	834	1256	684	.295

	R	H	RBI	Avg.
Sioux Falls	776	1183	676	.284
Norfolk	783	1191	655	.281
Sioux City	747	1085	642	.279
Worthington	677	1137	547	.274
Mitchell	613	982	544	.252

Team Fielding

	PO	A	E	DP	Pct.
Sioux Falls	3119	1349	258	80	.945
Sioux City	2908	1379	258	92	.943
Mitchell	2983	1430	271	68	.942
Norfolk	3137	1333	279	85	.941
Lincoln	3113	1322	278	90	.941
Worthington	2937	1342	351	77	.924

Individual Batting Leaders
(Minimum 340 At Bats)

	G	AB	R	H	Avg.
Connors, Howard, WO	82	362	62	132	.365
Wernet, Ed, SF	94	354	86	128	.362
Krueger, Hans, LI	109	463	92	161	.348
Morgan, William, NO	119	468	125	160	.342
Kakaloris, Ted, LI	119	486	107	166	.342

Individual Fielding Leaders
(More Than 100 Games)

	POS	G	PO	A	E	Pct.
Tucker, SF	1b	110	966	62	17	.974
Finders, NO	2b	119	382	362	30	.960
Earl, SF	3b	112	112	185	38	.886
Hennessy, SF	ss	104	224	285	62	.891
Dyke, SF	of	112	194	8	9	.962
Krueger, LI	of	109	167	7	7	.961
Morgan, NO	of	119	266	12	13	.956
Hower, NO	c	114	752	64	12	.985

Individual Pitching Leaders
(150 or More Innings)

	G	W–L	Pct.	IP
Bobeck, NO	29	19–3	.864	207
Scott, SF	26	17–6	.760	192
Kempe, SF	33	19–7	.731	227
Davis, NO	30	16–9	.640	166
Miller, LI	40	21–12	.636	257

HOME RUNS
William Morgan, NO—17

RUNS BATTED IN
Ted Kakaloris, LI—114

HITS
Wendell Finders, NO—167

RUNS
Bob Dillinger, LI—139

ERA
Lawrence Kempe, SF—3.02

WINS
John Miller, LI—21

LOSSES
Phipps, WO—15

INNINGS PITCHED
John Miller, LI—257

STRIKEOUTS
John Miller, LI—208

All-Star Team

1b—Pete Monahan, Sioux City
2b—Wendell Finders, Norfolk
3b—Ted Kakaloris, Lincoln
ss—Floyd McDaniel, Lincoln
of—Ed Wernet, Sioux Falls
of—William Morgan, Norfolk
of—Hans Krueger, Lincoln
c—Karl Hower, Norfolk
utility—Gottlieb Leipelt, Mitchell
p—John Miller, Lincoln
p—Leonard Bobeck, Norfolk
manager—Elmer "Doc" Bennett, Norfolk

1940

Lincoln and Mitchell dropped from the league, which reduced it to four teams. Sioux City then moved to Mitchell on July 24. The league

1940 All-Star Team

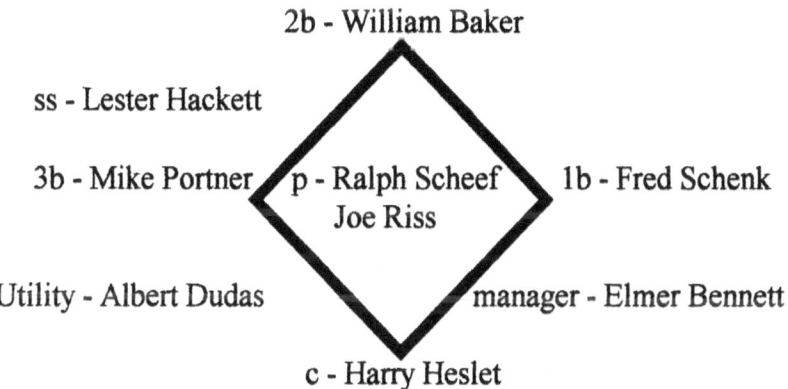

of - Tony Koenig

of - Russell Burns   of - John Lucas

2b - William Baker

ss - Lester Hackett

3b - Mike Portner   p - Ralph Scheef   1b - Fred Schenk
                     Joe Riss

Utility - Albert Dudas   manager - Elmer Bennett

c - Harry Heslet

schedule was played in four quarters. Norfolk won the first, second and fourth quarter, with Sioux Falls winning the third quarter. The Norfolk Yankees also finished the regular season by winning eight in a row. Unfortunately, that momentum fizzled in the playoffs as Sioux Falls upset the Yankees four games to two. Sioux Falls had finished a distant second in the regular season by losing six of their last seven games.

Frank Wagner of Sioux Falls came within one batter of a perfect game on August 30 when a Mitchell hitter reached first on an error. Wagner led the league in both wins and strikeouts.

Norfolk had three quarters of the infield on the All-Star Team. The Yankees also had the leading home run leader, Russell Burns, with 17 dingers.

1940

Final Standings

	W	L	Pct.	GB	Affiliations
Norfolk Yankees	73	39	.652	—	New York Yankees
Sioux Falls Canaries	59	58	.504	16½	None
Worthington Cardinals	50	59	.459	21½	St. Louis Cardinals
Sioux City Soos/Mitchell Kernels	44	70	.386	30	None

Playoffs

Sioux Falls defeated Norfolk, four games to two.

Team Batting

	AB	R	H	HR	SB	BB	SO	Avg.
Norfolk	4035	774	1181	59	163	444	645	.292
Sioux Falls	4152	613	1113	27	136	479	673	.268
Worthington	3878	557	1018	25	97	410	722	.263
Mitchell	3941	487	1030	33	76	436	688	.261

Team Fielding

	G	PO	A	E	DP	PB	Pct.
Norfolk	113	2962	1236	238	89	30	.948
Mitchell	115	3023	1489	265	94	11	.944
Sioux Falls	118	3082	1434	288	77	13	.940
Worthington	110	2893	1233	307	81	23	.931

Individual Batting Leaders
(Minimum 355 At Bats)

	G	AB	R	H	HR	SB	RBI	Avg.
Lucas, John, WO	105	419	81	149	6	27	70	.356

Class D Era (1939–1941)

	G	AB	R	H	HR	SB	RBI	Avg.
Koenig, Tony, SF	118	431	99	144	7	52	77	.334
Connors, Howard, SF	95	380	65	126	5	7	47	.332
Burns, Russel, NO	113	437	93	144	17	25	87	.330
Dugy, Robert, NO	111	477	112	154	5	17	62	.323

Individual Fielding Leaders
(More Than 90 Games)

	POS	G	PO	A	E	DP	Pct.
Schenk, NO	1b	113	1017	56	31	79	.972
Baker, NO	2b	113	260	321	48	62	.923
Earl, SF	3b	118	124	225	26	11	.931
Hodan, SF	ss	115	242	295	46	51	.921
Lucas, WO	lf	105	163	14	6	2	.962
Bocek, NO	cf	111	193	17	4	2	.981
Duby, NO	rf	111	140	8	6	1	.959
Fenner, SF	c	90	528	75	2	8	.996

Earned Run Average Leaders
(150 Or More Innings)

	G	W	L	Pct.	IP	R	ER	ERA
Wagner, SF	38	17	10	.630	232	81	54	2.10
Davis, NO	27	15	8	.652	198	77	53	2.41
Riss, WO/SF	25	15	5	.750	173	61	52	2.71
Sterling, NO	28	14	6	.700	176	78	53	2.71
Scheff, WO	33	14	6	.700	215	95	67	2.81

All-Star Team

1b—Fred Schenk, Norfolk
2b—William Baker, Norfolk
3b—Mike Portner, Norfolk
ss—Lester Hackett, Worthington
of—Russell Burns, Norfolk
of—Tony Koenig, Sioux Falls
of—John Lucas, Worthington
c—Harry Heslet, Norfolk
Utility—Albert Dudas, Worthington
p—Ralph Scheef, Worthington
p—Joe Riss, Sioux Falls
manager—Elmer "Doc" Bennett, Norfolk

Batting Leaders

HOME RUNS
Burns, Russel, NO—17
Heslet, Harry, NO—9
Schenk, Fred, NO—9
Grayston, Ed, MI—8
Several with 7

RUNS BATTED IN
Schenk, Fred, NO—97
Burns, Russel, NO—87
Koenig, Tony, SF—77
Lucas, John, WO—70
Several with 66

STOLEN BASES
Koenig, Tony, SF—52
Bohanan, Leo, SF—34
Baker, William, NO—27
Lucas, John, WO—27
Portner, Mike, NO—24

HITS
Bohanan, Leo, SF—158

Dugy, Robert, NO -154
Baker, William, NO—152
Lucas, John, WO—149
Several with 144
DOUBLES
Burns, Russel, NO—25
Dudas, Albert, WO—25
Baker, William, NO—23
Bohanan, Leo, SF—23
White, Clyde, MI—22
TRIPLES
Burns, Russel, NO—13
Lucas, John, WO—13
Bohanan, Leo, SF—12
Schenk, Fred, NO—12
Enger, Gordon, WO—9
TOTAL BASES
Burns, Russel, NO—246
Bohanan, Leo, SF—217
Lucas, John, WO—207
Schenk, Fred, NO—205
Koenig, Tony, SF—199
RUNS
Dugy, Robert, NO—112
Koenig, Tony, SF—99
Bohanan, Leo, SF—94
Baker, William, NO—93
Burns, Russel, NO—93
BASES ON BALLS
Fenner, Robert, SF—105
Koenig, Tony, SF—86
Burns, Russel, NO—65
Crider, Orrin, SF—61
Portner, Mike, NO—60
STRIKEOUTS
Hodan, Arthur, SF—112
Burns, Russel, NO—107
Perry, Paul, MI—90
Loewe, Harold, NO—85
Lucas, John, WO—70

Pitching Leaders

GAMES
Wagner, SF—38
Wehde, MI—38
Lindsey, MI—33
Scheff, WO—33
Papei, WO—31
WINS
Wagner, SF—17
Davis, NO—15
Riss, WO/SF—15
Sterling, NO—14
Scheff, WO—14
LOSSES
Lindsey, MI—15
Nelson, WO—13
Perry, MI—12
Johnson, SF—11
Papei, WO—10
INNINGS PITCHED
Wagner, SF—232
Scheff, WO—215
Davis, NO—198
Sterling, NO—176
Riss, WO/SF—173
BASE ON BALLS
McEntee, SF—98
Sterling, NO—92
England, SF—83
Perry, MI—74
Scheff, WO—72
STRIKEOUTS
Wagner, SF—193
Sterling, NO—174
Scheff, NO—174
Riss, WO/SF—159
Davis, NO—139
WILD PITCHES
England, SF—20
Several with 8

1941

The four quarters were gone in favor of a straight schedule with playoffs at the end of the season. Norfolk was again the team to beat and finished two and a half games ahead of Cheyenne.

In the playoffs Norfolk beat third-place Sioux City three games to two to advance to the finals against fourth-place Pueblo, who had defeated Cheyenne by the same margin. Mother Nature gave the Pueblo Rollers the championship. Pueblo was leading the series three games to two when torrential rains turned the Norfolk diamond into a lake and made play impossible for several days. The teams had agreed not to extend the playoffs beyond September 15, so Pueblo was awarded the crown. The Rollers had been the hottest team in the second half of the season and carried that forward into the playoffs. Pueblo's Bernard Steele led the league in batting average (.383), runs scored (188) and hits (158). The first baseman was named to the All-Star Team as well.

On December 7, 1941, the Japanese bombed Pearl Harbor. The Western League became one of the first casualties of the war as play was suspended for several seasons. In fact, many minor leagues followed suit until the war was over.

1941 All-Star Team

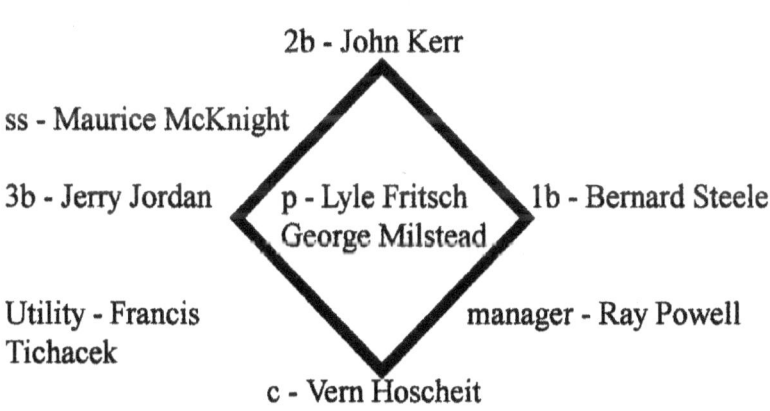

of - Orin Crider

of - Frank Bocek   of - Albert Dudas

2b - John Kerr

ss - Maurice McKnight

3b - Jerry Jordan   p - Lyle Fritsch / George Milstead   1b - Bernard Steele

Utility - Francis Tichacek   manager - Ray Powell

c - Vern Hoscheit

1941
Final Standings

	W	L	Pct.	GB	Affiliations
Norfolk Yankees	64	44	.593	—	New York Yankees

	W	L	Pct.	GB	Affiliations
Cheyenne Indians	59	44	.573	2½	None
Sioux City Soos	54	56	.491	11	St. Louis Cardinals
Pueblo Rollers	52	54	.491	11	St. Louis Browns
Sioux Falls Canaries	51	56	.477	12½	None
Denver Bears	42	68	.382	23½	None

Playoffs

Norfolk defeated Sioux City, three games to two.
Pueblo defeated Cheyenne, three games to two.

Finals

Pueblo defeated Norfolk, three games to two.

Team Batting

	AB	R	H	HR	SB	BB	SO	Avg.
Norfolk	3704	611	1009	39	128	487	589	.272
Pueblo	3658	570	985	15	97	463	533	.269
Cheyenne	3603	626	929	46	110	484	562	.256
Denver	3673	529	892	19	118	437	668	.243
Sioux Falls	3462	489	839	7	164	511	556	.242
Sioux City	3789	455	859	9	133	445	644	.227

Team Fielding

	G	DP	PB	PO	A	E	Pct.
Cheyenne	103	88	26	2767	1326	179	.956
Norfolk	108	59	32	2840	1195	221	.948
Sioux City	110	98	31	2926	1331	245	.946
Pueblo	106	85	34	2744	1275	241	.943
Denver	110	82	27	2799	1258	260	.940
Sioux Falls	107	76	34	2766	1180	281	.934

Individual Batting Leaders
(Minimum 335 At Bats)

	G	AB	R	H	HR	SB	RBI	Avg.
Bernard Steele, PU	102	412	88	158	3	22	87	.383
Frank Bocek, NO	101	397	86	137	8	15	92	.345
Mike Kowal, PU	91	356	50	109	2	20	74	.306
Gene Ready, NO	104	377	74	113	8	11	62	.300
Fred Hanis, NO	107	394	61	118	2	16	66	.299

Individual Fielding Leaders
(More Than 100 Games)

	POS	G	PO	A	E	DP	Pct.
Robert Benish, SC	1b	110	1018	46	15	85	.986

Class D Era (1939–1941)

	POS	G	PO	A	E	DP	Pct.
John Kerr, CH	2b	96	305	308	25	63	.961
Fred Hanis, NO	3b	102	129	175	28	12	.920
Maurice McKnight, CH	ss	103	196	351	31	58	.946
Mike Kowal, PU	of	91	185	2	2	1	.989
Carlisle Kopp, SC	of	104	177	6	4	1	.979
Dick Murphy, PU	of	104	163	10	5	3	.972
Richard Tichacek, SC	c	84	458	59	13	10	.975

Earned Run Average Leaders
(150 Or More Innings)

	G	W-L	Pct.	IP	R	ER	ERA
Frank Wagner, SF	40	11–18	.379	238	107	57	2.15
George Milstead, CH	25	19–5	.792	217	77	55	2.28
Clinton Wise, SC	25	8–12	.400	182	80	48	2.37
Robert Bergin, PU	37	16–10	.615	206	95	59	2.57
Ralph Rosengarten, NO	31	15–5	.750	181	86	52	2.58

All-Star Team
1b—Bernard Steele, Pueblo
2b—John Kerr, Cheyenne
3b—Jerry Jordan, Cheyenne
ss—Maurice McKnight, Cheyenne
of—Orin Crider, Sioux City
of—Frank Bocek, Norfolk
of—Albert Dudas, Sioux City
c—Vern Hoscheit, Norfolk
Utility—Francis Tichacek, Sioux City
p—Lyle Fritsch, Sioux City
p—George Milstead, Cheyenne
manager—Ray Powell

Batting Leaders
HOME RUNS
Babe Alford, NO—10
Mel Bergman, CH—10
John Metz, CH—10
Several with 8

RUNS BATTED IN
Frank Bocek, NO—92
Bernard Steele, PU—87
Jerry Jordan, CH—74
Mike Kowal, PU—74
Fred Hanis, NO—66

STOLEN BASES
Tony Keonig, SC—42

John Kerr, CH—29
Orin Crider, SC—28
Carlisle Kopp, SC—27
Harold Bradley, DE—25

HITS
Bernard Steele, PU—158
Frank Bocek, NO—137
Jerry Jordan, CH—132
Harold Bradley, DE—118
Fred Hanis, NO—118

DOUBLES
Frank Bocek, NO—25
Bernard Steele, PU—24
Albert Dudas, SC—21
James Griffin, NO—21
Joe Muffoletto, NO—20

TRIPLES
Frank Bocek, NO—20
Harold Wilson, PU—15
Bernard Steele, PU—14
Babe Alford, NO—10
Harold Bradley, DE—10
Dick Murphy, PU—10
Lester Newkirk, CH—10

TOTAL BASES
Frank Bocek, NO—226
Bernard Steele, PU—219

Jerry Jordan, CH—178
Harold Wilson, PU—165
Mel Bergman, CH—161

RUNS
Bernard Steele, PU—88
Frank Bocek, NO—86
William Haddican, DE—86
James Griffin, NO—85
Dick Murphy, PU—83

BASES ON BALLS
William Haddican, DE—91
John Metz, CH—80
Gene Ready, NO—78
Dick Murphy, PU—72
Several with 68

STRIKEOUTS
Babe Alford, NO—82
John Metz, CH—82
Joe Muffoletto, NO—81
Mel Bergman, CH—80
Several with 71

GAMES
Frank Wagner, SF—40
Robert Bergin, PU—37
James Cleghorn, DE—37
William Evans, CH—33
Several with 32

COMPLETE GAMES
George Milstead, CH—22
Robert Bergin, PU—19
James Cleghorn, DE—19
Joe Riss, SC—18
Frank Wagner, SF—18

BALKS
Meyer Buntz, NO—2
Gene Byrd, DE—2
James Dyck, NO—2

Max England, SF—2
John Riley, PU—2

WINS
George Milstead, CH—19
Robert Bergin, PU—16
James Cleghorn, DE—13
Joe Riss, SC—13
Walter Nasalik, NO—13

LOSSES
Frank Wagner, SF—18
James Cleghorn, DE—13
John Riley, PU—13
William Evans, CH—13
Several with 12

INNINGS PITCHED
Frank Wagner, SF—238
James Cleghorn, DE—219
George Milstead, CH—217
Robert Bergin, PU—206
Joe Riss, SC—192

BASE ON BALLS
Max England, SF—141
James Cleghorn, DE—136
Joe Riss, SC—116
William Evans, CH -113
Several with 100

STRIKEOUTS
Robert Bergin, PU—183
Joe Riss, SC—168
Robert Larson, DE—166
Walter Nasalik, NO—143
Max England, SF -142

WILD PITCHES
Max England, SF—21
Robert Bergin, PU—13
Joe Riss, SC—11
Leon Fiderlick, NO—11
Several with 9

6
After the War (1947–1958)

The Second World War ended in 1945, but it wasn't until 1947 that the Western League began again. The league came back with a Class A status. The energetic and ambitious U.S. Senator Edward C. Johnson from Colorado was named as president. Franchises were awarded in Denver, Des Moines, Lincoln, Omaha, Pueblo and Sioux City. Denver hadn't had a professional team in 15 years. Each of the teams had major league affiliations, too. One-hundred-and-forty games were scheduled.

The revived league caught a couple of clubs without fields to play on, so a mad scramble ensued to get ready for the season. The lack of fields resulted in a delay in the playing schedule, which was sort of like putting dessert before the meal. Both Lincoln and Des Moines were starting from scratch and had to rely on their local communities to build parks for their teams. Lincoln fans threatened an injunction to prevent the club and city from building a new park at one locale, so another site had to be picked before construction began. Omaha rented an American Legion stadium across the Missouri River in Council Bluffs and played home games there while a stadium was being built in Omaha.

Concerned about gambling, league officials decided not to allow players to mingle with fans before, during or after games, except for the press and club officials. The rule proved hard to enforce, however. The league had a salary limit of $5,700 and a player limit of 19 per squad.

Johnson Revives Western League

When the Western League named Edwin C. Johnson as its president in 1947, it chose an experienced politician. The former governor of Colorado had been a United States senator since 1936. Johnson set out to revive the league in 1946, so he was the natural choice as its new president. "I have no money to put in the venture, but I will give everything I have—time, and effort and hard work," he said. It took him six months.

Johnson played baseball in high school and became an avid fan of the game. He also knew baseball law. "Baseball is the perfect example of the American way of life," he maintained. "It is democracy in operation. I have grown to love the game."

Johnson remained as president of the league for eight seasons. During his reign he insisted on competent umpiring and responsible behavior on the field.

1947

The Sioux City Soos cruised to the league pennant in 1947. The Shaughnessy playoffs were a totally different story. Sioux City beat fourth-place Omaha in the first round, while third-place Pueblo whipped Des Moines. In the seven-game finale, Pueblo upset the Soos four games to one. Pueblo was managed by Walter Alston, who would go on to lead the Dodgers to seven World Series appearances and four world championships. Pueblo's Preston Ward led the league in runs scored and RBI. The first baseman went to the majors the next season and played nine seasons there with five different teams. The Dodgers also had outfielder Carmen Mauro, who went on to four years in the majors with four teams.

Manager Joe Becker, who played two seasons for the Cleveland Indi-

The Sioux City Soos won the Western League pennant in 1947. The players were: (first row, from left) Werener Strunk, John Uber, Joseph Ahearn, Edward Martin, Sam Webb, John Niggeling, Joseph Becker, Larry Miggins, Nick Andrimidas; (second row, from left) Ed Wagner, Frank Turci, Dave Garcia, Mel Harpuda, Ray Carlson, John Metkovitch, Tony Jaros, Don Schoenborn and Don Weeler. Sitting in front is batboy Allan Desmond. (Photograph courtesy of the National Baseball Hall of Fame, Cooperstown, N.Y.)

ans, guided Sioux City to the pennant. The Soos also had Sam "Red" Webb, the winningest pitcher in the league, with 19 victories. Webb's talents were recognized with a contract with the New York Giants for two seasons. And the Soos had Tony Jaros, who led the league in homers (24). Des Moines was led by talented pitcher Herb Chmiel, with his 14 victories, and Les Peden, who hit for the cycle once during the season. Peden got a trial with the Washington Senators a few years later. Clifford Aberson powered the Des Moines Bruins with 20 homers. That power led him to the Cubs for three seasons, where he found the home run harder to hit. Omaha's Eddie Kazak got the call from St. Louis the next season, and he became their regular third baseman for a couple of years. In all, he spent five years in the majors. Another Omaha player who put some time in the majors was John Bucha. The catcher played three seasons with St. Louis and Detroit. Pitcher John Crimian, who won 14 games that season, also got a call to the majors, but he never achieved success, as he was 5–9 in four seasons with Detroit, Kansas City and the St. Louis Cardinals. Omaha's Charlie Bishop led the league in strikeouts with 133, which helped lead him to the majors in 1952 for four seasons.

During the season a strange-but-true play occurred. Omaha was playing at Council Bluffs. Omaha's Ed Lewinski hit a shot to left field that appeared to go over the high screen in left, but as he turned toward second base he saw a ball headed to the infield. He held up at second. Fans began screaming at the umps. Leftfielder Joe King had hidden a baseball in his uniform and threw it against the wall in hopes that everyone thought it was the hit ball. The trickery worked—except for a couple of eagle-eyed fans. Lewinski was awarded a home run, and King was fined $50 by the league president.

In the first season, Lincoln managed to attract 43,000 fans, as people were slow to return to the park. By the next season, Lincoln had more than doubled their attendance figures.

1947

Final Standings

	W	L	Pct.	GB	Affiliations
Sioux City Soos	81	49	.623	—	New York Giants
Des Moines Bruins	75	52	.591	4½	Chicago Cubs
Pueblo Dodgers	70	58	.547	10	Brooklyn Dodgers
Omaha Cardinals	67	62	.519	13½	St. Louis Cardinals
Denver Bears	54	75	.419	21½	New York Yankees
Lincoln Athletics	38	89	.299	36½	Philadelphia Athletics

Playoffs

Sioux City defeated Omaha, three games to one.
Pueblo defeated Des Moines, three games to one.

Finals

Pueblo defeated Sioux City, four games to one.

Team Batting

	AB	R	H	HR	BB	SO	SB	Avg.
Pueblo	4459	820	1247	60	610	663	78	.280
Omaha	4362	736	1211	64	500	463	63	.278
Des Moines	4373	770	1204	87	557	670	85	.275
Sioux City	4369	664	1167	93	500	816	94	.267
Denver	4344	678	1117	58	563	745	63	.257
Lincoln	4013	469	910	23	511	582	54	.227

Team Fielding

	G	DP	PB	PO	A	E	Pct.
Pueblo	129	127	19	3319	1470	212	.958
Sioux City	130	106	15	3372	1449	228	.955
Omaha	131	125	23	3335	1450	232	.954
Des Moines	129	97	24	3339	1465	246	.951
Lincoln	127	100	21	3134	1392	237	.950
Denver	130	111	22	3334	1459	304	.940

Individual Fielding Leaders
(More Than 100 Games)

	POS	G	PO	A	E	DP	Pct.
Ward, Preston, PU	1b	125	1067	76	17	110	.985
Bundy, Robert, PU	2b	111	305	305	30	71	.953
Henningsen, Raymond, OM	3b	114	117	208	17	24	.950
Genovese, George, OM	ss	112	220	561	44	77	.947
Conroy, Michael, OM	of	101	183	9	3	2	.985
Krage, Edward, PU	of	121	234	9	5	1	.980
Cherry, Robert, DE	of	114	166	16	6	4	.968
Wheeler, Donald, SC	c	111	578	66	9	12	.986

Individual Batting Leaders
(Minimum 403 At Bats)

	G	AB	R	H	HR	SB	RBI	Avg.
Lewinski, Edmund, OM	114	439	79	152	13	0	105	.346
Conroy, Michael, OM	131	555	117	190	0	24	55	.342

After the War (1947–1958)

	G	AB	R	H	HR	SB	RBI	Avg.
Clarkson, Reginald, PU	125	508	112	170	5	8	65	.335
Ward, Preston, PU	125	465	120	151	17	5	121	.325
Peden, Leslie, DM	124	486	107	157	18	5	106	.323

Earned Run Average Leaders
(154 Or More Innings)

	G	W-L	Pct.	IP	R	ER	ERA
Crimian, John, OM	33	14–9	.609	173	67	55	2.86
Webb, Samuel, SC	31	19–7	.731	201	94	68	3.04
Uber, John, SC	29	14–7	.667	165	81	60	3.27
Harris, Charles, LI	23	10–11	.476	174	78	65	3.36
Kuhlman, Robert, DM	28	10–8	.556	168	82	63	3.38

All-Star Team
1b—Preston Ward, Pueblo
2b—Eddie Kazak, Omaha
3b—Les Peden, Des Moines
ss—Ray Carlson, Sioux City
of—Michael Conroy, Omaha
of—Carmen Mauro, Des Moines
of—Reggie Clarkson, Pueblo
c—John Bucha, Omaha
utility—Ray Henningsen, Omaha
utility—Russ Burns, Des Moines
p—Sam Webb, Sioux City
p—Herb Chmiel, Des Moines
manager—Joe Becker, Sioux City

Attendance
Des Moines—152,027
Omaha—138,308
Denver—124,923
Sioux City—113,036
Pueblo—80,163
Lincoln—43,464

Batting Leaders
HOME RUNS
Jaros, Anthony, SC—24
Aberson, Clifford, DM—20
Kazak, Edward, OM—20
Peden, Leslie, DM—18
Ward, Preston, PU—17

RUNS BATTED IN
Ward, Preston, PU—121
Peden, Leslie, DM—106
Lewinski, Edmund, OM—105
Jaros, Anthony, SC—94
Badgett, Paul, DE—90

STOLEN BASES
Martin, Edward, SC—25
Conroy, Michael, OM—24
Harpuder, Melvin, SC—21
Vernillo, John, LI—20
Burgess, William, DE—17

HITS
Conroy, Michael, OM—190
Clarkson, Reginald, PU—170
Garcia, David, SC—157
Peden, Leslie, DM—157
Lewinski, Edmund, OM—152

DOUBLES
Lewinski, Edmund, OM—37
Clarkson, Reginald, PU—36
Peden, Leslie, DM—33
Ward, Preston, PU—30
Several with 27

TRIPLES
Ward, Preston, PU—21
Kamler, Richard, OM—16
Conroy, Michael, OM 14
Clarkson, Reginald, PU—12
Mauro, Carmen, DM—12

TOTAL BASES
Ward, Preston, PU—274
Peden, Leslie, DM—258
Jaros, Anthony, SC—257
Lewinski, Edmund, OM—250
Several with 245

RUNS
Ward, Preston, PU—120
Conroy, Michael, OM—117
Clarkson, Reginald, PU—112
Mauro, Carmen, DM—107
Peden, Leslie, DM—107

BASES ON BALLS
Henningsen, Raymond, OM—103
Harpuder, Melvin, SC—101
Ward, Preston, PU—98
Crawford, Duane, DE—97
Krage, Edward, PU—95

STRIKEOUTS
Metkovich, John, SC—107
Palmer, Jack, DE—107
Garcia, David, SC—89
Carlson, Raymond, SC—81
Cherry, Robert, DE—81

Pitching Leaders

GAMES
Johnson, R., DE—49
Melignano, Carmine, DE—41
Alexander, Robert, DE—36
Jacobs, Anthony, DM—35
Several with 34

COMPLETE GAMES
Alexander, Robert, DE—17
Webb, Samuel, SC—17
Chimiel, Herb, DM—15
Several with 14

SHUTOUTS
Bonness, William, DM—3
Harris, Charles, LI—3
Strunk, Werner, SC—3
Several with 2

WINS
Webb, Samuel, SC—19
Shepard, William, PU—15
Chimiel, Herb, DM—14
Crimian, John, OM—14
Uber, John, SC—14

LOSSES
Melignano, Carmine, DE—14
Brightwell, William, PU—13
Alexander, Robert, DE—12
Bender, Sheldon, LI—12
Revels, Robert, DE—12

INNINGS PITCHED
Alexander, Robert, DE—219
Webb, Samuel, SC—201
Shepard, William, PU—194
Lown, Omar, PU—190
Schoenborn, Donald, SC—181

BASE ON BALLS
Lown, Omar, PU—133
McCullough, Wilbur, OM—113
Kuhlman, Robert, DM—110
Bishop, Charles, OM—107
Shepard, William, PU—95

STRIKEOUTS
Bishop, Charles, OM—133
Lown, Omar, PU—129
Alexander, Robert, DE—128
Schallock, Arthur, PU—117
Several with 105

WILD PITCHES
Revels, Robert, DE—17
Bishop, Charles, OM—15
Melrvin, Calvin, LI—15
Several with 14

1948

In 1948 Omaha continued to play in Council Bluffs, pending completion of its beautiful new home, the million-dollar Omaha Municipal Stadium, a park of Class AAA caliber. Denver also completed a new stadium in August.

The Des Moines Bruins took the pennant ahead of the Denver Bears.

After the War (1947–1958)

Denver played in Bears Stadium in 1948, but the stadium later became known as Mile High Stadium and the home of the Denver Broncos. (Photograph courtesy of Jay Sanford)

Both teams attracted more than 200,000 fans. In fact, the Bears set the league attendance record with a crowd of 12,752 on September 3. Sioux City and Lincoln tied for third place, so a one-game playoff was played to determine playoff positions. The Soos blanked the Athletics 6–0 to earn third place. After knocking off Denver in the first round, Sioux City again faced Lincoln in the finals of the playoffs after the Athletics eliminated first-place Des Moines. The Soos continued their dominance of the Athletics and won the finale four games to two.

Des Moines was helped both by players coming up to the majors and going down from there. For example, Leon "Red" Treadway had played for the New York Giants for two years during the war, so he had some much needed experience to help the new players. The leading pitcher in 1948 was Anthony Jacobs, who received a brief trial in the majors with the Cubs and Cardinals. Denver's Maury Donovan hit for the cycle in a game against Lincoln.

Lincoln was led in 1948 by pitcher Bobby Shantz, who racked up a league-leading 18 victories and led the league in strikeouts with his great curveball. Plus, he had great control. In one game at Des Moines he threw only 17 called balls in nine innings. His stellar performance was rewarded by a promotion to the majors the following season with the Philadelphia Athletics. In 1952 he pulled off 11 straight wins to give him a 24–7 record on the season with the Athletics. The next season the lefty suffered an arm

Manager Mike Gazella argues a call with umpire Russ Kimpel during a 1948 contest. (Photograph courtesy of Jay Sanford)

injury which turned him into a relief pitcher. In all, he pitched for 16 more seasons in the majors, winning more than 100 games and playing in two World Series with the New York Giants.

Swats Hits Nine Dingers in Nine Days!

Carl "Swats" Sawatski led the league in homers with 29 in 1948. His hottest streak came in July when he hit nine homers in nine days. And on August 28 he drove in seven runs in one game! He played another season for Des Moines before getting a call from the Cubs.

Swats had a roller coaster career between the majors and minors. He was sent back to the minors for the 1951 and 1952 seasons before the Cubs brought him back in 1953. Then he was dealt to the White Sox for a season. He was back in the minors in 1955 and 1956. He went to Milwaukee for the 1957 season and got to play in the World Series. The following season he was traded after 10 games to the Philadelphia Phillies, where he became the regular catcher. Philadelphia traded him to St. Louis and he played there for four seasons.

Carl "Swats" Sawatski caught for the Des Moines Bruins in 1948 before he went on to an 11-year major league career. (Photograph courtesy of Jay Sanford)

In all, Sawatski played 633 major league games over 11 seasons with a career .242 batting average. He also swatted 58 homers.

Mighty Mite Played for Lincoln

Lincoln's Nellie Fox was named to the All-Star Team in 1948, which earned him a call up to Philadelphia. The Athletics dealt "Mighty Mite" to the White Sox, where he flourished.

In 1956 Luis Aparicio became the shortstop for the Sox, and he and

Nellie became a great double-play combination. The duo helped the Sox to the World Series in 1959, the team's first series since 1919, when the players threw the series.

Fox was named to 12 All-Star teams and was the premiere second baseman of the decade. He finished his career as a playing coach with Houston. His only shortcoming was not being named to the Hall of Fame.

Turk Wins 17 for Pueblo

Omar "Turk" Lown was an All-Star pitcher for Pueblo in 1948 after winning 17 games.

His call to the majors came in 1951 with the Cubs, who tried unsuccessfully to use him as a starter. When they switched him to relief duty he became a much better hurler and began saving and winning games. In 1957 he led the National League with 67 appearances.

Lown went to the Reds before going to the White Sox in 1958. As a Sox pitcher he helped the team to the pennant and World Series, where he didn't allow a run in three appearances in 1959.

Labine Shines with Shutouts

Pueblo's Clem Labine led the league in shutouts in 1948. Perhaps it was a sign of things to come.

Labine got his first call to the Brooklyn Dodgers in 1950 and became a regular during the 1952 season. Although the righthander was used mostly as a reliever, he recorded two significant shutouts during his time with the Dodgers. The first was a shutout of the Giants in the playoffs in 1951. The second was a 10-inning shutout of the Yankees in Game Two of the 1956 World Series.

The Rhode Island–born pitcher led the National League in appearances for three years in a row starting in 1955. In all, he pitched for 13 seasons in the majors.

1948

Final Standings

	W	L	Pct.	GB	Affiliations
Des Moines Bruins	76	64	.542	—	Chicago Cubs
Denver Bears	70	67	.511	4½	None
Lincoln Athletics	69	68	.504	5½	Philadelphia Athletics
Sioux City Soos	69	68	.504	5½	New York Giants
Pueblo Dodgers	69	70	.496	6½	Brooklyn Dodgers
Omaha Cardinals	62	78	.443	14	St. Louis Cardinals

Playoffs

Lincoln defeated Sioux City, 6–0, two days after the regular season to determine playoff position.
Lincoln defeated Des Moines, three games to two.
Sioux City defeated Denver, three games to two.

Finals

Sioux City defeated Lincoln, four games to two.

Team Batting

	AB	R	H	HR	SB	BB	SO	Avg.
Denver	4767	824	1387	50	41	643	601	.291
Sioux City	4657	839	1309	110	69	641	273	.281
Pueblo	4703	777	1290	85	114	612	748	.274
Lincoln	4670	707	1255	69	67	555	758	.269
Des Moines	4828	783	1285	92	61	619	763	.266
Omaha	4764	762	1260	94	77	588	802	.264

Individual Fielding Leaders
(More Than 100 Games)

	POS	G	PO	A	E	DP	Pct.
Gorman, Herbert, PU	1b	139	1040	77	17	110	.985
Henningsen, Ray, DE	2b	102	265	278	18	64	.968
Jackson, Ransom, DM	3b	118	113	245	33	29	.916
Genovese, George, DE	ss	135	261	508	51	96	.938
Treadway, T. Leon, DM	of	105	250	13	3	1	.989
Pavlick, William, SC	of	125	333	14	6	2	.983
Kamler, Richard, OM	of	109	181	6	6	1	.969
Novick, Walter, LI	c	115	621	86	9	11	.987

Earned Run Average Leaders
(154 Or More Innings)

	G	W–L	Pct.	IP	R	ER	ERA
Jacobs, Anthony, DM	33	11–8	.579	169	76	51	2.72
Shantz, Robert, LI	28	18–7	.720	214	77	67	2.82
Kelly, R., DM	28	14–7	.667	200	83	65	2.93
Bowman, Roger, SC	30	11–8	.579	174	84	64	3.31
Uber, John, SC	35	12–15	.444	201	111	81	3.63

Team Fielding

	G	DP	PB	PO	A	E	Pct.
Des Moines	142	143	21	3623	1613	227	.958

	G	DP	PB	PO	A	E	Pct.
Lincoln	137	107	19	3501	1529	226	.957
Sioux City	138	91	10	3469	1361	234	.954
Pueblo	140	126	13	3562	1441	247	.953
Omaha	141	110	27	3603	1475	259	.951
Denver	138	136	20	3524	1620	286	.947

Individual Batting Leaders
(Minimum 434 At Bats)

	G	AB	R	H	HR	SB	RBI	Avg.
Treadway, T. Leon, DM	106	449	99	158	0	23	55	.352
Gorman, Herbert, PU	139	505	113	172	20	12	103	.341
Beringhele, Basil, DE	132	497	80	162	4	2	87	.326
Jackson, Ransom, DM	132	485	100	156	6	7	76	.322
Hofman, Robert, SC	120	501	104	160	10	7	72	.319

All-Star Team
1b—Herb Gorman, Pueblo
2b—Nellie Fox, Lincoln
3b—Ransom Jackson, Des Moines
ss—George Genovese, Denver
of—Larry Miggins, Omaha
of—Billy Pavlik, Sioux City
of—Leon "Red" Treadway, Des Moines
c—Carl Sawatski, Des Moines
utility—Bob Wellman, Lincoln
utility—Ed Martin, Sioux City
p—Omar "Turk" Lown, Pueblo
p—Bobby Shantz, Lincoln
manager—Mike Gazella, Denver

Attendance
Denver—283,377
Des Moines—232,038
Omaha—147,130
Lincoln—127,462
Pueblo—116,304
Sioux City—112,381
Total—1,018,692
Playoffs—77,630

Batting Leaders
HOME RUNS
Sawatski, Carl, DM—29
Limmer, Louis, LI—28
Gilbert, Harold, SC—26
Miggins, Lawrence, OM—26
Several with 21

RUNS BATTED IN
Gilbert, Harold, SC—114
Sawatski, Carl, DM—111
Gorman, Herbert, PU—103
Wellman, Robert, LI—102
Reash, Robert, DE—97

STOLEN BASES
Kirk, Thomas, LI—23
Treadway, T. Leon, DM—23
Babcook, James, PU—20
Conroy, Michael, OM—20
Several with 19

HITS
Wellman, Robert, LI—173
Gorman, Herbert, PU—172
Fox, J. Nelson, LI—170
Skeen, Wilmer, DE—167
Beringhele, Basil, DE—162

DOUBLES
Gorman, Herbert, PU—45
Hofman, Robert, SC—38
Wellman, Robert, LI—36
Genovese, George, DE—34
Gilbert, Harold, SC—33

TRIPLES
Columbo, Michael , SC—16
Fox, J. Nelson, LI—14
Kirk, Thomas, LI—13
Pavlick, William, SC—13
Several with 12

TOTAL BASES
Gorman, Herbert, PU—291
Gilbert, Harold, SC—272
Pavlick, William, SC—251
Fox, J. Nelson, LI—250
Several with 238

RUNS
Genovese, George, DE—119
Gilbert, Harold, SC—115
Pavlick, William, SC—114
Gorman, Herbert, PU—113
Reash, Robert, DE—106

BASES ON BALLS
Genovese, George, DE—125
Gilbert, Harold, SC—117
Gorman, Herbert, PU—96
Pavlick, William, SC—87
Henningsen, Ray, DE—82

STRIKEOUTS
Kerns, Russell, DM—109
Jaros, Anthony, OM—91
Kirk, Thomas, LI—90
Boehm, Edward, LI—80
Allperto, Joseph, LI—77

Pitching Leaders

GAMES
Schmidt, Donald, PU—45
Williams, Merlin, DE—44
Glaser, Raymond, OM—38
Andromidas, Nicholas, SC—36
Brewer, Samuel, SC—36

COMPLETE GAMES
Wells, John, LI—23
Shantz, Robert, LI—19
Kelly, R., DM—18
Hufford, Clinton, DE—17
Lown, Omar, PU—17

SHUTOUTS
Labine, Clement, PU—3
Several with 2

WINS
Shantz, Robert, LI—18
Lown, Omar, PU—17
Wells, John, LI—15
Several with 14

LOSSES
Uber, John, SC—15
Lee, Roy, DE—14
Glaser, Raymond, OM—13
Bernardi, Francis, LI—12
Bower, Albert, LI—12

INNINGS PITCHED
Williams, Merlin, DE—221
Shantz, Robert, LI—214
Lee, Roy, DE—209
Hufford, Clinton, DE—201
Uber, John, SC—201

BASE ON BALLS
Uber, John, SC—119
Remke, John, OM—118
Lown, Omar, PU—112
Lee, Roy, DE—103
Hufford, Clinton, DE—102

STRIKEOUTS
Shantz, Robert, LI—212
Brewer, Samuel, SC—169
Wells, John, LI—158
Andromidas, Nicholas, SC—157
Remke, John, OM—145

WILD PITCHES
Lee, Roy, DE—16
Remke, John, OM—16
Lown, Omar, PU—13
Martin, W., DE—13
Several with 11

1949

In 1949 an expansion was planned for two more teams, but Wichita was unable to provide playing facilities for the season. Then Cedar Rapids failed to make a new application at the midsummer meeting.

Pitchers took the spotlight in 1949. Early in the season, Des Moines' hurler Bob Kuhlman pitched a no-hitter against Sioux City. On August 16 another Des Moines pitcher, Elvin "Srubby" Stabefeld, repeated the feat. Stabefeld walked the first batter, then retired the next 27 Pueblo hitters in 89 pitches. In spite of the efforts by Des Moines pitchers, Lincoln took the pennant, finishing three-and-a-half games ahead of the Denver Grizzlies and the Pueblo Dodgers. The Grizzlies set a single-game record the last day of the regular season when 18,523 paying customers jammed the stadium in a game against Pueblo. The total helped the league reach its highest yearly attendance in history—1,363,854.

Because of a tie for second, Denver and Pueblo met in a one-game playoff before the regular playoffs began. The Grizzlies won 5–3, thanks to a six-hit effort by pitcher George Uhle. He helped his own cause by delivering a two-run triple in Denver's big four-tally sixth inning. Catcher Walt Linden contributed a couple of hits and could have won the batting title, but the game didn't count toward the regular season statistics. Lincoln was disappointing in the playoffs, as it could only manage one win over the Des Moines Bruins; the Bruins were managed by Stan Hack, who played 16 years for the Chicago Cubs. Meanwhile, the Pueblo Dodgers knocked off the Denver Bears in the other playoffs. Pueblo and Des Moines took the playoffs to a seventh game. The final game was marred by a trio of errors, which led to as many runs for Pueblo and a victory over Des

The Denver Grizzlies ended up finishing second in 1949. Pictured are: (front row) bat boy, Jaderlund, Tanner, Weisenburger, Johnson, Tedeschi; (middle row) Browne, Angelone, Grose, St. Pierre, Uhle, Rambone, DeCarlo; (back row) McComas, Linden, Cooper, Bennett, Barkelew, Harmon, Jester and Behm, trainer. (Photograph courtesy of Jay Sanford)

Moines. Les Peden of Des Moines led all hitters in the playoffs with a .516 average. Unfortunately, cold weather during the playoffs resulted in a 30 percent drop in attendance.

Denver was led to the pennant by all-star pitcher Ernie Johnson. The righthander would pitch in the majors for nine seasons beginning the next season. Pueblo's Ken Lehman led the league in strikeouts that season. A couple of years later he made it to the majors, where he played for five seasons. The Dodgers were also led by Vic Marasco, who led the league in hitting and RBI. Teammate Marion Fricano had the best winning percentage with his 10–2 record. Fricano would get his call to the majors in 1952 with Philadelphia, and he would pitch four seasons in the big leagues. Joe Presko of Omaha was one of the pitching leaders in 1949 with his 14–9 record. He would go on to six seasons in the majors with St. Louis and Detroit.

Shoeless Tanner Scores Homer

Chuck Tanner was one of the leading hitters in the league in 1949 with the Denver Bears. One of his hits was an inside-the-park homer minus a shoe, which he lost coming around third base.

After laboring nine years in the minors, he finally made it to the majors in 1955 with Milwaukee. He played for nine seasons and never amounted to much. However, when he turned to managing, he was quite good. By 1970 he was managing in the majors with the White Sox.

Tanner found much more success in managing when he joined Pittsburgh in 1977. He engineered the Pirates to a World Series championship in 1979. Tanner then managed the Braves for three seasons before being fired for the first time as a manager. He decided to retire.

Chuck Tanner (left) and Ernie Johnson played for Denver in 1949. (Photograph courtesy of Jay Sanford)

1949

Final Standings

	W	L	Pct.	GB	Affiliations
Lincoln Athletics	74	64	.536	—	Philadelphia Athletics
Denver Grizzlies	71	68	.511	3½	Boston Braves
Pueblo Dodgers	71	68	.511	3½	Brooklyn Dodgers
Des Moines Bruins	70	70	.500	5	Chicago Cubs
Omaha Cardinals	68	71	.489	6½	St. Louis Cardinals
Sioux City Soos	63	76	.453	11½	New York Giants

Playoffs

Denver defeated Pueblo in a one-game playoff for second.
Des Moines defeated Lincoln, three games to one.
Pueblo defeated Denver, three games to one.

Finals

Pueblo defeated Des Moines, four games to three.

Individual Hitting Leaders
(Minimum 434 At Bats)

	G	AB	R	H	RBI	Avg.
Vic Marasco, PU	131	512	89	169	121	.330
Linden, DE	121	452	81	147	95	.325
Yelen, SC	101	358	51	115	71	.321
Lou Limmer, LI	135	484	100	152	105	.314
Chuck Tanner, DE	124	465	92	146	53	.314

Winning Percentage Leaders

	G	W–L	Pct.	IP
Fricano, PU	15	10–2	.833	87
Johnson, DE	20	15–5	.750	167
Uhle, DE	22	10–5	.667	140
Lovenguth, LI	34	17–10	.630	225
Garlock, OM	22	11–7	.611	132

All-Star Team

1b—Fred Richards, Lincoln
2b—Joe Torpey, Pueblo
3b—Stan Jok, Sioux City
ss—Bobby Stewart, Lincoln
of—Rocco Ippolito, Lincoln
of—Bob Jaderland, Denver
of—Victor Marasco, Pueblo
c—Walter Linden, Denver
p—Ernie Johnson, Denver
p—Ken Lehman, Pueblo
Manager of the Year—Jimmy De Shong, Lincoln

Attendance

Denver—463,039
Omaha—277,370
Des Moines—210,204
Lincoln—149,159
Pueblo—138,726
Sioux City—125,356
Total—1,363,854
Playoffs—54,282

Batting Leaders

HOME RUNS
Lou Limmer, LI—29
RUNS BATTED IN
Vic Marasco, PU—121

HITS
Fred Richards, DM—178

RUNS
James Williams, PU—126

Pitching Leaders

WINS
Elvin Stabelfeld, DM—17
Lynn Lovenguth, LI—17
Walter Cox, SC—17

STRIKEOUTS
Ken Lehman, PU—203

1950

The league expanded to eight teams in 1950, with the Colorado Springs Sky Sox and Wichita Indians being added. The schedule was also expanded from 140 to 154 games. African-Americans returned to the league for the first time since 1886. War broke out in Korea in 1950, but the police action did not have any immediate impact on minor league baseball. In May, flooding in Lincoln put Sherman Field under seven feet of water, and the team was forced to transfer its home series to the road.

Omaha finished first in 1950. Like previous playoffs, winning the pennant didn't ensure success in postseason. Omaha didn't muster a win in the five-game series with fourth-place Wichita. Sioux City then slid past Wichita, three games to one, to win the playoffs.

Omaha's Bob Mahoney led the league with 20 wins that season. He was twice given a try in the majors without any success. Better success in the majors came to Omaha's Wally Moon, who played 12 seasons with the Cardinals and Dodgers. Vern Fear, with Des Moines, was the leading hurler in 1950, but he only pitched four games with the Cubs in 1952. The league's leading hitter was Bill Taylor of Sioux City with a .346 batting average. Taylor played five seasons in the majors as a pinch hitter. In fact, he led the National League in pinch hits in 1955 with the Giants. Pete Whisenant, with Denver, collected 15 hits in 22 at bats during a three day series in July against Pueblo. And George Moskovich, with Lincoln, hit for the cycle against Denver.

One of the major league veterans in the league was Pat Seerey with Colorado Springs. He had played eight seasons in the majors with Cleveland and the Chicago White Sox in the 1940s.

Denver finished fifth in 1950. Team members were: (front row) Nubin, Morgan, bat boys, Holden, Behm, trainer; (middle row) Stewart, Tanner, DeCarlo, Jester, Williams, Kuczek, Della Monica, Browne, manager; (back row) Hartley, Womack, Hofmann, Taylor, Staub, Whisenant, Dittmer, Uhle and McWhorter. (Photograph courtesy of Jay Sanford)

Turley Was Jim Dandy Hurler

Wichita's Bob Turley struck out hitters with regularity to become one of the strikeout leaders in the Western League. That skill led him to a successful major league career.

Turley got his first call to the majors in 1951 and became a regular with the St. Louis Browns in 1953. He became a winning pitcher after joining the Yankees in 1955. In 1958 he went 21-7 and won the Cy Young Award. He finished the season by being named as the Most Valuable Player in the World Series.

The righthander retired after 12 seasons in the majors with a 101-85 record—a winner.

1950
Final Standings

	W	L	Pct.	GB	Affiliations
Omaha Cardinals	96	58	.623	—	St. Louis Cardinals
Sioux City Soos	89	65	.578	7	New York Giants
Des Moines Bruins	84	70	.545	12	Chicago Cubs
Wichita Indians	77	77	.500	19	St. Louis Browns
Denver Bears	75	79	.487	21	Boston Braves
Colorado Springs Sky Sox	72	82	.468	24	Chicago White Sox

After the War (1947–1958) 229

	W	L	Pct.	GB	Affiliations
Lincoln Athletics	69	85	.448	27	Philadelphia Athletics
Pueblo Dodgers	54	100	.351	42	Brooklyn Dodgers

Playoffs

Wichita defeated Omaha, three games to none.
Sioux City defeated Des Moines, three games to two.

Finals

Sioux City defeated Wichita, three games to one.

Team Batting

	AB	R	H	HR	SB	BB	SO	Avg.
Denver	5317	956	1516	87	61	760	703	.285
Sioux City	5210	935	1417	164	59	811	758	.272
Colorado Springs	5213	925	1398	114	37	850	753	.268
Omaha	5163	843	1354	73	84	702	719	.262
Des Moines	5010	759	1288	77	21	715	642	.257
Lincoln	5141	740	1300	67	51	714	680	.253
Pueblo	5141	760	1295	77	134	636	707	.252
Wichita	5118	796	1282	88	83	808	745	.250

Team Fielding

	G	DP	PB	PO	A	E	Pct.
Omaha	155	149	26	4009	1677	203	.966
Des Moines	155	164	10	3938	1721	245	.959
Pueblo	156	170	31	3969	1688	248	.958
Sioux City	157	127	12	3996	1702	257	.957
Lincoln	156	148	10	3992	1619	254	.957
Colorado Springs	156	172	20	3940	1814	294	.951
Wichita	155	132	19	4011	1666	293	.951
Denver	154	154	11	3988	1755	306	.949

Individual Fielding Leaders (More Than 100 Games)

	POS	G	PO	A	E	DP	Pct.
Zernia, Harvey, OM	1b	138	1244	73	18	113	.987
Moskovich, George, LI	2b	151	415	387	22	95	.973
Grammas, C. Peter, CS	3b	102	98	208	25	20	.924
McAlester, Fred, OM	ss	155	230	507	39	88	.950
Schramka, Paul, DM	of	148	290	18	7	3	.978
Holden, Daniel, DE	of	138	253	12	6	2	.978
Whisenant, Thomas, DE	of	117	288	20	8	3	.975
Katt, Raymond, SC	c	132	717	70	16	6	.980

Earned Run Leaders
(154 Or More Innings)

	G	W–L	Pct.	IP	R	ER	ERA
Fear, Luvern, DM	39	15–5	.750	181	74	57	2.83
Kucab, John, LI	31	16–12	.571	261	99	86	2.97
Cohan, Jack, OM	27	13–10	.565	212	96	70	2.97
Rubert, Octavia, OM	32	17–8	.680	226	93	77	3.07
Bowes, Mason, LI	32	15–15	.500	247	115	91	3.32

Individual Batting Leaders
(Minimum 450 At Bats)

	G	AB	R	H	HR	SB	RBI	Avg.
Zernia, Harvey, OM	138	532	102	169	7	5	75	.318
Womack, Dallas, DE	154	545	115	173	17	5	112	.317
Tanner, Charles, DE	154	619	111	195	7	2	86	.315
Whisenant, Thomas, DE	118	481	125	150	24	14	119	.312
Grammas, C. Peter, CS	127	501	107	156	9	6	74	.311

All-Star Team

1b—Harvey Zernia, Omaha
2b—Eddie Samcoff, Sioux City
3b—Pete Grammas, Colorado Springs
ss—Fred McAlister, Omaha
of—Bill Taylor, Sioux City
of—Tom Whisenant, Denver
of—Bob Balcena, Wichita
of—Pat Seerey, Colorado Springs
c—Nick Adzick, Omaha
c—Bruce McWhorter, Denver
p—Robert Mahoney, Omaha
p—Octavio Rubert, Omaha
p—John O'Donnell, Wichita
p—Mason Bowes, Lincoln

Attendance

Denver—379,180
Omaha—218,393
Des Moines—147,549
Sioux City—143,237
Wichita—126,729
Colorado Springs—107,264
Pueblo—91,299
Lincoln—68,884
Total—1,282,535
Playoffs—33,067
No All-Star Game

Batting Leaders

HOME RUNS
Taylor, William, SC—30
Whisenant, Thomas, DE—24
Spencer, Daryl, SC—23
Gardner, William, SC—22
Henley, Gail, SC—22

RUNS BATTED IN
Whisenant, Thomas, DE—119
Gardner, William, SC—118
Womack, Dallas, DE—112
Huff, Roy, OM—111
Juelke, Conrad, CS—110

STOLEN BASES
Heckel, Ashton, PU—24
Balcena, Robert, WI—19
Caffery, Robert, WI—18
Henter, Gordon, PU—17
Several with 16

HITS
Tanner, Charles, DE—195
Gardner, William, SC—176
Holden, Daniel, DE—176
Womack, Dallas, DE—173
Several with 170

After the War (1947–1958)

DOUBLES
Rutenbar, George, CS—51
Holden, Daniel, DE—40
Spencer, Daryl, SC—36
Taylor, William, SC—36
Several with 34

TRIPLES
Juelke, Conrad, CS—14
Huff, Roy, OM—13
Balcena, Robert, WI—12
Several with 11

TOTAL BASES
Gardner, William, SC—288
Whisenant, Thomas, DE—276
Spencer, Daryl, SC—273
Several with 268

RUNS
Holden, Daniel, DE—131
Whisenant, Thomas, DE—125
Balcena, Robert, WI—119
Womack, Dallas, DE—115
Several with 111

BASES ON BALLS
Womack, Dallas, DE—125
Balcena, Robert, WI—119
Caffery, Robert, WI—119
Samcoff, Edward, SC—114
Boehm, Edward, SI—105

STRIKEOUTS
Seerey, J. Patrick, CS—92
Maul, Allan, SC—89
Spencer, Daryl, SC—82
Balcena, Robert, WI—79
Elder, George, WI—78

Pitching Leaders

GAMES
Jester, Virgil, DE—59
Williams, M., DE—53
Bordt, William, WI—41
Carbonaro, Joseph, PU—40
Turley, Robert, WI—40

COMPLETE GAMES
Kucab, John, LI—28
Bowes, Mason, LI—19
Carbonaro, Joseph, PU—19
Cohan, Jack, OM—19
Cox, Walter, SC—19

SHUTOUTS
Clear, Elwood, OM—4
Several with 3

WINS
Mahoney, Robert, OM—20
Kamis, James, CS—17
Rubert, Octavia, OM—17
Several with 16

LOSSES
Carbonaro, Joseph, PU—16
Zavitka, James, PU—15
Bowes, Mason, LI—15
Kellner, Walter, LI—14
Turley, Robert, WI—14

HOME RUNS ALLOWED
Sayers, David, SC—28
Kamis, James, CS—25
Shandor, Theodore, CS—24
Dahlke, Jerome, CS—23
Carey, Elwood, LI—21

INNINGS PITCHED
Kucab, John, LI—261
Bowes, Mason, LI—247
Carbonaro, Joseph, PU—240
Rubert, Octavia, OM—226
Several with 224

BASES ON BALLS
Carbonaro, Joseph, PU—175
Bishop, Charles, SC—142
Thompson, Glenn, DE—131
Clear, Elwood, OM—119
Turley, Robert, WI—118

STRIKEOUTS
Mahoney, Robert, OM—162
Bishop, Charles, SC—156
Turley, Robert, WI—153
Thompson, Glenn, DE—152

WILD PITCHES
Bishop, Charles, SC—11
Carbonaro, Joseph, PU—11
Turley, Robert, WI—11

Pilgram, William, WI—10
Several with 9

BALKS
Dahlke, Jerome, CS—13

Baczewski, Frederick, DM—9
Taylor, Bryon, DE—9
Helmer, Harry, OM—9
Several with 8

1951

The playoff jinx continued in 1951. Omaha finished two games ahead of Denver for the pennant, but the Cardinals fell in the first round of the playoffs to the Sioux City Soos. Then the Soos whipped Denver, three games to one, in the playoffs. Sioux City had the leading hitter in the league for awhile, as Sam Hairston hit .389, but he was called up to the White Sox. Hairston's sons would also go on to play in the majors, too.

The leading pitcher in the league in 1951 was Omaha's Willard Schmidt. His 2.11 ERA led him to a promotion to the Cardinals the next season. He pitched another seven seasons for the Cardinals and Reds. Elroy Face had a great season, going 23–9 with Pueblo. Face went on to pitch 16 seasons in the majors, mainly with the Pirates. He led the National

The Omaha Cardinals won the Western League pennant in 1951. The players were: (front row, from left) batboy Billy Saint, Roy Huff, Hall Coffman, Earl Weaver, Jack Shirley, Bob Stephenson, batboy Billy Richardson; (middle row, from left) Harvey Zernia, Jim Neufeldt, Nick Adzick, Buddy Phillips, George Kissell, manager Russell Rac, Lou Ciola, George Eyrich; (back row, from left) John Grodzicki, Jim Hercinger, Tom Keating, Ken Boyer, Roy Pounds, Joe Chuka, Willard Schmidt and trainer Paul Kippels. (Photograph courtesy of the National Baseball Hall of Fame, Cooperstown, N.Y.)

After the War (1947–1958)   233

The Denver Bears finished second in 1951. The players were: (front row, from left) Osorio, Rivas, Vega, Palica, Roberts, Gregory and Ries; (second row) manager Andy Cohen, Lassalle, McWhorter, Williams, Bruton, Lewis, Jaderlund, trainer Behm; (back row) Isringhaus, Morgan, Wollpert, Frank Torre, Stewart, Schultz, Boles, Fierson.

League in saves on three different occasions and pitched in the 1960 World Series. Pueblo also had the leading hitter in George Freese, with a .338 average. He got a call from Detroit the next season for one game. Then he played a season for the Pirates in 1955 and again in 1961 with the Cubs. Denver had a couple of players who would later star in the majors. Bill Bruton, who played in the Negro Leagues, was named to the All-Star team in 1951. He went on to play a dozen seasons with Milwaukee and Detroit. Frank Torre also played for Denver in 1951. The brother of Joe Torre played for the Milwaukee Braves in two World Series in the 1950s.

Boyer Buoys Omaha

Ken Boyer was one of the leading hitters in the Western League in 1951 with Omaha. Four years later he was playing for the St. Louis Cardinals and distinguishing himself at third base.

When the Gold Glove Award was created, Boyer won the first four at third base. His best season came in 1964 when he led the Cardinals to a World Championship and was named Most Valuable Player of the National League.

Ken played 15 years in the majors and was part of the Cardinals' World Series team in 1964, while brother Clete played for 16 years in the majors. Ken also managed for three seasons. The Cardinals honored him by retiring his number (14) in 1984.

1951

Final Standings

	W	L	Pct.	GB	Affiliations
Omaha Cardinals	90	64	.584	—	St. Louis Cardinals
Denver Bears	88	66	.571	2	Boston Braves
Wichita Indians	84	68	.553	5	Cleveland Indians
Sioux City Soos	77	71	.520	10	New York Giants
Des Moines Bruins	73	78	.483	15½	Chicago Cubs
Pueblo Dodgers	74	80	.481	16	Brooklyn Dodgers
Colorado Springs Sky Sox	64	87	.424	24½	Chicago White Sox
Lincoln Athletics	57	93	.380	31	Philadelphia Athletics

Playoffs

Sioux City defeated Omaha, three games to one.
Denver defeated Wichita, three games to one.

Finals

Sioux defeated Denver, three games to one.

Team Batting

	AB	R	H	HR	SB	BB	SO	Avg.
Colorado Springs	5095	846	1396	99	53	732	692	.274
Denver	5173	785	1405	57	55	712	577	.272
Pueblo	5186	814	1399	64	152	676	757	.270
Sioux City	4952	736	1316	105	85	606	668	.266
Des Moines	5038	632	1291	67	62	619	694	.256
Omaha	5050	752	1274	76	71	704	748	.252
Wichita	4834	692	1154	81	105	788	777	.239
Lincoln	4945	642	1166	37	47	673	653	.238

Team Fielding

	G	DP	PB	PO	A	E	Pct.
Denver	156	145	15	4002	1714	196	.967
Omaha	155	175	20	3997	1611	207	.964
Wichita	153	150	18	3938	1624	214	.963
Sioux City	150	147	18	3797	1640	224	.960
Pueblo	155	163	17	4005	1726	246	.959
Des Moines	152	149	24	3942	1721	262	.956
Lincoln	151	127	13	3838	1541	259	.954
Colorado Springs	152	138	26	3842	1698	301	.950

Individual Fielding Leaders
(More Than 100 Games)

	POS	G	PO	A	E	DP	Pct.
Zernia, Harvey, OM	1b	100	764	55	10	88	.988
Roberts, Curtis, DE	2b	131	329	373	19	86	.974
Morgan, L., DE	3b	125	139	234	23	27	.942
Bressoud, Edward, SC	ss	141	256	395	35	68	.949
Colombo, Michael, SC	of	125	200	18	3	5	.986
Anderlik, Robert, DM	of	137	360	23	10	2	.975
Wakefield, Robert, DM	of	104	211	11	6	0	.974
McWhorter, Pierce, DE	c	116	574	64	8	11	.988

Earned Run Average Leaders
(154 Or More Innings)

	G	W–L	Pct.	IP	R	ER	ERA
Schmidt, Willard, OM	44	19–14	.576	252	80	59	2.11
Eyrich, George, OM	36	18–11	.621	275	96	73	2.39
Kotrany, Joseph, WI	38	13–8	.619	168	57	48	2.57
Face, Elroy, PU	35	23–9	.719	265	99	82	2.78
Rivas, Rafael, DE	30	11–4	.733	165	71	52	2.84

Batting Leaders
(Minimum 480 At Bats)

	G	AB	R	H	HR	RBI	SB	Avg.
Freese, George, PU	135	541	104	183	12	106	12	.338
Anderlik, Robert, DM	137	530	64	168	13	54	7	.317
Landenberger, Ken, CS	147	529	86	166	10	81	5	.314
Boyer, Ken, OM	151	565	87	173	14	90	11	.306
Morgan, Lucius, DE	150	566	94	172	4	85	6	.304

All-Star Team

1b—Joe Macko, Wichita
2b—Ron Samford, Sioux City
3b—George Freese, Pueblo
ss—Gus Gregory, Denver
of—Russell Rac, Omaha
of—Bob Anderlik, Des Moines
of—Bill Bruton, Denver
c—Harry Chiti, Des Moines
p—El Roy Race, Pueblo
p—Jack Shirley, Omaha
p—Mason Bowes, Lincoln
p—Rafael Rivas, Denver
manager—Joe Schultz, Wichita

Attendance

Denver—424,065
Omaha—162,592
Wichita—122,060
Colorado Springs—107,320
Pueblo—104,254
Sioux City—104,247
Des Moines—94,137
Lincoln—37,123
Total—1,155,798
Playoffs—41,570
No All-Star Game

Batting Leaders

HOME RUNS
Boles, Howard, DM—32
Lutz, Michael, WI—19
Seerey, James, CS—19
Rac, Russell, OM—17
Several with 16

RUNS BATTED IN
Freese, George, PU—106
Boles, Howard, DM—102
Rac, Russell, OM—102
Macko, Joseph, WI—96
Boyer, Ken, OM—90

STOLEN BASES
Carey, Lee, WI—39
Samford, Ronald, SC—29
Caloia, George, PU—26
Leap, C. Allen, PU—23
Bruton, William, DE—19

HITS
Freese, George, PU—183
Boyer, Ken, OM—173
Morgan, Lucius, DE—172
Samford, Ronald, SC—170
Anderlik, Robert, DM—168

DOUBLES
Morgan, Lucius, DE—44
Freese, George, PU—37
Hunter, Donald, PU—33
Leonard, Fred, CS—32
Ronning, Albert, PU—32

TRIPLES
Bruton, William, DE—27
Freese, George, PU—15
Kirk, Thomas, LI—14
Holden, Daniel, DE—12
Several with 11

TOTAL BASES
Freese, George, PU—286
Boles, Howard, DM—273
Boyer, Ken, OM—257
Samford, Ronald, SC—251
Morgan, Lucius, DE—248

RUNS
Samford, Ronald, SC—108
Bruton, William, DE—104
Freese, George, PU—104
Boles, Howard, DM—96
Several with 94

BASES ON BALLS
Reid, Robert, SC—114
Hunter, Donald, PU—113
King, James, WI—109
Carey, Lee, WI—105
Rac, Russell, OM—94

STRIKEOUTS
Skurski, Andrew, CS—120
Leap, C. Allen, PU—111
Rac, Russell, OM—106
Boles, Howard, DM—100
Carey, Lee, WI—89

Pitching Leaders

GAMES
Giddings, Robert, SC—59
Frantz, Vernon, PU—48
Osorio, Alberto, DE—48
Ciola, Louis, OM—46
Schmidt, Willard, OM—44

COMPLETE GAMES
Face, Elroy, PU—25
Bowes, Mason, LI—19
Eyrich, George, OM—19
Palica, Ambrose, DE—19
Schmidt, Willard, OM—19

SHUTOUTS
Coffman, Harold, OM—5
Foulk, Leon, DM—4
Several with 3

WINS
Face, Elroy, PU—23
Schmidt, Willard, OM—19
Eyrich, George, OM—18
Palica, Ambrose, DE—17
Cohen, Hyman, DM—16

LOSSES
Gohl, Vincent, LI—18
Yasinski, Edward, PU—17
Bowes, Mason, LI—16
Piccone, Mario, CS—15
Several with 14

HOME RUNS ALLOWED
Powell, William, CS—21
Romberger, Allen, LI—21
Several with 16

INNINGS PITCHED
Eyrich, George, OM—275
Face, Elroy, PU—265
Schmidt, Willard, OM—252
Cohen, Hyman, DM—236
Portocarrero, Arnold, LI—236

BASES ON BALLS
Piccone, Mario, CS—152
Ploetz, Ronald, SC—121
Yasinski, Edward, PU—121
Portocarrero, Arnold, LI—112
Schmidt, Willard, OM—108

STRIKEOUTS
Schmidt, Willard, OM—202
Face, Elroy, PU—171
Powell, William, CS—157
Piccone, Mario, CS—148
Eyrich, George, OM—139

WILD PITCHES
McCoy, Richard, PU—17
Brewer, Samuel, SC—13
Pounds, Roy, OM—12
Powell, William, CS—12
Piccone, Mario, CS—12

BALKS
Fassler, Leonard, SC—9
Rivas, Rafael, DE—8
Hoyle, LI—7
Trujillo, Ernest, WI—7
Brewer, Samuel, SC—6

1952

In 1952 Denver finally broke the playoff jinx that had followed the pennant winner for several years. The Bears edged out Colorado Springs for the pennant, then swept Omaha in the playoffs. The team also continued to lead the league in attendance by a wide margin as well, drawing more than 450,000 fans. Bears Stadium was the largest in the league, with a seating capacity of 19,000.

The Colorado Springs Sky Sox finished in second place in 1952. (Photograph courtesy of Jay Sanford)

Denver was led by pitcher Alberto Osorio, who won a league-leading 20 games. Omaha's Eddie Phillips led the league in hitting that season with a .320 average. He had a look-see by the Cardinals the next season. Ken Landenberger, with the Colorado Springs Sky Sox, was a triple leader that season in hits, runs scored and RBI. This performance earned him a call up to the White Sox at the end of the season. However, he didn't stay there. One player that did stick in the majors from the Sky Sox was pitcher Connie Johnson. Johnson got the call from the White Sox in 1953 and played six seasons in the majors.

Weaver Better at Managing

Earl Weaver was named to the All-Star Team in 1952 with Omaha. Weaver starred in the league for several years and was one of the leaders in runs scored in 1954, as he crossed home plate 124 times.

The second baseman never made it to the majors as a player. Instead, he turned to managing and wound up guiding the Baltimore Orioles for 17 seasons, taking the team to six first-place finishes and four World Series appearances. His 1970 team won the world championship.

Weaver retired after the 1986 season as one of the leading managers in the history of the game.

1952

Final Standings

	W	L	Pct.	GB	Affiliations
Denver Bears	88	66	.571	—	Pittsburgh Pirates
Colorado Springs Sky Sox	87	67	.565	1	Chicago White Sox
Omaha Cardinals	86	68	.558	2	St. Louis Cardinals
Sioux City Soos	83	71	.539	5	New York Giants
Pueblo Dodgers	81	73	.526	7	Brooklyn Dodgers
Wichita Indians	67	87	.435	21	Cleveland Indians
Lincoln Athletics	67	87	.435	21	Philadelphia Athletics
Des Moines Bruins	57	97	.370	31	Chicago Cubs

Playoffs

Denver defeated Sioux City, three games to one.
Omaha defeated Colorado Springs, three games to one.

Finals

Denver defeated Omaha, three games to one.

Team Batting

	AB	R	H	HR	BB	SO	SB	Avg.
Colorado Springs	5258	894	1454	112	737	722	44	.277
Pueblo	5196	841	1410	92	747	829	84	.271
Denver	5243	808	1417	83	737	737	79	.270
Sioux City	5093	779	1325	121	691	764	92	.260
Omaha	5061	728	1284	68	666	824	66	.254
Des Moines	5105	570	1269	32	580	554	47	.249
Lincoln	4996	654	1218	41	693	698	40	.244
Wichita	5061	761	1231	60	827	813	63	.243

Team Fielding

	G	DP	PB	PO	A	E	Pct.
Colorado Springs	154	142	24	4010	1766	193	.968
Denver	156	182	16	4019	1817	219	.964
Des Moines	155	188	30	3955	1826	242	.960
Sioux City	155	144	16	3953	1741	239	.960
Omaha	154	157	25	3972	1641	242	.959
Pueblo	154	191	20	3975	1696	264	.954
Wichita	154	148	34	3963	1608	267	.954
Lincoln	154	144	15	3918	1635	277	.952

Individual Fielding Leaders
(More Than 100 Games)

	POS	G	PO	A	E	DP	Pct.
Landenberger, Ken, CS	1b	147	1371	97	15	116	.990
Jacinto, Alvin, CS	2b	109	233	332	13	67	.978
Crosby, Jerry, CS	3b	113	90	204	17	14	.945
Gregory, Constantine, DE	ss	137	238	423	36	100	.948
Fucci, Victor, CS	of	131	307	19	6	4	.982
Wells, William E., CS	of	131	193	12	4	3	.981
Cordell, Richard, OM	of	116	187	2	4	0	.979
Hairston, Samuel, CS	c	129	763	82	10	16	.988

Earned Run Average Leaders
(154 Or More Innings)

	G	W–L	Pct.	IP	R	ER	ERA
Singleton, James, SC	33	14–7	.667	188	77	57	2.73
Picone, Mario, SC	26	15–7	.682	199	77	62	2.80
Pope, William, CS	23	12–5	.706	159	64	53	3.00
Schultz, George, DE	31	17–9	.654	238	97	84	3.18
Blaylock, Gary, OM	30	13–9	.591	177	77	63	3.20

Individual Batting Leaders
(Minimum 483 At Bats)

	Avg.	G	AB	R	H	HR	RBI	SB
Phillips, Edward, OM	.320	145	509	90	163	7	61	8
Hairston, Samuel, CS	.316	134	503	89	159	12	98	1
Landenberger, Ken, CS	.315	149	581	112	183	26	133	5
Ibanez, Amado, SC	.309	143	576	86	178	13	87	11
Yelen, Ernest, SC	.309	140	531	91	164	7	68	10

All-Star Team
1b—Ken Landenberger, Colorado Springs
2b—Earl Weaver, Omaha
3b—Chico Ibanez, Sioux City
ss—Sherwin Dixon, Omaha
of—Bill Pinkard, Denver
of—Norman Postolese, Pueblo
of—Raymond Berns, Sioux City
c—Sam Hairston, Colorado Springs
p—Connie Johnson, Colorado Springs
p—Alberto Osorio, Denver,
p—Edward Hrabcsak, Lincoln
p—Marvin Williams, Pueblo

Attendance
Denver—461,419
Colorado Springs—170,041
Omaha—137,378
Pueblo—122,746
Wichita—116,703
Sioux City—103,004
Des Moines—62,597
Lincoln—61,483
Total—1,235,371
Playoffs—34,883

Batting Leaders
HOME RUNS
Pinckard, William, DE—35
Crosby, Jerry, CS—26
Landenberger, Ken, CS—26
Harris, Boyd G., SC—23
McMillan, William, SC—20

RUNS BATTED IN
Landenberger, Ken, CS—133
Lamont, Leonard, PU—109
Pinckard, William, DE—108
Crosby, Jerry, CS—107
Berns, Raymond, SC—100

STOLEN BASES
Dixon, Sherwin, OM—34
Curry, Lacey, PU—30
Cleverly, James, WI—28
Leap, C. Allen, PU—22
Johnson, Raymond, SC—21

HITS
Landenberger, Ken, CS—183
Ibanez, Amado, SC—178
Postolese, Norman, PU—175
Fucci, Victor, CS—168
Yelen, Ernest, SC—164

DOUBLES
Landenberger, Ken, CS—39
Postolese, Norman, PU—38
Ries, Robert, DE—37
Zwainz, Richard, WI—35
Stewart, William, LI—32

TRIPLES
Postolese, Norman, PU—16
Curry, Lacey, PU—13
Moon, Wallace, OM—11
Mangini, Joseph, LI—11
Dickey, James, DE—10

TOTAL BASES
Landenberger, Ken, CS—314
Postolese, Norman, PU—263
Ibanez, Amado, SC—256
Pinckard, William, DE—251
Crosby, Jerry, CS—242

RUNS
Landenberger, Ken, CS—112
Cleverly, James, WI—110
Curry, Lacey, PU—109
Fucci, Victor, CS—106
Jacinto, Alvin, CS—100

After the War (1947–1958)

BASES ON BALLS
Cleverly, James, WI—112
King, James F., WI—112
Stewart, William, LI—107
McMillan, William, SC—107
Lamont, Leonard, PU—105

STRIKEOUTS
Pinckard, William, DE—118
Johnson, Raymond, SC—115
Dixon, Sherwin, OM—108
Leap, C. Allen, PU—105
Curry, Lacey, PB—103

Pitching Leaders

GAMES
Ciola, Louis, OM—65
Fustin, Kenneth, PU—54
Thomas, David F., OM—47
Giddings, Robert, SC—46
Kunel, Joseph, DM—46

COMPLETE GAMES
Johnson, C., CS—24
Giddings, Robert, SC—22
Mesa, Richard P., WI—20
Fracchia, Donald, SC—19
Strahs, Richard, CS—19

SHUTOUTS
Montgomery, Walter, OM—6
Osorio, Alberto, DE—6
Atkinson, Richard, OM—4
Giddings, Robert, SC—4
Romberger, Allen, LI—4
Several with 3

WINS
Osorio, Alberto, DE—20
Giddings, Robert, SC—19
Fustin, Kenneth, PU—19
Johnson, C., CS—18
Schultz, George, DE—17

LOSSES
Mesa, Richard P., WI—18

Romberger, Allen, LI—18
Montgomery, Walter, OM—16
Bruner, Jack, WI—15
Schneiders, Paul, DM—15

HOME RUNS ALLOWED
Erath, George, SC—23
Giddings, Robert, SC—18
Osorio, Alberto, DE—16
Johnson, C., CS—16
Several with 15

INNINGS PITCHED
Mesa, Richard P., WI—270
Giddings, Robert, SC—253
Johnson, C., CS—248
Schultz, George, DE—238
Strahs, Richard, CS—231

BASES ON BALLS
Williams, M.W., PU—172
Mesa, Richard P., WI—146
Fustin, PU—132
Fracchia, Donald, SC—118
Long, George, DM—117

STRIKEOUTS
Johnson, C., CS—233
Mesa, Richard P., WI—201
Picone, Mario, SC—166
Montgomery, Walter, OM—150
Several with 149

WILD PITCHES
Long, George, DM—17
Fustin, Kenneth, PU—16
Williams, M.W., PU—16
Mesa, Richard P, WI—14
Piktuzis, George, DM—13

BALKS
Vega, Rene, DE—6
Kumm, John, LI—5
Blaylock, Gary, OM—4
Rivas, Ragael—4
Several with 3

1953

On April 20, 1953, Jerry Crosby smashed four consecutive homers in consecutive innings to set a Western League record and lead Colorado

The Colorado Springs Sky Sox won the pennant in 1953. (Photograph courtesy of Jay Sanford)

Springs to a wild 20–16 win over Pueblo. He also singled in the game to earn 17 total bases in the game, another league record.

Denver tried to make it two championships in a row, but fell a game short to Colorado Springs for the pennant in 1953. In the first round of the Shaughnessy playoff, the Sky Sox were eliminated by upstart fourth-place Des Moines, who had a losing record in the regular season. Denver blanked Pueblo in the other playoffs. Des Moines then beat the Bears in the finals, four games to one.

Denver's Jake Thies tied with Omaha's Walt Montgomery for pitching honors. Thies later pitched for the Pirates for two seasons. Denver also had All-Star pitcher Nelson King, who played four years with Pittsburgh. The third-placed Pueblo Dodgers had Jim Gentile at first base. He was an All-Star that season. Later, "Diamond Jim" had one super season in the majors in which he hit 46 home runs, including five grand slams, two of which came in consecutive innings. However, his bright candle burned out quickly and he spent only seven full seasons in the majors. Lincoln's Norman Brown, who played a couple of seasons in the majors, led the league with 21 wins.

Attendance was beginning to slide in 1953 as Americans began to turn their attention elsewhere. Sioux City attracted just 45,412, compared to Denver's league high 322,128.

Landis Lands in Chicago

The Sky Sox were helped to the pennant by Jim Landis, who was named to the All-Star Team. The outstanding fielder also was one of the leading hitters in the league with his .311 average.

Landis made it to the Chicago White Sox a few years later. He scored six runs in the 1959 World Series. For the next five seasons he won the Gold Glove for his fielding in center. He was only average with the bat though.

After eight seasons with the Sox, he went to five other teams during his 11-year career.

1953

Final Standings

	W	L	Pct.	GB	Affiliations
Colorado Springs Sky Sox	95	59	.617	—	Chicago White Sox
Denver Bears	94	60	.610	1	Pittsburgh Pirates
Pueblo Dodgers	78	77	.503	17½	Brooklyn Dodgers
Des Moines Bruins	77	78	.497	18½	Chicago Cubs
Omaha Cardinals	74	80	.481	21	St. Louis Cardinals
Lincoln Chiefs	71	83	.461	24	Milwaukee Braves
Sioux City Soos	70	84	.455	25	New York Giants
Wichita Indians	58	96	.377	37	St. Louis Browns

Playoffs

Des Moines defeated Colorado Springs, three games to one.
Denver defeated Pueblo, three games to none.

Finals

Des Moines defeated Denver, three games to one.

Team Batting

	AB	R	H	HR	BB	SO	SB	Avg.
Colorado Springs	5335	875	1507	88	634	707	121	.282
Denver	5179	901	1462	123	768	691	49	.282
Pueblo	5188	795	1450	101	632	735	83	.279
Sioux City	5109	705	1286	89	654	822	130	.252
Omaha	5069	618	1231	59	646	630	50	.243
Des Moines	5042	687	1220	73	744	843	61	.242
Wichita	5088	676	1216	88	653	785	70	.239
Lincoln	5080	602	1215	41	670	646	44	.239

Team Fielding

	G	DP	PB	PO	A	E	Pct.
Denver	154	152	16	3963	1750	200	.966

	G	DP	PB	PO	A	E	Pct.
Colorado Springs	155	162	20	4018	1748	208	.965
Lincoln	154	146	24	4018	1682	227	.962
Omaha	154	184	22	4025	1763	244	.960
Des Moines	156	147	4	4001	1748	241	.960
Wichita	155	168	21	3980	1686	248	.958
Sioux City	154	158	20	3958	1718	274	.954
Pueblo	156	154	14	3972	1586	267	.954

Individual Fielding Leaders
(More Than 100 Games)

	POS	G	PO	A	E	DP	Pct.
Womack, Dallas, LI	1b	149	1301	75	22	114	.984
Weaver, Earl, OM	2b	139	344	389	17	112	.977
Konyar, Peter, WI	3b	121	117	232	22	26	.941
Honacki, Richard, WI	ss	123	210	386	32	73	.949
Rice, Francis, DE	of	147	375	16	1	3	.997
Postolese, Norman, PU	of	156	425	22	8	5	.982
Colombo, Michael, WI	of	150	267	25	6	2	.980
Kovach, Steven, WI	c	101	539	66	8	9	.987

Earned Run Average Leaders
(154 Or More Innings)

	G	W–L	Pct.	IP	R	ER	ERA
Thies, Vernon, DE	31	16–6	.727	196	84	53	2.43
Montgomery, Walter, OM	37	13–9	.591	196	73	53	2.43
Jackson, Lawrence, OM	22	10–9	.526	162	50	44	2.44
Mathieson, Robert, LI	27	7–10	.412	168	55	46	2.46
Wright, Roger, LI	46	10–10	.500	158	60	50	2.85

Individual Batting Leaders
(Minimum 465 At Bats)

	G	AB	R	H	HR	RBI	SB	Avg.
Pflasterer, Kent, PU	141	543	94	190	9	80	15	.350
Gorbous, Glen, PU	156	607	94	204	11	103	10	.336
Ries, Robert, DE	153	580	102	191	10	89	0	.329
Johnston, Leonard, CS	155	626	133	199	2	68	60	.318
Landis, James, CS	128	473	87	148	14	68	10	.313

All-Star Team

1b—Jim Gentile, Pueblo
2b—Curt Roberts, Denver
3b—Bob Ries, Denver
ss—Clyde Perry, Colorado Springs
of—Glen Gorbons, Pueblo
of—Jim Landis, Colorado Springs
of—Russell Rac, Omaha
of—Orinthal Anderson, Denver
c—Sam Hairston, Colorado Springs

c—Jack Shepard, Denver
utility—William Ley, Colorado Springs
p—Norman Brown, Lincoln
p—Nelson King, Denver
p—Jake Thies, Denver
p—Robert Zick, Des Moines
p—Joe Stupak, Sioux City
p—Karl Spooner, Pueblo
manager—Don Gutterridge,
  Colorado Springs

Attendance

Denver—322,128
Colorado Springs—141,117
Omaha—115,512
Pueblo—103,878
Des Moines—98,972
Lincoln—87,615
Wichita—68,683
Sioux City—45,412
Total—983,317
Playoffs—19,970
All-Star Game—7,447

Batting Leaders

HOME RUNS
Gentile, James, PU—34
Getter, Richard, SC—27
Crosby, Jerry, CS—25
Rice, Francis, DE—25
Rac, Russell, OM—23

RUNS BATTED IN
Crosby, Jerry, CS—115
Rhyne, Harold, CS—111
Getter, Richard, SC—110
Gorbous, Glen, PU—103
Several with 102

STOLEN BASES
Johnston, Leonard, CS—60
La Sala, Vincent, SC—31
Johnson, Raymond, SC—29
Springfield, William, WI—28
Ley, William, CS—21

HITS
Gorbous, Glen, PU—204
Johnston, Leonard, CS—199

Ries, Robert, DE—191
Pflasterer, Kent, PU—190
Postolese, Norman, PU—181

DOUBLES
Hairston, Sam, CS—42
Jacobs, Gerald, WI—39
Prescott, George, DE—38
Roberts, Curtis, DE—32
Several with 30

TRIPLES
Lee, Andrew, OM—15
Thurlby, Burdette, DM—13
Jones, James, SC—11
Gorbous, Glen, PU—10
Postolese, Norman, PU—9

TOTAL BASES
Gorbous, Glen, PU—286
Gentile, James, PU—280
Ries, Robert, DE—271
Jacobs, Gerald, WI—261
Several with 258

RUNS
Johnston, Leonard, CS—133
Roberts, Curtis, DE—126
Gentile, James, PU—115
Anderson, Orinthal, DE—105
Hancock, Fred, LI—105

BASES ON BALLS
Womack, Dallas, LI—137
La Sala, Vincent, SC—131
Kitsos, Christopher, DM—122
Crosby, Jerry, CS—106
Several with 97

STRIKEOUTS
Gentile, James, PU—135
Bridges, Marshall, SC—109
Johnson, Raymond, SC—105
Springfield, William, WI—101
Several with 99

Pitching Leaders

GAMES
King, Nelson, DE—50
Hamlin, Richard, CS—46
Wright, Roger, LI—46

Dewey, Paul, OM—44
Upchurch, James, WI—43

GAMES STARTED
Brown, Norman, LI—34
Stevens, Clyde, SC—31
Waters, M., PU—31
Pope, William, CS—30
Several with 28

COMPLETE GAMES
Brown, Norman, LI—28
Stupak, Joseph, SC—23
Waters, M., PU—23
Pope, William, CS—19
Zick, Robert, DM—19

SHUTOUTS
Brown, Norman, LI—5
Dewey, Paul, OM—4
Spooner, Karl, PU—4
Several with 3

WINS
Brown, Norman, LI—21
Stupak, Joseph, SC—19
Waters, M., PU—18
Several with 16

LOSSES
Hamlin, Richard, CS—20
Locke, Charles, WI—18
Upchurch, James, WI—15
Verbic, DM—14
Several with 13

HOME RUNS ALLOWED
Hamlin, Richard, CS—21

LeGros, Thomas, DM—17
Pope, William, CS—18
Hoffman, R., PU—16
Stupak, Joseph, SC—16

INNINGS PITCHED
Brown, Norman, LI—284
Hamlin, Richard, CS—259
Waters, M., PU—247
Locke, Charles, WI—242
Stupak, Joseph, SC—242

BASE ON BALLS
Locke, Charles, WI—149
Stevens, Clyde, SC—142
Hamlin, Richard, CS—129
Spooner, Karl, PU—115
Several with 108

STRIKEOUTS
Spooner, Karl, PU—198
Locke, Charles, WI—191
Waters, F., LI—173
Pope, William, CS—167
Zick, Robert, DM—138

WILD PITCHES
Hamlin, SC—19
Mahrt, James, SC—14
Several with 12

BALKS
Salgado, Ramon, DE—5
Sauer, Arthur, SC—4
Hamlin, Richard, CS—3
Locke, Charles, WI—3
Several with 2

1954

In 1954 Denver returned to the top of the league, winning the pennant by a wide margin over Des Moines. Nevertheless, Des Moines got the last laugh by beating Denver in the playoffs, three games to one. Omaha and Pueblo finished third and fourth, respectively, and managed just one win in the playoffs. Colorado Springs dropped from the sky like a meteor and finished last after being on top the season before.

Hy Cohen of Des Moines led the league in pitching, with a 1.88 ERA. He got a call from the Cubs the next season as reliever. Colorado Springs'

After the War (1947–1958)

The Denver Bears won the Western League in 1954. The team consisted of: (front row) Pritts, Lathorpe, Brookey, Weaver, manager Andy Cohen, Dahlke, Prescott, McCord, Rice; (back row) trainer Behm, Ippolito, Cobos, Figard, Browne, DeBenedetti, Garber, Churn, Bloxam, Drilling and Garmon. (Photograph courtesy of Jay Sanford).

Joe Kirrene led the league in hitting, with a .343 average. His league-leading performance earned him a call from the White Sox that season for nine games. Unfortunately, this was the extent of his major league experience, other than a single game in 1950. Omaha's Jim King was named to the All-Star Team, which led to a call from the Cubs the next season. The outfielder played 11 years in the majors.

Wills Steals the Show

Before Maury Wills made history in the majors, he was a leading base stealer in the Western League in 1954 when he swiped 28. Wills led the Western League in stolen bases in 1956. He also was one of the leaders in triples.

After eight seasons in the minors he finally made it to the Dodgers. Then he stole the show. In 1962 he stole 104 bases to break Ty Cobb's record, which was nearly fifty years old. In the league playoffs he was named as MVP, despite the Dodgers losing.

Wills was the stolen-base leader in the National League for six straight seasons before injuries slowed him. During his career he appeared in six All-Star Games.

White Rises from Hitter to President

Bill White of Sioux City was one of the best hitters in the league in 1954, as he led the league in homers, stolen bases and putouts to earn himself a spot on the All-Star team.

White went to the New York Giants two seasons later. The Giants traded him to St. Louis, where he earned six Gold Gloves playing first base. White was named to five All-star Teams during his 13 years in the majors.

After spending some time in the broadcast booth, White was named as president of the National League in 1989.

1954
Final Standings

	W	L	Pct.	GB	Affiliations
Denver Bears	94	56	.627	—	Pittsburgh Pirates
Des Moines Bruins	88	66	.571	8	Chicago Cubs
Omaha Cardinals	83	68	.550	11½	St. Louis Cardinals
Pueblo Dodgers	79	74	.516	16½	Brooklyn Dodgers
Sioux City Soos	78	75	.510	17½	New York Giants
Wichita Indians	76	77	.497	19½	Baltimore Orioles
Lincoln Chiefs	62	88	.413	32	Milwaukee Braves
Colorado Springs Sky Sox	48	104	.316	47	Chicago White Sox

Playoffs

Denver defeated Pueblo, three games to one.
Des Moines defeated Omaha, three games to one.

Finals

Des Moines defeated Denver, three games to one.

Team Batting

	AB	R	H	HR	BB	SO	SB	Avg.
Pueblo	5161	804	1436	92	665	971	106	.278
Denver	5069	944	1406	123	767	785	65	.277
Des Moines	5061	726	1353	126	625	686	50	.267
Colorado Springs	5091	729	1350	81	632	814	61	.265
Omaha	5001	663	1319	73	538	545	71	.263
Wichita	5135	741	1343	60	667	716	60	.262
Sioux City	5121	690	1341	140	577	828	72	.262
Lincoln	4991	669	1289	56	637	627	39	.258

Team Fielding

	G	DP	PB	PO	A	E	Pct.
Des Moines	155	164	17	3976	1726	183	.969

After the War (1947–1958)   249

	G	DP	PB	PO	A	E	Pct.
Wichita	154	128	13	4018	1623	193	.967
Omaha	152	142	23	3937	1707	211	.964
Denver	151	141	10	3920	1535	202	.964
Sioux City	154	144	22	3982	1712	243	.959
Colorado Springs	152	192	22	3840	1797	242	.959
Lincoln	151	102	11	3863	1518	231	.959
Pueblo	155	172	18	4024	1760	257	.957

Individual Fielding Leaders
(More Than 100 Games)

	POS	G	PO	A	E	DP	Pct.
Hertweck, Neal, OM	1b	137	1195	82	13	114	.990
Anderson, George, PU	2b	146	397	432	20	116	.976
Ries, Robert, OM	3b	134	138	308	24	29	.949
Honacki, Richard, WI	ss	139	257	391	23	65	.966
Pavlick, William, SC	of	121	272	15	3	2	.990
Prescott, George, DE	of	142	240	8	5	4	.980
Getter, Richard, SC	of	128	247	16	6	3	.978
Brookey, Melvin, DE	c	103	624	62	12	10	.983

Earned Run Average Leaders
(154 Or More Innings)

	G	W–L	Pct.	IP	R	ER	ERA
Cohen, Hyman, DM	27	16–6	.727	196	51	41	1.88
Kump, Ronald, OM	30	14–12	.538	217	78	55	2.28
Suarez, Armando, PU	43	15–7	.682	215	75	64	2.68
Elston, Donald, DM	35	17–10	.630	220	73	66	2.70
Clear, E. Robert, OM	39	20–11	.645	267	107	87	2.93

Individual Batting Leaders
(Minimum 465 At Bats)

	G	AB	R	H	HR	RBI	SB	Avg.
Kirrene, Joseph, CS	130	467	91	160	10	79	11	.343
DeBenedetti, Reno, DE	147	557	125	183	15	89	19	.329
De, Thaddeus, WI	137	517	78	166	5	88	8	.321
White, William, SC	154	573	120	183	30	92	40	.319
Davis, Willard, PU	146	549	78	175	19	108	11	.319

All-Star Team

1b—Bill White, Sioux City
2b—Earl Weaver, Denver
3b—Joe Kirrene, Colorado Springs
ss—Edward Winceniak, Des Moines
of—Jim King, Omaha
of—Ted Delguercio, Wichita
of—Bobby Prescott, Denver
c—Les Peden, Des Moines
p—Bob Garber, Denver

p—Hy Cohen, Des Moines
p—John O'Donnell, Wichita

Attendance

Denver—232,686
Omaha—150,131
Des Moines—113,691
Wichita—87,854
Pueblo—80,768
Lincoln—80,660
Sioux City—69,333
Colorado Springs—59,606
Total—874,729
Playoffs—16,394

Batting Leaders

HOME RUNS
While, William, SC—30
Getter, Richard, SC—27
Gentile, James, PU—26
Peden, Leslie, DM—26
King, James, OM—25

RUNS BATTED IN
Ippolito, Rocco, DE—131
King, James, OM—127
George Prescott, DE—121
Browne, Prentice, DE—109
Rhyne, Harold, CS—109

STOLEN BASES
White, William, SC—40
Wills, Maurice, PU—28
DeBenedetti, Reno, DE—19
Jeffers, Frank, PU—18
McLennan, Donald, OM—17

HITS
DeBenedetti, Reno, DE—183
White, William, SC—183
Storck, Frederick, PU—178
Davis, Willard, PU—175
Elser, Byron, OM—171

DOUBLES
McQuillen, Glenn, LI—41
DeBenedetti, Reno, DE—39
Jeffers, Frank, PU—39
Davis, Willard, PU—36
Browne, Prentice, DE—35

TRIPLES
Jeffers, Frank, PU—15
Winceniak, Edward, DM—12
Elser, Byron, OM—11
Springfield, William, WI—10
Wills, Maurice, PU—10

TOTAL BASES
White, William, SC—321
King, James, OM—284
DeBenedetti, Reno, DE—277
Davis, Willard, PU—274
Ippolito, Rocco, DE—265

RUNS
Prescott, George, DE—137
DeBenedetti, Reno, DE—125
Weaver, Earl, DE—124
White, William, SC—120
Ippolito, Rocco, DE—119

BASES ON BALLS
Prescott, George, DE—132
Springfield, William, WI—103
Weaver, Earl, DE—102
DeBenedetti, Reno, DE—94
Jacinto, Alvin, CS—93

STRIKEOUTS
Jeffers, Frank, PU—118
Speake, Robert, DM—115
Davis, Willard, PU—114
Wills, Maurice, PU—104
Rice, Francis, DE—104

Pitching Leaders

GAMES
Ciola, Louis, OM—49
Mazar, Peter, WI—49
Diemer, William, WI—48
Graves, James, SC—46
Wright, Roger, LI—46

GAMES STARTED
Clear, E. Robert, OM—34
Bush, Anderson, LI—30
O'Donnell, John, WI—30
Diemer, William, WI—29
Heim, Millard, OM—29

COMPLETE GAMES
Bush, Anderson, LI—24
Clear, E. Robert, OM—22
O'Donnell, John, WI—22
Garber, Robert, DE—19
Garmon, Charles, DE—18

SHUTOUTS
Elston, Donald, DM—9
Cohen, Hyman, DM—6
Clear, E. Robert, OM—5
Heim, Millard, OM—5
Menking, Paul, DM—5

WINS
Clear, E. Robert, OM—20
Bush, Anderson, LI—19
Garber, Robert, DE—19
Graves, James, SC—18
Several with 17

LOSSES
O'Donnell, John, WI—16
Howard, Roger, CS—15
Wilbur, Benjamin, SC—15
Rudolph, Frederick, CS—14
Yowell, Walter, CS—14

HOME RUNS ALLOWED
Wilbur, Benjamin, SC—25
Graves, James, SC—24
Garmon, Charles, DE—17

O'Donnell, John, WI—16
Diemer, William, WI—16

INNINGS PITCHED
Clear, E. Robert, OM—267
O'Donnell, John, WI—249
Bush, Anderson, LI—242
Garber, Robert, DE—242
Diemer, William, WI—240

BASES ON BALLS
Clear, E. Robert, OM—114
DeWitt, Clyde, PU—109
Diemer, William, WI—105
Suarez, Armando, PU—101
Kern, Eugene, PU—100

STRIKEOUTS
Elston, Donald, DM—171
Garmon, Charles, DE—160
Diemer, WI—160
Several with 145

WILD PITCHES
Howard, Roger, CS—18
Bradley, CS—15
Kern, Eugene, PU—13
Pane, Andrew, SC—12
Several with 11

BALKS
Keating, Thomas, LI—5
Several with 2

1955

Denver and Omaha left the league in 1955 for the American Association, which cut the league to six teams. Another change was O'Neill M. Hobbs from Pueblo, Colorado, taking over as league president.

Colorado Springs took the pennant in a close race to the finish, with Pueblo, Wichita and Des Moines in hot pursuit. The playoffs were close as well. First, the Wichita Indians and Des Moines Bruins had to play a game to decide third place. The Indians trounced the Bruins 21–3. The Bruins then upset the Sky Sox in the first round by taking the five-game series in four games. The Indians had a bit more trouble with second-place Pueblo but finally beat the Dodgers in the if-necessary game. That left Wichita again facing Des Moines, but this time for the title. It was no contest. The Indians swept the series.

The Sky Sox were led by Sam Hairston, who led the league in hitting with a .350 average, and Ron Cooper, who was the RBI leader. Robert Harrison of Wichita finished the 1955 season in fine style when he pitched a 2–0 no-hitter against Des Moines in the final round of the playoffs. Lincoln's Dick Hall led the league in pitching with a 2.24 ERA until he left for the Pirates for the remainder of the season. He pitched in the majors for 16 seasons. The reliever appeared in three World Series with the Orioles.

Fodge Earns Old Nickname

One of the leading pitchers in the league was Gene "Suds" Fodge with Des Moines. In his second year in the league Fodge became a starter and responded with four shutouts and 16 wins. "I lost six games by a run," he recalled.

During his minor league days he picked up his nickname. "Johnnie Briggs and me were roommates and we used to sip a few [beers]," he explained. "One day he called me Suds."

Fodge finally got his shot at the majors with the Cubs in 1968. He picked up his only victory in the majors against the Los Angeles Dodgers the first month of the season. The relief pitcher spent that season in the majors until the Cubs ran out of options on his contract and sold him to the Yankees, who sent him to Denver. He decided not to report and went to work for a living instead of playing ball.

Kirkland Kaboomed the Ball

Sioux City's Willie Kirkland slammed out 40 homers to lead the league in home runs and runs scored. It earned him honors on the All-Star Team.

The shortstop was turned into an outfielder when he went to the majors in 1958 with the Giants. He earned the nickname "Boom Boom" when he put his name in the record book by hitting three straight homers off the same pitcher. Then he added another for four consecutive dingers to tie another major league record.

In nine seasons Kirkland knocked out 148 four-base hits. Then he traveled to Japan for another six years before retiring from baseball.

1955
Final Standings

	W	L	Pct.	GB	Affiliations
Colorado Springs Sky Sox	81	69	.540	—	Chicago White Sox
Pueblo Dodgers	79	71	.527	2	Brooklyn Dodgers

	W	L	Pct.	GB	Affiliations
Wichita Indians	78	73	.517	3½	Baltimore Orioles
Des Moines Bruins	77	74	.510	4½	Chicago Cubs
Sioux City Soos	69	81	.460	12	New York Giants
Lincoln Chiefs	67	83	.447	14	Pittsburgh Pirates

Playoffs

Wichita defeated Des Moines in a game to decide third place.
Des Moines defeated Colorado Springs, three games to one.
Wichita defeated Pueblo, three games to one.

Finals

Wichita defeated Des Moines, three games to one.

Team Batting

	AB	R	H	HR	BB	SO	SB	Avg.
Colorado Springs	4976	845	1395	118	601	732	52	.280
Wichita	5036	758	1389	82	554	543	91	.276
Sioux City	4826	713	1297	140	619	753	42	.269
Pueblo	5063	752	1356	126	552	881	91	.268
Des Moines	4921	723	1250	148	655	901	59	.254
Lincoln	4851	720	1225	83	726	779	45	.253

Team Fielding

	G	DP	PB	PO	A	E	Pct.
Wichita	152	149	13	3899	1521	182	.968
Des Moines	152	181	28	3891	1751	224	.962
Colorado Springs	150	150	17	3826	1713	219	.962
Sioux City	151	122	19	3729	1572	217	.961
Lincoln	141	133	15	3821	1468	222	.960
Pueblo	150	181	22	3875	1603	238	.958

Individual Fielding Leaders
(More Than 100 Games)

	POS	G	PO	A	E	DP	Pct.
Hallow, George, WI	1b	143	1201	74	9	124	.993
Babcock, Rex, LI	2b	145	330	365	22	89	.969
Barbarito, Edward, WI	3b	147	116	312	19	37	.957
Bellino, Raymond, DM	ss	145	262	493	39	107	.951
Rice, Francis, LI	of	150	416	15	8	3	.982
Smith, Robert, SC	of	102	176	16	4	0	.980
Glenn, Scott, PU	of	123	315	29	9	6	.975

Earned Run Average Leaders
(154 Or More Innings)

	G	W–L	Pct.	IP	R	ER	ERA
Hall, Richard, LI	19	12–5	.706	153	47	38	2.24
Fodge, Gene, DM	36	16–10	.615	225	82	57	2.28
Harrison, Robert, WI	32	14–12	.538	206	67	55	2.40
McMinn, Glen, PU	29	9–7	.563	182	84	59	2.92
Pane, Andrew, SC	22	12–8	.600	152	78	55	3.26

Individual Batting Leaders
(Minimum 465 At Bats)

	G	AB	R	H	HR	RBI	SB	Avg.
Hairston, Sam, CS	142	546	107	191	6	91	2	.350
Conde, Ramon, CS	134	494	70	171	11	84	1	.346
Senties, Juan, WI	142	545	82	180	13	94	14	.330
Almenares, Pedro, PU	135	498	71	164	22	91	4	.329
Moore, Clarence, PU	150	591	112	194	11	80	17	.328

All-Star Team
1b—Ken Landerberger, Colorado Springs
2b—Robert McKee, Des Moines
3b—Ed Barbarito, Wichita
ss—Clarence Moore, Pueblo
of—Willie Kirkland, Sioux City
of—Domenick DiTusa, Colorado Springs
of—Francis Rice, Lincoln
c—Sam Hairston, Colorado
c—Miguel Gaspar, Wichita
p—Andrew Pane, Sioux City
p—Bob Harrison, Wichita

Attendance
Wichita—94,862
Lincoln—90,024
Des Moines—88,181
Colorado Springs—87,527
Pueblo—73,941
Sioux City—62,902
Total—497,437
Playoffs—14,034

Batting Leaders
HOME RUNS
Kirkland, Willie, SC—40
Cooper, Ronald, CS—35
Cunningham, David, DM—30
McDaniel, James, DM—24
Several with 22

RUNS BATTED IN
Cooper, Ronald, CS—117
Kirtland, Willie, SC—116
Senties, Juan, WI—94
Cunningham, David, DM—93
Sheets, Eugene, CS—93

STOLEN BASES
Springfield, William, WI—46
Moore, Clarence, PU—17
Kirkland, Willie, SC—14
Senties, Juan, WI—14
Several with 13

HITS
Moore, Clarence, PU—194
Hairston, Sam, CS—191
Senties, Juan, WI—180
Barbarito, Edward, WI—176
Kirkland, Willie, SC—158

DOUBLES
Rice, Francis, LI—41
Sheets, Eugene, CS—40
Hairston, Sam, CS—38

Conde, Ramon, SC—35
Barbarito, Edward, WI—32

TRIPLES
Moore, Clarence, PU—12
Glenn, John, PU—10
Gnagy, Max, CS—8
Springfield, William, W—7
Several with 6

TOTAL BASES
Kirkland, Willie, SC—315
Cooper, Ronald, CS—278
Barbarito, Edward, WI—272
Moore, Clarence, PU—272
Cunningham, David, DM—271

RUNS
Kirkland, Willie, SC—117
Gnagy, Max, CS—115
Moore, Clarence, PU—112
Hairston, Sam, CS—107
Cunningham, David, DM—104

BASES ON BALLS
Cunningham, David, DM—104
Adkins, Theodore, LI—103
Rice, Francis, LI—98
Gnagy, Max, CS—95
Springfield, William, WI—86

STRIKEOUTS
Cooper, Ronald, CS—114
Rice, Francis, LI—107
Cunningham, David, DM—105
Babcock, Rex, LI—103
McDaniel, James, DM—101

Pitching Leaders

GAMES
Warren, Thomas, WI—49
Hamlin, Richard, SC—39
O'Donnell, John, WI—39
Wright, R., PU—39
Drilling, Richard, LI—37

GAMES STARTED
Barclay, Curtis, SC—29
Fodge, Gene, DM—29
Stanka, Joe, DM—28
Several with 26

COMPLETE GAMES
Barclay, Curtis, SC—22
Fodge, Gene, DM—20
Harrison, Robert, WI—18
Stanka, Joe, DM—17
Zanni, Dominick, SC—17

SHUTOUTS
Fodge, Gene, DM—4
McMinn, Glen, PU—4
Anderson, Robert, DM—3
Stanka, Joe, DM—3
Several with 2

WINS
Stanka, Joe, DM—17
Fodge, Gene, DM—16
Barclay, Curtis, SC—16
Zanni, Dominick, SC—15
Several with 14

LOSSES
O'Donnell, John, WI—15
Graves, James, SC—13
Hamlin, Richard, SC—13
Several with 12

HOME RUNS ALLOWED
Drilling, Richard, LI—29
Barclay, Curtis, SC—25
O'Donnell, John, WI—25
Graves, James, SC—22
Several with 19

INNINGS PITCHED
Fodge, Gene, DM—225
Barclay, Curtis, SC—219
Zanni, Dominick, SC—211
Stanka, Joe, DM—210
Harrison, Robert, WI—206

BASES ON BALLS
Harrison, Robert, WI—140
Bell, William, LI—133
Hamlin, Richard, SC—105
Anderson, Robert, DM—90
Fodge, Gene, DM—89

STRIKEOUTS
Harrison, Robert, WI—270
Stanka, Joe, DM—148
Hall, Richard, LI—137

Brown, John, LI—129
Zanni, Dominick, SC—128

WILD PITCHES
Hamlin, Richard, SC—17

Harrison, Robert, WI—17
Pope, William, CS—13
Bell, William, LI—12
Brown, John, LI—12

1956

The Western League added teams from Albuquerque and Amarillo to bring it back to eight teams for the 1956 campaign. The season was divided into two halves. Lincoln won the first half, while Amarillo won the second. The two faced each other in a seven-game series. Lincoln won it in five games. Topeka was the only team to have attendance over 100,000.

Lincoln was lifted to the title by the most powerful hitter in the league's history. Dick Stuart walloped 66 homers, with 158 RBI, for Lincoln—both league records. Lincoln also had all-star pitcher Bennie Daniels, who was called up to the majors the next season and who pitched nine seasons with Pittsburgh and Washington. Al Weygandt of Topeka also had a banner year hitting home runs (49). During one 10-game road trip he hammered 14 of the four baggers with 30 RBI. Topeka also had All-Star catcher Sammy Taylor, who was called up to the majors for six seasons. Teammate Marshall Bridges did him one year better as he pitched seven seasons in the majors for four different teams. The relief pitcher was 23–15 in the majors. He led the Western League in wins with 18 that season. Amarillo's Art Cuitti was the leading run scorer and hitter in the league, with a .364 average and 132 tallies.

Dr. Strangeglove Sets Homer Record

Some players have been described as all field, no bat. Dick Stuart was the opposite—all bat, no field. He earned the nickname "Dr. Strangeglove" because nobody knew if he'd catch the ball.

During his record 66 homer performance he reportedly hit one 610 feet in Pueblo. The next season he hit 47 homers with three different minor league teams.

Pittsburgh called him up in 1958, and he hit 16 homers in 67 games to earn a regular job despite his fielding woes. Dr. Strangeglove went to Boston in 1963 and led the American League in RBI with 118. He ended up playing for a decade in the majors, with appearances in two World Series.

1956
Final Standings
First Half

	W	L	Pct.	GB	Affiliations
Lincoln Chiefs	45	27	.625	—	Pittsburgh Pirates
Topeka Hawks	44	28	.611	1	Milwaukee Braves
Pueblo Dodgers	39	32	.549	5½	Brooklyn Dodgers
Amarillo Gold Sox	38	32	.543	6	None
Des Moines Bruins	35	36	.493	9½	Chicago Cubs
Colorado Springs Sky Sox	34	36	.486	10	Chicago White Sox
Albuquerque Dukes	26	44	.371	18	New York Giants
Sioux City Soos	22	48	.314	22	St. Louis Cardinals

Second Half

	W	L	Pct.	GB
Amarillo Gold Sox	49	20	.710	—
Lincoln Chiefs	39	27	.591	8½
Des Moines Bruins	37	31	.544	11½
Albuquerque Dukes	33	37	.471	16½
Colorado Springs Sky Sox	32	36	.471	16½
Pueblo Dodgers	29	38	.433	19
Topeka Hawks	26	40	.394	21½
Sioux City Soos	27	43	.386	22½

Playoffs

Lincoln defeated Amarillo, four games to one.

Team Batting

	AB	R	H	HR	BB	SO	SB	Avg.
Amarillo	4706	909	1357	192	642	775	57	.288
Colorado Springs	4726	789	1338	140	587	819	43	.283
Pueblo	4616	764	1290	149	532	832	82	.279
Topeka	4668	806	1304	176	568	901	72	.279
Albuquerque	4631	744	1287	75	760	852	56	.278
Lincoln	4772	934	1311	208	746	996	105	.275
Des Moines	4700	781	1284	121	647	841	33	.273
Sioux City	4673	717	1228	144	577	848	29	.263

Team Fielding

	G	DP	PB	PO	A	E	Pct.
Des Moines	139	140	19	3573	1479	184	.965
Lincoln	141	149	21	3655	1506	193	.964

	G	DP	PB	PO	A	E	Pct.
Pueblo	138	125	31	3524	1330	190	.962
Colorado Springs	139	110	27	3567	1416	207	.960
Topeka	138	113	20	3571	1351	209	.959
Sioux City	140	113	29	3526	1474	299	.956
Albuquerque	142	136	24	3599	1519	236	.956
Amarillo	139	123	23	3569	1430	234	.953

Individual Fielding Leaders
(Minimum 100 Games)

	POS	G	PO	A	E	DP	Pct.
Jackson, LI	1b	113	919	96	10	111	.999
Toothman, Kenneth, LI	2b	128	299	347	21	103	.969
Russell, PU	3b	138	140	214	29	21	.924
Fassler, Walter, SC	ss	108	196	311	24	54	.955
Griffith, Paul, CS	of	118	228	15	4	2	.984
Soraci, Charles, PU	of	127	195	8	5	1	.976
Jeffers, Frank, PU	of	104	193	12	5	2	.976
Barragan, AM	c	107	686	61	9	13	.988

Earned Run Average Leaders
(100 Or More Innings)

	G	W–L	Pct.	IP	R	ER	ERA
Swanson, Donald, DM	18	8–5	.615	125	62	44	3.17
O'Donnell, John, TO	42	15–11	.577	209	77	76	3.32
Coen, Michael, AM	34	17–9	.654	208	100	80	3.46
Arias, Rodolfo, CS	35	8–5	.615	142	70	56	3.55
Blanton, Hugh, AM	24	12–5	.706	116	57	47	3.65

Individual Batting Leaders
(Minimum 456 At Bats)

	G	AB	R	H	HR	RBI	SB	Avg.
Cutti, Arthur, AM	138	514	132	187	46	139	3	.364
Van de Hey, L., AL	140	549	80	197	10	110	2	.359
Taylor, Samuel, TO	132	525	116	188	28	123	4	.358
Miley, Sammy, LI	123	496	95	170	13	80	21	.343
Griffith, Paul, CS	134	517	119	174	10	62	11	.337

All-Star Team

1b—Ken Landenberger, Sioux City
2b—Ken Toothman, Lincoln
3b—Don Russell, Pueblo
ss—Maury Wills, Pueblo
of—Art Cuitti, Amarillo
of—Eddie Haas, Des Moines
of—Dick Stuart, Lincoln
c—Sammy Taylor, Topeka
c—Kenneth Worley, Pueblo
p—Marshall Bridges, Topeka
p—Reggie Lee, Albuquerque

p—Bennie Daniels, Lincoln
p—Michael Coen, Amarillo

Attendance

Topeka—103,938
Albuquerque—94,176
Lincoln—92,554
Amarillo—77,628
Des Moines—67,973
Colorado Springs—59,282
Pueblo—51,496
Sioux City—40,734
Total—587,781
Playoffs—13,037

Batting Leaders

HOME RUNS
Stuart, Richard, LI—66
Weygandt, Allen, TO—49
Cuitti, Arthur, AM—46
Stanley, Lawrence, PU—42
Di Tusa, Richard, CS—37

RUNS BATTED IN
Stuart, Richard, LI—158
Cuitti, Arthur, AM—139
Taylor, Samuel, TO—123
Weygandt, Allen, TO—116
Di Tusa, Richard, CS—115

STOLEN BASES
Wills, Maurice, PU—34
Toothman, Kenneth, LI—33
Miley, Sammy, LI—21
McDaniel, James, TO—19
Schimchak, William, TO—13

HITS
Van de Hey, L., AL—197
Taylor, Samuel, TO—188
Cuitti, Arthur, AM—187
Johnson, Ernest, DM—181
Griffith, Paul, CS—174

DOUBLES
Hairston, Samuel, CS—38
Taylor, Samuel, TO—38
Shields, William, AM—37
Van de Hey, L., AL—36
Bell, Charles, AM—35

TRIPLES
Griffith, Paul, CS—12
Syngel, Emil, PU—12
Grenald, Reginald, LI—10
Wills, Maurice, PU—8
Taylor, Samuel, TO—8

TOTAL BASES
Stuart, Richard, LI—385
Cuitti, Arthur, AM—350
Taylor, Samuel, TO—326
Weygandt, Allen, TO—315
Shields, William, AM—302

RUNS
Cuitti, Arthur, AM—132
Stuart, Richard, LI—131
Toothman, Kenneth, LI—121
Griffith, Paul, CS—119
Taylor, Samuel, TO—116

BASES ON BALLS
Lundgren, Charles, AL—123
Stanley, Lawrence, PU—117
Griffith, Paul, CS—104
Burnett, Arthur, SC—93
Weygandt, Allen, TO—89

STRIKEOUTS
Stuart, Richard, LI—171
Strichek, Donald, AL—130
Weygandt, Allen, TO—128
Stanley, Lawrence, PU—121
McDaniel, James, TO—109

Pitching Leaders

GAMES
Cray, Vernon, SC—57
Venable, Glenn, AM—48
Ready, Charles, PU—45
Williams, Don, LI—44
Hoffmeister, Paul, DM—43

GAMES STARTED
Bridges, Marshall, TO—31
Sherry, Lawrence, PU—31
Heman, Russell, CS—28
Daniels, Benny, LI—28
Several at 27

COMPLETE GAMES
Bridges, Marshall, TO—19
Coen, Michael, AM—17
Heman, Russell, CS—14
O'Donnell, John, TO—14
Sherry, Lawrence, PU—13

SHUTOUTS
Coen, Michael, AM—4
Daniels, Benny, LI—4
Several at 3

WINS
Bridges, Marshall, TO—18
Daniels, Benny, LI—15
O'Donnell, John, TO—15
Drilling, Richard, AL—14
Heman, Russell, CS—14

LOSSES
Shandor, Theodore, AL—15
Fishter, Rogers, SC—14
Heman, Russell, CS—14
Thiem, Theodore, SC—14
Sherry, Lawrence, PU—13

HOME RUNS ALLOWED
Tugerson, James, AM—34
Heman, Russell, CS—30
O'Donnell, John, TO—28
Atkinson, Richard, SC—27
Sherry, Lawrence, PU—25

INNINGS PITCHED
Bridges, Marshall, TO—242
O'Donnell, John, TO—209
Sherry, Lawrence, PU—209
Coen, Michael, AM—208
Heman, Russell, CS—208

BASE ON BALLS
Bridges, Marshall, TO—154
Lee, J. Reginald, LI—145
Sherry, Lawrence, PU—132
Rowe, Donald, LI—112
Heman, Russell, CS—110

STRIKEOUTS
Bridges, Marshall, TO—213
Heman, Russell, CS—186
Sherry, Lawrence, PU—184
Lee, J. Reginald, LI—183
Coen, Michael, AM—171

WILD PITCHES
Lee, J. Reginald, LI—18
Hines, W. Eugene, PU—15
Hoffman, Myron, LI—13
Ready, Charles, PU—13
Cray, Vernon, SC—12

1957

Three of the teams in the league had no major league affiliate, which was perhaps a premonition. The split season was gone and so were the playoffs. Lincoln won the pennant by a game over Amarillo in a close race. Both teams managed to attract over 100,000 fans, but none of the other teams in the league could get that many people to come to their parks.

Lincoln was led by Sammy Miley, who hit .374 to lead the league. Hugh Blanton also picked up 20 wins with Lincoln. And Don Williams appeared in 60 games in relief to chalk up 15 victories for the league victors. Williams would eventually find his way to the majors as a reliever with Pittsburgh and Kansas City for three seasons. Lincoln's All-Star pitcher Joe Gibbon bettered Williams by playing 13 years in the majors with four National League teams. Another Lincoln pitcher to make it to the bigs was John Lamabe, who won 13 games for Lincoln. The righthander became a journeyman relief pitcher for six major league teams in eight seasons. Topeka had a couple of star players, too. John Stadnicki picked up 23 wins on the season. Chuck Cottier was the Hawks' All-Star second baseman that season. He went on to a nine-year career in the majors and managed the Seattle Mariners for three seasons as well. Then Cottier coached for the Chicago Cubs. Amarillo's Clay Dalrymple made the All-Star team in 1957. By 1960 he was in the majors with Philadelphia. The receiver caught a dozen years in the majors with the Phillies and Orioles. Pueblo's Dick Tracewski was one of the leading hitters in the league. The middle infielder made it to the Dodgers in 1962 and spent eight years in the majors. He was all field, as he hit just .213 in the bigs.

Strange Scoring Play

One of the strangest plays ever in Western League history occurred in 1957. The game pitted Lincoln against Sioux City.

With Sioux City at bat, Artie Burnett was walked and then scored when Bob Rikard hit a double. However, he failed to tag home. Unaware Burnett had failed to touch home, base umpire Tom Dunn called time and asked for the ball. While he was examining the ball, the Lincoln catcher, Harry Dunlop, called for it. Burnett's teammates sent him back to touch the bag. The umpire failed to respond to the catcher and Burnett scored. Manager Larry Shepard protested the call, but plate umpire Jack Wagner allowed the run. However, Lincoln went on to win the game despite the call, and the protest was dropped.

1957

Final Standings

	W	L	Pct.	GB	Affiliations
Lincoln Chiefs	98	56	.636	-	Pittsburgh Pirates
Amarillo Gold Sox	97	57	.630	1	None
Topeka Hawks	87	64	.576	9½	Milwaukee Braves
Sioux City Soos	71	82	.464	26½	None
Colorado Springs Sky Sox	68	86	.442	30	Chicago White Sox
Albuquerque Dukes	66	88	.429	32	None
Pueblo Dodgers	66	88	.429	32	Brooklyn Dodgers
Des Moines Demons	60	92	.395	37	Chicago Cubs

Team Batting

	AB	R	H	HR	BB	SO	SB	Avg.
Amarillo	5256	953	1577	127	655	730	45	.300
Albuquerque	5309	827	1513	85	681	858	31	.285
Colorado Springs	5171	875	1453	137	749	780	40	.281
Pueblo	5198	815	1450	99	672	854	96	.279

	AB	R	H	HR	BB	SO	SB	Avg.
Topeka	5085	921	1408	235	727	973	51	.277
Des Moines	5089	750	1379	72	737	856	41	.271
Lincoln	5097	797	1381	125	658	855	86	.271
Sioux City	5084	827	1357	133	729	902	48	.267

Team Fielding

	G	DP	PB	PO	A	E	Pct.
Amarillo	154	171	20	3944	1592	183	.968
Albuquerque	154	175	26	4017	1609	202	.965
Sioux City	153	145	19	3903	1584	213	.963
Colorado Springs	154	144	34	3941	1700	224	.962
Pueblo	155	156	28	3943	1583	221	.962
Des Moines	153	160	35	3918	1589	229	.960
Topeka	151	170	20	3902	1655	240	.959
Lincoln	154	150	29	3994	1507	244	.958

Individual Fielding Leaders
(Minimum 100 Games)

	POS	G	PO	A	E	DP	Pct.
Landenberger, SC	1b	102	881	66	8	90	.992
Melendez, Wilfredo, LI	2b	117	268	302	10	80	.983
Bockman, J. Edward, AM	3b	121	80	262	18	30	.950
Bell, AL	ss	104	216	321	34	86	.940
Tanner, Rudolph, TO	of	127	279	12	5	1	.983
Rice, Francis, SC	of	139	362	24	8	2	.980
Goodell, John, AM	of	116	171	5	4	0	.978
Engel, Ray, TO	c	131	694	75	7	11	.991

Earned Run Average Leaders
(154 Or More Innings)

	G	W–L	Pct.	IP	R	ER	ERA
Blanton, E. Hugh, AM	33	20–9	.690	258	206	82	2.86
Perez, G., LI	30	15–6	.714	204	84	67	2.96
Lamabe, John, LI	28	13–7	.650	167	78	59	3.18
Umbricht, James, TO	29	13–8	.619	178	87	64	3.24
Stadnicki, John, TO	35	23–6	.793	226	95	82	3.34

Individual Batting Leaders
(Minimum 477 At Bats)

	G	AB	R	H	HR	RBI	SB	Avg.
Pinkston, Alfred, AM	141	554	104	206	23	133	2	.372
Coles, Charles, AL	154	604	122	208	26	121	2	.344

After the War (1947–1958) 263

	G	AB	R	H	HR	RBI	SB	Avg.
De Benedetti, Rene, AL	154	565	105	193	11	111	5	.342
Pascal, Robert, DM	144	499	107	170	18	115	5	.341
Shields, William, AM	154	615	127	200	12	90	16	.325

All-Star Team

1b—Bob Pascal, Des Moines
2b—Chuck Cottier, Topeka
3b—Mike Krsnich, Topeka
ss—Ray Webster, Amarillo
of—Leonard Williams, Topeka
of—Chuck Coles, Albuquerque
of—Al Pinkston, Amarillo
c—Clay Dalrymple, Amarillo
utility—Jim McDanniel, Topeka
utility—Gene Sheets, Colorado Springs
p—Kenneth Yoke, Amarillo
p—Joe Gibbon, Lincoln
p—John Stadnicki, Topeka
p—Hugh Blanton, Amarillo
manager—Eddie Bockman, Amarillo

Attendance

Amarillo—102,210
Lincoln—100,190
Albuquerque—92,236
Topeka—88,014
Des Moines—79,965
Sioux City—46,851
Colorado Springs—45,184
Pueblo—40,887
Total—595,537

Batting Leaders

HOME RUNS
Williams, Leonard, TO—43
Pokel, James, TO—41
McDaniel, James, TO—36
Krsnich, Michael, TO—33
Stuart, Richard, LI—31

RUNS BATTED IN
Pinkston, Alfred, AM—133
Coles, Charles, AL—121
Pokel, James, TO—120
McDaniel, James, TO—116
Pascal, Robert, DM—115

STOLEN BASES
Malec, Stanley, LI—35
Tracewski, Richard, PU—23
Gnagy, Max, SC—16
Shields, William, AM—16
Browne, William, PU—13

HITS
Coles, Charles, AL—208
Pinkston, Alfred, AM—206
Shields, William, AM—200
Dargle, Theodore, AL—197
De Benedetti, Reno, AL—193

DOUBLES
Dargle, Theodore, AL—49
Pinkston, Alfred, AM—41
Hunter, Donald, AM—39
Almenares, Pedro, PU—37
Pascal, Robert, DM—35

TRIPLES
Goodell, John, AM—14
Tracewski, Richard, PU—14
Coles, Charles, AL—12
Dargle, Theodore, AL—11
Burnett, Arthur, SC—9

TOTAL BASES
Coles, Charles, AL—342
Williams, Leonard, TO—335
Pinkston, Alfred, AM—328
McDaniel, James, TO—295
Dargle, Theodore, AL—289

RUNS
Webster, Raymond, AM—136
Shields, William, AM—127
Murray, Frank, AM—125
Coles, Charles, AL—122
McDaniel, James, TO—122

BASES ON BALLS
Gnagy, Max, SC—129
Pascal, Robert, DM—128
De Benedetti, Rene, AL—112

Burnett, Arthur, SC—109
McDaniel, James, TO—107

STRIKEOUTS
Robertson, Daryl, TO—127
Pokel, James, TO—124
Lynk, Daniel, PU—123
Stuart, Richard, LI—117
Williams, Leonard, TO—115

Pitching Leaders

GAMES
Williams, Don, LI—60
Osorio, Alberto, AL—54
Arias, Rodolfo, CS—53
Blasko, Joseph, SC—52
Ready, Charles, PU—48

GAMES STARTED
Blanton, E. Hugh, AM—32
Yoke, Ken, AM—32
Franco, William, SC—31
Jones, Sherman, SC—29
Michalec, James, AL—28

COMPLETE GAMES
Blanton, E. Hugh, AM—24
Yoke, Ken, AM—24
Stadnicki, John, TO—19
Several with 18

SHUTOUTS
Gibbon, Joseph, LI—4
Blanton, E. Hugh, AM—3
Stadnicki, John, TO—3
Several with 2

WINS
Stadnicki, John, TO—23
Blanton, E. Hugh, AM—20
Yoke, Ken, AM—20
Several with 15

LOSSES
Jones, Sherman, SC—16

Ramos, Richard, CS—15
Stenhouse, David, DM—13
Schaffernoth, DM—12
Several with 11

HOME RUNS ALLOWED
Franco, William, SC—33
Moton, SC—29
Jones, Sherman, SC—24
Perez, George, LI—24
Wegner, Robert, PU—22

INNINGS PITCHED
Yoke, Ken, AM—262
Blanton, E. Hugh, AM—258
Franco, William, SC—244
Several with 221

BASE ON BALLS
Jones, Sherman, SC—145
Stenhouse, David, DM—121
Schaffernoth, J., DM—109
Blasko, Joseph, SC—102
Several with 101

STRIKEOUTS
Stenhouse, David, DM—184
Perez, George, LI—168
Jones, Sherman, SC—165
Bell, W., LI—151
Stadnicki, TO—146

WILD PITCHES
Blasko, Joseph, SC—16
Stenhouse, David, DM—16
Arias, Rodolfo, CS—14
Bell, W., LI—13
Schaffernoth, J., DM—13

HIT BATTERS
Gilbert, H., AL—13
Davies, AL—10
Graham, TO—10
Mason, AL—10
Hine, PU—9

1958

1958 was a memorable year for the Colorado Springs Sky Sox, as the team won the championship and set nine modern league records. Too bad it would be their last. The records included runs scored, RBI, hits, doubles, average, least amount of shutouts suffered and three individual records: batting average, most hits in two games and most hits in three games. While the Sky Sox were hot on the field, the team was cold in the stands. In their last game of the season the team drew just 2,459 fans.

The Sky Sox were powered to the pennant with some good hitters that led the team to a .313 average, which was 18 percentage points higher than any other team. Jim McAnany hit .400 that year. Stan Johnson was the next best hitter on the Sky Sox with his .364 average. He had a trial in the majors. One of the leading pitchers in the league was Dave Stenhouse with a 2.91 ERA. He later pitched three seasons with the Washington Senators. Sky Sox pitcher Hal Trosky, Jr. pitched a no-hitter that season as well, which earned him brief trip to the White Sox that season. Lincoln finished in third place and was helped by All-Star pitcher Al Jackson, who was the leading pitcher in the league with 18 wins and an ERA just over 2. The lefty went on to a decade in the majors, mainly with the new expansion Mets. He had a losing lifetime record of 67–99 with the new team.

McAnany Tops .400

Outfielder Jim McAnany led the Colorado Springs Sky Sox in 1958 by hitting .400, with 26 homers and 117 RBI, which led to his call up to the Chicago White Sox. However, McAnany didn't record enough at bats to lead the league in hitting. His best performance came on June 18. The outfielder knocked in 10 runs in a 17–15 win over Sioux City.

He spent five seasons with the White Sox, where he was used primarily as a pinch hitter. He was unable to hit the long ball in 93 games there.

1958
Final Standings

	W	L	Pct.	GB	Affiliations
Colorado Springs Sky Sox	87	60	.592	–	Chicago White Sox
Amarillo Gold Sox	84	63	.571	3	None
Lincoln Chief	75	71	.514	11½	Pittsburgh Pirates
Pueblo Dodgers	73	74	.497	14	Chicago Cubs
Albuquerque Dukes	71	75	.486	15½	Cincinnati Reds
Sioux City Soos	69	77	.473	17½	None
Topeka Hawks	65	82	.442	22	Milwaukee Braves
Des Moines Bruins	61	83	.424	24½	Los Angeles Dodgers

Team Batting

	AB	R	H	HR	BB	SO	SB	LOB	Avg.
Colorado Springs	5152	1057	1615	133	726	729	61	1233	.313
Pueblo	5097	845	1436	115	643	847	43	1155	.282
Amarillo	5099	886	1423	109	718	905	76	1258	.279
Sioux City	4989	834	1387	162	682	893	60	1168	.278
Topeka	4932	780	1293	139	694	906	67	1155	.262
Lincoln	4826	688	1262	88	567	912	86	1090	.262
Albuquerque	4858	713	1229	102	592	980	75	1081	.253
Des Moines	4648	594	1168	50	531	725	52	1026	.251

Team Fielding

	G	DP	PB	PO	A	E	Pct.
Amarillo	148	159	12	3841	1628	196	.965
Des Moines	144	124	28	3663	1543	194	.964
Albuquerque	147	154	19	3808	1686	214	.963
Colorado Springs	147	135	18	3816	1554	229	.959
Sioux City	146	123	22	3781	1522	236	.957
Pueblo	148	135	19	3888	1674	248	.957
Topeka	148	140	45	3791	1496	247	.955
Lincoln	146	132	24	3797	1764	262	.955

Individual Fielding Leaders
(Minimum 100 Games)

	POS	G	PO	A	E	DP	Pct.
Upright, AM	1b	146	1233	91	18	130	.987
Streeter, AM	2b	141	363	423	31	104	.962
Koshorek, TO	3b	112	90	201	17	22	.945
Terry, Lazaro, AL	ss	108	215	333	24	83	.958
Bullard, George, TO	of	108	232	7	5	1	.980
Hicks, William, CS	of	112	189	3	4	2	.980
McAnany, CS	of	119	299	12	7	2	.978
Tate, Teddy, AM	c	114	637	83	4	14	.994

Earned Run Average Leaders
(Minimum 150 Innings Pitched)

	G	W	L	Pct.	IP	R	ER	ERA
Jackson, A., LI	31	18	9	.667	230	99	53	2.07
Stenhouse, David, PU	28	16	8	.667	207	91	67	2.91
Lines, Richard, LI	24	10	6	.625	160	70	56	3.15
Carrillo, Pedro, AL	29	17	6	.739	206	82	75	3.28
Brantley, CS		15	6	.714	193	96	73	3.40

Individual Batting Leaders
(Minimum 456 At Bats)

	G	AB	R	H	HR	RBI	Avg.
Hicks, William, CS	115	465	119	177	9	69	.381
Johnson, Stanley, CS	142	560	120	204	12	110	.364
Upright, R.T., AM	146	554	106	190	17	116	.343
Pinkston, Alfred, AM	148	606	114	204	24	126	.337
Cuitti, Arthur, CS	122	456	101	153	24	119	.336

All-Star Team
1b—R.T. Upright, Amarillo
2b—Gerald Streeter, Amarillo
3b—Daniel Lynk, Sioux City
ss—Don Prohovich, Colorado Springs
of—Jim McAnany, Colorado Springs
of—Stan Johnson, Colorado Springs
of—Bill Hicks, Colorado Springs
c—Ron Henry, Topeka
c—Charles Staniland, Sioux City
p—Al Jackson, Lincoln
p—Dick Lines, Lincoln
p—Pedro Carrillo, Albuquerque
p—Hugh Blanton, Amarillo

Attendance
Amarillo—85,931
Albuquerque—81,702
Lincoln—67,604
Colorado Springs—61,091
Sioux City—55,921
Topeka—43,686
Pueblo—39,179
Des Moines—35,039
Total—470,153

Batting Leaders
HOME RUNS
Lynk, Daniel, SC—37
Cook, R. Clifford, AL—32
McAnany, James, CS—26
Staniland, Charles, SC—26
Washington, Anthony, LI—25

RUNS BATTED IN
Pinkston, Alfred, AM—126
Cuitti, Arthur, CS—119
McAnany, James, CS—117
Upright, R.T., AM—116
Cook, R. Clifford, AL—115

STOLEN BASES
Javier, Manuel, LI—27
Rosell, Martin, AL—22
Shields, William, AM—20
Washington, Anthony, LI—19
Several with 17

HITS
Johnson, Stanley, CS—204
Pinkston, Alfred, AM—201
Syngel, Emil, PU—192
Upright, R.T., AM—190
Connally, G. Wayne, PU—182

DOUBLES
Pinkston, Alfred, AM—44
Shields, William, AM—40
Connally, G. Wayne, PU—38
Johnson, Stanley, CS—35
Pascal, Robert, SC—34

TRIPLES
Jackson, Louis, PU—14
Several with 11

TOTAL BASES
Pinkston, Alfred, AM—330
Johnson, Stanley, CS—297
Lynk, Daniel, SC—290
Upright, R.T., AM—288
McAnany, James, CS—284

RUNS
Johnson, Stanley, CS—120
Hicks, William, CS—119
Pinkston, Alfred, AM—114
Streeter, Gerald, AM—113
McAnany, James, CS—108

BASES ON BALLS
Prohovich, Donald, CS—123
Kuehl, Karl, AL—116

Goodell, John, AM—113
Pascal, Robert, SC—113
Kitos, Christopher, PU—96

STRIKEOUTS
Javier, Manuel, LI—158
Cook, R. Clifford, AL—146
Streeter, Gerald, AM—131
Tedesco, Joseph, SC—106
Goodell, John, AM—105

Pitching Leaders

GAMES
Pringle, AM—61
Doss, TO—51
Hemric, SC—51
Singleton, SC—49
Bauta, LI—48

GAMES STARTED
Blanton, AM—31
Johnson, J.A., AM—31
DeMars, TO—29
Jackson, A., LI—29
Several with 28

COMPLETE GAMES
Carrillo, AL—18
Stenhouse, PU—17
Jackson, A., LI—16
Cooke, AL—15
Senerchia, SC—13

SHUTOUTS
Carrillo, AL—5
Jackson, A., LI—4
Lines, LI—4
Ehrke, DM—3
Stenhouse, PU—3
Several with 2

WINS
Blanton, AM—20

Jackson, A., LI—18
Carrillo, AL—17
Stenhouse, PU—16
Brantley, CS—15

LOSSES
Hribar, DM—15
Doss, TO—14
Schomer, PU—14
Several with 12

INNINGS PITCHED
Blanton, AM—240
Jackson, A., LI—230
Johnson, J.A., AM—216
Stenhouse, PU—207
Carrillo, AL—206

HOME RUNS ALLOWED
Shandor, SC—27
Senerchia, SC—25
Blanton, AM—24
Brantley, CS—22
Several with 21

STRIKEOUTS
Carrillo, AL—177
DeMars, TO—177
Stenhouse, PU—176
Trosky, CS—165
Jackson, A., LI—162

WILD PITCHES
DeMars, TO—21
Hribar, DM—18
Hemric, SC—16
Cook, AL—15
Senerchia, SC—15

HIT BATTERS
Davolio, SC—11
Trosky, CS—11
Singleton, SC—10
Several with 8

1959

League attendance figures continued to fall like autumn leaves in 1958. The fall from 595,000 to 483,000 came for many reasons. People were finding television more compelling than going to watch live baseball. Other sports were becoming more popular, too. Travel expenses were a problem, as the league was spread over six states. The final nail in the coffin was the decision by Major League teams not to grant the league any working agreements in 1959. According to one sports writer, the boycott came informally and in secrecy. "We can't operate as a Class A league without working agreements, and there aren't enough to go around," said Western League president Neil Hobbs.

The minor league farm system continued to decline over the next few years, and other leagues became casualties as well. Some of the cities in the league shifted to a new league in 1959. Des Moines, Lincoln, Sioux City and Topeka went to the Three-I League. Amarillo went to the Texas League.

The Western League went into a long hibernation.

7

The Independent Phase (1995–Present)

After a 36-year lapse, the Western League was revitalized as an Independent league. Founded in 1994 by Portland businessman Bruce L. Engel, the league began play in 1995. All teams would be independently owned and operated and not affiliated with major league baseball. The caliber of play in the Western Baseball League has been rated Double A by major league scouts assigned to scout the league. Because Independent owners are responsible for the entire operating budget and control all aspects of the operation, the Independent teams are much more responsive and sensitive to the local market. If anything, the Independent minor league product is more enjoyable and rewarding than its major league–controlled counterpart. The players are paid comparable minor-league salaries, and the teams operate in a similar manner.

1995

In the inaugural season of 1995 the league consisted of eight teams: Bend (Ore.) Bandits, Grays Harbor (Wash.) Gulls, Surrey (B.C.) Glaciers and Tri-City (Wash.) Posse in the Northern Division; and four California teams in the Southern Division—Long Beach Riptide, Palm Springs Suns, Salinas Peppers and Sonoma County Crushers.

The season was divided into two halves. Surrey and Salinas took the first-half titles. Salinas continued its winning ways in the second half, while Surrey crashed like the Stock Market in 1929. Tri-City, which had finished last in the first half, and Bend tied for first in the second half, forcing a one-game playoff, which was won 9–5 by Tri-City. In the playoffs, division champ Salinas cooled off and lost to Long Beach. Tri-City swept by Surrey. Long Beach won the championship series over Tri-City, three games to one. Eddie Christian was named MVP for the series, as he went 4-for-4 and became the hero when he singled in the winning run in the 10th inning, giving Long Beach the first-ever Western Baseball League championship.

The Riptide was led by pitcher John Weglarz, who led the league in ERA and strikeouts, and was named pitcher of the year. The righthander pitched a no-hitter during the season, as well as a game in which he struck out 18. And Christian hit .339 on the season.

The Player of the Year was Kyle Washington, who was in triple-crown contention all year and won the batting crown with a .367 average. He was second in home runs with 17, and just five RBIs shy of the league lead with 74. He also led the WBL in slugging percentage (.647), and was second in extra-base hits (43) and on-base percentage (.443).

Dave Holt of the Salinas Peppers was named manager of the year after compiling a 60–30 record over the season. He had the most disciplined, fundamentally sound team in the league and was able to consistently get the most from his players. No postseason All-Star team was named.

1995

Final Standings
First Half
Division Standings

North Division	W	L	PCT	GB	South Division	W	L	PCT	GB
Surrey	26	16	.619	—	Salinas	27	18	.600	
Bend	22	23	.489	5.5	Long Beach	24	21	.533	3.0
Grays Harbor	18	26	.409	9.0	Palm Springs	21	22	.488	5.0
Tri-City	18	27	.400	9.5	Sonoma County	21	24	.467	6.0

Second Half
Division Standings

North Division	W	L	PCT	GB	South Division	W	L	PCT	GB
*Tri-City	27	19	.587	—	Salinas	33	12	.733	
Bend	26	20	.565	1.0	Long Beach	28	17	.622	5.0
Grays Harbor	13	33	.283	14.0	Sonoma County	23	22	.511	10.0
Surrey	12	36	.250	16.0	Palm Springs	22	25	.468	12.0

*Tri-City defeated Bend, 9–5, in a one-game playoff for the second-half Northern Division title.

Playoffs
Divisional Playoff Series
North: Tri-City defeated Surrey, two games to none.
South: Long Beach defeated Salinas, two games to none.

League Championship Series
Long Beach defeated Tri-City, three games to one.

All-Star Game
South 8, North 6
MVP: Rich Aldrete, Salinas (South)
W-Tim Gower, Salinas (South), L-Ned Darley, Bend (North)

Attendance
Regular Season—551,399
Playoffs—14,156
All-Star Game—3,176

Team Pitching

	W-L	ERA	H	CG	ShO	SV	HR	BB	SO
Salinas	60–30	3.37	776	7	9	30	48	248	565
Tri-City	45–46	3.87	848	18	10	19	52	249	606
Long Beach	52–38	3.96	847	17	2	25	53	234	533
Palm Springs	43–47	4.36	795	14	5	17	50	349	624
Bend	48–43	4.50	907	8	5	25	59	281	588
Surrey	38–52	4.53	815	23	5	17	65	385	644
Sonoma County	44–46	4.55	813	8	2	20	50	344	656
Grays Harbor	31–59	5.58	943	15	1	6	73	334	444

Team Hitting

	AB	R	H	HR	BB	SO	SB	CSt	Avg.
Bend	3256	551	929	65	366	601	85	39	.285
Long Beach	3130	529	890	53	391	536	102	41	.284
Sonoma County	3111	505	876	57	284	563	93	55	.282
Salinas	3093	517	851	66	264	575	121	53	.275
Palm Springs	3066	436	838	64	269	660	131	49	.273
Grays Harbor	3123	514	836	77	278	648	74	38	.268
Tri-City	3027	429	779	27	311	496	134	57	.257
Surrey	3000	407	745	41	261	581	80	48	.248

Individual Hitting Leaders
(Minimum 243 At Bats)

	G	AB	R	H	HR	RBI	Avg.
Washington, Kyle, SNC	80	289	67	107	17	75	.370
Tedder, Scott, BND	88	340	68	119	4	57	.350
Christian, Eddie, LB	83	333	66	113	1	50	.339
Aldrete, Rich, SLN	87	332	54	112	6	54	.337
Barbara, Don,	61	221	31	74	5	48	.335

Individual Pitching Leaders
(Minimum 120 Innings Pitched)

	W-L	ERA	IP	H	B	SO
Weglarz, John, TRI	11–5	1.87	149	119	41	162
Patton, John, SLN	11–6	2.01	134	108	53	112
Reardon, Kevin, SLN	14–2	2.29	138	109	27	93
Strong, Joe, SUR	8–9	2.75	131	120	48	129
Singleton, Scott, LB	9–5	2.88	147	124	34	112

Hitting Leaders

HOME RUNS
Williams, Paul, GRH—22
Hendricks, Steve, GRH—17
Taylor, Sam, SLN—17
Pridy, Todd, SLN—17
Washington, Kyle, SNC—17

RBI
Williams, Paul, GRH—79
Koehler, Jim, BND—78
Hendricks, Steve, GRH—76
Washington, Kyle, SNC—75
Murphy, Jim, SUR—62

STOLEN BASES
Scott, Shawn, TRI—42
McGowan, Marcus, BND—40
Norman, Kenny, SLN—36
Peguero, Jose, PSP—28
Christian, Eddie, LB- 27

HITS
Tedder, Scott, BND—119
Koehler, Jim, BND—116
Christian, Eddie, LB—113
Aldrete, Rich, SLN—112
Several Players Tied at 107

DOUBLES
Koehler, Jim, BND—33
Brice, Billy, BND—29
Gagliano, Manny, GRH 27
Christian, Eddie, LB—27
Rosario, Victor, SNC—27

TRIPLES
McGowan, Marcus, BND—10
Taylor, Sam, SLN—8
Norman, Kenny, SLN 8

Sheppard, Don, SLN—7
Scott, Shawn, TRI—6

ON-BASE PERCENTAGE
Tedder, Scott, BND—.452
Washington, Kyle, SNC—.446
Barbara, Don, LB—.421
Christian, Eddie, LB—.421
Several Players Tied at .406

SLUGGING PERCENTAGE
Washington, Kyle, SNC—.651
Bobo, Elgin, SLN—.564
Koehler, Jim, BND—.557
Williams, Paul, GRH—.530
Several Players Tied at .526

EXTRA-BASE HITS
Koehler, Jim, BND—50
Gagliano, Manny, GRH—43
Washington, Kyle, SNC—43
Hendricks, Steve, GRH—42
Taylor, Sam, SLN—41

RUNS SCORED
McGowan, Marcus, BND—73
Tedder, Scott, BND—68
Koehler, Jim, BND—68
Robinson, Don, LB—68
Washington, Kyle, SNC—67

Pitching Leaders

WINS
Reardon, Kevin, SLN—14
Peltzer, Kurt, LB—13
Patton, John, SLN—11
Weglarz, John, TRI—11
McKinley, Leif, BND—10

SAVES
Gower, Tim, SLN—25
Darley, Ned, BND—23
Graham, Richie, TRI—19
Corona, John, LB—17
Langley, Lee, SNC—17
Weglarz, John, TRI—162
McKinley, Leif, BND—129
Strong, Joe, SUR—129
Peltzer, Kurt, LB—118
Singer, Tom, BND—116

STRIKEOUTS
Weglarz, John, TRI—162
McKinley, Leif, BND—129
Strong, Joe, SUR—129
Peltzer, Kurt, LB—118
Singer, Tom, BND—116

GAMES
Diaz, Armando, SNC—46
Gower, Tim, SLN—45
Langley, Lee, SNC—44
Several Players Tied at 35

SHUTOUTS
Weglarz, John, TRI—5
Several Players Tied at 2

COMPLETE GAMES
Weglarz, John, TRI—10

Strong, Joe, SUR—9
Peltzer, Kurt, LB—8
Patterson, Jim, GRH—7
Several Players Tied at 5

INNINGS PITCHED
Peltzer, Kurt, LB—163.1
Weglarz, John, TRI—149.0
Singleton, Scott, LB—147.0
Johnson, Steve, TRI—141.2
McKinley, Leif, BND—141.0

LOSSES
Patterson, Jim, GRH—11
Several Players Tied at 9

WALKS
Rhodes, Ricky, SUR—66
O'Dea, Brett, PSP—57
Bene, Bill, PSP—54
Patton, John, SLN—53
Hokuf, Ken, SNC—51

HOME RUNS ALLOWED
Peltzer, Kurt, LB—17
McKinley, Leif, BND—14
Brown, Duane, SUR—14
Patterson, Jim, GRH—12
Haas, David, SLN—12

1996

Surrey folded after the first season, and in 1996 the Reno Chukars were added as an expansion franchise to keep the league at eight teams.

As in 1995, Tri-City finished last in the first half, won the second half, swept the divisional playoff, then lost to Long Beach in the finals, three games to one. Long Beach's Alan Burke was named Championship Series MVP. Long Beach was led all season by the Pitcher of the Year, Paul Anderson, who was among league leaders in many categories.

In his debut season in professional baseball, Butch Hughes guided the first-year Chukars to the first-half Northern Division title and a 48–42 record during the regular season, third best in the league.

The Player of the Year was Salinas' Rick Prieto, who was among the league leaders in most major offensive categories, including batting average (sixth, .338), runs (first, 83), hits (first, 123), doubles (tied for third, 27), triples (tied for first, 10), stolen bases (fifth, 30), stolen-base percentage (first .968, 30-for-31), and on-base percentage (fifth, .410). Defensively, he played 54 games in the outfield (without an error) and 34 games at second base. He was the only player to be named Player of the Week twice.

1996

Final Standings
First Half Division Standings

North Division	W	L	PCT	GB	South Division	W	L	PCT	GB
Reno	24	21	.533	—	Salinas	26	19	.578	—
Grays Harbor	23	22	.511	1.0	Palm Springs	23	22	.511	3.0
Bend	22	23	.489	2.0	Long Beach	22	23	.489	4.0
Tri-City	20	25	.444	4.0	Sonoma County	20	25	.444	6.0

Second Division Standings

North Division	W	L	PCT	GB	South Division	W	L	PCT	GB
Tri-City	25	20	.556	—	Long Beach	32	13	.711	—
Reno	24	21	.533	1.0	Salinas	28	17	.622	4.0
Grays Harbor	17	28	.378	8.0	Palm Springs	23	22	.511	9.0
Bend	17	28	.378	8.0	Sonoma County	14	31	.311	18.0

Attendance

Regular Season—483,229
Playoffs—15,232
No All-Star Game

Playoff Results
Divisional Playoff Series

North: Tri-City defeated Reno, two games to none.
South: Long Beach defeated Salinas, three games to two.

League Championship Series

Long Beach defeated Tri-City, three games to one.

Post Season All-Star Team
as voted by general managers, field managers, and coaches

1b—Todd Pridy, Salinas
2b—Chris Grubb, Grays Harbor
3b—Frank Valdez, Palm Springs
ss—Ryan Rutz, Tri-City
of Ray Harvey, Grays Harbor
of—Shawn Scott, Tri-City
of—Sam Taylor, Salinas
DH—David Mowry, Sonoma County
Util—Rick Prieto, Salinas
c—Carl Nichols, Reno
p—Paul Anderson, Long Beach
p—Jose Salcedo
p—Tim Gower, Salinas
p—Mark Tranberg, Long Beach
p—Ben Weber, Salinas

Team Pitching

	W–L	ERA	H	CG	ShO	SV	HR	BB	SO
Tri-City	45–45	3.83	791	10	5	22	45	328	694
Palm Springs	45–44	3.84	870	9	4	18	61	284	535
Long Beach	54–36	3.86	824	15	6	26	45	240	558
Salinas	54–35	4.19	797	3	1	26	64	293	585
Grays Harbor	40–50	4.77	886	9	1	18	84	377	718
Sonoma City	34–56	5.13	957	3	1	21	65	346	609
Bend	39–51	5.18	899	9	2	21	107	318	587
Reno	48–42	5.32	966	11	2	19	76	316	491

Team Hitting

	AB	R	H	HR	BB	SO	SB	CSt	Avg.
Reno	3146	559	952	79	304	679	89	56	.303
Salinas	3113	543	923	77	290	527	92	53	.296
Grays Harbor	3149	469	893	56	315	513	98	63	.284
Long Beach	3060	491	850	62	345	496	95	49	.278
Tri-City	3135	448	868	61	272	591	110	64	.277
Bend	3172	489	877	78	296	704	84	39	.276
Palm Springs	3004	425	810	49	333	546	148	93	.270
Sonoma Cty	3147	449	817	85	347	721	60	30	.260

Individual Hitting Leaders
(Minimum 243 At Bats)

	G	AB	R	H	HR	RBI	Avg.
Grubb, Chris, GRH	80	282	42	103	4	30	.365
Harvey, Ray, GRH	68	273	62	99	11	55	.363
Pridy, Todd, SLN	87	315	63	109	21	63	.346
Valdez, Frank, PSP	88	325	47	112	8	62	.345
Miller, Roy, RNO	72	262	60	90	8	53	.344

Individual Pitching Leaders
(Minimum 70 Innings)

	W–L	ERA	IP	H	BB	SO
Salcedo, Jose, TRI	7–3	2.11	111	77	42	97
Burcham, Tim, PSP	5–7	2.56	102	98	21	95
Anderson, Paul, LB	12–4	2.68	117	112	13	83
Tranberg, Mark, LB	9–3	2.93	135	128	38	113
Rolish, Chad, PSP	10–7	3.37	139	140	58	94

Batting Leaders

HOME RUNS
Todd Pridy, SLN—21
David Mowry, SC—20
Carl Nichols, RNO—20
Jim Koehler, BND—17
Donald Harris, BND—14

The Independent Phase (1995–Present)

RUNS BATTED IN
Carl Nichols, RNO—89
Ray DeLeon, SLN—83
Brian Kooiman, SLN—76
David Mowry, SC—76
Tim Moore, LB—69

STOLEN BASES
Shawn Scott, TC—43
Cobi Cradle, LB—36
Vince Harris, GH—31
Chad Ponegalek, PSP—31
Rick Prieto, SLN—30

HITS
Rick Prieto, SLN—123
Sam Taylor, SLN—121
Shawn Scott, TC—119
Tim Cooper, RNO—116
David Mowry, SC—113

DOUBLES
David Mowry, SC—30
Carl Nichols, RNO—29
Rick Prieto, SLN—27
Jon Fuller, SC—27
John Casey, LB—26

TRIPLES
Rick Prieto, SLN—10
Tim Cooper, RNO—10
Roy Miller, RNO—10
Eddie Comeaux, RNO—8
Several Players Tied at 7

ON-BASE PERCENTAGE
Todd Pridy, SLN—.454
Ray Harvey, GH—.441
Marcus McGowan, BND—.420
Chris Grubb, GH—.420
Rick Prieto, SLN—.410

SLUGGING PERCENTAGE
Todd Pridy, SLN—.616
David Mowry, SC—.587
Ray Harvey, GH—.586
Roy Miller, RNO—.584
Carl Nichols, RNO—.579

EXTRA-BASE HITS
David Mowry, SC—50
Carl Nichols, RNO—50
Tim Cooper, RNO—43
Several at 42

RUNS
Rick Prieto, SLN—83
Cobi Cradle, LB—77
Tim Cooper, RNO—75
Sam Taylor, SLN—68
Marcus McGowan, BND—67

Pitching Leaders

WINS
Ben Weber, SLN—12
Paul Anderson, LB—12
Mike Smith, LB—11
Brian Doughty, RNO—11
Chad Rolish, PSP—10

SAVES
Tim Gower, SLN—24
John Corona, LB—21
Rich Graham, TC—18
Bob Ayrault, RNO—15
Steve Grennan, BND—13

STRIKEOUTS
Chris Sheehan, TC—135
Chris Kotes, GH—128
John Patton, SLN—123
Mark Tranberg, LB—113
Tony Coscia, SC—106

GAMES
Tim Gower, SLN—52
Eric Estes, GRH—43
Hank Sprinkle, PS—41
Rich Graham, TC—40
Steve Grennan, BND—38

COMPLETE GAMES
Mike Smith, LB—5
Paul Anderson, LB—5
Several at 4

SHUTOUTS
Several at 1

INNINGS PITCHED
Ben Weber, SLN—148.1
Ruben Niebla, PS—140.2
Chad Rolish, PS—139.0
Mark Tranberg, LB—135.0
John Patton, Salinas—135.0

LOSSES
Pat Leahy, GRH—10

Ruben Niebla, PS—9
Several at 8

WALKS
John Patton, SLN—67
Chris Kotes, GH—62
Derek Baker, RNO—61
Chad Rolish, PS—58
Brook Smith, SC—52

HOME RUNS ALLOWED
Pat Leahy, GRH—18
Sam Knowland, BND—17
Dennis Shrum, BND—15
Chris White, BND—15
Ricky Talbott, BND—14

1997

Before the 1997 season began, the Palm Springs Suns elected to sit out while they worked toward a move to Oxnard, California, where they became the Pacific Suns. The league expanded once again, adding the Chico Heat, who would surpass all expectations by setting a season attendance record and winning the championship.

Sonoma County moved from worst in 1996 (34–56) to first in 1997 (56–34) but lost to Chico in the Southern Division playoffs. Sonoma County was led by manager Dick Dietz, who was named Manager of the Year. Chico won the playoff finals against heavy hitting Reno thanks partly to John Coats, who was named Series MVP.

Reno had a remarkable trio of hitters who all hit better than .400 — Todd Takayoshi (.407), who was named Player of the Year, Andy Tarpley (.404), and Brett Jenkins (.400). The Pitcher of the Year was Mike

The Chico Heat celebrate after winning the Western League championship in 1997. (Photograph by Kim Curtis)

Smith from the Mission Viejo Vigilantes. Smith was among the league's top five in wins (10, tied for fourth), ERA (2.95, second), strikeouts (109, tied for fifth), winning percentage (.714, fifth) and opponent batting average (.213, first). The league also featured Bret Barberie, who played in the majors for Montreal and other teams. The Mission Viejo player was one of the top hitters of the league.

1997

Final Standings
First Half Division Standings

North Division	W	L	PCT	GB	South Division	W	L	PCT	GB
Reno	30	15	.667	—	Sonoma County	29	16	.644	—
Grays Harbor	24	21	.533	6.0	Salinas	23	22	.511	6.0
Tri-City	18	27	.400	12.0	Chico	21	24	.467	8.0
Bend	17	28	.378	13.0	Misson Viejo	18	27	.400	11.0

Second Half Division Standings

North Division	W	L	PCT	GB	South Division	W	L	PCT	GB
*Grays Harbor	25	20	.556	—	Sonoma County	27	18	.600	—
Reno	25	20	.556	—	Chico	24	21	.533	3.0
Bend	22	23	.489	3.0	Mission Viejo	21	24	.467	6.0
Tri-City	16	29	.356	9.0	Salinas	20	25	.444	7.0

*Grays Harbor won second-half tie-breaker.

Attendance

Regular Season—610,202
Playoffs—21,083
No All-Star Game

Playoff Results Divisional Playoff Series

North: Reno defeated Grays Harbor, two games to one.
South: Chico defeated Sonoma County, two games to one.

League Championship Series

Chico defeated Reno, three games to one.

Postseason All-Star Team
as voted by general managers, field managers, and coaches

1b—David Mowry, Sonoma County
2b—Chris Grubb, Grays Harbor
3b—Andy Tarpley, Reno
ss—John Casey, Sonoma County
of—Mark Charbonnet, Bend
of—Sam Taylor, Mission Viejo
of—Corey Paul, Chico
DH—Todd Takayoshi, Reno

c—Jon Fuller, Sonoma County
p—Mike Smith, Mission Viejo
p—Eric Miller, Sonoma County
p—Brian Doughty, Reno
p—Kris Frank, Sonoma County
p—Chris White, Bend

1997 All-Star Team

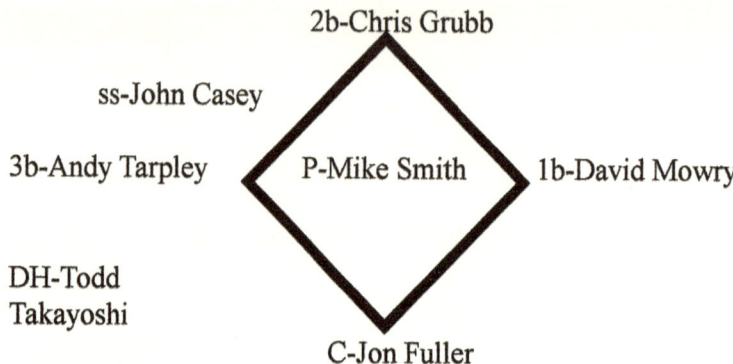

of-Mark Charbonnet
of-Sam Taylor
of-Corey Paul
2b-Chris Grubb
ss-John Casey
3b-Andy Tarpley
P-Mike Smith
1b-David Mowry
DH-Todd Takayoshi
C-Jon Fuller

P-Eric Miller
P-Brian Doughty
P-Kris Frank
P-Chris White

Final Official Team Totals
Team Pitching

	W–L	ERA	H	CG	SHO	SV	HR	BB	SO
Tri-City	34–56	4.47	850	3	6	21	75	330	621
Sonoma County	56–34	4.63	858	7	2	29	83	358	715
Chico	45–45	4.66	874	5	6	18	59	329	602
Salinas	43–47	4.70	923	10	4	14	82	310	551
Grays Harbor	49–41	4.79	885	9	8	22	94	318	582
Bend	39–51	4.90	902	9	5	17	94	339	603
Mission Viejo	39–51	4.94	848	10	3	20	91	318	570
Reno	55–35	5.81	969	4	2	22	84	374	585

Team Batting

	AB	R	H	HR	BB	SO	SB	CSt	Avg.
Reno	3295	724	1063	115	406	611	116	42	.323

The Independent Phase (1995–Present) 281

	AB	R	H	HR	BB	SO	SB	CSt	Avg.
Sonoma County	3190	587	946	104	381	613	65	32	.297
Salinas	3106	475	875	79	321	621	151	59	.282
Grays Harbor	3119	521	877	77	356	684	60	48	.281
Mission Viejo	3107	457	863	88	297	522	64	39	.278
Bend	3120	478	855	67	253	650	131	47	.274
Chico	3150	556	859	104	372	630	80	33	.273
Tri-City	2980	376	771	28	290	498	152	86	.259

Individual Hitting Leaders
(Minimum 243 At Bats)

	G	AB	R	H	HR	RBI	Avg.
Takayoshi, Todd, RNO	83	337	88	137	11	88	.407
Tarpley, Andy, RNO	87	317	92	128	15	82	.404
Jenkins, Brett, RNO	62	240	59	96	17	55	.400
Charbonnet, Mark, BND	78	319	54	115	15	58	.361
Barberie, Bret, MV	72	274	46	95	11	40	.347

Individual Pitching Leaders
(Minimum 72 Innings Pitched)

	W-L	ERA	IP	H	BB	SO
Frank, Kristopher, SNC	8–2	2.48	73	57	39	92
Smith, Mike, MV	10–4	2.95	125	98	42	109
Niebla, Ruben, TRI	8–6	3.05	112	108	36	76
Burlingame, Ben, BND	6–10	3.20	132	120	27	127
Novoa, Rafael, CHO	11–3	3.69	117	120	57	58

Hitting Leaders

HOME RUNS
Rendina, Mike, GRH—24
Mowry, David, SNC—23
Hansen, Terrel, CHO—22
Pridy, Todd, SNC—22
Several Players Tied at 2

RBI
Takayoshi, Todd, RNO—88
Tarpley, Andy, RNO—82
Mowry, David, SNC—82
Burke, Alan, MV—77
Ellis, Paul, RNO—75

STOLEN BASES
Comeaux, Eddie, SLN—43
Duncan, Andres, BND—33
Pfeifer, Scott, RNO—32
McGowan, Marcus, BND—27
Rhein, Jeff, CHO—27

HITS
Takayoshi, Todd, RNO—137
Tarpley, Andy, RNO—128
Francisco, David, RNO—120
Mowry, David, SNC—117
Charbonnet, Mark, BND—115

DOUBLES
Takayoshi, Todd, RNO—28
Tarpley, Andy, RNO—28
Hosey, Steve, SLN—24
Burke, Alan, MV—23
Casey, John, SNC—23

TRIPLES
Rhein, Jeff, CHO—6
Sanchez, David, GRH—6
Several Players Tied at 5

ON-BASE PERCENTAGE
Tarpley, Andy, RNO—.499

Takayoshi, Todd, RNO .490
Jenkins, Brett, RNO—.486
Ellis, Paul, RNO—.464
Shepherd, Bodie, SLN—.437

SLUGGING PERCENTAGE
Jenkins, Brett, RNO—.717
Hansen, Terrel, CHO—.674
Tarpley, Andy, RNO—.666
Hosey, Steve, SLN—.642
Pridy, Todd, SNC—.627

EXTRA-BASE HITS
Tarpley, Andy, RNO—48
Mowry, David, SNC—45
Shamburg, Ken, CHO—43
Roberts, John, RNO—43
Hosey, Steve, SLN—43

RUNS SCORED
Tarpley, Andy, RNO—92
Takayoshi, Todd, RNO—88
Casey, John, SNC—80
Several Players Tied at 74

Pitching Leaders

WINS
Genke, Todd, SNC—12
Novoa, Rafael, CHO—11
Doughty, Brian, RNO—11
Several Players Tied at 10

SAVES
Miller, Eric, SNC—22
Dawley, Joey, CHO—14
Grebe, Brett, TRI—13
Kishita, Kirt, MV—12
Martineau, Brian, GRH—11

STRIKEOUTS
Burlingame, Ben, BND—127
Coscia, Tony, SNC—125
White, Chris, BND—119

Smith, Mike, MV—109
Patton, John, SNC—109

GAMES
Stoecklin, Anthony, BND—51
Martineau, Brian, GRH—45
Plooy, Eric, GRH—45
Bryant, Adam, CHO—43
Lynn, John, BND—42

COMPLETE GAMES
Anderson, Paul, MV—7
Burlingame, Ben, BND—6
Goedhart, Darrell, GRH—5
Several Players Tied at 3

SHUTOUTS
Burlingame, Ben, BND—2
Ehler, Daniel, MV—2
Several Players Tied at 1

INNINGS PITCHED
Ritchie, Wally, SLN—136.1
White, Chris, BND—136.0
Burlingame, Ben, BND—132.1
Anderson, Paul, MV—132.1
Doughty, Brian, RNO—130.2

LOSSES
Burlingame, Ben, BND—10
Singleton, Scott, MV—10
Several Players Tied at 9

WALKS
Carl, Todd, RNO—58
Novoa, Rafael, CHO—57
White, Darell, RNO—53
White, Chris, BND—52
Patton, John, SNC—52

HOME RUNS ALLOWED
Carrasco, Carlos, SLN—21
Ritchie, Wally, SLN—18
Reid, Rayon, GRH—17
Singleton, Scott, MV—17
Anderson, Paul, MV—15

1998

In 1998 the Salinas Peppers dropped from the league. The Pacific Suns, who played as the Palm Springs Suns in 1995 and 1996 but sat out in 1997, returned to keep the number of active teams at eight.

The Chico Heat set Independent league records for best record (63–29, .708) and attendance (132,052) but were swept by eventual league champion Sonoma County in the semi-finals, three games to none. Sonoma County won its first league title with a three-game sweep of the Western Warriors in the finals. The team was led by Player of the Year Todd Pridy, who led the league in hitting (.408), on-base percentage (.478) and slugging percentage (.665).

The league's biggest story in 1998 was the Warriors' 68-game road trip (75 including playoffs), which resulted when the Grays Harbor Gulls ceased operation and the league took over the club. Surprisingly, the Warriors won the Northern Division's second-half title, then took three of four from the Reno Chukars in the Northern Division playoff. The team was managed by Charlie Kerfeld, who was named Manager of the Year for his efforts. Kerfeld was a pitcher for four seasons in the National League for Houston and Atlanta. Mike Smith of Mission Viejo was voted Pitcher of the Year for the second season in a row. The righthander was 10–6 with a 3.52 ERA and 121 strikeouts in 138 innings. He was named Pitcher of the Week three times.

1998

First-Half Standings

North Division	W	L	Pct.	GB
Reno Chukars	25	20	.556	—
Bend Bandits	24	21	.533	1.0
Western Warriors	20	25	.444	5.0
Tri-City Posse	18	27	.400	7.0

South Division	W	L	Pct.	GB
Chico Heat	30	15	.667	—
Sonoma County Crushers	26	19	.578	4.0
Mission Viejo Vigilantes	24	21	.533	6.0
Pacific Suns	13	32	.289	17.0

Second-Half Standings

North Division	W	L	Pct.	GB
Western Warriors	23	22	.511	—
Tri-City Posse	21	24	.467	2.0
Reno Chukars	20	25	.444	3.0
Bend Bandits	19	25	.432	3.5

South Division	W	L	Pct.	GB
Chico Heat	33	11	.750	—

The Western League

South Division	W	L	Pct.	GB
Mission Viejo Vigilantes	25	20	.556	8.5
Sonoma County Crushers	23	22	.511	10.5
Pacific Suns	15	30	.333	18.5

Playoff Results

North: Western defeated Reno, three games to one.
South: Sonoma County defeated Chico three games to none.

League Championship Series

Sonoma County defeated Western, three games to none.

Attendance

Regular Season—577,375
Playoffs—12,246
All-Star Game—4,297

All-Star Game

North 8, South 3
MVP: Randy Kapano, Bend (North)
W-Jeff Howell, Reno (North); L-Scott Navarro, Chico (South)
HR-Toddy Pridy, Sonoma County (South); Jun Fuller, Western (North)

Postseason All-Star Team

1b—Todd Pridy, SC
2b—Quentin Harley, Chico
3b—Eric White, SC
ss—Lino Connell, Western
of—Mark Charbonnet, Bend
of—Brett Jenkins, Reno
of—Vernon Spearman, SC
c—Jon Fuller, Western
p—Collin Kerley, Bend
p—Scott Navarro, Chico
p—Jeff Sobkoviak, Chico
p—Tony Coscia, SC
p—Mike Smith, MV
DH—Alan Burke, MV

1998 All-Star Team

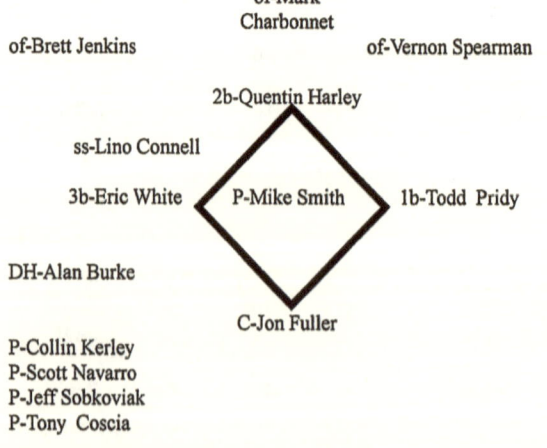

of-Mark Charbonnet
of-Brett Jenkins
of-Vernon Spearman
2b-Quentin Harley
ss-Lino Connell
3b-Eric White
P-Mike Smith
1b-Todd Pridy
DH-Alan Burke
C-Jon Fuller
P-Collin Kerley
P-Scott Navarro
P-Jeff Sobkoviak
P-Tony Coscia

Team Pitching

	W-L	ERA	H	CG	ShO	SV	HR	BB	SO
Chico	63–26	3.47	764	3	4	34	48	330	530
Mission Viejo	49–41	4.34	840	9	6	24	76	301	578
Sonoma County	49–41	4.51	851	12	6	19	66	375	715
Western	43–47	4.97	885	2	3	24	88	349	599
Pacific	28–62	4.99	873	17	2	8	84	355	566
Bend	43–46	5.16	828	10	1	21	67	418	675
Tri-City	39–51	5.25	974	3	1	20	71	325	539
Reno	45–45	5.91	1004	4	1	18	109	354	496

Team Batting

	AB	R	H	HR	BB	SO	SB	CSt	Avg.
Reno	3274	662	988	87	452	544	116	36	.302
Bend	3144	539	935	91	272	633	181	71	.297
Sonoma County	3111	538	902	61	385	582	88	28	.290
Western	3071	522	875	91	322	546	93	45	.285
Chico	3108	554	868	99	352	619	86	41	.279
Tri-City	3115	459	866	54	384	601	146	51	.278
Mission Viejo	3087	493	848	82	377	586	61	44	.275
Pacific	2994	343	737	44	263	587	76	43	.246

Individual Hitting Leaders
(Minimum 243 At Bats)

	G	AB	R	H	HR	RBI	Avg.
Pridy, Todd, SNC	90	358	82	146	21	94	.408
Dowler, Dee, RNO	63	293	62	114	4	45	.389
Charbonnet, Mark, BND	89	357	70	130	22	85	.364
Spearman, Vernon, SNC	89	369	89	134	2	34	.363
Connell, Lino, WES	89	370	66	134	10	56	.362

Individual Pitching Leaders
(Minimum 72 Innings Pitched)

	W-L	ERA	IP	H	BB	SO
Neier, Chris, CHO	8–2	2.94	86	73	14	49
Thurmond, Travis, SNC	6–5	3.05	112	99	66	134
Sobkoviak, Jeff, CHO	7–0	3.24	114	112	42	48
Navarro, Scott, CHO	10–4	3.34	121	119	40	66
Krahenbuhl, Ken, PAC	4–5	3.51	82	92	14	51

Hitting Leaders

HOME RUNS
Kapano, Randy, BND—25
Jenkins, Brett, RNO—23
Burke, Alan, MV—23
Charbonnet, Mark, BND—22
Several at 21

RUNS BATTED IN
Jenkins, Brett, RNO—94
Pridy, Todd, SNC—94
Burke, Alan, MV—92
Charbonnet, Mark, BND—85
Several at 76

STOLEN BASES
Mashore, Justin, CHO—45
Spearman, Vernon, SNC—40
Dowler, Dee, RNO—37
Lofton, Jame, TRI—33
Powell, Gordon, BND—32

HITS
Pridy, Todd, SNC—146
Connell, Lino, WES—134
Spearman, Vernon, SNC—134
Charbonnet, Mark, BND—130
Several at 122

DOUBLES
Charbonnet, Mark, BND—31
Vasquez, Chris, WES—31
Pridy, Todd, SNC—29
Connell, Lino, WES—26
White, Eric, SNC—25

TRIPLES
Connell, Lino, WES—9
Spearman, Vernon, SNC—8
Sanchez, David, WES—7
Dowler, Dee, RNO—7
Several at 5

ON-BASE PERCENTAGE
Pridy, Todd, SNC—.478
Jenkins, Brett, RNO—.449
Kliner, Josh, RNO—.447
Takayoshi, Todd, RNO—.440
Spearman, Vernon, SNC—.439

SLUGGING PERCENTAGE
Pridy, Todd, SNC—.665
Charbonnet, Mark, BND—.658
Kapano, Randy, BND—.635
Jenkins, Brett, RNO—.630
Burke, Alan, MV—.584

EXTRA-BASE HITS
Charbonnet, Mark, BND—57
Vasquez, Chris, WES—52
Pridy, Todd, SNC—50
Burke, Alan, MV—48
Connell, Lino, WES—45

RUNS
Spearman, Vernon, SNC—89
Mashore, Justin, CHO—88
Hagy, Gary, RNO—82
Pridy, Todd, SNC—82
Rodarte, Raul, BND—73

Pitching Leaders

WINS
Kerley, Collin, BND—12
Salcedo, Jose, CHO—11
Coscia, Tony, SNC—10
Navarro, Scott, CHO—10
Smith, Mike, MV—10

SAVES
Dawley, Joey, CHO—26
Peterson, Mark, WES—20
Darley, Ned, TRI—17
Stoecklin, Tony, BND—13
Belovsky, Josh, MV—13

STRIKEOUTS
Flynt, William, BND—134
Thurmond, Travis, SNC—134
Coscia, Tony, SNC—131
Patton, John, SNC—130
Smith, Mike, MV—121

GAMES
Escamilla, Jaime, WES—49
Mahlberg, John, WES—47
Peterson, Mark, WES—46
Several Players Tied at 45

COMPLETE GAMES
Smith, Mike, MV—6
Kerley, Collin, BND—5
Moeller, Dennis, PAC—5

Thurmond, Travis, SNC—4
Several at 3
SHUTOUTS
Smith, Mike, MV—3
Thurmond, Travis, SNC—3
Navarro, Scott, CHO—2
Several at 1
INNINGS PITCHED
Kerley, Collin, BND—147.2
Smith, Mike, MV—138.0
Flynt, William, BND—136.1
Coscia, Tony, SNC—132.1
Several at 125.0

LOSSES
Pool, Matt, RNO—9
Several at 8
WALKS
Meier, Patrick, BND—74
Patton, John, SNC—69
Thurmond, Travis, SNC—66
Grennan, Steve, BND—62
Sugar, Dylan, PAC—60
HOME RUNS ALLOWED
Moeller, Dennis, PAC—17
Howatt, Jeff, RNO—17
Pool, Matt, RNO—16
Several at 14

1999

Early in 1999 the Western Baseball League decided to move league offices to Chico, California, from Portland, Oregon, to be more geographically central to all locations within the league, which had three teams in California and one each in Nevada, Utah and Washington. The league owners also retained the services of Bob Linscheid and Associates, an organization management firm specializing in marketing and professional sports management. Bob Linscheid, the former vice president and general manager of the Chico Heat, was named general manager for the league. This move by league owners began the implementation of the league's plan for expansion and increased corporate marketing. "I'm confident the investment the owners are making will enhance the league's existing foundation and provide a catalyst for the Western Baseball League's future prosperity and expansion," said Linscheid.

While the league wanted an expansion, it first had to face a cutback, as four teams dropped out and two were added for the 1999 season. Gone were the Bend Bandits, Mission Viejo Vigilantes, Pacific Suns and Western Warriors. New teams included Zion Pioneerzz and Sacramento Steelheads. This left the league at six teams, so the north and south divisions were abandoned in favor of one division and no split season.

The Chico Heat were hot early in the season, winning 11 straight. Manager Bill Plummer, a former Cincinnati player for the Big Red Machine, guided the Heat to the pennant again. The playoffs saw the first place vs. fourth place and second place vs. third place. No surprises occurred, as first-place Chico Heat and second-place Tri-City Posse won their first-round playoffs and met in the finals. The surprise came in the finals when Tri-City, who finished 15 games behind the Heat in the regular season, overcame Chico three-games to one to win the championship. The Posse were led by Wally Backman, a former 14-year major league veteran.

Pitcher of the Year honors were tied between Ryan Bowen, Sacramento Steelheads, and Chris White, Chico Heat. Player of the Year honors went to Justin Drizoz of the Reno BlackJacks. Manager of the Year went to Plummer.

Drizos was the All-Star MVP. He registered his best season in 1999 with a .351 batting average, 104 hits and 24 home runs, and he drove in 85 runs. Drizos also led the league with a slugging percentage of .676, while battling for the Triple Crown.

Dietz Decides to Retire

In November 1999 Sonoma County Crushers manager Dick Dietz decided to retire. Dietz had the longest tenure in the modern Western Baseball League and won the most games of any manager in the league's history (180).

"We really enjoyed our four years with Dick. He led us into the playoffs the past three years and won the championship in 1998," said Club President Bob Fletcher.

Dietz played eight years in the major leagues with the Giants, Dodgers and Braves. The catcher played on the 1970 National League All-Star team.

1999

Final Standings

	W	L	Pct.	GB
Chico Heat	63	27	.700	—
Tri-City Posse	48	42	.533	15
Zion Pioneerzz	41	49	.456	22
Sonoma County Crushers	41	49	.456	22
Reno BlackJacks	41	49	.456	22
Sacramento Steelheads	36	54	.400	27

Playoffs

Chico defeated Reno, three games to two.
Tri-City defeated Sonoma County, three games to none.

Finals

Tri-City defeated Chico, three games to one.
Championship Series MVP: Nelson Simmons, Tri-City

Attendance

Regular Season—505,591
Playoffs—23,110
All-Star Game—3,485

All-Star Game

North 6, South 1
MVP—Justin Drizos, Reno

Postseason All-Star Team

1b—Justin Drizos, Reno
2b—Sergio Guerrero, Reno
3b—Bo Durkac, Chico
ss—Tim Cooper, Chico
of—Mark Charbonnet, Zion
of—Vernon Spearman, Sonoma County
of—Kevin Ellis, Tri-City
DH—Terrel Hansen, Chico
Utility—Raul Rodarte, Tri-City
C- Grant Fithian, Sonoma County
p—Chris White, Chico
p—Kurt Takahashi, Sonoma County
p—Tom Bergan, Chico
p—Ryan Bowen, Sacramento
p—Josh Montgomery, Chico
p—Randy Phillips, Reno
p—Marcus Moore, Zion

1999 All-Star Team

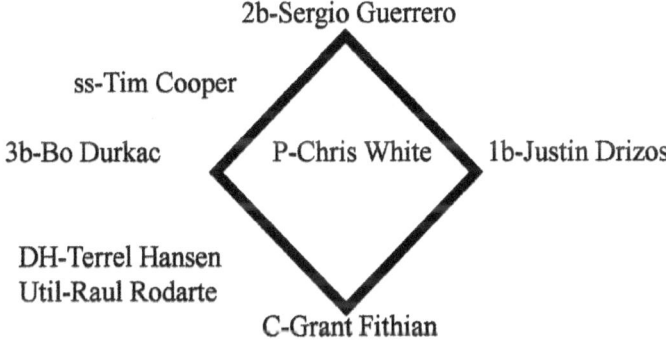

of-Mark Charbonnet
of-Vernon Spearman
of-Kevin Ellis
2b-Sergio Guerrero
ss-Tim Cooper
3b-Bo Durkac
P-Chris White
1b-Justin Drizos
DH-Terrel Hansen
Util-Raul Rodarte
C-Grant Fithian
P-Kurt Takahashi
P-Tom Bergan
P-Ryan Bowen
P-Josh Montgomery
P-Randy Phillips
P-Marcus Moore

Team Batting

	AB	R	H	HR	BB	SO	SB	CS	Avg.
Reno	3193	616	981	87	437	573	101	47	.307

	AB	R	H	HR	BB	SO	SB	CSt	Avg.
Zion	3242	642	968	110	408	660	141	38	.299
Tri-City	3157	583	937	83	393	489	114	48	.297
Chico	3151	610	920	101	400	606	83	30	.292
Sonoma County	3130	566	886	68	469	580	109	31	.283
Sacramento	3087	553	865	54	435	649	97	55	.280

Team Pitching

	W-L	ERA	H	CG	ShO	SV	HR	BB	SO
Chico	63-27	4.17	797	4	5	26	53	408	540
Tri-City	48-42	5.18	830	5	2	20	69	427	629
Sonoma County	41-49	5.73	941	4	2	21	90	398	591
Zion	41-49	5.95	959	8	3	18	93	457	585
Reno	41-49	6.49	1019	3	3	12	101	393	622
Sacramento	36-54	6.58	1011	4	0	16	97	459	590

Hitting Leaders

AVERAGE
Kevin Ellis, TC—.366
Dee Dowler, RNO—.365
Travis McClendon, ZI—.362
Sergio Guerrero, RNO—.354
Ricky Otero, ZI—.353

RUNS
Mike Nadeau, CHO—90
Vernon Spearman, SC—89
Ricky Otero, ZI—81
Tim Cooper, CHO—79
Justin Drizos, RNO—78

HITS
Mark Charbonnet, ZI—130
Sergio Guerrero, RNO—130
Kevin Ellis, TC—121
Eric White, SC—115
Ricky Otero, ZI—114

DOUBLES
Bo Dodson, SAC—28
Kevin Ellis, TC—27
Raul Rodarte, TC—27
Nelson Simmons, TC—27
Several with 26

TRIPLES
Josk Kliner, RNO—10
Ricky Otero, ZI—6
Tim Cooper, CHO—6
Dee Dowler, RNO—6
Several with 5

HOME RUNS
Mark Charbonnet, ZNO—28
Justin Drizos, RNO—24
Tim Cooper, CHO—19
Terrel Hansen, CHO—19
Several with 14

RUNS BATTED IN
Mark Charbonnet, ZI—103
Justin Drizos, RNO—85
Raul Rodarte, TC—79
David Sanchez, RNO—77
Bo Durkac, CHO—77

BASES ON BALLS
Todd Pridy, SC—75
Justin Drizos, RNO—73
Bo Dodson, SAC—67
Mike Rendina, SC—67
Vernon Spearman, SC—66

SLUGGING PERCENTAGE
Justin Drizos, RNO—676
Mark Charbonnet, ZI—663
Raul Rodarte, TC—610
Terrel Hansen, CHO—579
Bo Dodson, SAC—576

STOLEN BASES
Vernon Spearman, SC—55
Trovin Valdez, RNO—33

Ricky Otero, ZI—31
Kalin Foulds, ZI—30
Mike Nadeau, CHO—26

Pitching Leaders

ERA (MINIMUM 72
  INNINGS PITCHED)
Tom Bergan, CHO—2.93
Chris White, CHO—3.21
Ryan Bowen, SAC—3.56
Kurt Takahashi, SC—3.71
Marcus Moore, ZI—3.87

WINS
Chris White, CHO—10
Ryan Bowen, SAC—9
Kurt Takahashi, SC—9
Tom Beran, CHO—9
Jeff Sobkoviak, CHO—9

LOSSES
Reggie Leslie, TC/SAC
Several with 8

SAVES
Josh Montgomery, CHO—19
Rich Linares, RNO—9
Kirt Kishita, SC—7
Several with 6

INNINGS
Reggie Leslie, TC/SAC—139
Mike Smith, ZI—128.1
Will Flynt, TC—125.2
Jeff Sobkoviak, CHO—119.2
Randy Phillips, RNO—118.1

GAMES
Rich Linares, RNO—48
Bobby Cowan, TC—46
Adam Bryant, CHO—45
Rick Powalski, RNO—45
Dave Johnson, CHO—42

STRIKEOUTS
Reggie Leslie, TC/SAC—123
Kurt Takahashi, SC—119
Marcus Moore, ZI—114
Will Flynt, TC—109
Randy Phillips, RNO—104

WALKS
Reggie Leslie, TC/SAC—71
Jared Ewen, SC—67
Marcus Moore, ZI—64
Will Flynt, TC—59
Tom Bergan, CHO—56

SHUTOUTS
Tom Bergan, CHO—2
Several with 1

2000

The Western League was hoping to get back to eight teams as the Yuma Bullfrogs and Valley Vipers from Arizona were granted a franchise for the 2000 season. The Yuma franchise was to play its home games in Desert Sun Stadium. The Vipers would play in Scottsdale Stadium and would be managed by Cy Young Award winner Bob Welch. "The league is doing better now than it has in its history," Linscheid said. "Moving into Arizona will put us on the national map." Only two of the original six franchises remain, but Linscheid said that was a natural part of the business.

Owners in the league agreed to expand to ten teams in 2001. A franchise costs $400,000, and startup costs are about a million dollars. While 25 players from the Western League were offered minor-league contracts for 1999 spring training, the league was spared from having its top players called up to larger clubs in the middle of a season. League rules state teams cannot have more than nine players who have five or more years of professional experience. Also, teams must have at least four rookies.

In March 2000 the Sonoma County Crushers signed former Major Leaguer Kevin Mitchell, who was voted the National League's Most Valuable Player in 1989. Mitchell joined former teammate Jeffrey Leonard. The two played together with the Giants from mid–1987 through 1988.

Another former major leaguer signed that same month. Free agent utility player Tony Phillips agreed to terms to play the 2000 season with the Valley Vipers. "This is an opportunity to rehab in a quality environment, at home, and with people I enjoy being with," stated Phillips. "Baseball is in my blood. This will be a fun way to share what I've learned about it."

In April 2000 the Sonoma County Crushers signed ex-major leaguer and Bay Area native Curtis Goodwin for the 2000 season. Goodwin has played with five different major league teams throughout his career. Most recently, the speedy outfielder played for the Chicago Cubs and the Toronto Blue Jays in 1999.

Scottsdale Stadium would be the home of the Valley Vipers in 2000. The stadium is also used by the San Francisco Giants for spring training and the Arizona Fall League. (Photograph courtesy of the Scottsdale Stadium.)

8
League Records

The records in this chapter are based on the best information available. Before 1900, extensive records were not kept on the league. Career records were not compiled.

Batting Records

LONGEST CONSECUTIVE GAME STREAK
421 Games—Ed Hall, Davenport

BATTING AVERAGE
Highest, Season
*.464—James Macullar, Topeka, 1887
.431—Glasscock, St. Paul, 1896
*Walks were counted as base hits in 1887, so averages were inflated.

HOME RUNS
Most, Season
66—Richard Stuart, Lincoln, 1956
Most, Game
4—Jack Crooks, Omaha, 1889; Jerry Crosby, Colorado Springs, 1953; Grant Fithian, Sonoma County, 1999
Most, Successive Games
7—Many
Most, Inning
2—Many

TRIPLES
Most, Season
25—Nig Shaner, Lincoln, 1925
Most, Game
3—Many
Most, Inning
2—Chuck Hostetler, Wichita, 1952

DOUBLES
Most, Season
100—Lyman Lamb, Tulsa, 1924
Most, Game
5—Jim Blakesley, Wichita, 1921
Most, Inning
2—Bob Reash, Denver, 1948

BASE HITS
Most, Season
274—Jack Lelivelt, Omaha, 1921
Most, Game
7—Hoover, Lincoln, 1887
Most, Consecutive
11—Several

TOTAL BASES
Most, Season
458—Royce "Mule" Washburn, Tulsa, 1924
Most, Game
17—Jerry Corsby, Colorado Springs, 1953
Most, Inning
8—Several

RBI
Most, Season
160—Stan Keyes, Des Moines, 1931
Most, Game
9—Mark Charbonnet, Zion, 1999; Paul Williams, Grays Harbor, 1995

Most, Inning
5—Bob Powell, Denver, 1948

RUNS SCORED
Most, Season
217—William Wright, Grand Rapids, 1894

SACRIFICE HITS
Most, Season
75—Bill Davidson, Sioux City, 1914
Most, Game
2—Several

STRIKE OUTS
Most, Season
171—Richard Stuart, Lincoln, 1956
Most, Game
5—Many

BASES ON BALLS
Most, Season
135—Pat Seerey, Colorado Springs
Most, Game
5—Tony Scruggs, Long Beach, 1995

CONSECUTIVE GAME HITTING STREAK
69—Joe Wilhoit, Wichita, 1919

HIT BY PITCHER
Most, Season
14—Dallas "Moose" Womack, Denver, 1950
Most, Game
3—Lou Brower, Oklahoma City, 1930; Caster Masterson, Sonoma County, 1997

STOLEN BASES
Most, Season
97—Mertes, Columbus, 1897
Most, Game
5—George Knothe, Pueblo, 1928; Trovin Valdez, Reno, 1999

Pitching Records

WINS
Most, Season
38—Bill Hutchinson, Minneapolis, 1896; George Boehler, Tulsa, 1922

Most, Successive
17—Frank Lamanski, Davenport, 1934

DEFEATS
Most, Season
30—Paige, Denver, 1906
Most, Successive
11—Walt Kellner, Lincoln, 1950

WINNING PERCENTAGE
Highest, Season (Minimum 20 decisions)
.923 (24-2)—Bud Tinning, Des Moines, 1931

EARNED RUN AVERAGE (MINIMUM 100 INNINGS)
Lowest, Season
1.30—Jot Goar, Indianapolis, 1897

COMPLETE GAMES
Most, Season
39—Bill Phillips, Indianapolis, 1898

GAMES
Most, Season
73—Frank Tubbs, Oklahoma City, 1928

MOST INNINGS
Most, Season
441—George Boehler, Tulsa, 1922
Most, Game
21—Howard Gregory, Lincoln, 1917
Most, Doubleheader
23—Pat Malone, Des Moines, 1925
Consecutive innings without giving up a run
32—D.C. "Mutt" Williams, Denver, 1924

MOST STRIKEOUTS
Most, Season
337—Paul Musser, Des Moines, 1917
Most, Game
20—Darrell "Cy" Blanton, St. Joseph, 1933

BASES ON BALLS
Most, Season
237—Oscar Roettger, Sioux City, 1922

Most, Game
15—Danny Stupur, Pueblo, 1950
Most, Inning
7—John Howe, Des Moines, 1950

HIT BATSMEN
Most, Season
30—Closman, Omaha
Most, Game
4—Several

WILD PITCHES
Most, Season
20—Herb Hall, Omaha, 1912
Most, Game
3—Bill Shepard, Pueblo, 1947

BALKS
Most, Season
15—Hal Kleine, Pueblo, 1950
Most, Game
7—Harry Helmer, Omaha, 1950

SAVES
Most, Season
26—Joey Dawley, Chico, 1998

SHUTOUTS
Most, Season
8—Leo Moon, Des Moines, 1925
In Succession
3—Bill Chappelle, Des Moines, 1905

NO-HITTERS
Gray, Buffalo, vs. Indianapolis, May 8, 1899
Doc Newton, Indianapolis, vs. Milwaukee, 1899
McDonald, Sioux City, vs. Denver, 1900
Norwood Gibson, Kansas City, vs. Omaha, 2–3, July 19, 1902
Jake Weimer/Norwood Gibson, Kansas City, vs. St. Joseph, 3–10 (10), Aug. 25, 1902
Jack Pfeister, Omaha, vs. St. Joseph, 1904
Eddie Cicotte, Des Moines, vs. Omaha, 1906
Adolph Vollendorf, Pueblo, vs. Des Moines, 1906
Edward Eyler, Lincoln, vs. Des Moines, 1906
Pat Ragan, Omaha, vs. Lincoln, 4–1, June 26, 1907
John Jones, Lincoln, vs. Sioux City, 2–0, June 10, 1908
C. A. "Runty" Rhodes, Omaha, vs. Norfolk, 3–0, Aug. 27, 1908
Frank Lange, Des Moines, vs. Lincoln, 1–0, Sept. 27, 1909
Fred Olmstead, Denver, vs. St Joseph, 10–0, June 15, 1910
G.V. "Penny" Farthing, Lincoln, vs. Topeka, 1–0, Aug. 8, 1910
Frank Miller, Des Moines, vs. Topeka, 1910
Charlie Jackson, St. Joseph, vs. Sioux City, 7–0, April 21, 1911
Bucky O'Brien, Denver, vs. Lincoln, 5–1, July 4, 1911
Jeff Clark, Sioux City, vs. Des Moines, 1–0, Sept. 12, 1911
Heinie Steiger, Sioux City, vs. Denver, 4–0, Sept. 17, 1911
Gene Cochreham, Topeka, vs. Omaha, 1–0, Sept. 16, 1912
Chief Johnson, St. Joseph, Sioux City, Sept. 16, 1912
Harry Smith, Lincoln, vs. Wichita, 7–0, April 27, 1913
Harry "Bugs" Grover, Omaha, vs. Sioux City, 7–0, May 10, 1914
Arthur "Dazzy" Vance, St. Joseph, vs. Wichita, 2–1, May 30, 1915
Cy Lambert, Topeka, vs. St. Joseph, 4–0, June 26, 1916
Frank Graham, St. Joseph, vs. Wichita, June 15, 1917
John Nabors, Denver, vs. Sioux City, 1–0, July 22, 1917
Wally Waldbauer, Wichita, vs. Omaha, 4–0, June 10, 1918
Frank Sparks, Tulsa, vs. Joplin, 6–0, June 15, 1919
Howard Gregory, Wichita, vs. 5–1, Aug. 31, 1919
Emilio Palmero, Omaha, vs. Joplin, 1–0, May 13, 1920
Hub Pruett, Tulsa, vs. St. Joseph, 6–0, Aug. 27, 1921
Johnny Baker, St. Joseph, vs. Topeka, 11–0, Sept. 21, 1921

Dan Tipple, Omaha, vs. Des Moines, 3–0, Sept. 21, 1922
Russ Pence, Tulsa, vs. Omaha, 22–0, July 24, 1925
Roy "Snake" Allen, Oklahoma City, vs. Wichita, 6–0, Sept. 1, 1924
Jim Marquis, St. Joseph, vs. Omaha, 1924
Art Stokes, Des Moines, vs. Denver, 1924
James Marquis, St. Joseph, vs. Omaha, 4–0, June 7, 1925
Frank Tubbs, Oklahoma City, vs. Lincoln, 9–0, May 21, 1927
Steve Ellis, Oklahoma City, vs. Omaha, 7–1, Aug. 3, 1927
Nelson Greene, Des Moines, vs. Amarillo, 3–0 (7), July 27, 1928
Lena Stiles, Tulsa, vs. Des Moines, 6–0, June 30, 1929
John Paul Jones, Oklahoma City vs. Omaha, 13–0, Aug 30, 1931
Cy Blanton, St. Joseph, vs. Joplin, 9–0, July 27, 1933
Fred Newton, Rock Island, vs. Omaha, 5–1, Aug. 2, 1934
Herman Drefs, St. Joseph, vs. Davenport, 2–0, Sept. 25, 1934
Bill Prince, Davenport, vs. Cedar Rapids, 2–1, June 12, 1937
Bob Perry, Cheyenne, vs. Sioux Falls, 2–0, May 18, 1941
Robert Bergen, Pueblo, vs. Norfolk, 3–0, May 21, 1941
Bob Kuhlman, Des Moines, vs. Sioux City, June 8, 1947
Elvin Stabelfeld, Des Moines, vs. Pueblo, 7–0, Aug. 16, 1949
Vern Fear, Des Moines, vs. Denver, 5–0, July 21, 1950
Don Stephens, Omaha, vs. Denver, 5–0, Aug. 25, 1950
Leon Foulk, Des Moines, vs. Denver, 5–0, July 27, 1951
Mason Bowes, Lincoln, vs. Omaha, 3–0, April 24, 1952
Jack Bruner, Witchita, vs. Lincoln, 7–0, April 30, 1952
Mario Picone, Sioux City, vs. Des Moines, 3–0, July 3, 1952
Richard Strahs, Colorado Springs, vs. Lincoln, 3–0, July 27, 1952
Norman Bell, Lincoln, vs. Des Moines, 1–0, June 19, 1953
Karl Spooner, Pueblo, vs. Denver, 2–0, July 28, 1953
Charles Locke, Wichita vs. Sioux City, 6–1, Sept. 12, 1953
Dominick Zanni, Sioux City, vs. Denver, 3–0, June 5, 1954
Orinthan Anderson, Lincoln, vs. Omaha, lost 1–0, Sept. 10, 1954
Robert Harrison, Wichita, vs. Des Moines, 2–0, Sept. 14, 1955
Richard Atkinson, Sioux City, vs. Topeka, 2–0, June 5, 1956
Donald Rowe, Lincoln, vs. Amarillo, 1–0, Aug. 9, 1956
Daniels, Lincoln, vs. Amarillo, lost 1–0, Aug. 12, 1956
Hal Trosky, Jr., Colorado Springs, vs. Des Moines, June 15, 1958
Dave Stenhouse, Pubelo, vs. Topeka, June 20, 1958
Kurt Pelzer, Long Beach, vs. Tri-City, 3–1, July 29, 1995
Kerry Woodson, Sonoma County, vs. Surrey, 4–0, Aug. 9, 1995
John Weglarz, Tri-City, vs. Palm Springs, 1–0, Aug. 10, 1995
Ton Bergan, Chico, vs. Zion, 3–0, June 4, 1999

Fielding Records

FIRST BASEMEN
Percentage, Season
.995—Pete Monahan, Sioux City, 1936; Cory Parker, Surrey, 1995
Putouts, Season
1,768—Jack Lelivelt, Omaha, 1921
Putouts, Game
21—Bill Sweeney, Wichita, 1926
Assists, Season
153—Doc Thomas
Assists, Game
5—Herb Gorman, Pueblo, 1948; Lou Limmer, Lincoln, 1949

Total Chances, Game
22—Roy Brown, Des Moines, 1921
Total Chances, Successive Without an Error
591—Ed Lowell, 1930
Errors, Season
38—Caruthers, Grand Rapids, 1894
Errors, Game
5—Jim Oglesby, Des Moines, 1930
Double Plays, Season
186—William Wano, Pueblo, 1928
Double Plays, Game
5—Many

SECOND BASEMEN
Percentage
.983—Wilfredo Melendez, Lincoln, 1957
Putouts, Season
515—Fred Weed, Sioux City, 1906
Assists, Season
563—Royce "Mule" Washburn, Tulsa, 1921
Total Chances, Game
15—Marty Kaelin, Colorado Springs, 1950
Total Chances, Successive Without an Error
132—Pat Kelly, Denver, 1928
Errors, Season
102—Ace Stewart, Sioux City, 1894
Errors, Game
5—George "Red" Andreas, Sioux City, 1908
Double Plays, Season
155—Frankie Fuller, Pueblo, 1928
Double Plays, Game
4—Several

THIRD BASEMEN
Percentage
.967—Robert "Specs" Moore, Oklahoma City, 1926
Putouts, Season
256—W.A. Audtrey, Omaha, 1908
Putouts, Game
7—Chuck Gorman, Denver, 1926
Assists, Season
479—Jimmy Austin, Omaha, 1907
Assists, Game
8—Several

Total Chances, Game
11—Les Peden, Des Moines, 1947
Errors, Season
74—Everett, Detroit, 1894
Errors, Game
4—Several
Double Plays, Season
34—Ed Grimes, Tulsa, 1928
Double Plays, Game
43—Joe Kirrene, Colorado Springs, 1954

SHORTSTOPS
Percentage
.966—Richard Honacki, Wichita, 1954
Putouts, Season
465—Eddie Gagnier, Lincoln, 1910
Putouts, Game
9—Chuck Carroll, Omaha, 1926
Assists, Season
616—Joe Berger, Pueblo, 1911
Assists, Game
13—Hal Rhyne, Sr., Des Moines, 1921
Total Chances, Game
15—Hal Ryne, Sr., Des Moines; Fred McAlister, Omaha, 1950
Errors, Season
101—Everett, Detroit, 1894
Errors, Game
5—Peewee Lewis, Tulsa, 1926; Eddie Hock, Oklahoma City, 1926
Double Plays, Season
165—George Knothe, Pueblo, 1928
Double Plays, Game
5—Jimmy Morgan, Wichita, 1950

OUTFIELDERS
Percentage
.997—Robert Ries, Denver, 1953
Putouts, Season
486—George Harper, Oklahoma City, 1921
Putouts, Game
9—Several
Assists, Season
54—Henry Ginglardi, Sioux City, 1923
Assists, Game
3—Several

Errors, Season
57—Lohman, Milwaukee, 1894
Errors, Game
3—Jack McComas, Denver, 1949; Joe Kelly, Amarillo, 1927
Double Plays, Season
10—Charley Bates, Des Moines, 1932

CATCHERS
Percentage
.995—Paul Coppes, Palm Springs/Grays Harbor, 1996
Putouts, Season
942—Samuel Taylor, Topeka, 1956
Putouts, Game
20—Earle Burcker, Sr., St. Joseph, 1933; Al Kluttz, Omaha, 1947
Assists, Season
210—John Gossett, St. Joseph, 1912
Assists, Game
6—Several
Errors, Season
93—McFarland, Toledo, 1894
Errors, Game
4—Several
Passed Balls, Season
24—Ed Tickey, Pueblo
Double Plays, Season
22—Jimmy Long, Wichita, 1928
Double Plays, Game
2—Les Peden, Des Moines, 1949

PITCHERS
Percentage
1.000—Many
Putouts, Season
39—Harry White, Sioux City, 1913
Putouts, Game
4—Lew Fauth, Lincoln, 1949
Assists, Season
160—Pat Bohannon, Denver, 1907
Assists, Game
12—Oscar Roettger, Sioux City, 1922
Total Chances, Game
13—Oscar Roettger, Sioux City, 1922
Errors, Season
11—Norman Fox, Sioux City, 1949
Errors, Game
3—Many

Double Plays, Season
13—Billy Hargrove, Pueblo, 1928

Team Records
PENNANTS
7—Des Moines, 1906, 1909, 1910, 1915, 1917, 1931, 1948
Most in Succession
3—Denver, 1909–11; Norfolk, 1939–41

VICTORIES
Most, Season
111—Denver, 1911
Fewest, Season (120 or more game schedule)
26—Muskogee, 1933
Most in Succession
19—Wichita, 1921

DEFEATS
Most, Season
125—Topeka, 1910
Most in Succession
18—Pueblo, 1940

GAMES
Fastest Single Game
52 minutes—Omaha vs. Des Moines, Sept. 10, 1908 (first game of a doubleheader)
Fastest Doubleheader
1 hour, 46 minutes—Omaha vs. Des Moines, Sept. 10, 1909 (both games nine innings)
Most, Innings
17—Sept. 15, 1950, Sioux City vs. Des Moines
Longest Nine-Inning Game (Time)
4 hours, 13 minutes—Bend vs. Tri-City (20–15), July 25, 1998
Longest Extra-Inning Game (Time)
5 hours, 25 minutes—Sonoma County vs. Palm Springs (7–6), Aug. 7, 1996

WINNING PERCENTAGE
Highest
.776—Topeka, 1887 (83–24)
Lowest
.214—Amarillo, 1933 (26–95)

Lowest for a Pennant Winner
.536—Lincoln, 1949 (76–64)

MOST CONSECUTIVE SHUTOUTS
6—Lincoln, 1909 (Streak: Sept. 10, 5–0 and 3–0, over Denver; Sept. 11, 5–0 and 6–0, over Pueblo; Sept 14, 7–0 over Des Moines; and Sept. 15, 3–0, over Des Moines)

Club Batting

PERCENTAGE
*.390—Topeka, 1887
.354—Indianapolis, 1895
*Walks were counted as hits.

HITS
Most, Season
1,992—Tulsa, 1924
Most, Game
50—Lincoln vs. Wichita, Aug. 8, 1887
Most, Game by Both Clubs
65—Lincoln (50) vs. Wichita (15), Aug. 8, 1887
Most, Doubleheader
52—Des Moines vs. Omaha, Sept. 23, 1931
Fewest, Doubleheader
2—Denver (one in each game) vs. Sioux City, Aug. 5, 1948
Most in Succession
11—Des Moines vs. Omaha, fourth inning, Sept. 2, 1926

SACRIFICE HITS
Most, Season
298—Denver, 1910

RUNS
Most, Season
1,260—Tulsa, 1924
Most, Game
46—Lincoln, 1887 (Lincoln defeated Wichita 46–7)
Most, Game by Both Clubs
53—Lincoln (46) vs. Wichita (7), Aug. 8, 1887
Most, Doubleheader
51—Des Moines (29–22) vs. Omaha (6–9), Sept. 13, 1931

Most, Inning
17—Wichita vs. Pueblo, April 21, 1932.
Most, Inning by Both Clubs
18—Des Moines (14) vs. St. Joseph (4), 14th, June 9, 1932

TOTAL BASES
Most, Season
3,188—Tulsa, 1924

HOME RUNS
Most, Season
202—Tulsa, 1929
Most, Game
7—Tulsa, 1924 and 1929
Most, Game by Both Clubs
11—Tulsa (7) vs. Des Moines (4), May 12, 1940

TRIPLES
Most, Season
135—Amarillo, 1928
Most, Game
5—Pueblo, 1949

DOUBLES
Most, Season
508—Tulsa, 1924
Most, Game
13—Tulsa, 1925

STOLEN BASES
Most, Season
389—Des Moines, 1906
Most, Game
11—Pueblo, 1949

LEFT ON BASES
Most, Season
1,267—Sioux City, 1950
Most, Game
19—Denver vs. Tulsa, 1928

Team Fielding

PERCENTAGE
.974—Chio, 1998

PUTOUTS
Most, Season
4,631—Wichita

ASSISTS
Most, Season
2,301—Pueblo, 1911
Most, Game
33—Des Moines, 1921

ERRORS
Most, Season
446—Topeka, 1910
Most, Game
10—Several
Most, Inning
4—Sioux City vs. Lincoln, July 30, 1947

Most Successive Errorless Innings
57—Lincoln, Aug. 11–16, 1917

DOUBLE PLAYS
Most, Season
222—Pueblo, 1928
Most, Game
5—Several

TRIPLE PLAYS
Most, Season
3—Wichita, 1921
Most, Unassisted
1—Omaha (Phil Cooney, second base) vs. Denver, July 6, 1917

Teams of the Western League

Albuquerque, NM	1956–58
Amarillo, TX	1927–28, 1956–58
Bartlesville, OK	1933
Bend, OR	1995–98
Buffalo, NY	1899
Cedar Rapids, IA	1934–37
Cheyenne, WY	1941
Chico, CA	1997–99
Cleveland, OH	1885
Colorado Springs, CO	1901–05, 1916, 1950–58
Columbus, OH	1892, 1896–99
Council Bluffs, IA	1935
Davenport, IA	1934–37
Denver, CO	1886–88, 1900–17, 1922–32, 1941, 1947–54
Des Moines, IA	1900–37, 1947–58
Detroit, MI	1894–99
Emporia, KS	1887
Fort Wayne, IN	1892
Grand Rapids, MI	1894–97
Grays Harbor, WA	1995–97
Hastings	1887
Hutchison, KS	1888, 1917–18, 1933
Indianapolis	1885, 1892, 1894–99
Joplin, MO	1917–21, 1933
Kansas City, MO	1885, 1887, 1892, 1894–99, 1901–03
Keokuk, IA	1885, 1935
Leadville, CO	1886
Leavenworth, KS	1886–88
Lincoln, NE	1886–88, 1906–17, 1924–27, 1939–40, 1947–1958
Long Beach, CA	1995–96
Milwaukee, WI	1885, 1892, 1894–99, 1902–03

Minneapolis, MN	1892, 1894–99
Mission Viejo, CA	1997–98
Mitchell, SD	1939–40
Muskogee, OK	1933
Newton, KS	1888
Norfolk, NE	1939–41
Oklahoma City, OK	1918–32
Omaha, NE	1885, 1887, 1892, 1900–36, 1947–54
Palm Springs, CA	1995–96, 1998
Peoria, IL	1902–03
Pueblo, CO	1900, 1905–09, 1911, 1928–32, 1941, 1947–58
Reno, NV	1996–99
Rock Island, IL	1934–37
Sacramento, CA	1999
St. Joseph, MO	1886–87, 1898, 1900–05, 1910–26, 1930–35
St. Paul, MN	1892, 1895–99, 1901
Salinas, CA	1995–97
Sioux City, IA	1884, 1900, 1904–23, 1934–37, 1939–41, 1947–58
Sioux Falls, SD	1939–41
Sonoma County, CA	1995–99
Springfield, MO	1933
Surrey, BC	1995
Toledo, OH	1885, 1892, 1894–95
Topeka, KS	1886–87, 1909–16, 1918, 1929–31, 1933–34, 1956–58
Tri-City, WA	1995–99
Waterloo, IA	1936–37
Western, WA	1998–99
Wichita, KS	1887, 1909–33, 1950–55
Worthington, MN	1939–40
Zion, Utah	1999

9

League Officials

Presidents

J. Roy Carter, 1939–41
Emerson W. Dickerson, 1917–18
Bruce L. Engel, 1995–98
Dale D. Gear, 1926–35
Thomas J. Hickey, 1900–01
O'Neill M. Hobbs, 1955–58
Byron Bancroft "Ban" Johnson 1894–1899
Edwin C. Johnson, 1947–54
Bob Linscheid, 1999–2000
Dr. A.J. McLaughlin, 1936–37
Norris O'Neil, 1905–16
Michael H. Sexton, 1902–04
Ted Sullivan, 1885
Albert R. Tearney, 1919–25
J.H. Threw, 1887
Frank C. Zehrung, 1917

Managers

Spencer Abbott, Tulsa, 1919–20; Pueblo, 1928–29; Omaha, 1930; Des Moines, 1936
Charles "Babe" Adams, Hutchinson, 1917
C.H. Adkins, Denver, 1922
William "Nin" Alexander, 1887
Robert Allen, Detroit, 1897; Indianapolis, 1898–99
Ned Allen, Tulsa, 1929
Sled Allen, Amarillo, 1928
Walter Alston, Pueblo, 1947
Bill Alvord, Fort Wayne, 1892
Ferrell Anderson, Omaha, 1954

George "Red" Andreas, Sioux City, 1912, 1920–21
Jay Andrews, Des Moines, 1900; Sioux City, 1904; St. Joseph, 1912–13
Charles Arbogast, Omaha, 1912–13
Charlie Babb, Wichita, 1913
Lennie Backer, Waterloo, 1937
Eugene Bailey, St. Joseph, 1930
Dave Bancroft, Sioux City, 1936
Frank Bandle, Omaha, 1887
John Barnes, Minneapolis, 1894–95
Billy Barnie, Milwaukee, 1892
Monty Basgall, Lincoln, 1958
Buddy Bates, Wichita, 1955–56
Joe Battin, Cleveland, 1885
John Beall, Sioux City, 1900; Minneapolis, 1901
Ollie Beard, Detroit, 1898
Joseph Becker, Sioux City, 1947–48
Lester Bell, Lincoln, 1953
Elmer "Doc" Bennett, Norfolk, 1939–40
Joe Berger, Wichita, 1917–22; Denver, 1924–27; Waterloo, 1936
Marty Berghammer, Tulsa, 1925–29; Sioux City, 1936
Bruno Betzel, Topeka, 1930
James Bivin, Pueblo, 1951
Del Bissonette, Des Moines, 1937
Edward Bockman, Amarillo, 1957–58
Everett Boone, St. Joseph, 1930
Lute Boone, Des Moines, 1928
John Brandon, Leavenworth, 1887
Ralph Brandon, Sioux Falls, 1939

League Officials

Andy Cohen, in his strike-zone uniform, managed the Denver Bears from 1951 to 1954. (Photograph courtesy of Jay Sanford)

Petey Brausen, Omaha, 1927
Dick Breen, Oklahoma City, 1920–21; Des Moines, 1922; St. Joseph, 1926–27
Herbert Brett, Wichita, 1954
Lou Brower, Oklahoma City, 1930
Eddie Brown, Omaha, 1932
James Brown, Albuquerque, 1958
Tom Brown, Denver, 1901
Earl Browne, Denver, 1950
Earle Brucker, St. Joseph, 1934–35
William Bryan, Hutchinson, 1888
Barney Burch, Omaha, 1921–22, 1927–29
Jimmy Burke, Tulsa, 1921
R.R. Burke, Denver, 1907
William Burrell, Rock Island, 1937; Lincoln, 1955

John Butler, Denver, 1931; Des Moines, 1933
Walter Carlisle, Pueblo, 1909
Jack Carney, Toledo, 1894
John Carney, Grand Rapids, 1896; Sioux City, 1905–06
Mark Christman, Wichita, June 8, 1953
Keith Clark, Omaha/Rock Island, 1936
Josh Clarke, Sioux City, 1913–15; Lincoln, 1924–25
Robert Clear, Sioux City, May 15, 1956
Bill Clymer, Tulsa, 1921
Jack Coffey, Denver, 1914–15; Des Moines, 1917–21
Andrew Cohen, Denver, 1951–54
John "Shano" Collins, Des Moines, 1926–27, 1930
Charles Comiskey, St. Paul, 1895–99
Tom Connelly, Amarillo, 1928
Wid Conroy, Hutchinson, 1917
Jack Conway, Colorado Springs, 1955–56
Richard Cooley, Topeka, 1907, 1909–10, 1914
Fred Corey, Hastings, 1887
Johnny "Red" Corriden, Des Moines, 1924–25
Otis "Doc" Crandall, Wichita, 1927–28; Des Moines, 1935
L.M. Cretors, Leavenworth, 1888
Clarence "Cap" Crossley, Cedar Rapids, 1935–37
Nick Cullop, Albuquerque, 1957
Charles Cushman, Milwaukee, 1894
Jack Dalton, Joplin, 1917
Bert Daniels, St. Joseph, 1918
Claude Davenport, Des Moines, 1929–30
John Davenport, Sioux City, 1955
George Davis, Des Moines, 1911
O. C. "Red" Davis, Mitchell, 1939
Yank Davis, Joplin, 1917
Thomas Delhanty, Denver, 1903
Otto Denning, Colorado Springs, July 1, 1951
James Deshong, Lincoln, 1948–50

Tom Delhanty played and managed Denver in 1903. His brother, "Big Ed" Delhanty, was named to the Hall of Fame. Bottom: Bill Everitt, whose name was spelled incorrectly as "Everett" by many, managed Denver and Colorado Springs teams from 1901 to 1906. (Photograph courtesy of Jay Sanford)

Charles Dexter, St. Joseph, 1905; Des Moines, 1908
Cletus Dixon, Oklahoma City, 1931; Davenport, 1934–36
A.J. Dolan, St. Joseph, 1919
William Dorsey, Topeka, July 14, 1957
William Douglas, St. Joseph, 1905
Jack Doyle, Des Moines, 1906
Lewis Drill, Pueblo, 1907
Hugh Duffy, Milwaukee, 1902
Edward Dugan, Hutchinson, 1888
Joseph Dunn, Denver, 1922
George Dwyer, Des Moines, 1909–10; Lincoln, 1912
C. Bruce Edwards, Des Moines, June 24, 1953
Jack Egan, Oklahoma City, 1922
Joe Ellick, Kansas City, 1887
George Ellis, Grand Rapids, 1895–96
Clyde Engel, Topeka, 1916
William Everitt, Denver, 1901, 1905–06; Colorado Springs, 1902–03, 1904
Art Ewoldt, Topeka, 1933–34
Jimmy Ewoldt, Topeka, 1934
Pop Eyler, Denver, 1903
Bob Fenner, Sioux Falls, 1940–41
Louis Finney, Lincoln, 1953
Chauncey Fisher, Omaha, 1898
Gene Fisher, Oklahoma City, 1922
Tuffy Fiske, Denver, 1905
John Fitzpatrick, Davenport, 1937; Pueblo, 1948
Tom Fleming, Sioux City, 1904
Lee Fohl, Des Moines, 1928–29
William Fox, Lincoln, 1908–09; Omaha, 1910
Jim Franklin, Buffalo, 1899
David Garcia, Sioux City, 1954
Jim Garry, Buffalo, 1899
Harry Gaspar, Sioux City, 1915–16
Alex Gaston, Des Moines, 1934
Michael Gazella, Denver, 1948
Dale Gear, Topeka, 1912–14
Chick Genovese, Sioux City, 1951
Ralph Gibson, St. Joseph, 1905
Billy Gilbert, Denver, 1923

Jack Glasscock, St. Paul, 1896; Sioux City, 1900; Minneapolis, 1901
Robert Glenalvin, Detroit, 1894, 1896
Walton Goldsby, Topeka, 1887
Johnny Gonding, Omaha, 1914
George Graham, Wichita, 1914
Jack Graney, Des Moines, 1922
Frank Graves, Detroit, 1897–98
Ed Grayston, Mitchell, 1940
Guy Green, Lincoln, 1908
Howard Gregory, Wichita, 1922–26; Oklahoma City, 1928; Wichita, 1931; Topeka, 1931
Francis "Pug" Griffin, Omaha, 1929, 1931–33; Pueblo, 1932; Lincoln, 1939; Pueblo, 1941
John Griffin, Wichita, 1887
Wes Griffin, St. Joseph, 1934
Art Griggs, Omaha, 1924–25; Wichita, 1928–32
Pete Groft, Oklahoma City, 1930
Donald Gutteridge, Colorado Springs, 1952–53
Stanley Hack, Des Moines, 1948
Frank Haley, Lincoln, 1925; St. Joseph, 1931–32
Pat Haley, Wichita, 1926
Russ Hall, St. Joseph, 1902
William Hallman, Denver, 1904
James Hamilton, Joplin, 1920–21
Bubbles Hargraves, Cedar Rapids, 1934
Bill Harrington, Keokuk, 1885; Indianapolis, 1892
William Hart, Peoria, 1902
Roy Hartsfield, Des Moines, 1958
Roy Hartzell, Denver, 1917
Buddy Hassett, Colorado Springs, 1950
Ray Hathaway, Pueblo, 1950, 56–57
George Hausmann, Wichita, 1953
Ed Hawk, Wichita/Muskogee, 1933
George Hay, Omaha, 1885
Jack Hendricks, Denver, 1910–13
Ed Hengle, Hastings, 1887
Fred Henry, Omaha, 1927
Belden Hill, Des Moines, 1900
William Hoffer, Des Moines, 1904
Jack Holland, Wichita, 1909; St. Joseph, 1910, 1912–17; Oklahoma City, 1918–19
Albert Hollingsworth, Omaha, 1950
Ed Holly, Sioux City/St. Joseph, 1917
James "Ducky" Holmes, Sioux City, 1906–09, 1912–13; Lincoln, 1916–17; Sioux City, 1918
Golden Holt, Pueblo, 1954–55
George Hughes, Wichita, 1912–13
Billy Hulen, Pueblo, 1900; Colorado Springs, 1901
Rudy "Boss" Hulswitt, Joplin, 1918–19
James Humphries, Oklahoma City, 1920
Ira Hutchinson, Colorado Springs, 1957
Harold Irelan, Des Moines, 1934
Charles Irwin, Denver, 1908
Frank Isabell, Des Moines, 1910–16; Wichita, 1917
Alvin Jacinto, Colorado Springs, Aug. 5, 1954
Jimmy Jackson, Topeka, 1915–16
William Jackson, Omaha, 1918–19
Otto Jacobs, Hutchinson, 1918
Charles Jones, Denver, 1902, 1908–09
Coburn Jones, Denver, 1941
Hugh Jones, Lincoln, 1915
Dick Juvenal, Newton, 1888
James Keesey, Des Moines, 1947
James Keith, Lincoln, 1888
John Kelleher, St. Joseph, 1920
M. J. Kelley, Des Moines, 1907
Joe Kelly, St. Joseph, 1926
Joe Kelly, Amarillo, 1927; Oklahoma City, 1930
Mike Kelly, Des Moines, 1901
Doc Kennedy, Cleveland, 1885
John Kerr, Cheyenne, 1941
George Kissell, Omaha, 1951–53
Louis Klein, Des Moines, 1956
Jack Knight, Denver, 1928
Clifford Knox, Rock Island, 1934
Tony Koenig, Sioux Falls, 1941
Ed Konetchy, Omaha, 1923
Marty Krug, Omaha, 1915–17
Lyman Lamb, Tulsa, 1925

Kenneth Landenberger, Sioux City, 1957
Bill Lattimore, Topeka, 1916
John Lavan, Lincoln, 1927
T.L. Lawrence, Cleveland, 1885
Lester Layton, Wichita, May 27, 1954
Bob Leadley, Grand Rapids, 1897
Lefty Leifield, Oklahoma, 1929
Jack Lelivelt, Omaha, 1920–23; Tulsa, 1924; St. Joseph, 1925
Walter Linden, Lincoln, Aug. 30, 1953
Howard Lindimore, Topeka, 1931
Mickey Livingston, Colorado Springs, 1954
Dick Lloyd, Lincoln, 1914
Tom Loftus, Milwaukee, 1885; Columbus, 1896, 1898–99
Dennis Long, Toledo, 1895
Herman Long, Des Moines, 1905–06
Dutch Lorbeer, Sioux City, 1937
Robert Lowe, Denver, 1903
Fred Luderus, Oklahoma City, 1923–28, 1932
Ed MacGregor, Toledo, 1892
Connie Mack, Milwaukee, 1897–99
Nick Maddox, Wichita, 1913–14
Fergy Malone, Hastings, 1887
Jim Manning, Kansas City, 1892, 1894–99
Rube Marquard, Wichita/Muskogee, 1933
Runt Marr, Joplin, 1933
Hershel Martin, Des Moines, 1957
Pepper Martin, Des Moines, July 7, 1955
Ray Martin, Worthington, 1940
H. Masterson, Colorado Springs, 1905
Joe Mathes, St. Joseph, 1924; Des Moines, 1925
Walter "Chink" Mattick, Sioux City, 1922
William McCahan, Pueblo, 1953
Robert McClintock, Denver, 1887
William McClintock, Denver, 1888
Joe McDermott, Worthington, 1939; Omaha/Council Bluffs, 1935
James McGill, Denver, 1914–15
Fred McGuire, St. Joseph, 1907

Bobby Lowe managed Denver in 1903.

Matty McIntyre, Lincoln, 1915
Ed McKean, Colorado Springs, 1905
Byron McKibben, St. Joseph, 1900–02
Marty McManus, Denver, 1947
Red McQuillen, Lincoln, Aug. 6, 1954
George McQuinn, Topeka, 1958
Frank Metz, Sioux City, 1920–22

League Officials

Ralph Michaels, Waterloo, 1936
George Miller, Minneapolis, 1897
Clarence Mitchell, Omaha/Rock Island, 1936
William Mizeur, Cedar Rapids, 1934
Dan Moell, Oklahoma City, 1920
R.G. Mohn, Omaha, 1930
George Mold, Wichita, 1887
Pete Monahan, Sioux City, 1937, 1939
Fred Moore, Topeka, 1911
Charles Morton, Minneapolis, 1892
Ray Mueller, Sioux City, 1952–53; Pueblo, 1958
Tony Mullane, Detroit, 1898
Charles Mullen, Lincoln, 1913–14
Ed Murphy, Minneapolis, 1895
Billy Nash, Buffalo, 1899
Johnny Nee, Topeka/Hutchinson, 1918
Charles "Kid" Nichols, Kansas City, 1902–03
Rebel Oakes, Denver, 1916–17
Dan O'Leary, Toledo, 1885
Harold Ott, Sioux City, 1956
Yip Owens, St. Joseph, 1921
Eddie Palmer, Sioux City, 1923; Denver, 1929–30

Jay Parker, Sioux City, 1904
Riley Parker, Rock Island, 1934
Bradley Patterson, Kansas City, 1887
Hamilton Patterson, Pueblo, 1908; Wichita, 1915
George Payne, Worthington, 1940
Jimmy Payton, Topeka, 1929; Pueblo, 1930–31; Wichita, 1932; Keokuk, 1935
Leslie Peden, Des Moines, 1954–55
Ned Pettigrew, Oklahoma City, 1925, 1930
George Pfister, Pueblo, 1953
J.J. Philbin, Omaha, 1887
Malcolm Picket, Omaha, 1934
Hugh Poland, Sioux City, 1950
Ray Powell, Norfolk, 1941
Gale Pringle, Amarillo, Sept. 1, 1958
Mark Purtell, Hutchinson/Bartlesville, 1933
Wray Query, Sioux City, 1923
Joe Quinn, Des Moines, 1902–04
Art Rasmussen, Lincoln, 1924
Charles Reynolds, Hastings, 1887
Frank Richert, Topeka, 1911
L.A. Ripperton, Amarillo, 1928
Bill Rodgers, Denver, 1922, 1931; Des Moines, 1931–32
George Rohe, St. Joseph, 1903
Ulysses Rohrer, Hastings, 1887
Charles Root, Des Moines, 1950
William "Pa" Rourke, Omaha, 1898, 1900–10, 1912–15, 1917
David Rowe, Lincoln, 1887; Omaha, 1892
J.F. Runeir, St. Joseph, 1900
Jimmy Ryan, St. Paul, 1901; Colorado Springs, 1904
James Savage, Topeka, 1915; Joplin, 1917
Skeeter Scalzi, Colorado Springs, 1958
Gus Schmelz, Columbus, 1892; Minneapolis, 1898
Charley Schmidt, Sioux City, 1919
W. Schneider, Terre Haute, 1895; Columbus, 1896
Herman Schulte, Lincoln, 1947
Joe Schultz, Sr., Springfield, 1933

Frank Selee ran Pueblo for four years.

This drawing honored George Tebeau when he died. (Courtesy of Jay Sanford)

Joseph Schultz, Wichita, 1950–51
Karl Segrist, Omaha, 1927
Frank Selee, Pueblo, 1906–09
Hank Severeld, Omaha/Rock Island, 1936
Charles Shaffer, St. Joseph, 1911
Theodore Shandor, Sioux City, June 22, 1958
Dan Shannon, Buffalo, 1899
Bill Sharsig, Indianapolis, 1892, 1894
Lawrence Shepard, Lincoln, 1956–57
William Shipke, Omaha, 1911
William Shriver, Pueblo, 1905
Francis Skaff, Lincoln, 1951
Larry Spahr, Denver, 1915
Walter Smallwood, Pueblo, 1931–32
Earl Smith, Denver, 1932
H.C. "Doc" Smith, Omaha, 1931
Red Smith, Topeka, 1957
Wally Smith, St Joseph, 1922–23
George Stallings, Detroit, 1896, 1898–99
Charles Steven, Amarillo, 1956
Edward Stewart, Colorado Springs, June 5, 1954
Odie Strain, Wichita/Muskogee, 1933
Louis Stringer, Des Moines, 1957
Harry Strohm, Des Moines, 1953
J.C. "Con" Strothers, Detroit, 1895–96
Joe Sugden, St. Joseph, 1930
B.F. Sullivan, Emporia, 1887
Denny Sullivan, St. Joseph, 1916
James Sullivan, Lincoln, 1909, 1911
Ted Sullivan, Kansas City, 1885
Karl Swanson, Rock Island, 1935
Robert Swift, Albuquerque, 1956
Jack Tanner, Colorado Springs, 1905
Tommy Taylor, Rock Island, 1935
George Tebeau, Columbus, 1897–98; Grand Rapids, 1899; Denver, 1900; Kansas City, 1901; Denver, 1904
Rocky Tedesco, Sioux City, 1958
A.M. Thompson, St. Paul, 1892
Henry Thompson, Denver, 1909
Burdett Thurlby, Des Moines, July 4, 1955
Richard Tichacek, Sioux City, 1941
James "Cat" Tierney, Pueblo, 1929
Frank Tobin, Oklahoma City, 1931
Alfred Todd, Des Moines, 1951
Harold Toso, Albuquerque, July 20, 1957
Jay "Babe" Towne, Sioux City, 1910–11
Tom Tucker, Omaha, 1898
Larry Twitchell, Milwaukee, 1895–96
Robert Unglaub, Lincoln, 1911
George Vanderbeck, Detroit, 1895
Ollie Vanek, Omaha, 1947–48
Howard Wakefield, Lincoln, 1924
Bobby Wallace, Wichita, 1917
Clyde Wares, Wichita, 1915
Bill Watkins, Indianapolis, 1885; Sioux City, 1894; Indianapolis, 1895–98
Buck Weaver, Denver, 1901
Skeeter Webb, Colorado Springs, 1951
E.D. Webster, St. Joseph, 1904
Perry Werden, Minneapolis, 1899
Frank "Dutch" Wetzel, Omaha, 1934
Edward Wheeler, Sioux City, 1907
Kemp Wicker, Des Moines, 1953
Whitey Wietelmann, Lincoln, 1954

League Officials

William "Pa" Rourke managed the longest in the Western League—17 years!

Walt Wilmer, Minneapolis, 1897
Walter Wilmot, Minneapolis, 1896, 1898
Parke Wilson, Denver, 1902
Red Wilson, Wichita/Muskogee, 1933
William Wilson, Peoria, 1903
William "Hack" Wilson, Sioux City Cowboys, 1935
Ralph Winegarner, Wichita, 1953
William "Rasty" Wright, Grand Rapids, 1894
Archie Yelle, Des Moines, 1928
Jimmy Zinn, Sioux City, 1940
Ed Zinram, St. Joseph, 1905
Dutch Zwilling, Lincoln, 1926; St. Joseph, 1933; Sioux City, 1933

10
All-Time Players and Team

Many players in the Western League put together some stellar performances during their stay in the league. The following players could make up an All-Time All-Star Team:

First Base

Dick Stuart, Lincoln. The slugger holds the all-time record for homers in a season, with 66 in 141 games in 1957. He knocked in 158 RBI that season, the second highest in the history of the league. Unfortunately, he also set the all-time record for strikeouts, with 171 in a season.

Second Base

Royce "Mule" Washburn, Wichita, Tulsa. Washburn was a leading hitter in the league for several seasons with Wichita and Tulsa. He had a career year in 1924 with Tulsa when he led the league in homers and set the all-time league record with 458 total bases.

Honorable Mention: Earl Weaver, Denver. Weaver was twice an All-Star with the league, in 1952 and 1954. During those years he was one of the leading hitters, too.

Third Base

Les Peden, Des Moines. Peden was twice an All-Star in the league at two different positions. In 1947 he was named to the All-Star Team as its third baseman. During the season he averaged .323 batting and .944 fielding. In 1954 he was named to the All-Star Team as a catcher. That season he hit 26 homers and averaged .310 batting.

Shortstop

Buster Chatam, Pueblo. Chatam had a great year with Pueblo in 1929 when he had the highest batting average in the league (.386) before he was sold to Portland of the Pacific Coast League. He also contributed 13 homers, 10 triples and 32 doubles that season.

Honorable Mention: Maury Wills, Pueblo. The speedster led the league in stolen bases in 1956 on his way to an All-Star selection. Wills was quite a hitter for a shortstop and put up these numbers in 1956: .302 batting average, 33 doubles, eight triples and 10 homers.

Outfielders

Lyman Lamb, Tulsa. Lamb set the all-time records for doubles when he hit a hundred of them in a season (in which he didn't miss a game) in 1924. He was also a good fielder and had just 12 errors that year for a .974 fielding average. In four seasons in the Western League he averaged .349 hitting.

Bill Congalton, Colorado Springs. The outfielder was one of the league leading hitters from 1902 to 1904. In 1903 he led the league with 184 hits, 245 total bases and a .363 batting average. The following season he again led the league with a .327 batting average.

Joe Wilhoit, Wichita. The outfielder had the longest hitting streak—69 games—in league history, which rocketed his batting average to .422 in 1919.

Honorable Mention: Russell Rac, Omaha. Rac was a two-time All-Star in 1951 and 1953. A consistent .300 hitter, he clouted 17 dingers in 1951 and 23 in 1953. He also had 102 RBI in 1951.

Catcher

Sam Hairston, Colorado Springs. Hairston broke the color barrier in the Western League in 1950. During five seasons he averaged .325 batting and was named to three All-Star teams.

Honorable Mention: Earle Brucher, St. Joseph. During his four seasons in the league he was one of the best fielding receivers in the league. In fact, he led the league in fielding in 1934. The following season he was named MVP when he recorded the second highest batting average on the season (.342).

Pitchers

George Boehler, Tulsa. The hurler tied the all-time record for wins (38) in 1922, while setting the all-time mark for innings pitched (441).

Hugh Blanton, Amarillo. Blanton won 52 games over three seasons in the league and was twice named to the All-Star Team in 1957 and 1958. In 1957 he led the league in ERA (2.86).

Honorable Mention: Joey Dawley, Chico, set the all-time record for saves (26) in 1998. Bill Hutchinson, Minneapolis, recorded a record-tying

38 wins 1896. Leo Moon, Des Moines, tossed eight shutouts in 1925. Bud Tinning, Des Moines, had a great season in 1931 when he won 24 games in 29 starts and only lost two games to set the all-time winning percentage record of .923 for a pitcher with more than 20 decisions.

Team

Denver set the all-time league record of 111 victories in 1911. The Grizzlies secured the pennant with about a month to go and finished with an 18-game lead.

Bibliography

Axelson, G.W. *The Life Story of Charles A. Comiskey.* Chicago, Illinois: The Reilly and Lee Co., 1919.
Bryson, Bill, and Housh, Leighton. *Through the Years with the Western League, Since 1885.* Washington: Western League, 1951.
Cleveland Plain Dealer
Dellinger, H.L. *From Dust to Dust: An Account of the 1885 Western League.* Kansas City, MO: Two Rivers Press, 1977.
Denver Post
Fort Worth Star-Telegram
Howe Sportsdata provided the statistics of the independent Western League.
Johnson, Lloyd, and Wolff, Miles. *The Encyclopedia of Minor League Baseball.* Durham, N.C.: Baseball America, 1997.
Microsoft Complete Baseball: The Ultimate Multimedia Reference for Every Baseball Fan. (CD-ROM) Microsoft Corporation, 1995.
Murdock, Eugene C. *Ban Johnson: Czar of Baseball.* Westport, Connecticut: Greenwood Press, 1982.
New York Post
Okkonen, Marc. *Minor League Baseball Towns of Michigan.* Detroit, MI: Thunder Bay Press, 1997.
Reach's Official Guides, many issues.
Richter, Francis C. *Richter's History and Records of Baseball: The American Nation's Chief Sport.* Philadelphia, Pennsylvania: The Dando Company, 1914.
Riley, James A. *The Biographical Encyclopedia of the Negro Baseball Leagues.* New York, New York: Carroll & Graf Publishers, Inc., 1994.
Seymour, Harold. *Baseball: The Early Years.* New York, New York: Oxford University Press, Inc., 1960.
Spaulding/Reach Guides, many issues.
Spink, Alfred H. *The National Game: A History of Baseball, America's Leading Outdoor Sport, From the Time It Was First Played Up to the Present Day.* St. Louis, Missouri: The National Game Publishing Company, 1910.
The Sporting Life, many issues.
The Sporting News, many issues.
Sports Collectors Digest. Krause Publications, July 16, 1993.
TSN Guides, many issues.

Index

Abernathy, Clifford 213
Adams, Charles "Babe" 81, 82
Admission 6
Albuquerque 256
Alexander, Nin 13
All-American Girls Professional Baseball League 152
Allen, R. 49
Allen, Roy 128
Allington, Bill 152
Alston, Walter 212
Amarillo 152, 160, 256, 260, 261, 269
American Association 5, 6, 11, 17, 21, 65, 70, 74, 77, 98, 101, 119, 135
American League 1, 2, 19, 36, 41, 44, 53, 56, 63, 65, 100, 144, 149, 153, 256
Anderson, Ollie 101
Anderson, Paul 274
Anfenger, Mike 178
Ansfinger, Milk 136
Anson, Cap 38
Aparicio, Luis 219
Athletic Park 38
Atlanta 283, 288
Austin, Jimmy "Pepper" 84

Backman, Wally 288
Bailey, Bill 140
Baker Bowl 115
Baldwin, Charles "Lady" 10-11
Baltimore 56, 238, 252, 261
Bancroft, Dave 191
Barberie, Bret 279
Barnes, Pearl "Casey" 58, 59

Bartlesville Bronchos 178
Bates, Charles 182
Batterson, Jake 179
Bayne, Bill "Beverly" 122
Beall, John 98
Bears Stadium 217, 237
Beck, Fred 128
Becker, Joe 212
Beckley, Jake 2, 14, 15, 17
Bednar, Andy 174
Bend 270, 287
Bennett, Charley 43
Bennett, Herschel 131
Berghammer, Marty 157, 161
Birkofer, Ralph 174
Bishop, Charlie 213
Bissell, Walt 59
Black, Bob 8
Black, Karl 136, 152
Black Sox 41, 79, 101
blacks 9
Blaeholder, George 140, 152, 153
Blakesley, Jim 128
Blanton, Cy 179
Blanton, Hugh 260
Bodie, Ping 140
Boehler, George 100, 131
Bornholdt, Barney 157
Borton, Babe 98
Boston 68, 70, 79, 94
Boston Braves 100
Boston Red Sox 122
Bott 140
Bottomley, Jim 125
Bowman, Ryan 288
Boyer, Ken 233
Boyer, Clete 233
Brain, Dave 62
Brennan, John 8

Bridges, Marshall 256
Briggs, Johnnie 252
Broadway Park 58
Brooklyn 10, 70, 108, 220
Brown, Joe 143, 148
Brown, Mordecai "Three-Finger" 2, 38, 67
Brown, Norman 242
Brown, Walter 164
Brucker, Earl 182, 186
Brush, John T. 34, 40
Bruton, Bill 233
Bucha, John 213
Buffalo 56
Burke, Alan 274
Burnett, Artie 261
Burns, Jack 161
Burns, Russell 204
Butcher, Hank 111, 115
Butte 60

Canadian League 53
Carlson, Floyd 178
Carter, J. Roy 200
Cedar Rapids 182, 186, 191, 195, 196, 221
Central League 114
Channell, Les 100
Chappelle, Bill 76
Chartak, Michael "Shotgun" 195
Chicago 28, 58, 60, 111
Chicago Cubs 46, 57, 60, 62, 67, 75, 90, 148, 165, 169, 170, 174, 213, 219, 220, 224, 227, 233, 247, 252, 261, 292
Chicago Colts 38
Chicago Whales 60
Chicago White Sox 56, 62, 67, 79, 101, 122, 124, 143,

Index

170, 174, 186, 191, 219, 220, 225, 238, 243, 247, 265
Chicago White Stockings 32
Chico 278, 283, 287
Chmiel, Herb 213
Christian, Eddie 271
Cicotte, Eddie 79
Cincinnati 17, 35, 40, 41, 53, 54, 62, 164
Cincinnati Commercial-Gazette 35
Cincinnati Reds 34, 41, 46, 220, 232, 287
Clarke, Fred 104
Cleveland 5, 6, 7, 8, 9, 17, 18, 56, 70, 153, 227
Cleveland Indians 111, 115, 152, 170, 212
Cline, Judy 156
Coats, John 278
Cobb, Ty 54, 132, 247
Coffey, Jack 104, 115
Cohen, Hy 246
Collins, Shano 147, 148
Colorado Springs 57, 62, 70, 71, 74, 76, 111, 140, 227, 237, 241, 242, 251, 264, 265
Columbus 19, 32, 43, 46, 49, 52, 53
Comiskey, Charles 1, 2, 34, 36, 40, 41, 49
Comiskey Park 111
Congalton, Bill 70, 71
Conway, James 20
Cook, James 79
Cooper, Ron 252
Corriden, John "Red" 90
Cottier, Chuck 261
Council Bluffs 186, 213, 216
Crawford, "Wahoo Sam" 2, 53
Crosby, Jerry 241
Crossley, Clarence "Cap" 195
Crimian, John 213
Crystal Glen Park 8
Cuitti, Art 256
Cullop, Nick 140
Cy Young Award 228

Dalrymple, Clay 261
Daniels, Pete 36
Davenport 28, 140, 182, 186, 191, 196

Davis, Alfonso 52-53
Davis, Stormy 152
Davis, Yank 131
Dean, Dizzy 2, 165-166
Dean, Paul 165
Denver 13, 17, 19, 25, 28, 29, 30, 33, 57, 58, 59, 63, 66, 67, 71, 74, 78, 79, 91, 94, 98, 100, 104, 107, 111, 118, 131, 132, 136, 140, 143, 148, 161, 174, 178, 211, 216, 217, 224, 225, 228, 232, 233, 237, 242, 246, 247, 251
Des Moines 23, 24, 28, 33, 38, 57, 59, 62, 75, 76, 77, 78, 79, 84, 86, 90, 97, 100, 101, 104, 107, 114, 115, 128, 136, 140, 143, 147, 148, 161, 164, 168, 170, 178, 182, 187, 188, 196, 211, 212, 213, 216, 217, 219, 242, 246, 251, 252, 269
Des Moines Register and Leader 57, 76
Detroit 10, 33, 34, 43, 49
Detroit Tigers 46, 76, 90, 115, 132, 144
Dickerson, E.W. 114, 118, 121
Dietz, Dick 278, 288
Dixon, Celtus 191
Dolan, Alvin 121
Dolan, Cozy 91
Donovan, Maury 217
Dooin, Charles "Red" 64
Drefs, Herman 182
Drescher, Joe 36
Drizoz, Justin 288
Duffy, Hugh 2, 68
Dugas, Gus 164
Dundon, Gus 67
Dunagan, Carl 164
Dunlop, Harry 261
Dunn, Tom 261
Dust Bowl 2
Dyer, Ben 111

East, Carlton 128
Eastern League 74
Emporia 20, 23
Engel, Bruce L. 270
Epps, Harold 186
Evansville 5
Everett, Bill 78
Ewing, Bob 62

Eyler, Elwood "Pop" 57, 59, 62

Faber, Urban "Red" 2, 94, 101
Fagan, Bill 30
Fairweather, Tom 195
Fear, Vern 227
Federal League 60, 94, 100
Fenlon, Art 90
Finders, Wendell 200
Fletcher, Bob 288
Fodge, Gene "Suds" 252
Fort Wayne 32
Fowler, John 9, 10
Fox, Nellie 219-220
Franklin, James 56
Freese, George 233
Fricano, Marion 225
Furchner, Al 83

Gaffney, John 24
Gazella, Mike 218
Gear, Dale 147, 188
Gehrig, Lou 141
Genins, F. 36
Gentile, Jim 242
Gibson, Josh 156
Glade, Fred 62
Glasscock, Jack 43, 44, 58, 60
Goat, Jot 46
Golt, W.F.C. 56
Gonzales, Ray 152
Goodwin, Curtis 292
Grand Rapids 6, 19, 34, 46, 49, 52, 53
Grays Harbor 270, 283
Gregory, Howard 115
Griffin, F.A. 143
Griggs, Art 140

Haid, Harold 143
Haines, Jesse 2, 119
Hairston, Sam 232, 252
Haley, Frank 174
Hall, Frank 195
Hall, Herb 140, 148
Harrison, Robert 252
Hart, "Bond Hill" Billy 13
Hartzell, Roy "Topsy" 66
Hastings 20
Haworth, Homer 143
Hausen, "Old Hoss" 59
Haynes, James 191
Hemphill, Frank 62
Hendricks, Jack 100, 103

Index 317

Herman, Babe 136
Hickey, Al 59
Hickey, Thomas Jefferson 57, 63
Hickey, W.E. "Bill" 59, 65
Higbee, Mabion 136
Hobbs, O'Neill M. 251, 269
Hock, Eddie 148
Hodges, Byrd 143
Hogriever, George 36, 40, 76
Holland, Jack 5
Holmes, Dusty 83
Holt, Dave 271
Holzhouser, Herm 143
Horan, Joe 136
Hornsby, Rogers 115
Houston 283
Hovlik, Ed 119
Howard, Del 749
Hubbell, Carl 2, 143, 144, 145
Huggins, Miller 71
Hughes, Butch 274
Hutchinson 28, 114, 115, 118, 119, 178
Hutchinson, Bill 44

Independence 164
Indianapolis 5, 6, 7, 8, 9, 32, 34, 36, 40, 43, 46, 47, 49, 50, 52, 56, 62, 66, 103, 104
Igae, Phillip 5

Jackson, Al 265
Jacksonville 33
Jacobs, Anthony 217
Jaros, Tony 213
Jenkins, Brett 278
Jensen, Forrest 164
Johnson, Ban 1, 2, 34-36, 37, 40, 44, 49, 50, 56
Johnson, Connie 238
Johnson, Edward C. 211, 212
Johnson, Ernie 225
Johnson, Harry 195
Johnson, Stan 265
Joplin 114, 131, 178
Jones, Burt "Cowboy" 28
Jones, Tex 109

Kallio, Rudy 115
Kane, Harry "Klondike" 59, 104
Kansas City 6, 7, 8, 9, 10,
19, 20, 21, 22, 28, 32, 34, 37, 40, 43, 49, 50, 57, 62, 65, 72, 74, 119, 131, 135, 260
Kansas State League 20
Kazak, Eddie 213
Kelly, Lynn 195
Kenna, Ed 70
Keokuk 6, 8, 9, 10, 186, 188
Kerfeld, Charlie 283
Keyes, Stan 164, 170
Keyser, Lee 164
Kight, Charley 59
Killiea, M.R. 49
Kim, C.M. 5
Kimpel, Russ 218
Kimsey, Chad 157
King, Jim 247
King, Joe 213
King, Nelson 242
Kirkland, Willie 252
Kirrene, Joe 247
Kling, Johnny "Noisy" 57, 62
Kroner, John 170
Kuhlman, Bob 224

Labine, Clem 220
Lahman, Cal 195
Lamabe, John 260
Lamanski, Frank 182
Lamb, Lyman 131, 140
Landenberger, Ken 238
Landis, Jim 242-243
Landis, Kenesaw Mountain 41, 79, 157
Lange, Fred 86
Langford, Elton 143, 152
Lawrence, T. 5
Lazzeri, Tony 2, 140, 141
Leadville 13, 14, 16, 17, 20
Leavenworth 13, 14, 20
Lehman, Ken 225
Leifield, Lefty 77
LeJeune, Larry 104
Lelivelt, Bill 128
Lelivelt, Jack 128, 139
Leonard, Emil "Dutch" 169
Lessenring, Clarence 59
Lewinski, Ed 213
Lincoln 13, 28, 33, 81, 84, 86, 100, 104, 111, 114, 118, 131, 139, 143, 191, 200, 203, 211, 213, 217, 227, 252, 256, 261, 261, 269
Linden, Walt 224
Linscheid, Bob 287, 291

Loftus, Tom 43, 49
Long, D.A. 34
Long, Herman "Germany" 20, 21, 22
Long Beach 270, 271, 274
Los Angeles Dodgers 252, 261, 288
Louisville 38, 53, 56, 62, 81, 111
Lown, Omar "Turk" 220
Luby, Hugh 191

Mack, Connie 2, 44, 49
Mahoney, Bob 227
Malone, Pat 148, 186
Manning, J.H. 49
Manush, Heinie 2, 132
Marasco, Vic 225
Marquard, Rube 178
Maupin, Henry 57
Maun, Ernest 136
Mauro, Carmen 212
May, Herbert 179
McAnany, Jim 265
McCormick, Harry "Moose" 107
McDowell, Jim 136
McFarland, Howard 182
McGilvray, Bill 79, 81
McGinnity, Joe "Iron Man" 2, 37
McGrew, John 161
McKeenan, J.W. 7
McLaughlin, A.J. 188
McNally, Glenn 136
McNeeley, W.E. Harry 59
McVey, Cal 29
Menefee, Jock 53
Merchants Park 156
Merz, Otto 111
Mexico 36
Miley, Sammy 260
Miller, Dakin "Dusty" 59
Miller, John 200
Miller, Roscoe 79
Milwaukee 6, 7, 8, 10, 28, 32, 34, 40, 43, 49, 62, 65, 68, 70, 74, 77, 225
Milwaukee Brewers 44, 100, 219, 233
Minneapolis 5, 6, 13, 32, 34, 38, 40, 43, 44, 49, 52, 53, 57, 62, 98
Mission Viejo 279, 283, 287
Mitchell 200, 203
Mitchell, Kevin 292

Montgomery, Walt 242
Montreal 279
Moon, Leo 148
Moon, Wally 227
Morse, Hugh 186
Moskovich, George 227
Mullane, Tony 40
Munson, Joe 152
Murphy, Edward 13
Muskogee 140, 178
Musser, Paul 115

Nashville 5, 6
National Agreement. 5, 56, 62
National Association 6, 65, 74
National Association of Professional Base Ball Leagues 63
National Baseball Hall of Fame 2, 10, 11, 17, 21, 37, 41, 44, 49, 53, 54, 59, 60, 67, 68, 94, 100, 104, 108, 115, 119, 125, 132, 141, 145, 166, 170, 171, 178, 186, 220
National Board of Arbitration 152
National League 11, 15, 21, 32, 34, 36, 37, 38, 44, 46, 47, 50, 56, 60, 62, 72, 108, 148, 171, 178, 247, 248, 283, 288, 292
Nebraska State League 1, 2, 196, 200
Negro American League 195
Nehf, Art 100
New York Giants 124, 144, 191, 213, 218, 248
New York Highlanders 84
New York Mets 265
New York Yankees 100, 108, 115, 132, 141, 174, 217, 228, 252
Newton 28
Nichols, Charles "Kid" 2, 22, 65, 72
Niggeling, John 170
night baseball 164
Norfolk 200, 204, 207
North, Louis 120
Northwestern League 1

Oakes, Rebel 111
Oberlin College 35

O'Brien, Bucky 94
O'Brien, Darby 13, 15
O'Brien, M.J. 49
O'Doul, Frank "Lefty" 115
O'Dowd, Joe 161
Oglesby, Jim 170
Oklahoma City 128, 135, 136, 139, 143, 144, 148, 152, 157, 161, 164, 174
Okmulgee 140
O'Leary, Dan 9
Omaha 5, 6, 7, 8, 20, 28, 33, 38, 39, 50, 57, 58, 60, 65, 67, 71, 74, 75, 81, 83, 86, 98, 124, 128, 132, 136, 140, 152, 161, 164, 178, 186, 188, 191, 211, 212, 213, 216, 227, 232, 233, 237, 238, 242, 246, 247, 251
O'Neill, Norris "Tip" 76, 111
Osorio, Alberto 238
O'Toole, Marty 90

Pacific Coast League 74, 115
Pacific Suns 278, 282, 287
Palm Springs 270, 278, 282
Palmer, Eddie 136
Palmero, Emilio 124
Parrott, Tom "Tacks" 59
Passeau, Claude 188
Pastime Park 6
Peden, Les 213, 225
Peoria 33
Pfeister, John "Jack the Giant Killer" 75
Philadelphia 6, 64, 115, 178
Philadelphia Athletics 44, 186, 217
Philadelphia Phillies 188, 219, 261
Phillips, Bill 40, 46
Phillips, Eddie 238
Phillips, Tony 292
Piet, Tony 170
Pittsburgh 15, 46, 104, 108
Pittsburgh Federals 111
Pittsburgh Pirates 44, 75, 77, 82, 91, 135, 161, 164, 165, 171, 174, 178, 225, 232, 242, 252, 256, 260
Player's League 32, 41
Plummer, Bill 287
Polly, Nick 191
Porter, Dykes 195

Prather, Agrus "Dutch" 191
Presko, Joe 225
Preston, Walter "Wizard" 59, 74
Price, Walter 59
Pridy, Todd 283
Prieto, Rick 274
Pueblo 57, 62, 76, 93, 94, 97, 140, 157, 161, 164, 170, 178, 207, 211, 212, 224, 225, 227, 233, 242, 246, 251, 256

Quincy 33

Rabbit, Joe 152
Ramsey, C.A. 125
Ray Doan's Colored All-Stars 195
Reach, A.J. 6
Reagan, Pat 83
Reilly, "Princeton Charlie" 59
Reno 274, 278, 283, 288
Rhodes, Dusty 83
Riley, Leon 161
Riverfront Park 25
Robinson, Jackie 9
Rock Island 33, 65, 182, 186, 191, 195, 196
Rossman, Claude 76
Rough Riders 11
Rourke, William "Pa" 81
Roush, Edd 100
Rowe, David 33
Ruth, Babe 37, 141, 156
Ryba, Mike 178

Sacramento 287
St. Joseph 9, 13, 17, 20, 33, 49, 50, 57, 62, 94, 100, 104, 108, 114, 121, 128, 131, 139, 140, 143, 148, 152, 164, 164, 165, 169, 182, 186
St. Louis 11, 13, 28, 213
St. Louis Browns 32, 84, 131, 149, 152, 228
St. Louis Cardinals 67, 121, 165, 174, 191, 232, 233, 238, 248
St. Louis Dispatch 2
St. Paul 5, 6, 8, 9, 28, 32, 38, 40, 41, 43, 44, 49, 56, 57, 62, 64, 71
Salinas 270, 274, 282
Salt Lake City Bees 141

Index

San Francisco Giants 288, 292
Saulpaugh, C.H. 49
Sawatski, Carl "Swats" 218, 219
Schalk, Roy 174
Schmelz, G.H. 49
Schmidt, Henry 70
Schmidt, Willard 232
Scottsdale Stadium 291, 292
Seattle Mariners 261
Seerey, Pat 227
Selee, Frank 67
Severeid, Hank 191
Sexton, Mike 65, 76, 148
Shaner, Walter 143
Shantz, Bobby 217
Shaughnessy playoff 186
Shepard, Larry 261
Sherman Field 227
Shirk, Len "Dad" 59
Sioux City 28, 32, 34, 36, 37, 38, 40, 58, 62, 78, 86, 89, 98, 104, 107, 114, 131, 135, 136, 139, 140, 182, 188, 191, 195, 200, 203, 207, 211, 212, 213, 217, 227, 232, 248, 252, 261, 269
Sioux Falls 200, 204
Smith, Tony 86
Smith, Mike 278, 283
Sommers, Andy 8
Sonoma County 270, 278, 283, 288, 291, 292
Southern League 6, 72
Spencer, Glen 161
Spink, Alfred H. 2, 13
Sporting Life 40, 44
Sporting News 56
Sportsman Park 8
Springfield, Missouri 178, 179
Springfield, Ohio 5, 140
Stabefeld, Elvin "Srubby" 224
Stadnicki, John 261
Steele, Bernard 207
Steinfeldt, Harry 46
Stenhouse, Dave 265
Stephens, George 32
Sterzer, Buck 104
Stewart, Asa "Ace" 38, 53
Stoner, Jim 157
Storti, Lin 161
Stuart, Dick 256

Sturdy, Guy 148, 149
Stuvengen, Charles 143
Sullivan, Jack 59
Sullivan, Tim 5, 6, 8, 13
Surrey 270, 274
Swigart, Oadis 195

Takayoshi, Todd 278
Tanner, Chuck 225
Tarpley, Andy 278
Taylor, Bill 227
Taylor, Howard 195
Taylor, Jack 67
Taylor, Sammy 256
Tearney, Al 121, 131
Tebeau, George "White Wings" 17, 19, 57, 60, 65
Tebeau, Oliver "Patsy" 17, 18, 19
Terre Haute 40, 43, 67, 68
Texas League 139, 174
The Sporting News 13
Theil, Buck 75
Theis, Jake 242
Thesenga, Arnold 195
Thomas, Fay 157
Thomas, John 91
Thompson, Fresco 140
Thompson, "Big" Sam 10
Three-I League 67, 121, 148, 195, 196, 269
Tinker, Joe 2, 59, 60, 63
Tinning, Bud 170
Tipple, Dan 132
Todt, Phil 128
Toledo 5, 6, 7, 8, 9, 34, 40, 43
Topeka 13, 17, 20, 21, 81, 86, 100, 114, 118, 119, 160, 161, 164, 256, 269
Toronto Blue Jays 292
Torre, Frank 233
Torre, Joe 233
Tracewski, Dick 261
Traffley, Bill 28
Treadway, Leon "Red" 217
Tri-City 270, 287, 288
Trosky, Hal, Jr. 265
Tubbs, Frank 148
Tulsa 121, 122, 124, 128, 131, 135, 136, 139, 140, 143, 148, 152, 157, 164, 174
Turley, Bob 228
Turpin, Hal 191

Uhle, George 224
umpires 6
Union Association 5, 11

Valley Vipers 291, 292
Van Fleet, Dwight 195
Vance, Dazzy 2, 104, 108
Vanderbeck, George A. 34, 49
Vaughn, Arky 2, 170-171
Veach, Willie "Peek-a-Boo" 11
Veterans Committee 10, 17, 60, 119, 132, 141
Vizard, J.H. 59

Waldron, Irv 65
Waddell, Rube 2, 53
Wagner, Jack 261
Wagner, Frank 204
Walker, Moses 9
Ward, Preston 212
Washburn, Royce 128, 140
Washington 44, 56
Washington, Kyle 271
Washington Park Stadium 6
Washington Senators 119, 169, 213, 256, 265
Waterloo 195, 196
Watson, George 100
Weaver, Earl 238
Webb, James "Skeeter" 191
Webb, Sam "Red" 213
Webster, Mons "Eddie" 59
Weglarz, John 271
Wehde, Wilbur 186
Weimer, Jake 65
Welch, Bob 291
Welch, Harry 86
Welday, Mike 79
Werden, Perry "Moose" 13, 20, 37, 40, 44
Western Association 1, 19, 28, 31, 32, 33, 34, 37, 65, 72, 74, 81, 86, 152, 164, 195
Western Warriors 287
Weygandt, Al 256
Whipple, T.H. 5
Whisenant, Pete 227
White, Bill 248
White, Chris 288
Whitfield, James 65
Wichita 20, 86, 93, 97, 111, 118, 119, 120, 121, 124, 128, 131, 132, 140, 152, 157, 164, 168, 170, 174, 178, 223, 227, 251
Wilcox, Jimmy 140
Wilhoit, Joe 121

Williams, D.C. "Mutt" 140
Williams, Don 260
Williams, Jimmy 50
Wills, Maury 247
Wilmot, Walter 43
Wilson, Hack 186
Wirtz, Elwood 161
Witherup, Roy 84
Wood, Charles 164

World Series 11, 41, 56, 101, 118, 148, 188, 218, 219, 220, 233, 238, 243, 252, 256
Worthington Cardinals 200

Yaryan, Clarence "Yam" 122, 124

Yde, Emil 135
Yuma 291

Zehrung, Frank 111, 114
Zeitz, Charlie 59
Zion 287
Zwilling, Dutch 94

www.ingramcontent.com/pod-product-compliance
Lightning Source LLC
Chambersburg PA
CBHW051208300426
44116CB00006B/477